PLAN YOUR TRIP

Welcome to Normandy
& D-Day Beaches 5

Normandy &
D-Day Beaches Map 6

Normandy & D-Day Beaches
Highlights 8

Paris City Guide 10

Lille City Guide 11

Need to Know 12

ROAD TRIPS

1 D-Day's
    Beaches   3 Days   17

2 Monet's
    Normandy   4 Days   27

3 Tour des
    Fromages   5 Days   35

4 In Flanders
    Fields   3 Days   43

DESTINATIONS

Normandy 52

Rouen 52

Dieppe 58

Côte d'Albâtre 59

Le Havre 62

Les Andelys 63

Bayeux 64

D-Day Beaches 67

Caen 71

Trouville & Deauville 74

Honfleur 76

Lille 82

Flanders & Artois 92

Arras 92

Battle of the Somme,
Flanders & Artois Memorials 94

Picardy 98

Amiens 98

ROAD TRIP ESSENTIALS

France Driving
Guide 105

France Travel
Guide 111

Language 119

Dramatic white cliffs, Étretat (p30)

WELCOME TO
NORMANDY &
D-DAY BEACHES

Northern France is primed with possibilities – whether that means sampling Norman cheeses, getting close to WWI and WWII history or simply moseying around Rouen's old town. And with its abundance of coast and countryside, it's a pleasure to drive, too.

It's a region with a long (and turbulent) history that is plain to see. The scars of war can still be traced on the fields of Flanders and the beaches of Normandy. Elsewhere, be awed by the landscapes and villages that inspired artists such as Claude Monet.

NORMANDY & D-DAY BEACHES

⭐

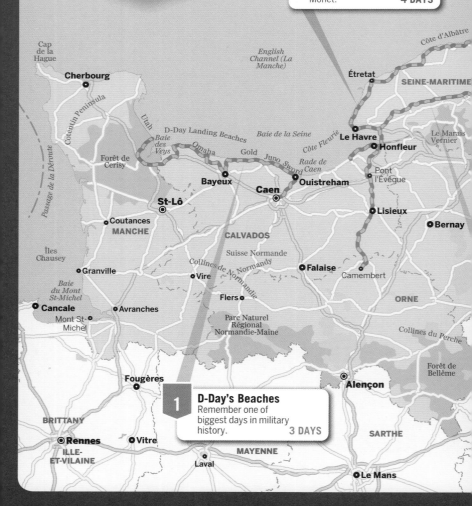

2 **Monet's Normandy**
Explore the landscapes and cities that inspired Monet. **4 DAYS**

Eastbourne

Cap de la Hague

Cherbourg

English Channel (La Manche)

Côte d'Albâtre

Étretat

SEINE-MARITIME

Cotentin Peninsula

Utah

D-Day Landing Beaches

Baie des Veys

Omaha

Gold

Juno Sword

Baie de la Seine

Côte Fleurie

Le Havre

Honfleur

Le Marais Vernier

Forêt de Cerisy

Bayeux

Caen

Rade de Caen

Ouistreham

Pont l'Évêque

Passage de la Déroute

St-Lô

Coutances

MANCHE

CALVADOS

Lisieux

Bernay

Îles Chausey

Granville

Suisse Normande

Collines de Normandie

Vire

Falaise

Camembert

ORNE

Baie du Mont St-Michel

Flers

Cancale

Avranches

Mont St-Michel

Parc Naturel Régional Normandie-Maine

Collines du Perche

Forêt de Bellême

Fougères

1 **D-Day's Beaches**
Remember one of biggest days in military history. **3 DAYS**

Alençon

BRITTANY

Rennes

Vitré

MAYENNE

Laval

SARTHE

Le Mans

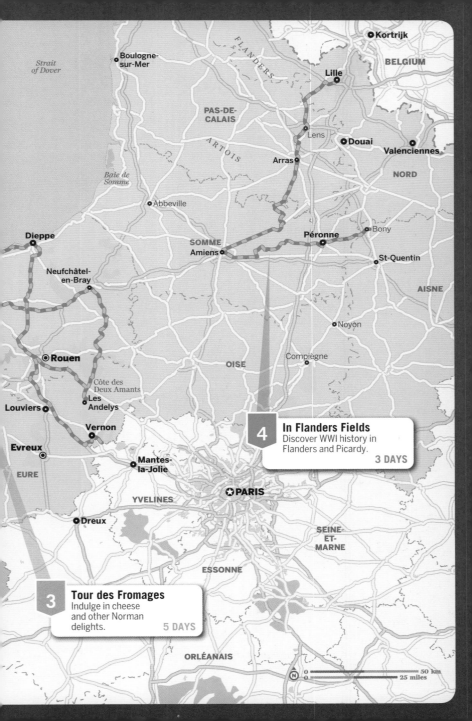

Strait
of Dover

Kortrijk

**Boulogne-
sur-Mer**

FLANDERS

Lille

BELGIUM

PAS-DE-
CALAIS

ARTOIS

Lens

Douai

Valenciennes

Arras

NORD

Baie de
Somme

Abbeville

Dieppe

SOMME
Amiens

Péronne

Bony

St-Quentin

Neufchâtel-
en-Bray

AISNE

Noyon

Rouen

OISE

Compiègne

Côte des
Deux Amants

Les
Andelys

Louviers

Vernon

4 **In Flanders Fields**
Discover WWI history in
Flanders and Picardy.
3 DAYS

Evreux

EURE

**Mantes-
la-Jolie**

PARIS

YVELINES

Dreux

SEINE-
ET-
MARNE

ESSONNE

3 **Tour des Fromages**
Indulge in cheese
and other Norman
delights. **5 DAYS**

ORLÉANAIS

0 ————— 50 km
0 ————— 25 miles

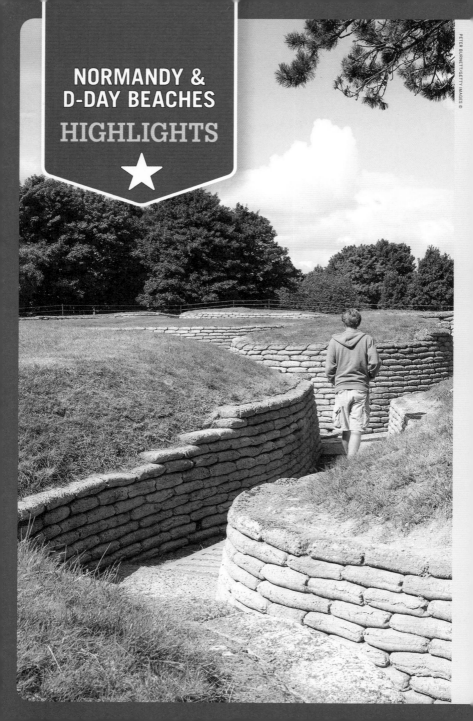

D-Day Beaches (right)
On 6 June 1944 the largest invasion the world has ever seen stormed the beaches of Normandy. Now known as D-Day, it marked the turning point of WWII. See the area on Trip ❶

Vimy Ridge (left)
Walk through one of the only surviving trench systems from WWI. See it on Trip ❹

Musée d'Art Moderne André Malraux (top right) This museum in Le Havre contains the best impressionist collection outside Paris. See it on Trip ❷

CITY GUIDE

Île de la Cité, Paris

PARIS

If ever a city needed no introduction, it's Paris – a trend setter, fashion former and style icon for centuries, and still very much at the cutting edge. Whether you're here to tick off the landmarks or seek out the secret corners, Paris fulfils all your expectations, and still leaves you wanting more.

Getting Around

Driving in Paris is a nightmare. Happily, there's no need for a car. The metro is fast, frequent and efficient; tickets cost €1.70 (day passes €6.70) and are valid on the city's buses. Bikes can be hired from 1800 Vélib (www.velib. paris.fr) stations; insert a credit card, authorise a €150 deposit and pedal away. Day passes cost €1; first 30 minutes free, subsequent 30 minutes from €2.

Parking

Meters don't take coins; use a chip-enabled credit card. Municipal car parks cost €2 to €3.50 an hour, or €20 to €25 per 24 hours.

Discover the Taste of Paris

Le Marais is one of the best areas for eating out, with its small restaurants and trendy bistros. Don't miss Paris' street markets: the Marché Bastille, rue Montorgueil and rue Mouffetard are full of atmosphere.

Live Like a Local

Base yourself in Montmartre for its Parisian charm, if you don't mind crowds. Le Marais and Bastille provide style on a budget, while St-Germain is good for a splurge.

Useful Websites

Paris Info (http://en.parisinfo. com) Official visitor site.

Lonely Planet (www. lonelyplanet.com/paris) Lonely Planet's city guide.

Secrets of Paris (www. secretsofparis.com) Local's blog full of insider tips.

Paris by Mouth (www. parisbymouth.com) Eat and drink your way round the capital.

Place du Général de Gaulle, Lille

LILLE

Lille may be France's most underrated major city. This once-tired industrial metropolis has transformed itself into a stylish, self-confident city with a strong Flemish accent. Three art museums, lots of stylish shops and a lovely old town make it well worth investigating.

Getting Around

Driving into Lille is incredibly confusing, even with a good map; just suspend your sense of direction and blindly follow the 'Centre Ville' signs. Lille's buses and two speedy metro lines run until about 12.30am. Tickets cost €1.50; a Pass' Journée (all-day pass) costs €4.

Parking

If you're driving, the best idea is to leave your vehicle at the park-and-ride at Champ de Mars on bd de la Liberté (open from 10am to 6pm or 7pm, closed Saturdays and Sundays, September to March), 1.2km northwest of the centre. It costs €3.25 a day and includes return travel for five people to central Lille on bus 12.

Discover the Taste of Lille

Lille's proximity to Alsace and Belgium has influenced its cuisine. Cosy *estaminets* (Flemish eateries) serve Lillois specialities such as *carbonade* (braised beef stewed with beer, spiced bread and brown sugar) and *potjevleesch* (jellied chicken, pork, veal and rabbit).

Live Like a Local

Most hotels are within striking distance of the city centre, but Lille's business focus means many are short on charm. On the plus side, rates drop at weekends.

Useful Website

Lille Tourisme (www.lilletourism.com) Comprehensive city site.

Road Trip Through Lille: ④

Destinations coverage: p82

NEED TO KNOW

CURRENCY
Euro (€)

LANGUAGE
French

VISAS
Generally not required for stays of up to 90 days (or at all for EU nationals); some nationalities need a Schengen visa.

FUEL
Petrol stations are common around main roads and larger towns. Unleaded costs from around €1.60 per litre; *gazole* (diesel) is usually at least €0.15 cheaper.

RENTAL CARS
ADA (www.ada.fr)

Auto Europe (www.autoeurope.com)

Avis (www.avis.com)

Europcar (www.europcar.com)

Hertz (www.hertz.com)

IMPORTANT NUMBERS
Ambulance (🖊15)

Police (🖊17)

Fire brigade (🖊18)

Europe-wide emergency (🖊112)

Climate

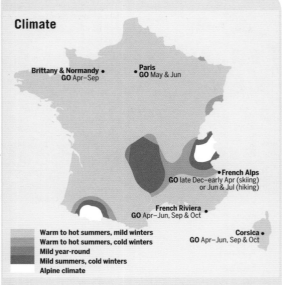

Brittany & Normandy •
GO Apr–Sep

• Paris
GO May & Jun

• French Alps
GO late Dec–early Apr (skiing) or Jun & Jul (hiking)

French Riviera •
GO Apr–Jun, Sep & Oct

Corsica •
GO Apr–Jun, Sep & Oct

- Warm to hot summers, mild winters
- Warm to hot summers, cold winters
- Mild year-round
- Mild summers, cold winters
- Alpine climate

When to Go

High Season (Jul & Aug)
» The main holiday season in France – expect traffic jams and big queues, especially in August.

» Christmas, New Year and Easter are also busy times to travel.

Shoulder Season (Apr–Jun & Sep)
» Balmy temperatures, settled weather and light crowds make this an ideal time to travel.

» Hotel rates drop in busy areas such as southern France and the Atlantic coast.

» The *vendange* (grape harvest) happens in early autumn.

Low Season (Oct–Mar)
» Expect heavy discounts on accommodation (sometimes as much as 50%).

» Snow covers the Alps and Pyrenees, as well as much of central France.

» Many sights and hotels close down for winter.

» Late December to March is high season in French ski resorts.

Daily Costs

Budget less than €100

» Double room in a budget hotel: €50–70

» Set lunchtime menus: €10–15

Midrange €100–200

» Double room in a midrange hotel: €70–120

» À la carte mains: €15–20

Top End over €200

» Luxury hotel room: €150–200

» Top-end restaurant meal: menus from €50, à la carte from €80

Eating

Cafes Coffee, drinks and bar snacks.

Bistros Serve anything from light meals to sit-down dinners.

Restaurants Range from simple *auberges* (country inns) to Michelin-starred wonders.

Vegetarians Limited choice on most menus; look out for *restaurants bios* in cities.

In this book, price symbols indicate the cost of a two-course set menu:

€	less than €20
€€	€20–40
€€€	more than €40

Sleeping

Hotels France has a wide range of hotels, from budget to luxury. Unless indicated otherwise, breakfast is extra.

Chambres d'hôte The French equivalent of a B&B; prices nearly always include breakfast.

Hostels Most large towns have a hostel operated by the FUAJ (Fédération Unie des Auberges de Jeunesse).

Price symbols indicate the cost of a double room with private bathroom in high season unless otherwise noted:

€	less than €80
€€	€80–180
€€€	more than €180

Arriving in France

Aéroport Roissy Charles de Gaulle (Paris)

Rental cars Major car-rental agencies have concessions at arrival terminals.

Trains, buses and RER To Paris centre every 15 to 30 minutes, 5am to 11pm.

Taxis €50 to €60; 30 minutes to Paris centre.

Aéroport d'Orly (Paris)

Rental cars Desks beside the arrivals area.

Orlyval rail, RER and buses At least every 15 minutes, 5am to 11pm.

Taxis €45 to €60; 25 minutes to Paris centre.

Mobile Phones

Most European and Australian phones work, but turn off roaming to avoid heavy data charges. Buying a French SIM card provides much cheaper call rates.

Internet Access

Wi-fi is available in most hotels and B&Bs (usually free, but sometimes for a small charge). Many cafes and restaurants also offer free wi-fi to customers.

Money

ATMs are available everywhere. Most major credit cards are accepted (with the exception of American Express). Larger cities have *bureaux de change*.

Tipping

By law, restaurant and bar prices are *service compris* (include a 15% service charge). Taxis expect around 10%; round up bar bills to the nearest euro.

Useful Websites

France Guide (www.franceguide.com) Official website run by the French tourist office.

Lonely Planet (www.lonelyplanet.com/france) Travel tips, accommodation, forum and more.

Mappy (www.mappy.fr) Online tools for mapping and journey planning.

France Meteo (www.meteo.fr) The lowdown on the French weather.

About France (www.about-france.com/travel.htm) Tips for driving in France.

For more, see Road Trip Essentials (p104).

Road Trips

1 **D-Day's Beaches 3 Days**
Follow the course of the WWII invasion on Normandy's beaches. (p17)

2 **Monet's Normandy 4 Days**
Investigate the origins of impressionism, from Étretat's cliffs to Monet's lily garden. (p27)

3 **Tour des Fromages 5 Days**
Fatten yourself up on this tour of Normandy's creamy cheeses. (p35)

4 **In Flanders Fields 3 Days**
The ghosts of the Great War still linger on the battlefields of northern France. (p43)

Cheese tour, Camembert (p37)
JUSTIN FOULKES/LONELY PLANET ©

D-Day's Beaches

1

Explore the events of D-Day, when Allied troops stormed ashore to liberate Europe from Nazi occupation. From war museums to landing beaches, it's a fascinating and sobering experience.

TRIP HIGHLIGHTS

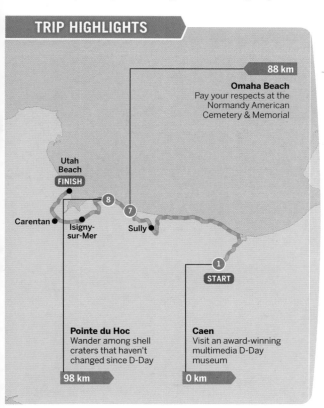

88 km

Omaha Beach
Pay your respects at the Normandy American Cemetery & Memorial

Utah Beach
FINISH

8 **7**

Carentan
Isigny-sur-Mer   Sully

1
START

Pointe du Hoc
Wander among shell craters that haven't changed since D-Day

98 km

Caen
Visit an award-winning multimedia D-Day museum

0 km

3 DAYS
142KM / 88 MILES

GREAT FOR...

BEST TIME TO GO
April to July, to avoid summer-holiday traffic around the beaches.

ESSENTIAL PHOTO
Standing next to the German guns at Longues-sur-Mer.

BEST FOR HISTORY
The Caen Mémorial provides you with a comprehensive D-Day overview.

Left: Normandy American Cemetery & Memorial (p68), Colleville-sur-Mer, Omaha Beach

1 D-Day's Beaches

The beaches and bluffs are quiet today, but on 6 June 1944 the Normandy
shoreline witnessed the arrival of the largest armada the world has ever
seen. This patch of the French coast will forever be synonymous with
D-Day (known to the French as Jour-J), and the coastline is strewn with
memorials, museums and cemeteries – reminders that though victory
was won on the Longest Day, it came at a terrible price.

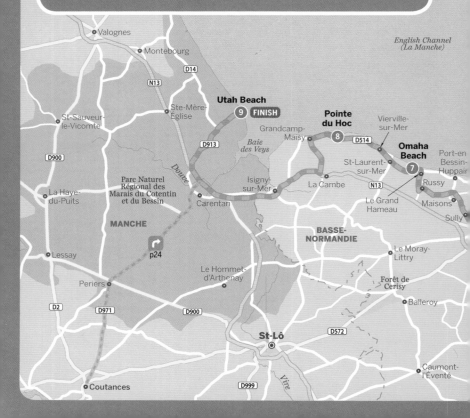

TRIP HIGHLIGHT

❶ Caen (p72)

Situated 3km northwest of Caen, the award-winning **Mémorial – Un Musée pour la Paix** (Memorial – A Museum for Peace; 📞02 31 06 06 44; www.memorial-caen.fr; esplanade Général Eisenhower; adult/child €19/11.50; ⏱9am-7pm daily mid-Feb–mid-Nov, 9.30am-6.30pm Tue-Sun mid-Nov–mid-Feb, closed 3 weeks in Jan) is a brilliant place to begin with some background on the historic events of D-Day, and the wider context of WWII. Housed in a purpose-designed building covering 14,000 sq metres, it's an immersive experience, using sound, lighting, film, animation and audio testimony to evoke the grim realities of war, the trials of occupation and the joy of liberation.

The visit begins with a whistle-stop overview of Europe's descent into total war, tracing events from the end of WWI through to the rise of fascism in Europe, the German occupation of France and the Battle of Normandy. A second section focuses on the Cold War. There's also an underground gallery dedicated to winners of the Nobel Peace Prize, located in bunkers used by the Germans in 1944.

On your way round, look out for an original Typhoon fighter plane and a full-size Sherman tank.

The Drive » From the museum, head northeast along Esplanade Brillaud de Laujardière, and follow signs to Ouistreham. You'll join the E46 ring road; follow it to exit 3a (Porte d'Angleterre), and merge onto the D515 and D84 to Ouistreham. Park on the seafront on bd Aristide Briand. In all it's a trip of 18km.

❷ Ouistreham

On D-Day, the sandy seafront around Ouistreham was code named **Sword Beach** and was the focus of attack for the British 3rd Infantry Division.

There are precious few reminders of the battle

LINK YOUR TRIP

Monet's Normandy
2 From the end of our Monet-themed trip at Fécamp, drive southwest on the A29 and A13 to Caen, a journey of just under 130km.

NORMANDY & D-DAY BEACHES 1 D-DAY'S BEACHES

19

D-DAY DRIVING ROUTES

There are several signposted driving routes around the main battle sites – look for signs for 'D-Day-Le Choc' in the American sectors and 'Overlord – L'Assaut' in the British and Canadian sectors. A free booklet called *The D-Day Landings and the Battle of Normandy,* available from tourist offices, has details on the eight main routes.

Maps of the D-Day beaches are available at *tabacs* (tobacconists), newsagents and bookshops in Bayeux and elsewhere.

now, but on D-Day the scene was very different: most of the surrounding buildings had been levelled by artillery fire, and German bunkers and artillery positions were strung out along the seafront. Sword Beach was the site of some of the most famous images of D-Day – including the infamous ones of British troops landing with bicycles, and bagpiper Bill Millin piping troops ashore while under heavy fire.

The Drive » Follow the seafront west onto rue de Lion, following signs for 'Overlord – L'Assaut' onto the D514 towards Courseulles-sur-Mer, 18km west. Drive through town onto rue de Ver, and follow signs to 'Centre Juno Beach'.

- - - - - - - - - -

❸ Juno & Gold Beaches

On D-Day, Courseulles-sur-Mer was known as **Juno Beach**, and was stormed mainly by Canadian troops. It

was here that the exiled French General Charles de Gaulle came ashore after the landings – the first 'official' French soldier to set foot in mainland Europe since 1940. He was followed by Winston Churchill on 12 June and King George VI on 16 June. A Cross of Lorraine marks the historic spot.

The area's only Canadian museum, **Juno Beach Centre** (☎02 31 37 32 17; www.junobeach.org; adult/child €7/5.50; ☻9.30am-7pm Apr-Sep, 10am-6pm Oct-Mar, closed Jan) has exhibits on Canada's role in the war effort and the landings, and offers guided tours of Juno Beach (€5.50) from April to October.

A short way west is **Gold Beach**, attacked by the British 50th Infantry on D-Day.

The Drive » Drive west along the D514 for 14km to Arromanches. You'll pass a car park and viewpoint marked with a statue of the Virgin Mary, which overlooks Port Winston and Gold Beach. Follow the road

into town and signs to Musée du Débarquement.

- - - - - - - - - -

❹ Arromanches (p71)

This seaside town was the site of one of the great logistical achievements of D-Day. In order to unload the vast quantities of cargo needed by the invasion forces without capturing one of the heavily defended Channel ports, the Allies set up prefabricated marinas off two landing beaches, code named **Mulberry Harbour**. These consisted of 146 massive cement caissons towed over from England and sunk to form a semicircular breakwater in which floating bridge spans were moored. In the three months after D-Day, the Mulberries facilitated the unloading of a mind-boggling 2.5 million men, four million tonnes of equipment and 500,000 vehicles.

At low tide, the stanchions of one of these artificial quays, **Port Winston** (named after Churchill), can still be seen on the sands at Arromanches.

Beside the beach, the **Musée du Débarquement** (Landing Museum; ☎02 31 22 34 31; www.musee-arromanches.fr; place du 6 Juin; adult/child €7.90/5.80; ☻9am-12.30pm & 1.30-5pm Oct-Apr, 9am-5pm May-Sep, closed Jan) makes for a very informative stop before visiting the beaches. Dioramas, models and two films explain the logistics and importance of Port Winston. Written material is available in 18 languages.

The Drive » Continue west along the D514 for 6km to the village of Longues-sur-Mer. You'll see the sign for the Batterie de Longues on your right.

- - - - - - - - - - - - -

⑤ Longues-sur-Mer (p72)

At Longues-sur-Mer you can get a glimpse of the awesome firepower available to the German defenders in the shape of two 150mm artillery guns, still housed in their concrete casements. On D-Day they were capable of hitting targets over 20km away – including

Gold Beach (to the east) and Omaha Beach (to the west). Parts of the classic D-Day film, *The Longest Day* (1962), were filmed here.

The Drive » Backtrack to the crossroads and head straight over onto the D104, signed to Vaux-sur-Aure/Bayeux for 8km. When you reach town, turn right onto the D613, and follow signs to the 'Musée de la Bataille de Normandie'.

- - - - - - - - - - - - -

⑥ Bayeux (p65)

Though best known for its medieval tapestry (see p64), Bayeux has another claim to fame: it was the first town to be liberated after D-Day (on the morning of 7 June 1944).

It's also home to the largest of Normandy's 18 Commonwealth military cemeteries – the **Bayeux War Cemetery**, situated on bd Fabien

Ware. It contains 4848 graves of soldiers from the UK and 10 other countries – including Germany. Across the road is a memorial for 1807 Commonwealth soldiers whose remains were never found. The Latin inscription reads: 'We, whom William once conquered, have now set free the conqueror's native land'.

Nearby, the **Musée Mémorial de la Bataille de Normandie** (Battle of Normandy Memorial Museum; www.bayeuxmuseum.com; bd Fabien Ware; adult/child €6/4; ☺9.30am-6.30pm May-Sep, 10am-12.30pm & 2-6pm Oct-Apr) explores the battle through photos, personal accounts, dioramas and a 25-minute film, screening in French and English.

The Drive » After overnighting in Bayeux, head northwest of town on the

D-DAY IN FIGURES

Code named 'Operation Overlord', the D-Day landings were the largest military operation in history. On the morning of 6 June 1944, swarms of landing craft – part of an armada of over 6000 ships and 13,000 aeroplanes – hit the northern Normandy beaches, and tens of thousands of soldiers from the USA, the UK, Canada and elsewhere began pouring onto French soil. The initial landing force involved some 45,000 troops; 15 more divisions were to follow once successful beachheads had been established.

The majority of the 135,000 Allied troops stormed ashore along 80km of beaches north of Bayeux code named (from west to east) Utah, Omaha, Gold, Juno and Sword. The landings were followed by the 76-day Battle of Normandy, during which the Allies suffered 210,000 casualties, including 37,000 troops killed. German casualties are believed to have been around 200,000; another 200,000 German soldiers were taken prisoner. About 14,000 French civilians also died.

For more background and statistics, see www.normandiememoire.com and www.6juin1944.com.

WHY THIS IS A CLASSIC TRIP
OLIVER BERRY, AUTHOR

You'll have heard the D-Day story many times before, but there's nothing quite like standing on the beaches where this epic struggle played out. D-Day marked the turning point of WWII and heralded the end for Nazism in Europe. Paying your respects to the soldiers who laid down their lives in the name of freedom is an experience that'll stay with you forever.

Top left: A large-calibre gun remains in situ at the Nazi's Atlantic Wall, Longues-sur-Mer
Left: Grave of an unknown soldier, Bayeux
Right: Utah Beach

A SOLDIER
OF THE
1939–1945
WAR
6TH JUNE 1944

CORMON FRANCIS/GETTY IMAGES ©

DENNIS K. JOHNSON/GETTY IMAGES ©

D6 towards Port-en-Bessin-Huppain. You'll reach a Super-U supermarket after about 10km. Go round the roundabout and turn onto the D514 for another 8km. You'll see signs to the 'Cimetière Americain' near the hamlet of Le Bray. Omaha Beach is another 4km further on, near Vierville-sur-Mer.

---

⑦ Omaha Beach (p70)

If anywhere symbolises the courage and sacrifice of D-Day, it's Omaha – still known as 'Bloody Omaha' to US veterans. It was here, on the 7km stretch of coastline between Vierville-sur-Mer, St-Laurent-sur-Mer and Colleville-sur-Mer, that the most brutal fighting on D-Day took place. US troops had to fight their way across the beach towards the heavily defended cliffs, exposed to underwater obstacles, hidden minefields and withering crossfire. The toll was heavy: of the 2500 casualties at Omaha on D-Day, over 1000 were killed, most within the first hour of the landings.

High on the bluffs above Omaha, the **Normandy American Cemetery & Memorial** (www.abmc.gov; Colleville-sur-Mer; ⊙9am-6pm mid-Apr–mid-Sep, to 5pm rest of year) provides a sobering reminder of the

DETOUR: COUTANCES

Start ⑨ Utah Beach

The lovely old Norman town of **Coutances** makes a good detour when travelling between the D-Day beaches and Mont St-Michel. At the town's heart is its Gothic **Cathédrale de Coutances** (parvis Notre-Dame; admission free; ⏰9am-7pm). Interior highlights include several 13th-century windows, a 14th-century fresco of St Michael skewering the dragon, and an organ and high altar from the mid-1700s. You can climb the lantern tower on a **tour** (adult/child €7/4; ⏰in French 11am & 3pm Mon-Fri, 3pm Sun Jul & Aug).

Coutances is about 50km south of Utah Beach by the most direct route.

human cost of the battle. Featured in the opening scenes of *Saving Private Ryan,* this is the largest American cemetery in Europe, containing the graves of 9387 American soldiers, and a memorial to 1557 comrades 'known only unto God'.

White marble crosses and stars of David stretch off in seemingly endless rows, surrounded by an immaculately tended expanse of lawn. The cemetery is overlooked by a large colonnaded memorial, centred on a statue dedicated to the spirit of American youth. Nearby is a reflective pond and a small chapel.

The Drive » From the Vierville-sur-Mer seafront, follow the rural D514 through quiet countryside towards Grandcamp-Maisy. After about 10km you'll see signs to 'Pointe du Hoc'.

TRIP HIGHLIGHT

⑧ Pointe du Hoc

West of Omaha, this craggy promontory was the site of D-Day's most audacious military exploit. At 7.10am, 225 US Army Rangers commanded by Lt Col James Earl Rudder scaled the sheer 30m cliffs, where the Germans had stationed a battery of artillery guns trained onto the beaches of Utah and Omaha. Unfortunately, the guns had already been moved inland, and Rudder and his men spent the next two days repelling counterattacks. By the time they were finally relieved on 8 June, 81 of the rangers had been killed and 58 more had been wounded.

Today the **site** (☎02 31 51 90 70; www.abmc.gov; admission free; ⏰9am-5pm), which France turned over to the US government in 1979, looks much as it did on D-Day, complete with shell craters and crumbling gun emplacements.

The Drive » Stay on the D514 to Grandcamp-Maisy, then continue south onto the D13 dual carriageway. Stay on the road till you reach the turn-off for the D913, signed to St-Marie-du-Mont/Utah Beach. It's a drive of 44km.

⑨ Utah Beach

The D-Day tour ends at St-Marie-du-Mont, aka **Utah Beach**, assaulted by soldiers of the US 4th and 8th Infantry Divisions. The beach was relatively lightly defended, and by midday the landing force had linked with paratroopers from the 101st Airborne. By nightfall, some 20,000 men and 1700 vehicles had arrived on French soil, and the road to European liberation had begun.

Today the site is marked by military memorials and the **Musée du Débarquement de Utah Beach** (Landing Museum; ☎02 33 71 53 35; www.utah-beach.com; Ste-Marie du Mont; adult/child €8/3.50; ⏰9.30am-7pm Jun-Sep, 10am-6pm Oct-May, closed Jan) inside the former German command post.

Right: Cathédrale de Coutances

Monet's Normandy

2

This eclectic trip takes art lovers on a fascinating spin around eastern Normandy. En route you'll hit the key landscapes and cities that inspired Monet, the father of impressionism.

TRIP HIGHLIGHTS

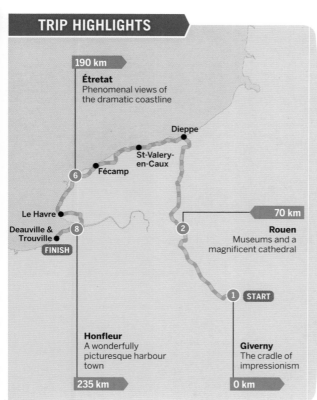

190 km

Étretat
Phenomenal views of the dramatic coastline

Dieppe

St-Valery-en-Caux

6 **Fécamp**

70 km

2

Rouen
Museums and a magnificent cathedral

Le Havre

Deauville & Trouville
8

FINISH

1 **START**

Honfleur
A wonderfully picturesque harbour town

235 km

Giverny
The cradle of impressionism

0 km

4 DAYS
290KM / 180 MILES

GREAT FOR...

BEST TIME TO GO
Any time from September to June for perfectly nuanced light.

ESSENTIAL PHOTO
Snap the truly extraordinary coastal vista from the cliff top in Étretat.

BEST FOR CULTURE
Rouen has plenty of top-quality museums and historic buildings.

Left: Jardins de Claude Monet (p29)

27

2 Monet's Normandy

Be prepared for a visual feast on this three-day trip around the eastern part of Normandy – the cradle of impressionism. Starting from the village of Giverny, location of the most celebrated garden in France, you'll follow in the footsteps of Monet and other impressionist megastars, taking in medieval Rouen, the dramatic Côte d'Albâtre, Le Havre, Honfleur and Trouville. This is your chance to see first-hand why so many painters were attracted to this place.

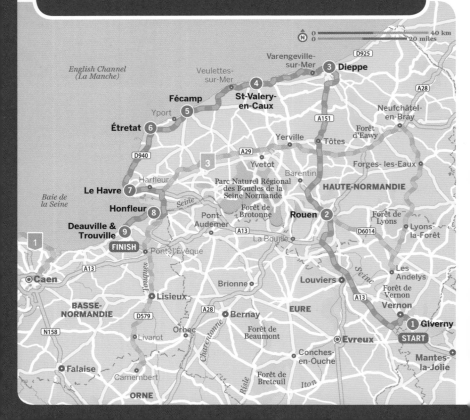

❶ Giverny

The tiny country village of Giverny is a place of pilgrimage for devotees of impressionism. Monet lived here from 1883 until his death in 1926, in a rambling house – surrounded by flower-filled gardens – that's now the immensely popular **Maison et Jardins de Claude Monet** (☎02 32 51 28 21; www. fondation-monet.com; adult/ child €9/5.50; ⏰9.30am-6pm Apr-Oct). His pastel-pink house and Water Lily studio stand on the periphery of the garden

LINK YOUR TRIP

3 Tour des Fromages

From Honfleur or Rouen you can embark on a gastronomic drive, and taste and learn about some of the best cheese in France at various cheese museums.

1 D-Day's Beaches

From Trouville, it's an easy 50km drive west to Caen, the obvious starting point for the D-Day beaches.

(called 'Clos Normand'), with its symmetrically laid-out gardens bursting with flowers.

The Drive » It's a 70km trip (one hour) to Rouen. Head to Vernon and follow signs to Rouen along the A13. A more scenic (but longer) route is via Les Andelys, along the east bank of the Seine.

❷ Rouen (p52)

With its elegant spires and atmospheric medieval quarter complete with narrow lanes and wonky half-timbered houses, it's no wonder that Rouen has inspired numerous painters, including Monet. Some of his works, including one of his studies of the stunning **Cathédrale Notre Dame** (p54), are displayed at the splendid **Musée des Beaux-Arts** (☎02 35 71 28 40; www. rouen-musees.com; esplanade Marcel Duchamp; adult/child €5/free; ⏰10am-6pm Wed-Mon), housed in a grand structure erected in 1870. Feeling inspired? Sign up for an art class with the tourist office (p57) and create your own Rouen Cathedral canvas from the very room in which Monet painted his series of that building.

If you're at all interested in architectural glories, the 14th-century **Abbatiale**

St-Ouen (place du Général de Gaulle; ⏰10am-noon & 2-6pm Tue-Thu, Sat & Sun), which is a marvellous example of the Rayonnant Gothic style, is a must-see abbey. Also don't miss **Église St-Maclou** (place Barthélémy) and the ornate **Palais de Justice** (Law Courts; rue aux Juifs) – both are typical examples of the Flamboyant Gothic style.

The Drive » Follow signs to Dieppe. Count on 45 minutes for the 65km trip.

❸ Dieppe (p58)

Sandwiched between limestone cliffs, Dieppe is a small-scale fishing port with a pleasant seafront promenade. Still used by fishing vessels but dominated by pleasure craft, the **port** makes for a bracing sea-air stroll. High above the city on the western cliff, the 15th-century **Château-musée** (☎02 35 06 61 99; www.dieppe.fr; rue de Chastes; adult/child €4/2; ⏰10am-noon & 2-6pm, closed Tue Oct-May) is the town's most imposing landmark and offers spectacular views of the coast. Inside, the museum, renovated in 2014, explores the city's maritime history. A highlight is the local scenes painted by artists such as Pissaro and Renoir. Monet immortalised **Pourville**, a seaside village on the western outskirts of Dieppe.

The Drive » Take the scenic coastal roads (D75 and D68), rather than the inland D925, via the resort towns of Pourville, Varengeville-sur-Mer, Quiberville, St-Aubin-sur-Mer, Sotteville-sur-Mer and Veules-les-Roses (35km, 45 minutes).

- - - - - - - - - - - - - -

④ St-Valery-en-Caux (p59)

You're now in the heart of the scenic Côte d'Albâtre (Alabaster Coast), which stretches from Dieppe southwest to Étretat. With its lofty bone-white cliffs, this wedge of coast is a geological wonder world that has charmed a generation of impressionists, including Monet. Once you get a glimpse of sweet little St-Valery-en-Caux, with its delightful port, lovely stretch of stony beach and majestic cliffs, you'll see why.

The Drive » Take the coastal road (D79) via Veulettes-sur-Mer. Count on an hour for the 36km trip.

- - - - - - - - - - - - - -

⑤ Fécamp (p60)

After all that driving along the Côte d'Albâtre, it's time to stop for a glass of Bénédictine at the **Palais de la Bénédictine** (☏02 35 10 26 10; www.benedictinedom. com; 110 rue Alexandre Le

Grand; adult/child €8/3.40; ⏱ticket sales 10.30-11.30am & 2.30-4.30pm mid-Dec–mid-Apr, longer hours mid-Apr–mid-Dec, closed early Jan–mid-Feb). Opened in 1900, this unusually ornate factory is where all the Bénédictine liqueur in the world is made. Self-guided tours take you to a minimuseum of 13th- to 19th-century religious art works and then to the production facilities (visible through glass), where you can admire copper alembics and touch and smell some of the 27 herbs used to make the famous *digestif*.

Be sure to drive up north to **Cap Fagnet** (110m; p60), which offers gobsmacking views of the town and the coastline.

The Drive » Follow signs to Étretat (17km, along the D940). You could also take the D940 and turn off onto the more scenic D11 (via Yport).

- - - - - - - - - - - - - -

TRIP HIGHLIGHT

⑥ Étretat (p61)

Is Étretat the most enticing town in Normandy? It's picture-postcard everywhere you look. The dramatic white cliffs that bookend the town, the **Falaise d'Aval** to the southwest and the **Falaise d'Amont** to the northeast, will stick in your memory. Once at the top, you'll pinch yourself to see

if it's real – the views are sensational. Such irresistible scenery made Étretat a favourite of painters, especially Monet, who produced more than 80 canvases of the scenery here.

The Drive » Follow signs to Le Havre (28km, along the D940 and the D147). Count on about half an hour for the journey.

- - - - - - - - - - - - - -

⑦ Le Havre (p62)

It was in Le Havre that Monet painted the defining impressionist view. His 1873 canvas of the harbour at dawn was entitled *Impression: Sunrise*. Monet wouldn't recognise present-day Le Havre. All but obliterated in September 1944 by Allied bombing raids, the city centre was totally rebuilt after the war by Belgian architect Auguste Perret. Make sure you visit the fantastic **Musée d'Art Moderne André Malraux** (MuMa; ☏02 35 19 62 62; 2 bd Clemenceau; adult/child incl audioguide €5/free; ⏱11am-6pm Mon-Fri, to 7pm Sat & Sun), which houses a truly fabulous collection of impressionist works – the finest in France outside of Paris, with canvases by Monet, Eugène Boudin, Camille Corot and many more. Then head to the fashionable seaside suburb of **Ste-Adresse**, just north of the centre –

Picture-perfect Étretat

another favourite retreat for Monet.

The Drive » Follow signs to Pont de Normandie, which links Le Havre to Honfleur (toll €5.50).

- - - - - - - - - - -

TRIP HIGHLIGHT

8 Honfleur (p76)

Honfleur is exquisite to look at. (No, you're not dreaming!) Its heart is the amazingly picturesque **Vieux Bassin** (Old Harbour),

from where explorers once set sail for the New World. Marvel at the extraordinary 15th-century wooden **Église Ste-Catherine** (place Ste-Catherine; ◷9am-5.15pm), complete with a roof that from the inside resembles an upturned boat, then wander the warren of flower-filled cobbled streets lined with wooden and stone buildings.

Honfleur's graceful beauty has inspired numerous painters, including Eugène Boudin, an early impressionist painter born here in 1824, and Monet. Their works are displayed at the **Musée Eugène Boudin** (☎02 31 89 54 00; www.musees-honfleur.fr; 50 rue de l'Homme de Bois; adult/child €5.60/4.10, late Jun-Sep €6.50/5; ◷10am-noon & 2-6pm Wed-Mon mid-Mar–Sep, 2.30-5.30pm Wed-Mon &

CLAUDE MONET

The undisputed leader of the impressionists, Claude Monet was born in Paris in 1840 and grew up in Le Havre, where he found an early affinity with the outdoors.

From 1867 Monet's distinctive style began to emerge, focusing on the effects of light and colour and using the quick, undisguised broken brushstrokes that would characterise the impressionist period. His contemporaries were Pissarro, Renoir, Sisley, Cézanne and Degas. The young painters left the studio to work outdoors, experimenting with the shades and hues of nature, and arguing and sharing ideas. Their work was far from welcomed by critics; one of them condemned it as 'impressionism', in reference to Monet's *Impression: Sunrise* when it was exhibited in 1874.

From the late 1870s Monet concentrated on painting in series, seeking to recreate a landscape by showing its transformation under different conditions of light and atmosphere. In 1883 Monet moved to Giverny, planting his property with a variety of flowers around an artificial pond, the Jardin d'Eau, in order to paint the subtle effects of sunlight on natural forms. It was here that he painted the *Nymphéas* (Water Lilies) series.

For more info on Monet and his work, visit www.giverny.org.

10am-noon Sat & Sun Oct–mid-Mar). The museum also features superb 19th- and 20th-century paintings of Normandy's towns and coasts by Dubourg and Dufy. An English audioguide costs €2.

The Drive » From Honfleur it's a 14km trip to Trouville along the D513 (about 20 minutes).

❾ Deauville & Trouville (p74)

Finish your impressionist road trip in style by heading southwest to the twin seaside resorts of Deauville and Trouville, which are only separated by a bridge but maintain distinctly different personalities. Exclusive, expensive and brash, Deauville is packed with designer boutiques, deluxe hotels and public gardens of impossible neatness, and is home to two racetracks and a high-profile American film festival.

Trouville, another veteran beach resort, is more down to earth. During the 19th century the town was frequented by writers and painters, including Monet, who spent his honeymoon here in 1870. No doubt he was lured by the picturesque port, the 2km-long sandy beach lined with opulent villas and the laid-back seaside ambience.

Right: Église Ste-Catherine (p31), Honfleur

Tour des Fromages

3

On this gastronomic drive you'll devour some of the best cheese in France and see where the seaside inspired artists, where Joan of Arc was executed and where Richard the Lionheart prowled.

TRIP HIGHLIGHTS

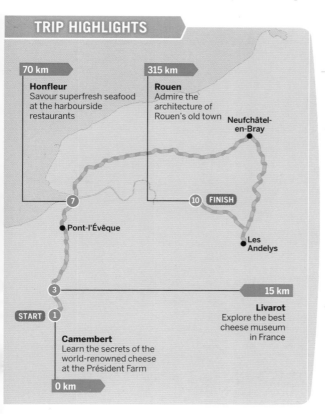

70 km

Honfleur
Savour superfresh seafood at the harbourside restaurants

315 km

Rouen
Admire the architecture of Rouen's old town

Neufchâtel-en-Bray

7

● Pont-l'Évêque

10 FINISH

● Les Andelys

3

15 km

START **1**

Livarot
Explore the best cheese museum in France

Camembert
Learn the secrets of the world-renowned cheese at the Président Farm

0 km

5 DAYS
315KM / 196 MILES

GREAT FOR...

BEST TIME TO GO

In May Pont L'Évêque celebrates all that is cheese during the Fête du Fromage.

 ESSENTIAL PHOTO

Snap a shot of the Seine from the platform near the Château Gaillard.

 BEST FOR HISTORY

Pay your respects to the memory of Joan of Arc in Rouen.

Left: French essentials: bread and cheese

35

3 Tour des Fromages

More cheese, please! It's said that in France there is a different variety of cheese for every day of the year. On this driving culinary extravaganza you'll taste, and learn about, some of the very finest of French cheeses. Cheese cravings sated, explore the backstreets of Rouen, build castles made of sand on the seashore and clamber up to castles made of stone in the interior.

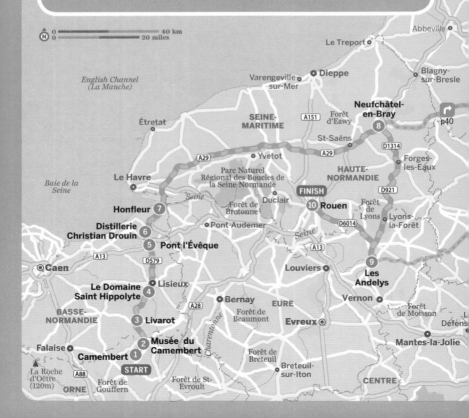

❶ Camembert (p77)

Thanks to a delicious soft cheese, the name Camembert is world famous, so it can be surprising to learn that Camembert is merely a small, picturesque, classic Norman village of half-timbered buildings. The big attraction here is of course the aforementioned cheese, and you can learn all about it during a guided tour of the **Maison du**

Camembert (🕿02 33 12 10 37; www.fermepresident. com; adult/child €3.50/1.50; ⊗10am-noon & 2-5pm daily May-Sep, Wed-Sun Apr & Oct, Fri-Sun mid-Feb–Mar, closed Nov–mid-Feb), an early-19th-century farm restored by Président, one of the region's largest Camembert producers.

The Drive ›› It's a 5km, 10-minute drive along the D246 and then the D16 from Camembert village to the Musée du Camembert in Vimoutiers.

❷ Musée du Camembert

Recently reopened after two years of extensive renovations, the small **Musée du Camembert** (🕿02 33 39 30 29; 10 Av du Général de Gaulle; adult/child €3/2; ⊗2-5.30pm Thu-Mon Apr-Oct), in the village of Vimoutiers, gives you the lowdown on the history and culture of the smelly stuff. It's a privately run affair; you might have to call for them to open up.

The Drive ›› It's another 10-minute drive north to Livarot, along the D579.

❸ Livarot

Although not as famous internationally as Camembert, Livarot is a big deal in France. The town where the cheese of the same name originated is home to probably the best cheese tour in Normandy. **Le Village Fromager** (L'Atelier Fromager; 🕿02 31 48 20 10; www.graindorge.fr; 42 rue du Général Leclerc; ⊗9.30am-1pm & 2-5.30pm Mon-Sat, 10.30am-1pm & 3-5.30pm Sun) offers a free tour and tasting at the Graindorge factory. A self-guided tour accompanied by multimedia displays leads through a series of whiffy viewing rooms where you can watch Livarot, Camembert and Pont l'Évêque being made.

After you've expanded your waistline on the cheese tour, work it all off again with a walk around the town. Its wobbly-wiggly half-timbered buildings make it a real charmer.

🔗 LINK YOUR TRIP

④ In Flanders Fields

The war memorials of northern France are a powerful symbol of the wastefulness of war. Amiens, the start of our Flanders Fields drive, is 120km from Rouen.

The Drive » Using the D579 it's only a 15km drive through leafy countryside to Le Domaine Saint Hippolyte, just on the outskirts of the village of St Martin de la Lieue (take the third exit off the roundabout at the entrance to the village).

④ Le Domaine Saint Hippolyte

There's fun for all the family at **Le Domaine Saint Hippolyte** (🖉02 31 31 30 68; www.domaine-saint -hippolyte.fr; rte de Livarot/ D579, St Martin de la Lieue; adult/child €5.90/free; ⏱10am-6pm Mon-Tue & Thu-Sat, to 7pm Wed), which is both a cheese producer and a retailer where you can witness the process behind turning milk into cheese. There's also a small museum and, most interestingly for children, a working farm where you can pat cows and stroll through the grounds to the river.

The Drive » A gentle countryside cruise of just over half an hour (31km) up the D45 and D101 will see you easing into Pont l'Évêque.

⑤ Pont l'Évêque

Since the 13th century this unpretentious little town with rivers meandering through its centre has been known for its eponymous cheese. Although two-thirds of the town was destroyed in WWII, careful reconstruction has brought much of it back to life. Half-timbered buildings line the main street and 1960s stained glass bathes the 15th-century **Église St-Michel** (place de l'Église) in coloured light.

There's no shortage of **cheese shops** in town.

If you're passing through over the second weekend in May, don't miss the **Fête du Fromage**, when the townsfolk throw a little party for cheese – only in France!

The Drive » To get to the Distillerie Christian Drouin, your next stop, head out of Pont l'Évêque in a northeasterly direction on the D675. At the roundabout on the edge of the town, take the third exit (rue Saint-Mélaine/ D677) and continue for about 2.5km until you see the farm on your left.

⑥ Distillerie Christian Drouin

In case you were starting to wonder if Normandy was merely a one-cheese pony, pay a visit to the **Distillerie Christian Drouin** (🖉02 31 64 30 05; www.calvados-drouin.com; rte de Trouville, Coudray-Rabut; ⏱9am-noon & 2-6pm), which will let you in on the delights of Norman cider and Calvados (that other classic Norman tipple). Entrance is free.

The Drive » It's a simple enough 17km drive along the D579 to Honfleur and your first sea views (yes, the sun will be out by the time you get there...).

TRIP HIGHLIGHT

⑦ Honfleur (p76)

Long a favourite with painters, Honfleur is arguably Normandy's most charming seaside town.

On the west side of the **Vieux Bassin** (Old Harbour), with its many pleasure boats, **quai Ste-Catherine** is lined with tall, taper-thin houses –

NORMAN CUISINE

Normandy may be the largest region of France not to contain a single vineyard, but its culinary wealth more than makes up for what it lacks in the wine department – besides, any self-respecting Norman would far rather partake in a locally produced cider or Calvados. This is a land of soft cheeses, apples, cream and an astonishingly rich range of seafood and fish. You simply shouldn't leave Normandy without trying classics like *coquilles St-Jacques* (scallops) and *sole dieppoise* (Dieppe sole). And whatever you do, don't forget your *trou normand* ('Norman hole') – the traditional break between courses for a glass of Calvados to cleanse the palate and improve the appetite for the next course!

Alleyway, Rouen (p40)

many protected from the elements by slate tiles – dating from the 16th to the 18th centuries. The **Lieutenance**, at the mouth of the old harbour, was once the residence of the town's royal governor.

Initially intended as a temporary structure, the **Église Ste-Catherine** (place Ste-Catherine; ✪9am-6pm) has been standing in the square for over 500 years. The church is particularly notable for its double-vaulted roof and twin naves, which from the inside resemble a couple of overturned ships' hulls.

The Drive » You've had nice, mellow country lanes so far. Time to speed things up for the 111km race (not too fast, please!) down the A29 to Neufchâtel-en-Brey.

❽ Neufchâtel-en-Bray

The small market town of Neufchâtel-en-Brey is renowned for its heart-shaped cheese called, imaginatively, Neufchâtel. To buy it in the most authentic way, try to time your arrival to coincide with the Saturday-morning **market**.

Appetite satisfied, it's now time for some culture. Check out the **Musée Mathon-Durand** (📞02 35 93 06 55; Grande Rue Saint-Pierre; adult/child €2.35/free; ✪3-6pm Tue-Sun), inside a gorgeous

DETOUR:
AMIENS

Start ⑧ Neufchâtel-en-Brey

One of France's most awe-inspiring Gothic cathedrals is reason enough to make a detour to Amiens, the comfy, if reserved, former capital of Picardy. The **Cathédrale Notre Dame** (place Notre Dame; north tower adult/child €5.50/free; ⊙cathedral 8.30am-6.15pm daily, north tower afternoon only Wed-Mon) is the largest Gothic cathedral in France and a Unesco World Heritage Site. Begun in 1220, the magnificent structure was built to house the **skull of St John the Baptist**. For more, see p98.

From Neufchâtel-en-Brey head 73km (one hour) down the A29 toll road. In order to rejoin the main part of the trip, take the A16 toll road via Beauvais (129km, one hour and 50 minutes) straight to stop 9, Les Andelys.

medieval building that once belonged to a knight. He's long since gone off to fight dragons in the sky, and today the house contains a small museum of local culture.

The Drive » The most obvious route between Neufchâtel-en-Brey and Les Andelys, is along the A28, but that means skirting around Rouen – time it badly and you'll be sitting in traffic breathing in carbon monoxide. Instead, take the more serene D921 back road. Going this way should take you about 80 minutes to cover the 75km.

⑨ Les Andelys (p63)

On a hairpin curve in the Seine lies Les Andelys (the 's' is silent), the old part of which is crowned by the ruins of Château Gaillard, the 12th-century hilltop castle of Richard the Lionheart.

Built from 1196 to 1197, **Château Gaillard** (☎02 32 54 41 93; adult/child €3.20/2.70; ⊙10am-1pm & 2-6pm Wed-Mon late Mar-early Nov) secured the western border of English territory along the Seine until Henry IV ordered its destruction in 1603. Fantastic views of the Seine's white cliffs can be enjoyed from the platform a few hundred metres up the one-lane road from the castle. The tourist office (p63) has

details on tours (€4.50) held at 4.30pm daily except Tuesday and at 11.30am on Sunday. Entry to the grounds is free.

The Drive » It's a 45km, 50-minute scamper (well, as long as you don't hit rush-hour traffic) down the D6014 to your final stop, Rouen.

- - - - - - - - - - - - - - -

TRIP HIGHLIGHT

⑩ Rouen (p52)

With its elegant spires, beautifully restored medieval quarter and soaring Gothic cathedral, the ancient city of Rouen is one of Normandy's highlights. It was here that the young French heroine Joan of Arc (Jeanne d'Arc) was tried for heresy.

Rouen's stunning **Cathédrale Notre Dame** (p54) is the famous subject of a series of paintings by Monet.

Rue du Gros Horloge runs from the cathedral west to **place du Vieux Marché**, where you'll find the thrillingly bizarre **Église Jeanne d'Arc**, with its fish-scale exterior. It sits on the spot where the 19-year-old Joan was burned at the stake.

Right: Château Gaillard, Les Andelys

In Flanders Fields

4

WWI history comes to life in this tour of the battlefields where Allied and German troops endured three years of trench warfare. Stopovers in Lille, Arras and Amiens offer an urban counterpoint.

TRIP HIGHLIGHTS

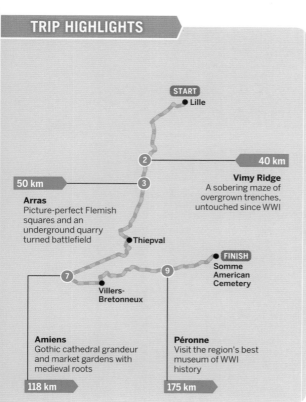

START ● Lille

2

40 km
Vimy Ridge
A sobering maze of overgrown trenches, untouched since WWI

50 km
3
Arras
Picture-perfect Flemish squares and an underground quarry turned battlefield

● Thiepval

7

9

● **FINISH**
Somme American Cemetery

● Villers-Bretonneux

Amiens
Gothic cathedral grandeur and market gardens with medieval roots

118 km

Péronne
Visit the region's best museum of WWI history

175 km

3 DAYS
225KM / 140 MILES

GREAT FOR...

BEST TIME TO GO
March to November; some sites close in winter.

ESSENTIAL PHOTO

The staggering list of missing soldiers' names at Thiepval.

BEST FOR HISTORY

Carrière Wellington, Arras' riveting quarry turned battlefield.

Left: WWI memorial, Vimy Ridge (p44)

4

In Flanders Fields

Shortly after WWI broke out in 1914, Allied troops established a line of resistance against further German advances in the northern French countryside near Arras, resulting in one of the longest and bloodiest standoffs in modern military history. This tour of Flanders and Picardy takes in France's most important WWI battle memorials, along with the great cities of Lille, Arras and Amiens.

① Lille (p82)

A convenient gateway to northern France's WWI battlefields, cosmopolitan Lille offers an engaging mix of grand architecture and Flemish culture. Stop in for dinner at an *estaminet* (traditional Flemish restaurant) and stroll around the gorgeous pedestrianised centre, where highlights include the **Vieille Bourse**, a 17th-century Flemish Renaissance extravaganza decorated with caryatids and cornucopia, and the neo-Flemish **Chambre**

de Commerce, crowned by a gilded clock atop a 76m-high spire.

The Drive » Take the N41, N47 and D55 45km southwest to Vimy Ridge.

TRIP HIGHLIGHT

② Vimy Ridge (p96)

More than any other site in northern France, the vast crater-pocked battlefield at Vimy allows visitors to imagine the horrors of trench warfare. A long tree-lined drive ushers you into the surreally serene landscape of

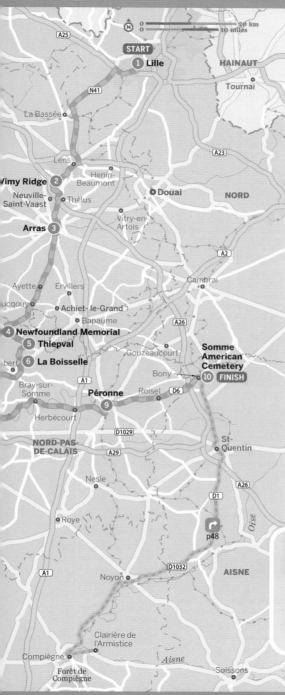

grass-covered century-old bunkers where 3598 Canadian soldiers lost their lives in April 1917 while taking 14km-long Vimy Ridge from the Germans. Climb to the ridgeline to see the striking allegorical **WWI memorial**, then visit the **welcome centre** (www.veterans.gc.ca/eng/memorials; ⏰10am-6pm, closed mid-Dec–mid-Jan) for a **guided tour** (⏰hourly 10am-5pm Tue-Sun Feb-Nov) of the tunnels and trenches, preserved exactly as they were when the guns fell silent.

The Drive » Follow the D55, N17 and D917 12km into Arras.

TRIP HIGHLIGHT

③ Arras (p92)

Contemplating the picture-perfect, reconstructed Flemish-style facades of Arras' two gorgeous market squares (**Grand' Place** and **Place des Héros**) today, it's hard to believe that the city centre was largely reduced to rubble in WWI. For a more palpable sense of Arras' wartime realities, head

LINK YOUR TRIP

1 **D-Day's Beaches**
Relive Europe's other great war on this tour of Normandy's D-Day sites.

1km southeast of town to **Carrière Wellington** (www.carriere-wellington.com; rue Delétoille; adult/child €6.80/3.10; ⏱tours 10am-12.30pm & 1.30-5pm, closed Christmas–mid-Jan), a remarkable quarry turned museum that served as the staging area for an ambitious Allied surprise attack on the Germans on 9 April 1917. Prior to the attack, a corps of 500 New Zealand miners worked round the clock for five months expanding Arras' medieval quarries to accommodate kitchens, a hospital and several thousand Commonwealth troops. Reminders of this chapter in history are everywhere, from Maori-language graffiti to candle burn marks from the Easter Mass celebrated underground the day before the troops surged from their subterranean hideout into the German front lines.

The Drive » Take the D919, D174 and D73 31km southwest to the Newfoundland Memorial, detouring briefly at kilometre 15 to the Ayette Indian and Chinese Cemetery, where Chinese and Hindi inscriptions mark the graves of Indian soldiers and Chinese noncombat labourers.

④ Newfoundland Memorial

On 1 July 1916 the volunteer Royal Newfoundland Regiment stormed entrenched German positions and was nearly wiped out. Like Vimy, the evocative **Beaumont-Hamel Newfoundland Memorial** preserves the battlefield much as it was at fighting's end. Climb to the bronze caribou statue for views of the shell craters, barbed-wire barriers and zigzag trenches that still fill with mud in winter. The on-site **welcome centre** (www.veterans.gc.ca/eng/memorials; ⏱9am-6pm) offers guided tours.

The Drive » Head 5km east-southeast on the D73 through tiny Beaumont-Hamel, across a pretty stream valley, past Ulster Tower Memorial (site of a Northern Irish war monument and a homey tearoom) and on to the easy-to-spot Thiepval memorial.

⑤ Thiepval

On a lonely, windswept hilltop, the towering **Thiepval memorial** to 'the Missing of the Somme' marks the site of a German stronghold that was stormed on 1 July 1916 with unimaginable casualties. Thiepval catches visitors off guard both with its monumentality and its staggering simplicity. Inscribed below the enormous arch, visible from miles around, are the names of 73,367 Commonwealth soldiers whose remains were never recovered or identified. A seemingly endless roll call of regiments runs down each column, with the alphabetised names of individual soldiers emphasising the relentless and arbitrary nature of war. The glass-walled **visitor centre** (⏱10am-6pm) has excellent displays describing the battle and its context.

The Drive » A 7km ride through rolling hills along the D151, and D20 brings you through La Boisselle to La Grande Mine.

⑥ La Boisselle

Just outside this hamlet, the 100m-wide, 30m-deep **Lochnagar Crater** looks like the site of a meteor impact. Colloquially known as **La Grande Mine**, it was created on 1 July 1916 by about 25 tonnes of ammonal laid by British sappers attempting to breach the German lines.

The Drive » Backtrack along the D20 to the D929, then turn left (southwest) 35km to Amiens.

TRIP HIGHLIGHT

⑦ Amiens (p98)

Amiens' pedestrianised city centre offers a delightful break from the battlefields. Climb the north tower of the 13th-century **Cathédrale Notre Dame** (place Notre Dame; north tower adult/child €5.50/free; ⏱cathedral 8.30am-6.15pm daily, north

THEIR NAME LIVETH
FOR EVERMORE

Thiepval memorial

tower afternoons Wed-Mon) for stupendous views of town, and don't miss the free 45-minute **light show** that bathes the façade in vivid medieval colours nightly in summer. (See p98 for more on the cathedral.)

Across the Somme River, gondola-like boats offer tours of Amiens' vast market gardens, the **Hortillonnages** (☎03 22 92 12 18; 54 bd Beauvillé; adult/ child €5.90/4.10; ☺2-5pm Apr-Oct), which have supplied the city with vegetables and flowers since the Middle Ages.

Literature buffs will love the **Maison de Jules Verne** (Home of Jules Verne; ☎03 22 45 45 75; www.amiens. fr/vie-quotidienne/culture; 2 rue Charles Dubois; adult/child €7.50/4; ☺10am-12.30pm

& 2-6.30pm Mon & Wed-Fri, 2-6.30pm Tue, 11am-6.30pm Sat & Sun), the turreted home where Jules Verne wrote many of his best-known works.

The Drive » Take the D1029 19km east to Villers-Bretonneux.

- - - - - - - - - - - -

❽ Villers-Bretonneux

During WWI, 46,000 of Australia's 313,000 volunteer soldiers met their deaths on the Western Front (14,000 others perished elsewhere). In the village of Villers-Bretonneux, the **Musée Franco-Australien** (Franco-Australian Museum; www.museeaustralien.com; 9 rue Victoria; adult/child €5/3; ☺9.30am-5.30pm Mon-Sat) displays a collection of

highly personal WWI Australiana, including letters and photographs that evoke life on the front. It is housed in a primary school that was built with funds donated by Australian schoolchildren.

The names of 10,982 Australian soldiers whose remains were never found are engraved on the base of the 32m-high **Australian National War Memorial** (www.cwgc.org; Villers-Bretonneux), 2km north of town. For the full effect of the imposing monument, climb up to the viewing platform. In front of the memorial is a large **Commonwealth cemetery**. The Anzac Day Dawn Service (www. anzac-france.com) is held here every 25 April at

47

DETOUR: THE RAILROAD CAR WHERE THE WAR ENDED

Start ⑩ Somme American Cemetery

On the 11th hour of the 11th day of the 11th month in 1918, WWI officially ended at **Clairière de l'Armistice** (Armistice Clearing), 7km northeast of the city of Compiègne, with the signing of an armistice inside the railway carriage of Allied supreme commander Maréchal Ferdinand Foch. In the same forest clearing, in a railroad car of similar vintage, the **Musée de l'Armistice** (www.musee-armistice-14-18.fr; adult/child €5/3; ⏰10am-5.30pm, closed Tue Oct-Mar) commemorates these events with memorabilia, newspaper clippings and stereoscopic photos that capture all the mud, muck and misery of WWI; some of the furnishings, hidden away during WWII, were the ones actually used in 1918.

From the Somme American Cemetery, take the D1044, D1 and D1032 86km southwest towards Compiègne, then follow signs 8km east along the N1031 and D546 to Clairière de l'Armistice.

5.30am. The ceremony pays homage to the 313,000 Australians who volunteered for overseas military service; 46,000 met their deaths on the Western Front.

The Drive » From the Australian memorial, take the D23 briefly north, then meander east through pretty rolling country, roughly paralleling the Somme River along the D71, D1 and D1017 into Péronne.

TRIP HIGHLIGHT

❾ Péronne

Housed in a massively fortified château, Péronne's award-winning museum, **Historial de la Grande Guerre** (Museum of the Great War; ☎03 22 83 14 18; www.historial.org; Château de Péronne, Péronne; adult/child incl audioguide €7.50/4; ⏰10am-6pm, closed mid-Dec–mid-Feb) tells the story of the war chronologically, with equal space given to the German, French and British perspectives on what happened, how and why.

The museum contains a unique collection of visually engaging material, including period films and the bone-chilling engravings by Otto Dix, which capture the aesthetic sensibilities, enthusiasm, native patriotism and

unimaginable violence of the time.

The lake behind the museum is a fine place for a stroll or picnic.

For excellent English-language brochures about the battlefields, visit Péronne's tourist office (p98), opposite the museum.

The Drive » The American cemetery is 24km east-northeast of Péronne via the D6, D406 and D57.

⑩ Somme American Cemetery

In September 1918, just six weeks before WWI ended, American units, flanked by their Commonwealth allies, launched an assault on the Germans' heavily fortified Hindenburg Line. Some of the fiercest fighting took place near the village of Bony. At the nearby **Somme American Cemetery** (www.abmc.gov; ⏰9am-5pm), criss-crossing diagonals of crosses and stars of David mark the graves of 1844 American soldiers who fell here; the names of 333 other men whose remains were never recovered are inscribed on the walls of the adjacent **Memorial Chapel**.

The Drive » From here, it's an easy drive back to Arras (69km via the A26), Lille (96km via the A26 and A1) or Amiens (98km via the A29).

Right: Cathédrale Notre Dame, Amiens (p46)

HEMIS.FR RM/GETTY IMAGES ©

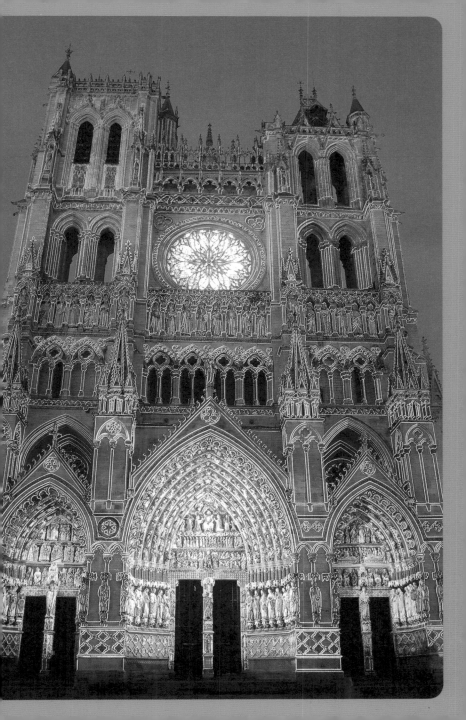

Destinations

Normandy (p52)
From the Norman invasion of England in 1066 to the D-Day landings of 1944, Normandy has long played an outsized role in European history.

Lille, Flanders & Somme (p82)
True, a tan is easier to come by along the Mediterranean, but when it comes to culture, cuisine, beer, shopping and dramatic views of land and sea – not to mention good old-fashioned friendliness – these regions compete with the best France has to offer.

Wine shop, Vieux Bassin, Honfleur (p76)

Normandy

Normandy's rich and often brutal past is brought vividly to life by the Bayeux Tapestry, world famous for its cartoon scenes of 11th-century life; and the cemeteries and memorials along the D-Day beaches, places of solemn pilgrimage.

History

Vikings invaded present-day Normandy in the 9th century, and some of them established settlements and adopted Christianity. In 911 French king Charles the Simple, of the Carolingian dynasty, and Viking chief Hrölfr agreed that the area around Rouen should be handed over to these Norsemen – or Normans, as they came to be known.

Throughout the Hundred Years War (1337–1453), the Duchy of Normandy seesawed between French and English rule. England dominated the region for some 30 years until France gained permanent control in 1450. In the 16th century Normandy, a Protestant stronghold, was the scene of considerable fighting between Catholics and Huguenots.

The liberation of Western Europe from Nazi occupation began on the beaches of Normandy on D-Day, 6 June 1944.

ℹ️ Getting There & Around

Car ferries link Dieppe with the English port of Newhaven; Le Havre and Ouistreham (Caen) with Portsmouth; and Cherbourg with Poole and Portsmouth and the Irish ports of Dublin and Rosslare.

Normandy is easily accessible by train from Paris – Rouen is just 70 minutes from Paris' Gare St-Lazare. Most major towns are accessible by rail, and with the **Visi'ter card** (www.ter-sncf.com) travel for one to four people around the Basse Normandie region is remarkably cheap on weekends and holidays. However, bus services between smaller towns are infrequent at best.

SEINE-MARITIME

The Seine-Maritime *département* stretches along the chalk-white cliffs of the Côte d'Albâtre (Alabaster Coast) from Le Tréport via Dieppe to Le Havre, France's second-busiest port (after Marseille). Its history firmly bound up with the sea, the region offers visitors a mix of small seaside villages and dramatic cliff-top walks.

When you fancy a break from the bracing sea air, head inland to the lively, ancient metropolis of Rouen, a favourite haunt of Monet and Simone de Beauvoir and one of the most intriguing cities in France's northeast.

Rouen

POP 110,700

With its soaring Gothic cathedral, beautifully restored medieval quarter, excellent museums and vibrant cultural life, Rouen is one of Normandy's most engaging destinations. The city has had a turbulent history. It was devastated by fire and plague several times during the Middle Ages, and was occupied by the English during the Hundred Years War. The young French heroine Joan of Arc (Jeanne d'Arc) was tried for heresy and burned at the stake in the central square in 1431. And during WWII, Allied bombing raids laid waste to large parts of the city, especially south of the cathedral.

Rouen

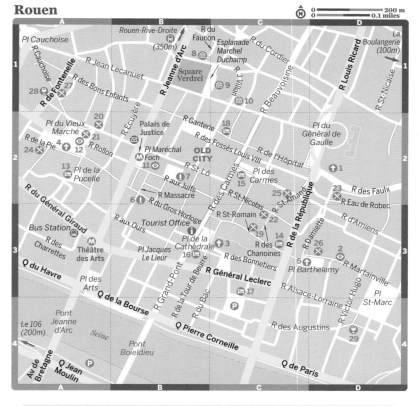

Rouen

⊙ Sights

1	Abbatiale St-Ouen...................... D2
2	Aître St-Maclou........................ D3
3	Cathédrale Notre Dame................ C3
4	Église Jeanne d'Arc.................... A2
5	Église St-Maclou C3
6	Gros Horloge........................... B2
7	Monument Juif.......................... B2
8	Musée de la Céramique B1
9	Musée des Beaux-Arts.................. C1
10	Musée Le Secq des Tournelles.......... C1
11	Palais de Justice....................... B2
12	Place du Vieux Marché................. A2

⊟ Sleeping

13	Hôtel de Bourgtheroulde............... A2
14	Hôtel de la Cathédrale C3
15	Hôtel des Carmes C2

16	Hôtel Le Cardinal...................... B3
17	Hôtel Vieille Tour C3
18	Le Vieux Carré C2

⊗ Eating

	Brasserie Paul .... (see 16)
19	Dame Cakes C3
20	Gill Côté Bistro........................ A2
21	Hallettes du Vieux Marché A2
22	La Rose des Vents C3
23	Le P'tit Bec D2
24	Les Nymphéas A2
25	L'Espiguette C2
26	Made in Normandy D3
27	Minute et Mijoté....................... A1

⊙ Drinking & Nightlife

28	La Boîte à Bières A1
29	Le Saxo............................... D4

ℹ Orientation

The heart of the old city is rue du Gros Horloge, which is two blocks north of the city centre's main east–west thoroughfare, rue Général Leclerc. The main shopping precinct is due north of the cathedral, on pedestrianised rue des Carmes and nearby streets.

- -

◉ Sights & Activities

North of the cathedral, parts of the city centre – especially between rue de la République and rue Jeanne d'Arc – still have a distinctly medieval aspect, with half-timbered buildings and cobblestone streets. Alleyways worth exploring include tiny rue des Chanoines, just 90cm wide.

At the tourist office, audioguides (€5) of the city and the cathedral are available in seven languages.

Cathédrale Notre Dame   Cathedral

(place de la Cathédrale; ⊙ 2-6pm Mon, 9am-7pm Tue-Sat, 8am-6pm Sun Apr-Oct, shorter hours Nov-Mar) Rouen's stunning Gothic cathedral, built between the late 12th and 16th centuries, was famously the subject of a series of canvasses painted by Monet at various times of the day and year. The 75m-tall Tour de Beurre (Butter Tower) was financed by locals in return for being allowed to eat butter during Lent – or so the story goes.

A free sound-and-light spectacular is projected on the facade every night from mid-June (at 11pm) to late September (at 9.30pm).

Gros Horloge   Clock Tower

(rue du Gros Horloge; adult/child €6/3; ⊙ 10am-1pm & 2-7pm Apr-Oct, 2-6pm Nov-Mar, closed Mon, last entry 1hr before closing) Spanning rue du Gros Horloge, the Great Clock's Renaissance archway has a gilded, one-handed medieval clock face on each side. High above, a Gothic belfry, reached via spiral stairs, affords spectacular views. The excellent audioguide is a great introduction to Rouen's colourful history and is available in eight languages.

Palais de Justice   Architecture

(place Maréchal Foch & rue aux Juifs) The ornately Gothic Law Courts, little more than a shell at the end of WWII, have been restored to their early-16th-century glory. The spire- and gargoyle-adorned courtyard is accessible on weekdays via a metal detector from pedestrianised rue aux Juifs. Visitors curious about the French justice system can sit in on a court session – under French law, most proceedings are open to the public.

Under the staircase at the courtyard's eastern end is the Monument Juif (Jewish Monument; rue aux Juifs), the only relic of Rouen's medieval Jewish community, which was expelled by Philippe le Bel in 1306. An impressive, stone-built Romanesque structure constructed around 1100, it is the oldest extant Jewish communal structure in Western Europe.

The tourist office runs two-hour tours (€6.50) at 3pm every Tuesday and at 10.30am on the last Friday of every month.

Place du Vieux Marché   Square

This is where Joan of Arc was executed for heresy in 1431. Dedicated in 1979, thrillingly modernist Église Jeanne d'Arc (⊙ 10am-noon & 2-6pm, closed Fri & Sun mornings), with its fish-scale exterior, stands on the spot where Joan was burned at the stake. The church's soaring interior is lit by some marvellous 16th-century stained glass.

Musée des Beaux-Arts   Art Museum

See p29.

Musée de la Céramique   Museum

(📞 02 35 07 31 74; www.rouen-musees.com; 1 rue du Faucon; adult/child €3/free, 3 museums adult €8; ⊙ 2-6pm Wed-Mon) The Ceramics Museum, housed in a 17th-century building with a courtyard, is known for its 16th- to 19th-century faience (tin-glazed earthenware) and porcelain.

Musée Le Secq des Tournelles   Museum

(📞 02 35 88 42 92; www.museelesecqdestournelles.fr; 2 rue Jacques Villon; adult/child €3/free, 3 museums adult €8; ⊙ 2-6pm Wed-Mon) Home to one of the world's premier collections of wrought iron, this museum showcases the skills of pre-industrial-age iron- and locksmiths. Housed in a desanctified 16th-century church.

Église St-Maclou   Church

(place Barthelemy; ⊙ 10am-noon & 2-5.30pm Sat & Sun) This Flamboyant Gothic church was built between 1437 and 1521 (and renovated in 2013) but much of the decoration dates from the Renaissance. Half-timbered houses inclined at curious angles can be found on nearby side streets.

Aître St-Maclou   Historic Quarter

(186 rue Martainville; ⊙ 9am-6pm) Decorated with lurid woodcarvings of skulls, crossbones,

Gros Horloge, Rouen

gravediggers' tools and hourglasses (a reminder that your time, my friend, is running out), this macabre ensemble of half-timbered buildings was used for centuries as a cemetery for plague victims. Built between 1526 and 1533, it now houses Rouen's École des Beaux-Arts (fine arts school).

Abbatiale St-Ouen — Church

See p29.

🛏 Sleeping

The tourist office can help you find a room (€3 fee).

Hôtel des Carmes — Hotel €

(☑ 02 35 71 92 31; www.hoteldescarmes.com; 33 place des Carmes; d €57-82, ste €83-108; 🐀) This sweet little hotel, built in 1850, offers 12 smallish but pleasant rooms that get cheaper the higher you climb (there's no lift). The annexe has two spacious suites.

La Boulangerie — B&B €

(☑ 06 12 94 53 15; www.laboulangerie.fr; 59 rue St-Nicaise; d incl breakfast €77-92, q incl breakfast €154; 🐀) Tucked into a quiet side street 1.2km northeast of the cathedral, this adorable B&B, above a historic bakery, has three pleasingly decorated rooms and, for stays of a week or more, apartments. Your charming hosts, Franck and Aminata, are a gold mine of local information.

Hôtel Vieille Tour — Hotel €

(☑ 02 35 70 03 27; www.hotelcentrerouen.fr; 42 place de la Haute Vieille Tour; d €55-85; 🐀) Central, friendly and good value, this hotel has 20 bright, quiet rooms with big windows and simple, practical furnishings. Situated in a postwar building facing 'Parking Cathédrale'.

Le Vieux Carré — Hotel €

(☑ 02 35 71 67 70; www.hotel-vieux-carre.com; 34 rue Ganterie; r €60-68; 🐀) Set around a little medieval courtyard, this quiet, half-timbered hotel has a delightfully old-fashioned *salon de thé* (tearoom) and 13 small, practical rooms, all of which were renovated in 2012 and '13.

Auberge de Jeunesse Robec — Hostel €

(☑ 02 35 08 18 50; www.fuaj.org; 3 rue de la Tour; dm/s/d incl breakfast €22.80/34/58; ⊙reception 8-11.45am & 5.30-10pm; 🐀) The two- to eight-bed rooms at this modern, 88-bed hostel are comfortable and functional. Situated 2km

east of the cathedral off route de Darnétal; from the city centre, take bus T2 or T3 to the 'Auberge de Jeunesse' stop.

Hôtel Le Cardinal — Hotel €€

(☑ 02 35 70 24 42; www.cardinal-hotel.fr; 1 place de la Cathédrale; s €78-98, d €88-118; 🐀) Facing the cathedral's famous west facade, this 15-room hotel is one of best midrange deals in central Rouen. All but two of the bright rooms have romantic cathedral views, and eight come with balconies or terraces.

Hôtel de la Cathédrale — Hotel €€

(☑ 02 35 71 57 95; www.hotel-de-la-cathedrale.fr; 12 rue St-Romain; s/d/q from €80/90/160; @ 🐀) Hiding behind a 17th-century half-timbered facade, this atmospheric hotel has 27 rooms with old-time French decor and modern bathrooms; most overlook a quiet, plant-filled courtyard.

★ Hôtel de Bourgtheroulde — Luxury Hotel €€€

(☑ 02 35 14 50 50; www.hotelsparouen.com; 15 place de la Pucelle; r €265-450; ✱🐀🏊) Rouen's finest hostelry serves up a mix of early-16th-century architecture – Flamboyant Gothic, to be precise – and sleek, modern luxury. The 78 rooms are spacious and gorgeously appointed. Amenities include a pool (19m), sauna and spa in the basement, and a lobby bar with live piano music on Saturday evening.

🍴 Eating

Rouen's main dining district, home to dozens of eateries and cafes, is around place du Vieux Marché and adjacent place de la Pucelle. East of the cathedral, there's a row of classy little restaurants along the northern side of rue Martainville, near Église St-Maclou.

★ La Rose des Vents — Modern French €

(☑ 02 35 70 29 78; 37 rue St-Nicolas; mains €15; ⊙noon-about 3pm Tue-Sat) Tucked away inside a retro secondhand shop, this stylish establishment is hugely popular with foodies and hipsters. Patrons rave about the two lunch mains, which change weekly according to what's available in the market. Reservations are highly recommended.

L'Espiguette — Bistro €

(☑ 02 35 71 66 27; 25 place St-Amand; weekday lunch menu €11.80, mains €13-19.80; ⊙noon-10pm Tue-Sat) This atmospheric bistro-cafe doesn't do culinary acrobatics, just pared-down French classics such as *entrecôte* (steak) and salads. The lunch *menu* is a great deal.

Le P'tit Bec
Modern French €

(☑ 02 35 07 63 33; www.leptitbec.com; 182 rue Eau de Robec; lunch menus €12.50-16; ⊙ noon-2.30pm Mon-Sat, 7-10.30pm Thu-Sat, plus 7-10.30pm Tue & Wed Jun-Aug; ☑) The down-to-earth menu is stuffed with *gratins* (cheese-topped dishes), salads, *œufs cocottes* (eggs with grated cheese baked in cream) and homemade pastries.

Dame Cakes
Patisserie €

(☑ 02 35 07 49 31; www.damecakes.fr; 70 rue St-Romain; lunch mains €11, menus €14.50-23.50; ⊙10.30am-7pm Mon-Sat; ☑) Walk through the historic, early 20th-century façade and you'll discover a delightfully civilised selection of pastries, cakes and chocolates. From noon to 3pm you can tuck into delicious quiches, *gratins* and salads in the attached *salon de thé*. Lovely.

Made in Normandy
French €€

(☑ 02 35 14 07 45; www.lemadeinnormandy.fr; 236 rue Martainville; menu €21.50; ⊙ noon-2pm & 7-9.30pm Thu-Mon) A candlelit, semiformal restaurant that serves outstanding French and Norman dishes, including succulent beef, fine fish and superb crème brulée.

Gill Côté Bistro
Bistro €€

(☑ 02 35 89 88 72; www.gill.fr; 14 place du Vieux Marché; 2-course menu €22.50; ⊙ noon-3pm & 7.30-10.30pm) Sleek contemporary design, traditional French and Lyonnaise cuisine, and wine by the glass (€4.20 to €5.90) are featured at this popular bistro, under the tutelage of renowned chef Gilles Tournadre.

Minute et Mijoté
Bistro €€

(☑ 02 32 08 40 00; http://minutemijote.canalblog.com; 58 rue de Fontenelle; menus lunch €16.50-21, dinner €26-31; ⊙ noon-2pm & 7.45-10pm Tue-Sat) This smart bistro, with its retro decor, is one of our favourite dining spots in Rouen. The trademark here is freshness and great value.

Brasserie Paul
Brasserie €€

(☑ 02 35 71 86 07; www.brasserie-paul.com; 1 place de la Cathédrale; lunch menu €16.90, gourmet menu €24; ⊙ 9.30am-11pm) A favourite of artists and philosophers since 1898, this is the classic Rouennaise brasserie. The service is starchy, the drapes are red velvet and the menu features several regional dishes.

Les Nymphéas
Gastronomic €€€

(☑ 02 35 89 26 69; www.lesnympheas-rouen.com; 7-9 rue de la Pie; weekday lunch menu €27, other menus €42-74; ⊙ 12.15-2pm Wed-Sun, 7-9pm Tue-Sat) With its formal tables arrayed under 16th-century beams, Les Nymphéas has long been a top address for fine dining. Young chef Alexandre Dessaux, in charge since 2013, serves up French cuisine that manages to be both traditional and creative. Reservations are a must on weekends.

Drinking & Nightlife

The bars and cafes around place du Vieux Marché and in the old town buzz from noon until the early hours. Rouen is also the centre of Normandy's gay life.

La Boîte à Bières
Bar

(www.laboiteabieres.fr; 35 rue Cauchoise; ⊙ 5pm-2am Tue-Sat) This friendly, often-crowded establishment, with walls plastered with memorabilia, is affectionately known as BAB. Serves 16 beers on tap and another 200 in bottles, including local *bières artisanales* (microbrews).

Le Saxo
Bar

(☑ 02 35 98 24 92; www.facebook.com/le.saxo.rouen; 11 place St-Marc; ⊙ 5pm-2am Mon-Sat) Le Saxo swings to jazz, blues, rock, reggae and world music, with free concerts by local bands on Friday and Saturday from 10pm to 1.30am (except in July and August). It hosts jazz jam sessions every other Thursday from 9pm. Serves 13 beers on tap and 120 by the bottle.

Le 106
Live Music

(☑ 02 32 10 88 60; www.le106.com; quai Jean de Béthencourt) Rouen's premier concert venue brings to the stage *musiques actuelles* (contemporary music) of every sort. Situated 2km west of the cathedral, on the other side of the river.

ℹ Information

Tourist Office (☑ 02 32 08 32 40; www.rouentourisme.com; 25 place de la Cathédrale; ⊙ 9am-7pm Mon-Sat, 9.30am-12.30pm & 2-6pm Sun & holidays May-Sep, 9.30am-12.30pm & 1.30-6pm Mon-Sat Oct-Apr) Housed in a 1500s Renaissance building facing the cathedral. Can provide English brochures on Normandy and details on guided tours in English (July and August). Rouen's only exchange bureau is at the back.

Place du Vieux Marché, Rouen (p54)
YADID LEVY / ALAMY ©

🛈 Getting Around

BICYCLE
Cy'clic (📞08 00 08 78 00; http://cyclic.rouen.fr)
Cy'clic, Rouen's version of Paris' Vélib', lets you
rent a city bike from 20 locations around town.
Credit-card registration for one/seven days costs
€1/5, plus a deposit of €150. Use is free for the
first 30 minutes; the 2nd/3rd/4th and subsequent half-hours cost €1/2/4 each.

CAR
Free parking is available near the Boulingrin metro
terminus, 1.5km northeast of the cathedral, and at
Parking du Mont Riboudet (next to the Palais des
Sports), 2.7km northeast of the cathedral; the lat-
ter is linked to the centre by buses T1, T2 and T3.

METRO & BUS
Rouen's public transport is operated by **Réseau
Astuce** (www.crea-astuce.fr). The 'metro' – in fact
a light-rail system – runs from 5am (6am on Sunday) to about 11pm and is useful for getting from
the train station to the centre of town. A single-
journey ticket on the metro or bus costs €1.50.

Dieppe

POP 32,700

A seaside resort since 1824, Dieppe hasn't
been chic for more than a century but the
town's lack of cuteness and pretension can
be refreshing. During WWII, the city was the
focal point of the only large-scale Allied raid
on Nazi-occupied France before D-Day.

Dieppe was one of France's most important ports in the 16th and 17th centuries,
when ships regularly sailed from here to
West Africa and Brazil. Many of the earliest French settlers in Canada set sail from
Dieppe.

👁 Sights & Activities

Château-Musée   Museum
See p29.

Cité de la Mer   Maritime Museum
(Estran; 📞02 35 06 93 20; www.estrancitedelamer.
fr; 37 rue de l'Asile Thomas; adult/child €7/3.50;
🕐9.30am-6pm Mon-Fri, 9.30am-12.30pm & 1.30-6pm
Sat & Sun) The 'City of the Sea' brings Dieppe's
long maritime and fishing history to life,
with kid-friendly exhibits that include model ships and a fish-petting *bassin tactile*. Sea
creatures native to the English Channel swim
in a dozen aquariums. Ask for an English-
language brochure at the ticket desk.

Dieppe Port   Historic Quarter
Still used by fishing vessels but dominated
by pleasure craft, the port is lined with evocative old buildings.

Beach   Beach
(👣) Dieppe's often-windy, 1.8km-long beach
is covered with smooth pebbles. The vast
lawns were laid out in the 1860s by that
seashore-loving imperial duo, Napoléon III
and his wife, Eugénie. The area has several
play areas for kids.

Dieppe Canadian War Cemetery   Cemetery
(www.cwgc.org) Many of the Canadians who
died in the Dieppe Raid of 1942 are buried
here. Situated 4km towards Rouen; from the
centre, take av des Canadiens (the continu-
ation of av Gambetta) south and follow the
signs.

🛏 Sleeping & Eating

There are a number of modest hotels facing
the beach, and quai Henri IV, along the north
side of the harbour, is lined with touristy
restaurants.

Les Arcades   Hotel €
(📞02 35 84 14 12; www.lesarcades.fr; 1-3 arcades
de la Bourse; d €72-88; 📶) Perched above a
colonnaded arcade from the 1600s, this
well-managed establishment enjoys a great

location across the street from the tourist office. The decor, in tans and browns, is nothing to write home about but 12 of the 21 rooms have fine port views.

À La Marmite Dieppoise Seafood €€

(☑ 02 35 84 24 26; 8 rue St-Jean; menus €21-44; ⊘ noon-2pm Tue-Sun, 7-9pm Tue-Sat) A Dieppe institution, this eatery is celebrated for its hearty *marmite dieppoise* (cream-sauce stew made with mussels, prawns and four kinds of fish; €30), served in a rustic dining room. Other specialities include Normandy-style fish and, from October to May, scallops.

ℹ Information

Tourist Office (☑ 02 32 14 40 60; www. dieppetourisme.com; Pont Jehan Ango; ⊘ 9am-1pm & 2-5pm Mon-Sat, plus 9.30am-1pm & 2-5.30pm Sun May-Sep) Has useful English brochures on Dieppe and nearby parts of the Côte d'Albâtre.

Côte d'Albâtre

Stretching along the Norman coast for 130km from Le Tréport southwest to Étretat, the vertical, bone-white cliffs of Côte d'Albâtre (Alabaster Coast; www.seine-maritime-tourism.com) are strikingly reminiscent of the limestone cliffs of Dover, just across the Channel. The dramatic coastline, sculpted over eons by the wind and the waves, is dotted with attractive villages, fishing harbours, resort towns, pebbly beaches and lovely gardens – and, for a bit of variety, two nuclear power plants (Paluel and Penly).

On the plateau above the cliffs, walkers can follow the dramatic long-distance GR21 hiking trail (www.gr-infos.com/gr21.htm), which parallels the coast from Le Tréport all the way to Le Havre. *Le Pays des Hautes Falaises* ('Land of the high cliffs'), a free map available at tourist offices, details 46 coastal and inland walking circuits ranging from 6km to 22km.

Cyclists might want to stop by a tourist office to pick up *Véloroute du Littoral,* a free map detailing coastal bike routes.

If you're driving west from Dieppe, take wherever possible the beautiful tertiary roads near the coast (eg the D75, D68, D79, D211 and D11), which pass through verdant, rolling countryside, rather than the inland D925 and D940, which is where road signs will try to direct you. One option for a lovely northeast-to-southwest coastal drive: feast on oysters in Pourville-sur-Mer before cruising to scenic Varengeville; Veules-les-Roses, a cute and very neat village with a seafront boardwalk; and handsome St-Valery-en-Caux, where attractions include a yacht harbour and a lovely beach. Continue to Veulettes-sur-Mer and Les Petites Dalles before reaching Fécamp.

St-Valery-en-Caux

This delightful village, 32km west of Dieppe, has a large fishing and pleasure port, a lovely beach and half-a-dozen hotels. It is also the site of a Franco-British WWII cemetery. In January 1945 a runaway troop train crashed here, killing 89 American soldiers.

⌂ Sleeping & Eating

La Maison des Galets Hotel €

(☑ 02 35 97 11 22; www.lamaisondesgalets.com; 6 rue des Remparts; s €50, d €70-80; ☎) The spacious lobby is classic 1950s, with leather couches

---

THE DIEPPE RAID

On 19 August 1942 a mainly Canadian force of more than 6000, backed up by 300 ships and 800 aircraft, landed on 20km of beaches between Berneval-sur-Mer and Varengeville-sur-Mer. The objectives: to help the Soviets by drawing Nazi military power away from the Eastern Front – so the film *Dieppe Uncovered* revealed in 2012 – to 'pinch' one of the Germans' new, four-rotor Enigma encoding machines (the effort failed). The results of the Dieppe Raid were nothing short of catastrophic: 73% of the men who took part ended up killed, wounded or missing in action. But lessons learned at great cost here proved invaluable in planning the Normandy landings two years later.

For insights into the operation, visit Dieppe's Memorial du 19 Août 1942 (www.dieppe-operationjubilee-19aout1942.fr; place Camille St-Saëns; adult/child €3/free; ⊘ 2-6.30pm Wed-Mon late May–Sep, 2-6pm Sat, Sun & holidays Apr–mid-May & Oct–mid-Nov, closed mid-Nov–Mar).

and lovely sea panoramas. Upstairs, the 14 rooms are simply furnished, with nautical touches and shiny, all-tile bathrooms. Situated 100m west of the casino.

Restaurant du Port
Seafood €€

(📞 02 35 97 08 93; 18 quai d'Amont; menus €26-46; ⏲ 12.15-2pm Tue-Sun, 7.30-9pm Tue, Wed, Fri & Sat) A treat for lovers of fish and seafood. À la carte offerings include oysters, fresh crab and turbot marinated in cream. The seafood platters (€43) are a sight to behold.

Fécamp
POP 28,660

Fécamp is a lively fishing port with an attractive harbour, dramatic cliffs and a long monastic history. It is best known for producing Bénédictine, a fiery 'medicinal elixir' concocted here by a Venetian monk in 1510. Lost during the Revolution, the recipe was rediscovered in the 19th century.

👁 Sights & Activities

Les Pêcheries
Museum

(Cité des Terre-Neuvas; quai Capitaine Jean Recher; adult/child €5/3; ⏲ 11am-5.30pm Fri-Wed, to 8pm Thu, closed Tue mid-Sep–mid-May) Set to open in 2015, Fécamp's new flagship museum showcases local history, the town's fishing industry, artists who were active here, and traditional Norman life. The dramatic, glassed-in observation platform on top offers great views of town. Situated in the middle of the harbour, 300m northwest of the tourist office.

Beach
Beach

Fécamp's 800m-long, smooth-pebble beach stretches southward from the narrow channel connecting the port with the open sea. In July and August you can rent catamarans, kayaks, paddle boats and windsurfers.

Cap Fagnet
Viewpoint

The highest point on the Côte d'Albâtre, Cap Fagnet (110m) towers over Fécamp from the north, offering fantastic views up and down coast. The site of a German blockhaus and radar station during WWII, today it's topped by a chapel and five wind turbines (there's a plan to erect 83 more turbines offshore). Cap Fagnet is a 1.5km walk from the centre.

Abbatiale de la Ste-Trinité
Abbey

(place des Ducs Richard; ⏲ 9am-7pm Apr-Sep, 9am-noon & 2-5pm Oct-Mar) Built from 1175 to 1220 by Richard the Lionheart, towering Abbatiale de la Ste-Trinité was the most important pilgrimage site in Normandy until the construction of Mont St-Michel, thanks to the drops of Jesus' blood that, legend has it, miraculously floated to Fécamp in the trunk of a fig tree. Across from the abbey are the remains of a fortified château built in the 10th and 11th centuries by the earliest dukes of Normandy. Situated 1.5km east of the beach.

Palais de la Bénédictine
Liqueur Factory

See p29.

🛏 Sleeping & Eating

Tourist-oriented crêperies and restaurants, many specialising in fish and mussels, line the south side of the port, along quai de la Vicomté and nearby parts of quai Bérigny.

Hôtel Vent d'Ouest
Hotel €

(📞 02 35 28 04 04; www.hotelventdouest.tm.fr; 3 rue Gambetta; s/d/tr €46/63/85) Small and welcoming, with a smart breakfast room and 15 pleasant rooms decorated in yellow and blue. Call ahead if you'll be checking in after 8pm. Situated 200m east (up the hill) from the port, next to Église St-Étienne.

La Marée
Seafood €€

(📞 02 35 29 39 15; www.restaurant-maree-fecamp. fr; 77 quai Bérigny; weekday menus €19-24; ⏲ noon-2pm Tue-Sun, 7.30-8.30pm or later Tue, Wed, Fri & Sat) Fish and seafood – that's all that matters at La Marée, Fécamp's premier address for maritime dining. Locals claim that you won't find better seafood anywhere in town.

ℹ Information

Tourist Office (📞 02 35 28 51 01; www.fecamp tourisme.com; quai Sadi Carnot; ⏲ 9am-6pm daily Apr-Oct, to 5.30pm Mon-Sat Nov-Mar; 📶) Has useful English-language brochures and maps, an iPad you can use to surf the internet, and free luggage lockers. Situated at the eastern end of the pleasure port, across the parking lot from the train station.

Smooth-pebble beach, Fécamp

ⓘ Getting Around

The tourist office rents bicycles for €9/14/40 per day/weekend/week.

Étretat

POP 1500

The small village of Étretat's dramatic scenery (it's framed by twin cliffs) made it a favourite of painters such as Camille Corot, Boudin, Gustave Courbet and Monet. With the vogue for sea air at the end of the 19th century, fashionable Parisians came and built extravagant villas. Étretat has never gone out of style and still swells with visitors every weekend.

⊙ Sights & Activities

The pebbly beach is separated from the town centre by a dyke. To the left as you face the sea, you can see the Falaise d'Aval, renowned for its free-standing arch – compared by French writer Maupassant to an elephant dipping its trunk in the sea – and the adjacent Aiguille, a 70m-high spire of chalk-white rock rising from the waves. Further along the cliff is a second natural arch known as La Manneporte. To reach the plateau above, take the steep footpath from the southwestern end of the beachfront.

To the right as you face the sea towers is the Falaise d'Amont, atop which a memorial marks the spot where two aviators were last seen before attempting to cross the Atlantic in 1927. The tourist office has a map of trails around town and can also provide details on sail-powered cruises aboard a two-masted schooner (March to October).

⏣ Sleeping

There are plenty of B&Bs in and around Étretat.

★ **Detective Hôtel**   Hotel €

(☑ 02 35 27 01 34; www.detectivehotel.com; 6 av Georges V; d €45-89; ☎) Run by a former detective, this clever establishment was inspired by the deductive exploits of Sherlock Holmes and Hercule Poirot. Each of the 14 charming rooms bears the name of a fictional gumshoe whose time and place have inspired the decor. In some, the first mystery you'll face is how to find the secret door to the hidden bathroom. Utterly original.

ⓘ Information

Tourist Office (☑ 02 35 27 05 21; www.etretat. net; place Maurice Guillard; ⊙ 9.30am-6.30pm daily mid-Jun–mid-Sep, 10am-noon & 2-6pm Mon-Sat mid-Sep–mid-Jun, open Sun during school holidays) Situated inside the town hall.

Le Havre

POP 177,300

A Unesco World Heritage Site since 2005, Le Havre is a love letter to modernism, evoking, more than any other French city, France's postwar energy and optimism. All but obliterated in September 1944 by Allied bombing raids that killed 3000 civilians, the centre was completely rebuilt by the Belgian architect Auguste Perret, whose bright, airy modernist vision remains, miraculously, largely intact. Attractions include one of France's finest art museums, renowned for its collection of impressionist works. Le Havre is a regular port of call for cruise ships.

◉ Sights & Activities

★ Musée d'Art Moderne
André Malraux
Art Museum

See p30.

Église St-Joseph
Church

(bd François 1er) Perret's masterful, 107m-high Église St-Joseph, visible from all over town, was built using bare concrete from 1951 to 1959. Some 13,000 panels of coloured glass make the soaring, sombre interior particularly striking when it's sunny.

Appartement Témoin
Architecture

(adult/child €3/free; ⊙ tours hourly 2-5pm Wed, Sat & Sun, plus 2pm Mon, Tue, Thu & Fri Jun-Sep) Furnished in impeccable early-1950s style, this lovingly furnished bourgeois apartment can be visited on a one-hour guided tour that starts at 181 rue de Paris (Maison du Patrimoine), a block north of Le Volcan.

Le Volcan
Cultural Centre

(Espace Oscar Niemeyer; www.levolcan.com; place Charles de Gaulle) Le Havre's most conspicuous landmark, designed by Brazilian architect Oscar Niemeyer and opened in 1982, is also the city's premier cultural venue. One look and you'll understand how it got its name, which means 'the volcano'. After extensive renovations the complex should reopen in 2015, with new performance spaces and an ultramodern *mediathèque* (multimedia library). Situated at the western end of the Bassin du Commerce, the city centre's former port.

⌂ Sleeping

Hôtel Oscar
Hotel €

(☑ 02 35 42 39 77; www.hotel-oscar.fr; 106 rue Voltaire; s €54-61, d €71-81; 🛜) A treat for architecture aficionados, this bright and very central hotel brings Auguste Perret's mid-20th-century legacy alive. The rooms are authentic retro, with hardwood floors and large windows, as is the tiny 1950s lounge. Reception closes at 9pm. Situated across the street from Le Volcan.

★ Hôtel Vent d'Ouest
Boutique Hotel €€

(☑ 02 35 42 50 69; www.ventdouest.fr; 4 rue de Caligny; d €100-150, q €170-215, apt €185; 🛜) Decorated with maritime flair, this stylish establishment has nautical memorabilia downstairs and 35 cream-walled, sisal-floored rooms upstairs; ask for one with a balcony. Facilities include a restaurant, fashionable tearoom, bar and sparkling spa. Situated across the street from Église St-Joseph.

✗ Eating

There's a cluster of restaurants in Quartier St-François, the area just south of the Bassin du Commerce – check out rue de Bretagne, rue Dauphine and rue du Général Faidherbe.

La Taverne Paillette
Brasserie €

(☑ 02 35 41 31 50; www.taverne-paillette.com; 22 rue Georges Braque; lunch menu €14.80, dinner menu €30.20; ⊙ noon-midnight) Solid brasserie food is the order of the day at this Le Havre institution – think big bowls of mussels, generous salads, gargantuan seafood platters and, in the Alsatian tradition, eight types of *choucroute* (sauerkraut). Situated five blocks north of Église St-Joseph, at the northeast corner of a park called Square St-Roch.

Bistrot des Halles
Bistro €

(☑ 02 35 22 50 52; 7 place des Halles Centrales; lunch menu €13.50, other menu €24.80; ⊙ noon-2.30pm & 7.30-11pm Mon-Sat, 9am-3pm Sun) For a very French dining experience, head to this Lyon-style bistro, decked out with old-time enamel publicity plaques. Specialities include steak, *magret de canard* (duck breast filet), *cassoulet* and large salads. Situated two blocks west of Le Volcan.

ℹ️ Information

Maison du Patrimoine (☎ 02 35 22 31 22; 181 rue de Paris; ☉1.45-6.30pm year-round, plus 10am-noon Apr-Sep) The tourist office's city-centre annexe has an exposition on Perret's postwar reconstruction of the city.

Normandie Change (41 chaussée Kennedy; ☉9am-12.30pm & 2-6.30pm Mon-Fri, to 5pm Sat) An exchange bureau half a block west of the southern end of rue de Paris.

Tourist Office (☎ 02 32 74 04 04; www.lehavre tourisme.com; 186 bd Clemenceau; ☉ 9.30am-6.30pm Apr-Sep, 10am-12.30pm & 2-6pm Oct-Mar) Has a map in English for a two-hour walking tour of Le Havre's architectural highlights and details on cultural events. Situated at the western edge of the city centre, one block south of the La Plage tram terminus.

ℹ️ Getting There & Away

Le Havre's car ferry terminal, situated 1km southeast of Le Volcan, is linked with the English port of Portsmouth by **DFDS Seaways** (www.dfdsseaways.co.uk). From late May to early September, **Brittany Ferries** (www.brittany-ferries.co.uk) also handles this route.

ℹ️ Getting Around

LiA (www.transports-lia.fr) Two tram lines, run by LiA, link the train station with the city centre and the beach. A single/all-day ticket costs €1.50/3.70. LiA also rents out **bicycles** (2hr/half day/full day €3/4/7) at four sites, including the main tourist office and the train station.

EURE

From Rouen, lovely day trips can be made to the landlocked Eure *département* (www.eure-tourisme.fr). The 12th-century Château Gaillard in Les Andelys affords a breathtaking panorama of the Seine, while the beautiful gardens of Claude Monet are at Giverny (p29), 70km southwest of Rouen.

Les Andelys

POP 8230

Some 40km southeast of Rouen, on a hairpin curve in the Seine, lies Les Andelys (the 's' is silent), crowned by the ruins of Richard the Lionheart's hilltop castle.

👁️ Sights

Château Gaillard   Château
See p40.

PONT DE NORMANDIE

The futuristic bridge Pont de Normandie (each way per car €5.40), which opened in 1995, stretches in a soaring 2km arch over the Seine between Le Havre and Honfleur. It's a typically French affair, as much sophisticated architecture as engineering, with two huge inverted-V-shaped columns holding aloft a delicate net of cables. Crossing it is quite a thrill – and the views of the Seine are magnificent. In each direction there's a narrow footpath and a bike lane.

🛏️ Sleeping & Eating

Hôtel de la Chaîne d'Or   Hotel €€
(☎ 02 32 54 00 31; www.hotel-lachainedor.com; 27 rue Grande, Petit Andely; r €95-150; 🛜) Packed with character, this little hideaway is rustically stylish without being twee. The 12 rooms are spacious, tasteful and romantic, with antique wood furnishings and plush rugs; some are so close to the Seine you could almost fish out the window.

Restaurant de la Chaîne d'Or   Gastronomic €€€
(☎ 02 32 54 00 31; www.hotel-lachainedor.com; 25 rue Grande, Petit Andely; weekday lunch menus €22-30, other menus €52-114; ☉noon-2pm & 7.30-8.30pm Thu-Tue year-round, closed Sun dinner & Tue mid-Oct–mid-Apr) A classy French restaurant that's one of the best for miles around. Specialities include fish and *ris de veau* (calf's sweetbread) and local favourite *tarte aux pommes flambées au Calvados* (flambéed apple pie). Reservations are recommended.

ℹ️ Information

Tourist Office (☎ 02 32 54 41 93; www.les andelys-tourisme.fr; rue Raymond Phélip; ☉10am-noon & 2-6pm Mon-Sat, 10am-1pm Sun, shorter hours Oct-Mar) In Petit Andely.

CALVADOS

The Calvados *département* (www.calvados-tourisme.com) stretches from Honfleur in the east to Isigny-sur-Mer in the west and includes Caen, Bayeux and the D-Day beaches. The area is famed for its rich pastures and farm products, including butter, cheese, cider and an eponymous apple brandy.

Bayeux

POP 13,350

Two cross-Channel invasions, almost 900 years apart, gave Bayeux a front-row seat at defining moments in Western history. The dramatic story of the Norman invasion of England in 1066 is told in 58 vivid scenes by the world-famous Bayeux Tapestry, embroidered just a few years after William the Bastard, Duke of Normandy, became William the Conqueror, King of England. And on 6 June 1944, 160,000 Allied troops, supported by almost 7000 naval vessels, stormed ashore along the coast just north of town – D-Day. Bayeux was the first French town to be liberated after D-Day (on the morning of 7 June 1944) and is one of the few places in Calvados to have survived WWII practically unscathed.

These days, it's a great spot to soak up the gentle Norman atmosphere. The delightful, flowery city centre is crammed with 13th- to 18th-century buildings, many of them half-timbered, and a fine Gothic cathedral.

Bayeux makes an ideal base for exploring the D-Day beaches.

◉ Sights

A 'triple ticket' good for all three of Bayeux' outstanding municipal museums costs €15/13.50 for an adult/child.

★ Bayeux Tapestry   Tapestry

(☑ 02 31 51 25 50; www.tapestry-bayeux.com; rue de Nesmond; adult/child incl audioguide €9/4; ⊙ 9am-6.30pm mid-Mar–mid-Nov, to 7pm May-Aug, 9.30am-12.30pm & 2-6pm mid-Nov–mid-Mar) The world's most celebrated embroidery depicts the conquest of England by William the Conqueror in 1066 from an unashamedly Norman perspective. Commissioned by Bishop Odo of Bayeux, William's half-brother, for the

Interior of the Cathédrale Notre Dame, Bayeux

NICOLAS THIBAULT/GETTY IMAGES ©

opening of Bayeux' cathedral in 1077, the 68.3m-long cartoon strip tells the dramatic, bloody tale with verve and vividness.

Fifty-eight action-packed scenes of pageantry and mayhem occupy the centre of the canvas, while religious allegories and illustrations of everyday 11th-century life, some of them naughty, adorn the borders. The final showdown at the Battle of Hastings is depicted in graphic fashion, complete with severed limbs and decapitated heads (along the bottom of scene 52). Halley's Comet, which blazed across the sky in 1066, appears in scene 32.

A 16-minute film gives the conquest historical, political and cultural context, including crucial details on the grooming habits of Norman and Saxon knights. Also well worth a listen is the lucid, panel-by-panel audioguide, available in 14 languages. A special audioguide for kids aged seven to 12 is available in French and English.

★ Musée d'Art et d'Histoire Baron Gérard
Museum

(MAHB; ☑02 31 92 14 21; www.bayeuxmuseum.com; 37 rue du Bienvenu; adult/child €7/4; ☺9.30am-6.30pm May-Sep, 10am-12.30pm & 2-6pm Oct-Apr) Opened in 2013, this is one of France's most gorgeously presented provincial museums. The exquisite exhibits cover everything from Gallo-Roman archaeology to medieval art to paintings from the Renaissance to the 20th century, including a fine work by Gustave Caillebotte. Other highlights include impossibly delicate local lace and Bayeux-made porcelain. Housed in the former bishop's palace.

Cathédrale Notre Dame
Cathedral

(rue du Bienvenu; ☺8.30am-7pm) Most of Bayeux' spectacular Norman Gothic cathedral dates from the 13th century, though the crypt (take the stairs on the north side of the choir), the arches of the nave and the lower parts of the entrance towers are 11th-century Romanesque. The central tower was added in the 15th century; the copper dome dates from the 1860s. First prize for tackiness has got to go to 'Litanies de la Sainte Vierge', a 17th-century, haut-relief retable in the first chapel on the left as you enter the cathedral.

Several plaques and stained-glass windows commemorate American and British sacrifices during the world wars. The first new cathedral bell in over 150 years, paid for by subscription and dedicated to 'peace and freedom', was added to the South Tower in 2014 to commemorate the 70th anniversary of D-Day.

Contact the tourist office for details on guided tours (adult/child €4/3), held in English at 10am and 2.15pm Monday to Friday in July and August.

Conservatoire de la Dentelle
Lace Workshop

(Lace Conservatory; ☑02 31 92 73 80; http://dentelledebayeux.free.fr; 6 rue du Bienvenu; ☺9.30am-12.30pm & 2.30-5pm, closed Sun & holidays) FREE Lacemaking, brought to Bayeux by nuns in 1678, once employed 5000 people. The industry is long gone, but at the Conservatoire you can watch some of France's most celebrated lacemakers create intricate designs using dozens of bobbins and hundreds of pins; a small shop sells some of their delicate creations. The half-timbered building housing the workshop, decorated with carved wooden figures, dates from the 1400s.

Musée Mémorial de la Bataille de Normandie
Museum

See p21.

Bayeux War Cemetery
Cemetery

See p21.

Mémorial des Reporters
Memorial

(bd Fabien Ware) This landscaped promenade, a joint project of the City of Bayeux and Reporters Without Borders (http://en.rsf.org), lists the names of more than 2000 journalists killed in the line of duty around the world since 1944. Situated just northwest of the Bayeux War Cemetery, a bit off bd Fabien Ware.

🛏 Sleeping

Bayeux has many excellent accommodation options. The tourist office can supply you with a list of nearby B&Bs.

Les Logis du Rempart
B&B €

(☑02 31 92 50 40; www.lecornu.fr; 4 rue Bourbesneur; d €60-100, tr €110-130; ☎) The three rooms of this delightful *maison de famille* ooze old-fashioned cosiness. Our favourite, the Bajocasse, has parquet floor and Toile de Jouy wallpaper. The shop downstairs is the perfect place to stock up on top-quality, homemade cider and *calvados* (apple brandy).

Hôtel d'Argouges
Hotel €€

(☑02 31 92 88 86; www.hotel-dargouges.com; 21 rue St-Patrice; d/tr/f €140/193/245; ☺closed Dec & Jan; ☎) Occupying a stately 18th-century residence with a lush little garden, this graceful hotel has 28 comfortable rooms with exposed beams, thick walls and Louis XVI–style furniture. The breakfast room, hardly changed since 1734, still has its original wood panels and parquet floors.

Hôtel Reine Mathilde
Hotel €€

(☑ 02 31 92 08 13; www.hotel-bayeux-reinemathilde. fr; 23 rue Larcher; d €85-125; 🛜) Superbly central, this friendly, family-run hotel has 23 smallish but comfortable rooms and its own restaurant. In the annexe, a converted barn by the river, the seven rooms are sleek and spacious.

Villa Lara
Luxury Hotel €€€

(☑ 02 31 92 00 55; www.hotel-villalara.com; 6 place de Québec; d €180-280, ste €290-510; ✳🛜) Built in 2012, this 28-room hotel, Bayeux' most luxurious, sports minimalist colour schemes, top-quality fabrics and decor that juxtaposes 18th- and 21st-century tastes.

Amenities include a bar and a gym. Most rooms have cathedral views.

✕ Eating

Local specialities to keep an eye out for include *cochon de Bayeux* (a local heritage pig breed). Near the tourist office, along rue St-Jean and rue St-Martin, there are a variety food shops and cheap eateries.

★ La Reine Mathilde
Patisserie €

(47 rue St-Martin; cakes from €2.20; ⊙ 9am-7.30pm Tue-Sun) This sumptuously decorated patisserie and *salon de thé* (tearoom), ideal for a sweet breakfast or relaxing cup of tea, hasn't changed much since it was built in 1898.

L'Assiette Normande
French €

(☑ 02 31 22 04 61; www.lassiettenormande.fr; 1-3 rue des Chanoines; lunch menu €10, other menus €13.90-34.50; ⊙ noon-3pm Tue-Sat & 7-11pm daily, closed Sun & Mon Dec-Mar) This rustic eatery is

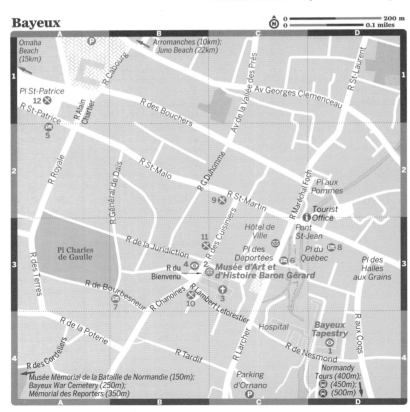

Bayeux

about straightforward French food – meat, fish and oysters – at reasonable prices. Kids under 12 get a half portion at half price.

Le Pommier Norman €€

(☑ 02 31 21 52 10; www.restaurantlepommier.com; 38-40 rue des Cuisiniers; lunch menus €15-18, other menus €21-39.50; ☺ noon-2pm & 7-9pm, closed Sun Nov-Feb; ☑) At this romantic restaurant, delicious Norman classics include steamed pollock and Caen-style tripe. A vegetarian menu – a rarity in Normandy – is also available, with offerings such as soybean steak in Norman cream.

Self-Catering

Marchés Food Market

(place St-Jean & place St-Patrice; ☺ 8am-12.30pm Wed & Sat) Stalls sell fresh edibles at place St-Patrice (Saturday morning) and right in front of the tourist office (Wednesday morning).

ℹ Information

Post Office (14 rue Larcher) Changes foreign currency.

Tourist Office (☑ 02 31 51 28 28; www.bayeux -bessin-tourisme.com; pont St-Jean; ☺ 9.30am-12.30pm & 2-6pm Mon-Sat) Covers both Bayeux and the surrounding Bessin region, including the D-Day beaches. Has a walking-tour map of town and bus and train schedules, and sells books on the D-Day landings in English. Charges €2 to book hotels and B&Bs.

Bayeux

◎ Top Sights

1	Bayeux Tapestry	D
2	Musée d'Art et d'Histoire Baron Gérard	C3

◎ Sights

3	Cathédrale Notre Dame	C3
4	Conservatoire de la Dentelle	B3

🛏 Sleeping

5	Hôtel d'Argouges	A2
6	Hôtel Reine Mathilde	C3
7	Les Logis du Rempart	B3
8	Villa Lara	D3

🍴 Eating

9	La Reine Mathilde	C2
10	L'Assiette Normande	B3
11	Le Pommier	B3
12	Marchés	A1

ℹ Getting Around

There's free parking at Parking d'Ornano, at the southern end of rue Larcher.

Vélos (☑ 02 31 92 89 16; www.velosbayeux. com; 5 rue Larcher; per half/full day €7.50/10; ☺ 8.30am-5pm or later, to 10pm in summer) offers year-round bike rental from a fruit and veggie store a few paces from the tourist office.

D-Day Beaches

Code-named 'Operation Overlord', the D-Day landings were the largest seaborne invasion in history. Early on the morning of 6 June 1944, swarms of landing craft – part of an armada of more than 6000 ships and boats – hit the beaches of northern Normandy and tens of thousands of soldiers from the US, the UK, Canada and elsewhere began pouring onto French soil.

The majority of the 135,000 Allied troops who arrived in France that day stormed ashore along 80km of beaches north of Bayeux code-named (from west to east) Utah, Omaha, Gold, Juno and Sword. The landings on D-Day – known as 'Jour J' in French – were followed by the 76-day Battle of Normandy, during which the Allies suffered 210,000 casualties, including 37,000 troops killed. German casualties are believed to have been around 200,000; another 200,000 German soldiers were taken prisoner. About 14,000 French civilians also died. Caen's Le Mémorial – Un Musée pour la Paix (p19) and Bayeux' Musée Mémorial (p21) provide a comprehensive overview of the events of D-Day. Dozens of villages near the landing beaches have museums focusing on local events; all but a few are privately owned.

If you've got wheels, you can follow the D514 along the D-Day coast or several signposted circuits around the battle sites – look for signs reading 'D-Day–Le Choc' in the American sectors and 'Overlord-L'Assaut' in the British and Canadian sectors. The area is also sometimes called the Côte de Nacre (Mother-of-Pearl Coast). A free booklet called *The D-Day Landings and the Battle of Normandy,* available from tourist offices, has details on the eight major visitors' routes.

Maps of the D-Day beaches are available at *tabacs* (tobacconists), newsagents and bookshops in Bayeux and elsewhere. All the towns along the coast have plenty of small hotels. When visiting the D-Day sites, do not leave valuables in your car as theft is not unknown here.

Quite a few excellent websites have details on D-Day and its context, including www.normandiememoire.com, www.6juin1944.com and www.normandie44lamemoire.com.

☞ Tours

A guided minibus tour – lots of local companies offer them – can be an excellent way to get a sense of the D-Day beaches and their place in history. The Bayeux tourist office (p67) can handle reservations.

Normandy Tours Guided Tour
(☑ 02 31 92 10 70; www.normandy-landing-tours.com; 26 place de la Gare, Bayeux; adult/student €62/55) Offers well-regarded four- to five-hour tours of the main sites starting at 8.15am and 1.15pm on most days, as well as personally tailored trips. Based at Bayeux' Hôtel de la Gare, facing the train station.

Normandy Sightseeing Tours Guided Tour
(☑ 02 31 51 70 52; www.normandy-sightseeing-tours.com; adult/child morning €45/25, full day €90/50) This experienced outfit offers morning tours of various beaches and cemeteries, as well as all-day excursions.

Tours by Mémorial –
Un Musée pour la Paix Minibus Tour
(☑ 02 31 06 06 45; www.memorial-caen.fr; adult/child morning €64/64, afternoon €81/64; ☺ 9am & 2pm Apr-Sep, 1pm Oct-Mar, closed 3 weeks in Jan) Excellent year-round minibus tours (four to five hours), with cheaper tours in full-size buses (€39) from June to August. Rates include entry to Le Mémorial – Un Musée pour la Paix. Book online.

ⓘ Getting There & Away

Bus Verts (www.busverts.fr) links Bayeux' train station and place St-Patrice with many of the villages along the D-Day beaches.

Bus 70 (two to four daily Monday to Saturday, more frequently and on Sunday and holidays in summer) goes to Colleville-sur-Mer (Omaha Beach and the American Cemetery; €2.40, 35 minutes); some services continue to Pointe du Hoc (€4.65) and Grandcamp-Maisy.

Bus 74 (bus 75 in July and August; three or four daily Monday to Saturday, more frequently and on Sunday and holidays in summer) heads to Arromanches (€2.50, 10 minutes), Gold Beach

(Ver-sur Mer; €3.65, 30 minutes) and Juno Beach (Courseulles-sur-Mer; €3.65, one hour).

Omaha Beach

The most brutal fighting on D-Day took place on the 7km stretch of coastline around Vierville-sur-Mer, St-Laurent-sur-Mer and Colleville-sur-Mer, 15km northwest of Bayeux, known as 'Bloody Omaha' to US veterans. Seven decades on, little evidence of the carnage unleashed here on 6 June 1944 remains except for the American cemetery and concrete German bunkers, though at very low tide you can see a few remnants of the Mulberry Harbour.

These days Omaha is a peaceful place, a beautiful stretch of fine golden sand partly lined with dunes and summer homes. Circuit de la Plage d'Omaha, trail-marked with a yellow stripe, is a self-guided tour along the beach.

Normandy American
Cemetery & Memorial Memorial
(www.abmc.gov; Colleville-sur-Mer; ☺ 9am-6pm mid-Apr–mid-Sep, to 5pm rest of the year) White marble crosses and stars of David stretch off in seemingly endless rows at the Normandy American Cemetery, situated on a now-serene bluff overlooking the bitterly contested sands of Omaha Beach. The visitor center has an excellent multimedia presentation on the D-Day landings, told in part through the stories of individuals' courage and sacrifice. English-language tours of the cemetery, also focusing on personal stories, depart daily at 2pm and, from mid-April to mid-September, at 11am.

This place of pilgrimage is one of the largest American war cemeteries in Europe. It contains the graves of 9387 American soldiers, including 33 pairs of brothers who are buried side-by-side (another 12 pairs of brothers are buried separately or memorialised here). Only about 40% of American war dead from the fighting in Normandy are interred in this cemetery – the rest were repatriated at the request of their families.

Overlooking the gravestones is a large colonnaded memorial centred on a statue called The *Spirit of American Youth*, maps explaining the order of battle and a wall honouring 1557 Americans whose bodies were not found (men whose remains were recovered after the memorial was inaugurated are marked with a bronze rosette). A small, white-marble

The Battle of Normandy

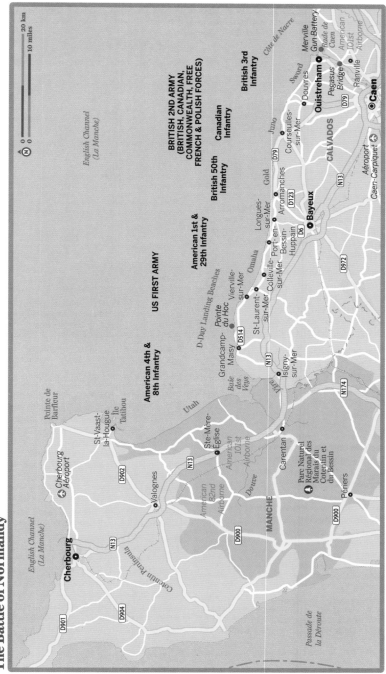

English Channel
(La Manche)

Pointe de
Barfleur

Cherbourg
Aéroport

St-Vaast-
la-Hougue

Île
Tatihou

D902

Valognes

N13

Ste-Mère-
Église

American
101st
Airborne

American
82nd
Airborne

Cherbourg

N13

D901

D904

Cotentin Peninsula

Douve

D900

MANCHE

Carentan

Parc Naturel
Régional des
Marais du
Cotentin et
du Bessin

Périers

D900

Passade de
la Déroute

N174

D972

Isigny-
sur-Mer

N13

D514

Grandcamp-
Maisy

Baie
des
Veys

Utah

Vire

Aure

Pointe
du Hoc

D-Day Landing Beaches

Vierville-
sur-Mer

St-Laurent-
sur-Mer

Omaha

Colleville-
sur-Mer

Port-en-
Bessin-
Huppain

Longues-
sur-Mer

Arromanches

D123

Gold

D79

Bayeux

D6

CALVADOS

Aéroport
Caen-Carpiquet

N13

Courseulles-
sur-Mer

Juno

Douvres

Sword

Merville

Ouistreham

Gun Battery

Pegasus
Bridge

Ranville

D79

Caen

Rade de
Caen

American
101st
Airborne

Côte de Nacre

English Channel
(La Manche)

**American 4th &
8th Infantry**

US FIRST ARMY

**American 1st &
29th Infantry**

**BRITISH 2ND ARMY
(BRITISH, CANADIAN,
COMMONWEALTH, FREE
FRENCH & POLISH FORCES)**

**British 50th
Infantry**

**Canadian
Infantry**

**British 3rd
Infantry**

N

0   20 km
0   10 miles

69

DANITA DELIMONT/GETTY IMAGES ©

chapel stands at the intersection of the cross-shaped main paths through the cemetery.

The Normandy American Cemetery & Memorial is 17km northwest of Bayeux; by car, follow the signs to the 'Cimetière Militaire Americain'.

Overlord Museum   Museum

(www.overlordmuseum.com; D514, Colleville-sur-Mer; adult/child €7.10/5.10; ⊗ 9.30am-5pm, closed Jan & Feb) Opened in 2013, this museum has a well-presented collection of restored WWII military equipment from both sides. Situated just up the hill from the American cemetery.

Pointe du Hoc

See p24.

Arromanches-les-Bains

The centre of Arromanches has a number of hotels, making it a possible base for exploring the area.

See p20 for more information about Arromanches' importance on D-Day.

◉ Sights

Arromanches 360°
Circular Cinema   Cinema

(☑ 02 31 06 06 44; www.arromanches360.com; chemin du Calvaire; admission €5; ⊗ 10am-between 5.30pm & 7pm, closed 3 weeks in Jan & Mon mid-Nov–mid-Feb) The best view of Port Winston and nearby Gold Beach is from the hill east of town, site of the new Arromanches 360° Circular Cinema, which screens archival footage of the Battle of Normandy; it is run by Caen's Le Mémorial – Un Musée pour la Paix.

Musée du Débarquement   Museum
See p20.

Juno Beach

Dune-lined Juno Beach, 12km east of Arromanches around Courseulles-sur-Mer, was stormed by Canadian troops on D-Day. See p20 for more.

Arromanches-les-Bains

⊙ Sights

Juno Beach Centre   Museum
See p20.

**Bény-sur-Mer Canadian
War Cemetery**   Cemetery
(www.cwgc.org) The Bény-sur-Mer Canadian War Cemetery is 4km south of Courseulles-sur-Mer near Reviers.

Longues-sur-Mer

Part of the Nazis' Atlantic Wall, the massive casemates and 150mm German guns near Longues-sur-Mer, 6km west of Arromanches, were designed to hit targets some 20km away, including both Gold Beach (to the east) and Omaha Beach (to the west). More than seven decades later, the mammoth artillery pieces are still in their colossal concrete emplacements – the only in situ large-calibre weapons in Normandy. For details on the tours in English (adult/child €7/3), available from April to October, contact the on-site Longues tourist office (☑02 31 21 46 87; www.bayeux-bessin-

tourisme.com; ⊙10am-1pm & 2-6pm, closed Nov-Mar). The site itself is always open.

Utah Beach

See p24.

Caen

POP 109,300
Founded by William the Conqueror in the 11th century, Caen – capital of the Basse Normandie region – was 80% destroyed during the 1944 Battle of Normandy. Rebuilt in the 1950s and '60s in the utilitarian style in vogue at the time, modern-day Caen nevertheless offers visitors a walled medieval château, two ancient abbeys and a clutch of excellent museums, including a groundbreaking museum of war and peace.

⊙ Sights

Caen's two great abbeys, Abbaye aux Hommes and Abbaye aux Dames, were founded in the mid-11th century by William the Conqueror and his wife, Matilda of Flanders, as part of a deal in which the Church pardoned these fifth cousins for their semi-incestuous marriage.

Pedestrianised place St-Sauveur, 500m southwest of the château, is home to some historic mansions. Another attractive area for a stroll is Caen's main shopping precinct, along and near pedestrians-only rue St-Pierre, just south of the park that surrounds the château.

★ Le Mémorial –
Un Musée pour la Paix   Memorial
See p19.

Château de Caen   Château
(www.chateau.caen.fr; ⊗ 8am-10pm) **FREE** Looming above the centre of the city, Caen's castle – surrounded by massive battlements and a dry moat – was established by William the Conqueror, Duke of Normandy, in 1060. Visitors can walk around the ramparts and visit the 12th-century Église St-Georges, transformed into an information centre in 2014, and the Échiquier (Exchequer), which dates from about 1100 and is one of the oldest civic buildings in Normandy. The Jardin des Simples is a garden of medicinal and aromatic herbs cultivated during the Middle Ages, some of them poisonous.

The 'Château' parking garage is underneath the entrance to the château. The following museums are inside the château:

➡ Musée des Beaux-Arts

(Fine Arts Museum; ☑ 02 31 30 47 70; www.mba.caen. fr; adult/child €3.20/2.20, incl temporary exhibition €5.20/3.20; ⊗ 9.30am-6pm Wed-Mon) This excellent and well-curated museum takes you on a tour through the history of Western art from the 15th to 21st centuries. The collection includes works by Rubens, Tintoretto, Géricault, Monet, Bonnard, Braque, Balthus and Dubuffet, among many others.

➡ Musée de Normandie

(☑ 02 31 30 47 60; www.musee-de-normandie.caen. fr; adult/child €3.20/free; ⊗ 9.30am-6pm, closed Tue Nov-May) This two-part museum presents traditional life in Normandy and the region's history and archaeology.

Abbaye-aux-Hommes   Abbey
(Abbaye-St-Étienne; ☑ 02 31 30 42 81; www.caen. fr/abbayeauxhommes; rue Guillaume le Conquérant; ⊗ church 9am-1pm & 2-6.30pm Mon-Sat, 2-6.30pm Sun, cloister 8.30am-5pm Mon-Fri, 9.30am-1pm & 2pm-5.30pm Sat & most Sun) Caen's most important medieval site is the Men's Abbey – now city hall – and, right next door, the magnificent, multi-turreted Église St-Étienne (St Stephen's Church), known for its Romanesque nave, Gothic choir and William the Conqueror's rebuilt tomb (the original was destroyed by a 16th-century Calvinist mob and, in 1793, by fevered revolutionaries). The complex is 1km southwest of the Château de Caen; to get there by car, follow the signs to the 'Hôtel de Ville'.

You can visit the cloister and the abbey church (11th, 13th and 17th centuries) on your own, but the only way to see the interior of the 18th-century monastery is to take a 1½-hour tour (adult €4.50 or €7, child free). From April to September, these begin daily at 10.30am, 2.30pm and 4pm; the rest of the year there are tours on weekdays at 10.30am and 2.30pm. English tours are only available in July and August, at 11am, 1.30pm and 4pm. Tickets are sold at the information desk inside the Hôtel de Ville (city hall).

Abbaye-aux-Dames   Abbey
(Abbaye-de-la-Trinité; ☑ 02 31 06 98 98; www.region-basse-normandie.fr/l-abbaye-aux-dames; place Reine Mathilde) Highlights at the Women's Abbey complex, once run by the Benedictines, includes Église de la Trinité – look for Matilda's tomb behind the main altar and the striking pink stained-glass windows beyond. Free tours (at 2.30pm and 4pm daily) take you through the interior, but you can snoop around the courtyard and the church on your own at other times, except during Mass. Situated 600m east of the Château de Caen.

🛏 Sleeping

Hôtel des Quatrans   Hotel €
(☑ 02 31 86 25 57; www.hotel-des-quatrans.com; 17 rue Gémare; d from €85; 🖥) This typically modern hotel has 47 comfy, unfussy rooms in white and chocolate. Promotional deals are often available online.

★ La Maison de Famille   B&B €€
(☑ 06 61 64 88 54; www.maisondefamille.sitew.com; 4 rue Elie de Beaumont; d €70-95, q €110-135; 🖥) Wow! This four-room B&B, overflowing with personality and charm, occupies three floors of an imposing town house 500m west of the Château de Caen. Added perks include a peaceful garden and private parking. From May to September there's a two-night minimum stay.

Caen

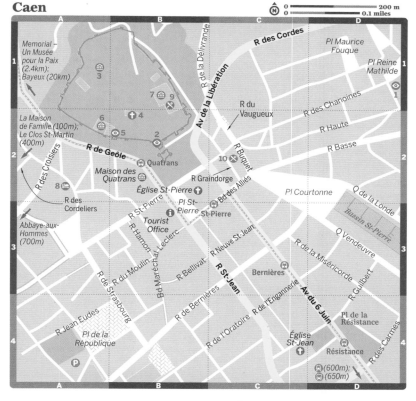

Le Clos St-Martin
B&B €€

(☑ 07 81 39 23 67; www.leclosaintmartin.com; 18bis place St-Martin; d €108-138; 🛜) Eighteenth-century grace is the order of the day at this delightfully atmospheric, four-room B&B.

✕ Eating

A variety of eateries line rue du Vaugueux, a couple of blocks east of the château, and nearby streets. More restaurants can be found three blocks to the southeast along quai Vandeuvre, facing the marina.

Café Mancel
Norman €

(☑ 02 31 86 63 64; www.cafemancel.com; Château de Caen; menus €18-36; ⊙ noon-2pm Tue-Sun, 7-10pm Tue-Sat) In the same building as the Musée des Beaux-Arts, stylish Café Mancel serves up delicious, traditional French cuisine – everything from pan-fried Norman-style

Caen

◎ Sights
1	Abbaye-aux-Dames	D1
2	Château de Caen	B2
3	Échiquier	A1
4	Église St-Georges	B2
5	Jardin des Simples	B2
6	Musée de Normandie	A2
7	Musée des Beaux-Arts	B1

🛏 Sleeping
8	Hôtel des Quatrans	A2

✕ Eating
9	Café Mancel	B1
10	Le Bouchon du Vaugueux	C2

beefsteak to hearty Caen-style *tripes*. Has a lovely sun terrace.

★ Le Bouchon
du Vaugueux　　　　　　　　Norman €€

(☑ 02 31 44 26 26; www.bouchonduvaugueux. com; 4 rue Graindorge; menus €21-33; ⊙ noon-2pm & 7-10pm Tue-Sat) Come and savour some spectacular modern cooking at this *bistrot gourmande* (gourmet bistro) – and enjoy a wonderful choice of wines (€3.50 to €5 a glass) from small producers all over France. Staff are happy to translate the chalk-board menu. Reservations recommended.

❶ Information

Tourist Office (☑ 02 31 27 14 14; www.caen-tourisme.fr; 12 place St-Pierre; ⊙ 9.30am-1pm & 2-6pm Mon-Sat Oct-Mar, 9.30am-6pm Mon-Sat, 10am-1pm Sun Apr-Sep) Helpful and efficient.

❶ Getting Around

Twisto runs the city's buses and the two tram lines, A and B, both of which link the train station with the city centre.

Abbaye-aux-Hommes (p72), Caen
ROY RAINFORD/GETTY IMAGES ©

Trouville & Deauville

The twin seaside towns of Trouville-sur-Mer (population 4900) and Deauville (population 4000), 15km southwest of Honfleur, are hugely popular with Parisians, who flock here year-round on weekends – and all week long from June to September and during Paris' school holidays.

Chic Deauville has been a playground of well-heeled Parisians ever since it was founded by Napoléon III's half-brother, the Duke of Morny, in 1861. Expensive, flashy and brash, it's packed with designer boutiques, deluxe hotels and meticulously tended public gardens, and hosts two race-tracks and the high-profile American Film Festival.

Unpretentious Trouville is both a veteran beach resort, graced with impressive mansions from the late 1800s, and a working fishing port. Popular with middle-class French families, the town was frequented by painters and writers during the 19th century (eg Mozin and Flaubert), lured by the 2km-long sandy beach and the laid-back seaside ambience.

◉ Sights & Activities

In Deauville, the rich and beautiful strut their stuff along the beachside Promenade des Planches, a 643m-long boardwalk that's lined with a row of 1920s cabins named after famous Americans (mainly film stars). After swimming in the nearby 50m Piscine Olympique (Olympic swimming pool; bd de la Mer; admission from €4.50; ⊙ closed 2 weeks in Jan & 1 week in Jun), filled with sea-water heated to 28°C, they – like you – can head to the beach, hundreds of metres wide at low tide; walk across the street to their eye-popping, neo-something mansion; or head down the block to the spectacularly Italianate casino.

Trouville, too, has a waterfront casino, wide beach and Promenade des Planches (boardwalk). At the latter, 583m long and outfitted with Bauhaus-style pavilions from the 1930s, you can swim in a freshwater swimming pool and windsurf; there's also a playground for kids. Trouville's most impressive 19th-century villas are right nearby.

Musée Villa Montabello　　　　　　Museum

(☑ 02 31 88 16 26; 64 rue du Général Leclerc, Trouville; adult/child €2/1.50; ⊙ 2-5.30pm Wed-Mon Apr–mid-Nov, from 11am Sat, Sun & holidays) In a fine mansion built in 1865, this municipal museum recounts Trouville's history and features works by Charles Mozin and Eugène Boudin. Situated 1km northeast of the tourist office, near the beach.

🎊 Festivals & Events

Deauville is renowned for horse racing at two *hippodromes* (racetracks): La Touques for flat races and Clairefontaine (www. hippodrome-deauville-clairefontaine.com) for flat, trotting and jumping races (steeplechases and hurdles). For details on events dates and venues, see www.deauvillecheval.com and www.hippodromesdedeauville.com.

Deauville Asian Film Festival   Film

(www.deauvilleasia.com) Running since 1999, this festival shows films from East, Southeast and South Asia. Held for five days in early March; tickets for one day/whole festival cost €12/35.

Deauville American Film Festival   Film

(www.festival-deauville.com) Deauville has a fair bit of Beverly Hills glitz so it's an appropriate venue for a festival celebrating American cinema, founded in 1975. Held for 10 days from early September; tickets cost €30/150 for one day/whole festival.

🛏 Sleeping

Trouville offers much better accommodation value than Deauville. Prices are highest – and reservations recommended – in July and August, and year-round on weekends and holidays; and lowest (we're talking half off) from October to Easter, except during Paris' school holidays, and most of the year on weekdays.

La Maison Normande   Hotel €

(📋 02 31 88 12 25; 4 place de Lattre de Tassigny, Trouville; d/q from €73/104; 🛜) The 17 rooms in this late-17th-century Norman house, decked out with copper pots and pans, vary considerably in size and style but all, though uninspiring, are eminently serviceable and offer good value. Situated six short blocks inland along rue Victor Hugo from Trouville's waterfront, across the street from Église Bonsecours.

★ L'Espérance   Hotel €€

(📋 02 31 88 26 68; www.lesperancehoteldeauville. com; 32 rue Victor Hugo, Deauville; d €130; 🛜) Hidden away inside an elegant town house, beyond the lovely public areas, are 10 doubles decorated with excellent taste. Prices at this family-run gem change day by day according to demand. Situated in the heart of Deauville, a block north of place Morny.

Le Fer à Cheval   Hotel €€

(📋 02 31 98 30 20; www.hotel-trouville.com; 11 rue Victor Hugo, Trouville; d/q €98/185; 🛜) Ensconced in three beautiful turn-of-the-20th-century buildings, this very welcoming hotel has 34 comfortable, modern rooms with big windows, equine-themed decor and bright bathrooms. Situated two short blocks inland from the riverfront.

🍴 Eating

In Trouville, there are lots of restaurants and buzzing brasseries along riverfront bd Fernand Moureaux; many specialise in fresh fish, mussels and seafood. The area has a fantastic atmosphere on summer evenings. Inland, check out the small restaurants and cafes along and near rue d'Orléans.

Deauville has a good selection of eateries scattered around town, with clusters around the tourist office and place Morny.

Tivoli Bistro   Bistro €€

(📋 02 31 98 43 44; 27 rue Charles Mozin, Trouville; menu €27.50; ⏲ 12.15-1.30pm & 7.15-9.30pm Fri-Tue) You won't find a cosier place in Trouville than this much-loved hideaway, tucked away on a narrow side street a block inland from the riverfront. It's famous for its delicious *sole meunière* (Dover sole) and exquisite homemade terrine.

Le Comptoir et la Table   Modern French €€

(📋 02 31 88 92 51; www.lecomptoiretlatable.fr; 1 quai de la Marine, Deauville; weekday lunch/dinner menus €15/30; ⏲ noon-2.30pm & 7-10.30pm Thu-Tue, daily Jul & Aug) Seasonal ingredients fresh from the market are transformed into delicious dishes, some of Italian inspiration, that are served in appealingly maritime surroundings. Specialities include risotto. Situated 600m northeast of the tourist office along rue Victor Hugo.

TOP TIP: FRESH OYSTERS

The Marché aux Poissons (Fish Market; bd Fernand Moureaux; ⊙ 8am-7.30pm) is *the* place in Trouville to head for a waterfront picnic of fresh oysters with lemon (from €10 to €12 a dozen) – or, if you'll be cooking, for whelks, sea urchins, prawns, shrimp and, of course, fish. Everything is super-fresh and since there are no middlemen, you pay reasonable prices and the fishermen get a fair share of the proceeds. Located on the waterfront 250m south of the casino.

Poissonnerie Pillet Saiter (www. poissonnerie-pilletsaiter.fr; bd Fernand Moureaux, Trouville; oysters per 12 €10-12), proud of having operated its own fishing boat since 1887, sells platters of seafood (by weight) and oysters (by the six or dozen) that you can eat at little tables.

🛍 Shopping

Deauville's town centre features elegant boutiques with posh window displays – check out the shops around the Casino and place Morny, and along rue Eugène Colas and rue Désiré-le-Hoc.

Trouville features less-glitzy wares along its main commercial street, rue des Bains, which runs inland from the waterfront.

ℹ Information

Deauville Post Office (rue Robert Fossorier) Exchanges currency. Situated half a block from the tourist office.

Deauville Tourist Office (📞 02 31 14 40 00; www.deauville.org; place de la Mairie; ⊙ 10am-6pm Mon-Sat, 10am-1pm & 2-5pm Sun) Has a trilingual walking-tour brochure with a Deauville map and can help find accommodation. The website has details on cultural events and horse races. Situated 800m west of the train station along rue Désiré le Hoc.

Trouville Tourist Office (📞 02 31 14 60 70; www.trouvillesurmer.org; 32 bd Fernand Moureaux; ⊙ 10am-6pm Mon-Sat, to 4pm Sun) Has a free map of Trouville and sells map-brochures for two self-guided architectural tours (€3.50) and two rural walks (€1) of 7km and 11km. Situated 200m north of pont des Belges.

ℹ Getting Around

Les Trouvillaises (📞 02 31 98 54 11; www.lestrouvillaises.fr; place Foch; bicycle per hour/day €5/14; ⊙ 9.30am-7.30pm mid-Mar–Oct, plus weekends & school holidays) Based near Trouville's casino (next to the footbridge/passenger ferry to Deauville), Les Trouvillaises rents out a variety of two- and four-wheel pedal-powered conveyances, including bicycles, tandems and carts, for both adults and children.

Honfleur

POP 8160

Long a favourite with painters such as Monet, Normandy's most charming port town is a popular day-trip destination for Parisian families. Though the centre can be over-run with visitors on warm weekends and in summer, it's hard not to love the rugged maritime charm of the Vieux Bassin (old harbour), which evokes maritime Normandy of centuries past.

In the 16th and 17th centuries, Honfleur was one of France's most important ports for commerce and exploration. Some of the earliest French expeditions to Brazil and Newfoundland began here, and in 1608 Samuel de Champlain set sail from Honfleur to found Quebec City.

ℹ Orientation

Honfleur is centred around the roughly rectangular Vieux Bassin and, along its southeast side, the Enclos, the once-walled old town. Église Ste-Catherine is northwest of the Vieux Bassin (up the hill).

👁 Sights & Activities

Honfleur is superb for aimless ambling, especially if you have a walking map from the tourist office. One option is to head north from the Lieutenance along quai des Passagers to Jetée de l'Ouest (Western Jetty), which forms the west side of the Avant Port, out to the broad mouth of the Seine. Possible stops include the Jardin des Personnalités, a park featuring figures from Honfleur history; the beach; and Naturospace (📞 02 31 81 77 00; www.naturospace.com; bd Charles V; adult/child €8.50/6.60; ⊙ 9.30am-1pm & 2-5.30pm Feb-Nov, closed Dec & Jan), a greenhouse filled with free-flying tropical butterflies that's situated 500m northwest of the Lieutenance.

The tourist office also has audioguides (€3.50; in English, French and German) for a 1½-hour walking tour of town.

Le Pass Musées (adult/child €10.10/7.10) gets you into all four municipal museums for the price of two.

Vieux Bassin   Historic Quarter

The old harbour, with its bobbing pleasure boats, is Honfleur's focal point. On the west side, quai Ste-Catherine is lined with tall, taper-thin houses – many protected from the elements by slate tiles – dating from the 16th to 18th centuries. The Lieutenance, at the mouth of the old harbour, was once the residence of the town's royal governor. Just northeast of the Lieutenance is the Avant Port, home to Honfleur's dozen fishing vessels, which sell their catch at the Marché au Poisson (Fish Market; Jetée de Transit; ☉ 8am-noon or later Thu-Sun).

Église Ste-Catherine   Church

(place Ste-Catherine; ☉ 9am-5.15pm or later) Initially intended as a temporary structure, this extraordinary wooden church was built by local shipwrights during the late 15th and early 16th centuries after its stone predecessor was destroyed during the Hundred Years War. Wood was used so money would be left over to strengthen the city's fortifications. From the inside, the remarkable twin naves and double-vaulted roof resemble two overturned ships' hulls. Situated a block

southwest (up the hill) from the northern end of the Vieux Bassin.

Clocher Ste-Catherine, the church's free-standing wooden bell tower, stands across the square from the facade. It is said to have been built away from the church to limit the damage from lightning strikes.

Les Maisons Satie   Museum

(☑ 02 31 89 11 11; www.musees-honfleur.fr; 67 bd Charles V & 90 rue Haute; adult/child €6.10/4.60; ☉ 10am-6pm Wed-Mon, last entry 1hr before closing) Like no other museum you've ever seen, this complex captures the whimsical spirit of the eccentric avant-garde composer Erik Satie (1866–1925), who lived and worked in Honfleur and was born in one of the two half-timbered *maisons Satie* (Satie houses). Visitors wander through the utterly original rooms, each hiding a surreal surprise, with a headset playing Satie's strangely familiar music. Situated 350m northwest of the northern end of the Vieux Bassin.

Musée Eugène Boudin   Art Museum

See p31.

Musée de la Marine   Maritime Museum

(☑ 02 31 89 14 12; www.musees-honfleur.fr; quai St-Etienne; adult/child incl Musée d'Ethnographie €3.90/2.70; ☉ 10am-noon & 2-6.30pm Tue-Sun Apr-Sep, 2.30-5.30pm Tue-Sun & 10am-noon Sat & Sun mid-Feb-Mar, Oct & Nov, closed Dec–mid-Feb) Has model sailing ships, nautically themed en-

CAMEMBERT COUNTRY

Some of the most enduring names in the pungent world of French *fromage* come from Normandy, including Pont L'Évêque, Livarot and, most famous of all, Camembert, all of which are named after towns south of Honfleur, on or near the D579.

It's thought that monks first began experimenting with cheesemaking in the Pays d'Auge area of Normandy sometime in the 11th century, but the present-day varieties didn't emerge until around the 17th century. The invention of Camembert is generally credited to Marie Harel, who was supposedly given the secret of soft cheesemaking by an abbot from Brie on the run from revolutionary mobs in 1790. Whatever the truth of the legend, the cheese was a huge success at the local market in Vimoutiers, and the *fabrication* of Camembert quickly grew from cottage production into a veritable industry. The distinctive round wooden boxes, in which Camembert is wrapped, have been around since 1890; they were designed by a local engineer to protect the soft disc during long-distance travel.

If you're interested in seeing how the cheese is made, you can take a tour of the Maison du Camembert (☑ 02 33 12 10 37; www.fermepresident.com; adult/child €3.50/1.50; ☉ 10am-noon & 2-5pm daily May-Sep, Wed-Sun Apr & Oct, Fri-Sun mid-Feb–Mar, closed Nov–mid-Feb), an early-19th-century farm restored by Président, one of the largest Camembert producers. It's in the centre of the town of Camembert, about 60km south of Honfleur.

gravings and watercolours, and a case that examines Honfleur's role in the 17th- and 18th-century *traite négrière* (slave trade). Situated on the eastern shore of the Vieux Bassin, in the deconsecrated 13th- and 14th-century Église St-Étienne.

Musée d'Ethnographie et
d'Art Populaire Normand   Museum
(www.musees-honfleur.fr; rue de la Prison; adult/child incl Musée de la Marine €3.90/2.70; ☺10am-noon & 2-6.30pm Tue-Sun, closed mid-Nov–mid-Feb) Offers a glimpse of domestic and economic life in 16th- to 19th-century Normandy through traditional costumes, furniture and housewares. Situated around the corner from Musée de la Marine, in two adjacent 16th-century buildings: a one-time prison and a house.

Chapelle Notre Dame de Grâce   Church
Built between 1600 and 1613, this chapel sits on the Plateau de Grâce, a wooded, 100m-high hill about 2km west of the Vieux Bassin. The area offers great views of the Seine estuary, Le Havre, Honfleur and the Pont de Normandie.

🛏 Sleeping

The tourist office and its website can help you get in touch with some 60 local B&Bs.

Ibis Budget   Hotel €
(☑08 92 68 07 81; www.ibisbudget.com; 2 rue des Vases; tr €64; ☏) Superbly situated just 400m southeast of the Vieux Bassin, this almost comically anonymous chain hotel has the cheapest beds in town – we mention it only because there's no youth hostel. The 63 rooms, strictly functional in white and green, come with a third bed overhead and tiny plastic bathroom pods. Prices drop on weekdays.

Hôtel du Dauphin   Hotel €
(☑02 31 89 15 53; www.hoteldudauphin.com; 10 place Pierre-Berthelot; d €73-102, q €160-175; ☏) Behind a 17th-century slate and half-timbered facade, this hotel and its annexe have 34 smallish, modern rooms with nautically themed bathrooms. The quads are pricey for what you get. Neither building has a lift. Situated one block west of Église Ste-Catherine.

La Petite Folie   B&B €€
(☑06 74 39 46 46; www.lapetitefolie-honfleur.com; 44 rue Haute; d €145-160, apt €185-295; ☏) Penny Vincent, an American who moved to France from San Francisco, and her French husband Thierry are the gracious hosts at this elegant town house, built in 1830 and still graced by the original stained glass and tile floors. Hard to believe, but this was beachfront property back then! There's a two-night minimum. Situated four short blocks northwest of the northern end of the Vieux Bassin.

À l'École Buissonnière   B&B €€
(☑06 16 18 43 62; www.a-lecole-buissonniere.com; 4 rue de la Foulerie; d incl breakfast €100-120; ☏) Occupying a former girls' school built in the 1600s, this welcoming B&B, lovingly restored, has five luxurious rooms with antique wood furnishings. For lunch, stop by the *bar à fromages* (cheese bar), or have them prepare a picnic lunch (€15). Bikes cost €15 a day. Situated three short blocks southwest of Église Ste-Catherine.

Le Fond de la Cour   B&B €€
(☑06 72 20 72 98; www.lefonddelacour.com; 29 rue Eugène Boudin; d €90-145; ☏) Watched over by three chickens, two cats, a dog and some koi, the six rooms (including a studio and a cottage) are light, airy and immaculate. The energetic Amanda, a native of Scotland, goes to great lengths to make you feel at home. Situated four blocks west of Église Ste-Catherine – follow rue du Puits.

✕ Eating

Some of Honfleur's finest restaurants, many featuring dishes plucked from the sea, are on place Hamelin and adjacent rue Haute, both just west of the northern end of the Vieux Bassin. There are more options up around Église Ste-Catherine. Budget places with watery views line quai Ste-Catherine, along the western side of the Vieux Bassin. East of the Vieux Bassin, there are more restaurants along rue de la Ville. Honfleur's dining spots often fill up, especially for dinner on weekends and during school holidays, so it's a good idea to phone in a reservation.

Vieux Bassin (p77), Honfleur

Au P'tit Mareyeur
French €€

(02 31 98 84 23; www.auptitmareyeur.fr; 4 rue Haute; lunch/dinner menu €28/35; noon-2pm & 7-10pm Thu-Mon, closed Jan) Under 17th-century beams, this 'semi-gastronomique' restaurant serves up Norman-style fish and langoustine, foie gras and *bouillabaisse honfleuraise* (fish and seafood stew with potatoes and saffron; €32); some of the side dishes feature South Indian spices. A new dining area opened upstairs in 2014. Situated two blocks northwest of the northern end of the Vieux Bassin.

L'Endroit
French €€

(02 31 88 08 43; 3 rue Charles et Paul Bréard; weekday lunch menu €21, other menu €28.50; noon-1.30pm & 7.30-9pm Thu-Mon) Normandy-grown heritage vegetables accompany the traditional French fish and meat dishes at L'Endroit, a classy and very well-regarded bistrot whose open kitchen lets you watch the chefs as they cook. Situated three blocks southeast of the southern end of the Vieux Bassin.

Le Gambetta
French €€

(02 31 87 05 01; 58 rue Haute; menu €25-35; noon-1.45pm & 7.15-9pm Wed-Sun) This traditional restaurant takes pride in resurrecting old recipes, some from the early 20th century, others from the Middle Ages. Specialities include fish, meat prepared on a *plancha* (grill) and scrumptious desserts. Situated four short blocks northwest of the northern end of the Vieux Bassin.

L'Écailleur
French €€

(02 31 89 93 34; www.lecailleur.fr; 1 rue de la République; weekday lunch menu €21, other menus €30-45; noon-2pm & 7-9pm Fri-Tue) Resembling a ship's wood-panelled interior, this stylish restaurant makes a lovely haven from the hustle. Specialities include turbot, *lotte* (monkfish) and *filet mignon du porc* (roasted tenderloin of pork). Situated at the southern tip of the Vieux Bassin.

L'Homme de Bois French €€

(02 31 89 75 27; 30-32 rue de L'Homme de Bois; menus €22-34; noon-2.30pm & 7-9.30pm) The rustic interior, complete with a fireplace, provides a relaxing backdrop for the locally caught fish, either grilled or prepared with delicate traditional sauces; *homard breton* (blue lobster) from the Carteret area; and excellent French-style steaks. Situated four short blocks northwest of the northern end of the Vieux Bassin.

Shopping

Honfleur is home to quite a few art galleries, some of them on the streets leading up the hill from Église Ste-Catherine (eg rue de l'Homme de Bois), others along rue Cachin, which is one long block south of the Vieux Bassin. A number of shops specialise in *brocante* (second-hand goods and antiques).

Information

There is no place in Honfleur to change money. **Tourist Office** (02 31 89 23 30; www.ot -honfleur.fr; quai Lepaulmier; 9.30am-12.30pm & 2-6pm Mon-Sat Sep-Jun, 9.30am-6pm Jul & Aug, also open 9.30am-5pm Sun Easter-Sep;) Has a free map detailing three enjoyable walking circuits, audioguides (€3.50) for a walking tour of town (in English, French and German), and bus schedules. Internet access costs €1 for 15 minutes. Situated a long block southeast of the Vieux Bassin, inside the ultra-modern Médiathèque (library) building.

Getting Around
Free parking is available next to Naturospace, which is 600m northwest of the Avant Port along bd Charles V.

Street-corner cafe, Honfleur

Lille, Flanders & Somme

In Lille and French Flanders, the down-to-earth Flemish vibe mixes easily with French sophistication and savoir faire. And in Picardy and Artois, WWI memorials and cemeteries marking the frontlines of 1916 render overseas visitors speechless time and again with their heart-breaking beauty.

History

In the Middle Ages, the Nord *département* (the sliver of France along the Belgian border; www.tourisme-nord.fr), together with much of Belgium and part of the Netherlands, belonged to a feudal principality known as Flanders (Flandre or Flandres in French, Vlaanderen in Flemish). Today, many people in the area still speak Flemish – essentially Dutch with some variation in pronunciation and vocabulary – and are very proud of their *flamand* culture and cuisine.

The area south of the Somme estuary and Albert forms the *région* of Picardy, historically centred on the Somme *département,* which saw some of the bloodiest fighting of WWI. The popular British WWI love song 'Rose of Picardy' was penned here in 1916 by Frederick E Weatherley.

ⓘ Getting There & Away

Lille, Flanders and Picardy are a hop, skip and a jump from southwest England. By train on the **Eurostar** (www.eurostar.com; promotional fares Lille–London start at just €88 return) Lille is just 70 minutes from London's St Pancras International train station. **Eurotunnel** (www.eurotunnel.com) can get you and your car from Folkestone to Calais, via the Channel Tunnel, in a mere 35 minutes. For those with sturdy sea legs, car ferries link Dover with Calais and Dunkirk.

On the Continent, superfast Eurostar and TGV trains link Lille with Brussels (35 minutes), and TGVs make travel from Lille to Paris' Gare du Nord (one hour) and Charles de Gaulle Airport (one hour) a breeze.

LILLE

POP 233,210

Lille (Rijsel in Flemish) may be France's most underrated major city. In recent decades this once-grimy industrial metropolis, its economy based on declining industries, has shrugged off its grey image and transformed itself into a glittering and self-confident cultural and commercial hub. Highlights for the visitor include an attractive old town with a strong Flemish accent, three renowned art museums, stylish shopping, some excellent dining options and a cutting-edge, student-driven nightlife scene. The Lillois have a well-deserved reputation for friendliness – and are so proud of being friendly that they often mention it!

Thanks to the Eurostar and the TGV, Lille makes an easy, environmentally sustainable weekend destination from London, Paris or Brussels.

History

Lille owes its name – once spelled L'Isle – to the fact that it was founded, back in the 11th century, on an island in the River Deûle. In 1667 the city was captured by French forces led personally by Louis XIV, who promptly set about fortifying his prize, creating the Lille Citadelle. In the 1850s the miserable conditions in which Lille's 'labouring classes' lived – the city was long the centre of France's textile industry – were exposed by Victor Hugo.

 Sights & Activities

Palais des Beaux Arts
Art Museum

(Fine Arts Museum; ☑ 03 20 06 78 00; www.pba-lille.fr; place de la République; adult/child €6.50/free; ☺ 2-5.30pm Mon, from 10am Wed-Sun; Ⓜ République-Beaux Arts) Lille's world-renowned Fine Arts Museum displays a truly first-rate collection of 15th- to 20th-century paintings, including works by Rubens, Van Dyck and Manet. Exquisite porcelain and faience (pottery), much of it of local provenance, is on the ground floor, while in the basement you'll find classical archaeology, medieval statuary and 18th-century scale models of the fortified cities of northern France and Belgium. Information sheets in French, English and Dutch are available in each hall.

Musée d'Art Moderne, d'Art Contemporain et d'Art Brut – LaM
Art Museum

(☑ 03 20 19 68 68; www.musee-lam.fr; 1 allée du Musée, Villeneuve-d'Ascq; adult/child €7/free; ☺ 10am-6pm Tue-Sun) Colourful, playful and just plain weird works of modern and contemporary art by masters such as Braque, Calder, Léger, Miró, Modigliani and Picasso are the big draw at this renowned museum and sculpture park in the Lille suburb of Villeneuve-d'Ascq, 9km east of Gare Lille-Europe. Take metro line 1 to Pont de Bois, then bus line 4 (10 minutes) to Villeneuve-d'Ascq-LaM.

La Piscine Musée d'Art et d'Industrie
Art Museum

(☑ 03 20 69 23 60; www.roubaix-lapiscine.com; 23 rue de l'Espérance, Roubaix; adult/child €5.50/free; ☺ 11am-6pm Tue-Thu, 11am-8pm Fri, 1-6pm Sat & Sun; Ⓜ Gare Jean Lebas) If Paris can turn a disused train station into a world-class museum (the Musée d'Orsay), why not transform an art deco municipal swimming pool (built 1927–32) – an architectural masterpiece inspired by civic pride and hygienic high-mindedness – into a temple of the arts? This innovative museum, 12km northeast of Gare

LILLE, FLANDERS & SOMME LILLE

Palais des Beaux Arts, Lille

Lille

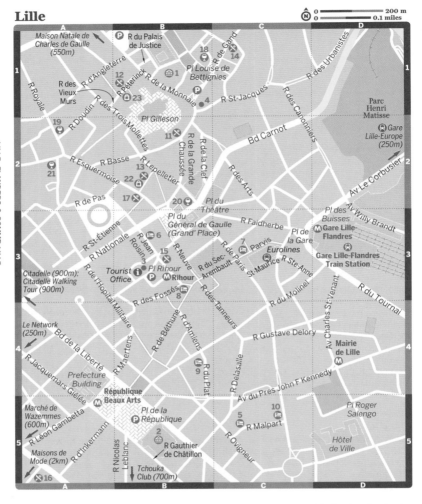

Maison Natale de Charles de Gaulle (550m)

R du Palais de Justice

R du Gand

Pl Louise de Bettignies

R des Urbanistes

R Royale

R d'Angleterre

R des Vieux Murs

R Péterinck

R de la Monnaie

R St-Jacques

R des Canonniers

Parc Henri Matisse

R Doudin

R des Trois Molettes

Pl Gilleson

R de la Grande Chaussée

R de la Clef

Bd Carnot

Gare Lille-Europe (250m)

R Esquermoise

R Basse

R Lepelletier

R des Arts

Av Le Corbusier

R de Pas

Av Willy Brandt

Pl du Théâtre

Pl des Buisses

Gare Lille-Flandres

Pl du Général de Gaulle (Grand' Place)

R Faidherbe

Pl de la Gare

R St-Étienne

R Nationale

R Jean Roisin

R Neuve

R de Paris

Parvis

Eurolines

Gare Lille-Flandres Train Station

Citadelle (900m); Citadelle Walking Tour (900m)

R de l'Hôpital Militaire

Tourist Office

Pl Rihour

Rihour

R du Sec-Arembault

St-Maurice

R Ste-Anne

R des Fossés

R des Tanneurs

R du Molinel

R du Tournai

Le Network (250m)

Bd de la Liberté

R Maertens

R de Béthune

R d'Amiens

R Gustave Delory

Av Charles St-Venant

Mairie de Lille

R Jacquemars Giélée

R Delasalle

Prefecture Building

République Beaux Arts

Pl de la République

R du Plat

Av du Prés John F Kennedy

Pl Roger Salengo

Marché de Wazemmes (600m)

R Léon Gambetta

R d'Inkermann

R Nicolas Leblanc

R Gauthier de Châtillon

R Malpart

R Ovigneur

Hôtel de Ville

Maisons de Mode (2km)

Tchouka Club (700m)

Lille-Europe in Roubaix, showcases fine arts, applied arts and sculpture in a delightfully watery environment.

Wazemmes
Neighbourhood

(M Gambetta) For an authentic taste of grassroots Lille, head to the ethnically mixed, family-friendly *quartier populaire* (working-class quarter) of Wazemmes, 1.7km southwest of place du Général de Gaulle, where African immigrants and old-time proletarians live harmoniously alongside penurious students and trendy *bobos* (bourgeois bohemians).

The neighbourhood's focal point is the cavernous Marché de Wazemmes, Lille's favourite food market. The adjacent outdoor market is the place to be on Sunday morning – it's a real carnival scene! Rue des Sarrazins and rue Jules Guesde are lined with shops, restaurants and Tunisian pastry places, many owned by, and catering to, the area's North African residents.

Wazemmes is famed for its many outdoor concerts and street festivals, including La Louche d'Or (Golden Ladle; 1 May), a soup festival that has spread to cities across Europe.

Lille

⊙ Sights
1 Musée de l'Hospice Comtesse B1
2 Palais des Beaux Arts B5

⊙ Activities, Courses & Tours
3 Flanders Battlefields Tour B3
4 Vieux Lille Walking Tour B1

⊙ Sleeping
5 Auberge de Jeunesse C5
6 Grand Hôtel Bellevue B3
7 Hôtel Brueghel C3
8 Hotel Kanaï B3
9 La Villa 30 .... B4
10 L'Hermitage Gantois C5

⊙ Eating
11 À l'Huîtrière B2

12 Au Vieux de la Vieille B1
13 La Petite Cour B2
14 Le Bistrot Lillois C1
   Le Comptoir 44 .... (see 14)
15 Le Pain Quotidien B3
16 Marché Sébastopol A5
17 Meert B2

⊙ Drinking & Nightlife
18 Café Oz – The
   Australian Bar B1
19 L'Illustration Café A2
20 Morel & Fils B2
21 Vice & Versa A2

⊙ Shopping
22 Fromagerie Philippe Olivier B2
23 L'Abbaye des Saveurs B1

Maison Natale de Charles de Gaulle — House Museum

(☑ 03 28 38 12 05; www.maison-natale-de-gaulle.org; 9 rue Princesse; adult/child incl audioguide €6/free; ⊙ 10am-noon & 2-5pm Wed-Sat, 1.30-5pm Sun) The upper-middle-class house in which Charles de Gaulle was born in 1890 is now a museum presenting the French leader in the context of his times, with an emphasis on his connection to French Flanders. Displays include de Gaulle's dainty baptismal robe and some evocative newsreels.

Musée de l'Hospice Comtesse — Art Museum

(☑ 03 28 36 84 00; 32 rue de la Monnaie; adult/child €3.50/free; ⊙ 10am-12.30pm & 2-6pm, closed Mon morning & Tue) Housed in a remarkably attractive 15th- and 17th-century poorhouse, this museum features ceramics, earthenware wall tiles, religious art and 17th- and 18th-century paintings and furniture. A rood screen separates the Salle des Malades (Hospital Hall) from a mid-17th-century chapel (look up to see a mid-19th-century painted ceiling).

Citadelle — Fortress

(☑ 03 20 21 94 39; Vauban-Esquermes; ☐ 12) At the northwestern end of bd de la Liberté, this massive star-shaped fortress was designed by renowned 17th-century French military architect Vauban after France captured Lille in 1667. Made of some 60 million bricks, it still functions as a French and NATO military base. Guided tours are available on Sundays in summer – contact the tourist office. This is the only way to see the inside of the Citadelle.

Outside the 2.2km-long ramparts is the city centre's largest park, where children will love the amusement park, playground and small municipal zoo.

☞ Tours

The tourist office (p91) runs various guided tours.

Citadelle Walking Tour — Walking

(tour €7.50; ⊙ 3pm & 4.30pm Sun Jun-Aug) This is the only way to see the inside of the Citadelle, usually a closed military zone. Sign up for the tour (in French) at least 72 hours ahead and bring a passport or national ID card. The tour lasts one hour.

Vieux Lille Walking Tour — Walking

(adult/child €11.50/9.50; ⊙ 10.15am Sat in English, 3pm daily in French) Departing from the tourist office, this walking tour takes in all the highlights of Lille's 17th- and 18th-century Old Town.

Flanders Battlefields Tour — WWI History

(tour €44; ⊙ 1-5pm Sat in English) Four-hour tour of several important WWI battle sites around Ypres (just across the Belgian border). Tours depart from the tourist office.

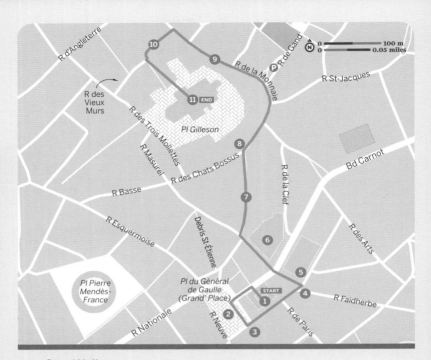

City Walk
Lille Discovery Stroll

START VIEILLE BOURSE
FINISH CATHÉDRALE NOTRE-DAME-DE-LA-TREILLE
LENGTH 1KM; ONE HOUR

The best place to begin is the **1 Vieille Bourse**, a Flemish Renaissance extravaganza ornately decorated with caryatids and cornucopia. Built in 1653, it consists of 24 separate houses set around a richly ornamented interior courtyard that hosts a used-book market. In warm weather locals often gather here to play *échecs* (chess).

West of the Vieille Bourse is **2 place du Général de Gaulle** (or 'Grand Place') where you can admire the 1932 art deco home of **3 La Voix du Nord** (the leading regional newspaper), crowned by a gilded sculpture of the Three Graces. The victory column (1845) in the fountain commemorates the city's successful resistance to the Austrian siege of 1792. On warm evenings, Lillois come here by the thousands to stroll, take in the atmosphere and sip a local beer. East of the Vieille Bourse, impressive **4 place du Théâtre** is dominated

by the Louis XVI–style **5 Opéra** and the neo-Flemish **6 Chambre de Commerce**, topped by a 76m-high spire sporting a gilded clock. Both were built in the early 20th century. Look east along rue Faidherbe and you'll see Gare Lille-Flandres at the other end.

Vieux Lille (Old Lille), proud of its restored 17th- and 18th-century brick houses, begins just north of here. Hard to believe, but in the late 1970s this quarter was a half-abandoned slum dominated by empty, dilapidated buildings. Head north along **7 rue de la Grande Chaussée**, lined with Lille's chic-est shops, and take a peek at **8 À l'Huîtrière** restaurant, an art deco masterpiece. Continue north along **9 rue de la Monnaie** (named after a mint constructed here in 1685), where old brick residences now house boutiques and the Musée de l'Hospice Comtesse.

Turning left (west) on tiny **10 rue Péterinck** and then left again will take you to the 19th-century, neo-Gothic **11 Cathédrale Notre-Dame-de-la-Treille**, which has a strikingly modern (some would say 'jarring') west facade (1999) that looks better from inside or when illuminated at night.

✦✦ Festivals & Events

The Braderie (p91), a flea-market extra-ordinaire, is held on the first weekend in September. Before the festivities you can join in the semi-marathon (www.semi marathon-lille.fr) that begins at 8.45am on Saturday, or a 10km run at 10.45am; both set off from place de la République.

Throughout the year, the varied art exhibitions associated with Lille 3000 (www. lille3000.com) 'explore the richness and complexities of the world of tomorrow'.

In the lead-up to Christmas, late November to 30 December, decorations and edible goodies are sold at the Marché de Noël (Christmas Market; www.noel-a-lille.com; place Rihour).

⌖ Sleeping

Most Lille hotels are at their fullest, and priciest, from Monday to Thursday.

Auberge de Jeunesse   Hostel €

(☎ 03 20 57 08 94; www.hifrance.org; 12 rue Malpart; dm incl breakfast €23; @ 🛜; Ⓜ Mairie de Lille, République-Beaux-Arts) This central former maternity hospital has 163 beds in rooms for two to eight, kitchen facilities and free parking. A few doubles have ensuite showers. Lockout is from 11am to 3pm (to 4pm Friday to Sunday).

Hotel Kanaï   Hotel €€

(☎ 03 20 57 14 78; www.hotelkanai.com; 10 rue de Bethune; d €75-140; ✳ @ 🛜; Ⓜ Rihour) In the heart of Lille's pedestrian zone, this enticing hotel offers reasonably priced rooms with a clean modern design; pick of the bunch are rooms 102 and 302, with large picture windows and plenty of natural light.

All come with coffee makers, attractive tiled bathrooms, crisp linen and excellent bedding. One complaint: there's no lift.

Grand Hôtel Bellevue   Historic Hotel €€

(☎ 03 20 57 45 64; www.grandhotelbellevue.com; 5 rue Jean Roisin; d €119-199; ✳ @ 🛜; Ⓜ Rihour) Grandly built in the early 20th century, this venerable establishment features 60 spacious rooms equipped with marble bathrooms, grey carpets, gilded picture frames and flat-screen TVs.

It's well worth springing for one of the better rooms with views of place du Général de Gaulle.

Hôtel Brueghel   Hotel €€

(☎ 03 20 06 06 69; www.hotel-brueghel-lille.com; 5 parvis St-Maurice; s €86-102, d €94-127; 🛜; Ⓜ Gare Lille-Flandres) The Brueghel is a dependable midrange hotel that occupies an appealing brick building halfway between Gare Lille-Flandres and the Grand' Place. The wood-panelled lobby has charm in spades, as does the creaky, tiny lift that trundles guests up to 65 rooms that have been recently modernised. Some south-facing rooms have sunny views of the adjacent church. A good deal.

La Villa 30   B&B €€

(☎ 03 66 73 61 30; www.lavilla30.fr; 24 rue du Plat; d incl breakfast €99-125; 🛜; Ⓜ République Beaux Arts) This five-room B&B is a safe bet. The fashion-forward style reflects the owner's love for contemporary interior design, with elegant furnishings, chocolate brown, beige and grey colour schemes, and modern bathrooms. One room has a balcony. It's in a quiet street near the Palais des Beaux Arts.

★ L'Hermitage Gantois   Historic Hotel €€€

(☎ 03 20 85 30 30; www.hotelhermitagegantois. com; 224 rue de Paris; d €234-455; @ 🛜; Ⓜ Mairie de Lille) This five-star hotel creates enchanting, harmonious spaces by complementing its rich architectural heritage – such as a Flemish-Gothic facade – with refined ultra-modernism. The 67 rooms are sumptuous, with Starck accessories next to Louis XV–style chairs and bathrooms that sparkle with Carrara marble. One of the four courtyards is home to a 220-year-old wisteria. The still-consecrated chapel was built in 1637.

✕ Eating

Lille (especially Vieux Lille) has a flourishing culinary scene. Keep an eye out for *estaminets* (traditional Flemish eateries, with antique knick-knacks on the walls and plain wooden tables) serving Flemish specialities.

Dining hot spots in Vieux Lille include rue de Gand – home to a dozen small, moderately priced French and Flemish restaurants – and rue de la Monnaie and its side streets.

⭐ Meert   Patisserie €
(📞 03 20 57 07 44; www.meert.fr; 27 rue Esquermoise; waffles from €3; ⏱ 9.30am-9.30pm Tue-Sat, 9am-6pm Sun; Ⓜ Rihour) A delightful spot for morning coffee or mid-afternoon tea, this elegant tearoom dating to 1761 is beloved for its retro decor and its *gaufres* (waffles) filled with sweet Madagascar vanilla paste. The tearoom's 1830s-vintage chocolate shop next door has a similarly old-fashioned atmosphere.

Le Pain Quotidien   Boulangerie €
(📞 03 20 42 88 90; www.lepainquotidien.fr; 35 place Rihour; mains €10-15; ⏱ 8am-9.15pm; Ⓜ Rihour) At this popular bakery, high-ceilinged interior rooms are flanked by display cases stacked floor to ceiling with jams, organic juices and scrumptious baked goods. In warm weather there's also outdoor seating on place Rihour, making this a prime spot for morning bowls of coffee, midday sandwiches and healthy salads, and afternoon snacks.

Le Bistrot Lillois   Flemish €
(📞 03 20 14 04 15; 40 rue de Gand; mains €10-15; ⏱ noon-2pm & 7.30-10pm Tue-Sat) This place owes its reputation to a menu based solidly on expertly prepared regional specialities. The highlight of the menu is *os à moëlle* (marrow bone), but other dishes worth trying include *carbonade flamande* (braised beef stewed with Flemish beer, spice bread and brown sugar) and *potjevleesch* (jellied chicken, pork, veal and rabbit).

Place du Général de Gaulle (Grand Place), Lille

Au Vieux de la Vieille   Flemish €

(📞 03 20 13 81 64; www.estaminetlille.fr; 2-4 rue des
Vieux Murs; mains €12-15; ⏱ noon-2pm & 7-10.30pm)
Although locals say that it used to be better, this *estaminet* (Flemish-style eatery)
remains one of the highly rated venues in
central Lille for regional cuisine. The fact it
has outdoor seating on picturesque cobble-
stoned place de l'Oignon is a plus.

Le Comptoir 44   Neobistro €

(📞 03 20 21 03 63; www.comptoir44.fr; 44 rue de
Gand; mains €13-19, lunch menu €16, dinner menu
€31; ⏱ noon-2.30pm & 7-10.30pm) Considering
its location on rue de Gand, this rustic chic
bistro could have been a typical tourist trap;
instead, well-prepared bistro classics and regional dishes go down a treat and are served
with a smile by a dynamic team.

La Petite Cour   Flemish €

(📞 03 20 51 52 81; www.lapetitecour-lille.fr; 17 rue
du Curé St-Étienne; mains €15-19, lunch menus €16-
19, dinner menu €28; ⏱ noon-2pm & 7.30-10.30pm
Mon-Thu, to 11.30pm Fri & Sat) You'd never guess
from outside that there's an atmospheric

dining room with brick walls, wooden
floors, high ceilings and a lovely inner
courtyard. Foodwise, it's no less impressive,
with a tempting array of Flemish staples,
salads as well as meat and fish dishes.

À l'Huîtrière   Seafood €€€

(📞 03 20 55 43 41; www.huitriere.fr; 3 rue des Chats
Bossus; mains €35-62, lunch menu €45, dinner menu
€98, oyster bar from €10; ⏱ noon-2pm & 7-9.30pm
Mon-Sat, noon-2pm Sun) On the 'Street of the
Hunchback Cats', this sophisticated restaurant is well known for its fabulous seafood
and wine cellar. For a lighter meal with a
lower price tag, sit at the oyster bar up front,
where stunning art deco trappings – including sea-themed mosaics and stained glass –
create a colourful, more relaxed atmosphere.

Self-Catering

Marché de Wazemmes   Market

(place de la Nouvelle Aventure; ⏱ 8am-2pm Tue-Thu,
to 8pm Fri & Sat, to 3pm Sun & holidays; Ⓜ Gambetta)
This beloved foodie space is 1.7km southwest of the tourist office, in Lille's working-
class quarter of Wazemmes.

Marché Sébastopol　　　　　Food Market

(place Sébastopol; ⊘ 7am-2pm Wed & Sat; Ⓜ République Beaux Arts) A popular food market.

🍷 Drinking & Nightlife

Lille has several drinking and nightlife areas. In Vieux Lille the small, stylish bars and cafes along streets such as rue Royale, rue de la Barre and rue de Gand are a big hit with chic 30-somethings. On Friday and Saturday nights, in the rue Masséna student zone, a university-age crowd descends on dozens of high-decibel bars along rue Masséna (750m southwest of the tourist office) and almost-perpendicular rue Solférino (as far southeast as Marché Sébastopol).

In the warm season, sidewalk cafes make the square in front of the Opéra, the place du Théâtre, a fine spot to sip beer and soak up the Flemish atmosphere.

L'Illustration Café　　　　　Bar

(www.bar-lillustration.com; 18 rue Royale; ⊘ 12.30pm-3am Mon-Sat, from 3pm Sun) Adorned with art nouveau woodwork and changing exhibits by local painters, this laid-back bar attracts artists, musicians, budding intellectuals and teachers in the mood to read, exchange weighty ideas, or just shoot the breeze. The mellow soundtrack mixes Western classical with jazz, French *chansons* and African beats.

L'Illustration Café, Lille
PATRICK FORGET/AGEFOTOSTOCK ©

Morel & Fils　　　　　Bar

(31-33 place du Théâtre; ⊘ 8am-11pm Mon-Sat, from 3pm Sun; Ⓜ Rihour) This bar-cafe diagonally across from Lille's Opéra features eclectic historical decor incorporating mannequins from its former life as a lingerie shop. Scan the facade for cannonballs dating back to the Austrian siege of 1792 (including one suggestively painted pink one).

Café Oz – The Australian Bar　　　Pub

(33 rue Louise de Bettignies; ⊘ 5pm-3am Mon-Sat) Footy and rugby on a wide screen, Australiana on the walls and cold bottles of Toohey's Extra Dry – what more could you ask for? Popular with English-speakers, including students, this place is packed when DJs do their thing from 9pm to 3am on Thursday, Friday and Saturday nights. It has a great warm-season terrace. Happy hour is 5pm to 9pm Monday to Saturday.

Vice & Versa　　　　　Gay Bar

(3 rue de la Barre; ⊘ 3pm-3am Mon-Sat, from 4pm Sun) The rainbow flies proudly at this well-heeled, sophisticated bar, which is as gay as it is popular (and it's very popular). Decor includes brick walls, a camp crystal chandelier and lots of red and green laser dots.

☆ Entertainment

Lille's free French-language entertainment guide *Sortir* (www.lille.sortir.eu, in French) is available at the tourist office, cinemas, event venues and bookshops.

Le Network　　　　　Disco

(www.network-cafe.net; 15 rue du Faisan; ⊘ 10.30pm-5.30am Tue & Wed, 9.30pm-5.30am Thu, 10.30pm-7am Fri & Sat, 7pm-5am Sun; Ⓜ République Beaux Arts) At Lille's hottest discotheque, you can sip beer and boogie in the main hall, presided over by two 5m-high statues from faraway lands, or in the baroque Venetian room, decked out with velvet settees and crystal chandeliers. The door policy is pretty strict – locals dress up – but tends to be a bit more relaxed for tourists. Situated 600m northwest of the Palais des Beaux-Arts.

Tchouka Club　　　　　Disco

(www.tchoukaclub.org; 80 rue Barthélemy Delespaul; ⊘ 11pm-7am Fri & Sat) This till-dawn gay and lesbian disco has photo-montage wall murals, plenty of flashing lights, buff barmen in tank tops and a soundtrack that's heavy on electro, house and techno. It's so packed after 1am that you may have trouble getting in. Relaxed dress code. Situated 700m due south of the Palais des Beaux-Arts.

🛍 Shopping

Lille's snazziest clothing and housewares boutiques are in Vieux Lille, in the area bounded by rue de la Monnaie, rue Esquermoise, rue de la Grande Chausée (a window-shopper's paradise!) and rue d'Angleterre. Keep an eye out for shops specialising in French Flemish edibles, including cheeses.

Maisons de Mode   Fashion

(☑03 20 99 91 20; www.maisonsdemode.com; 58/60 rue du Faubourg des Postes; ⊙2-7pm Wed-Sat) Cool, cutting-edge couture by promising young designers can be found in this cluster of studio-boutiques, about 2.5km southwest of the Palais des Beaux-Arts.

L'Abbaye des Saveurs   Food & Wine

(☑03 28 07 70 06; www.abbayedessaveurs.com; 13 rue des Vieux Murs; ⊙2-7pm Mon & Tue, 11am-7pm Wed-Sat, 11am-1.30pm Sun) A beer-lover's dream, this little shop features dozens of famous and more obscure local brews, from both the French and Belgian sides of the border.

Fromagerie Philippe Olivier   Food & Wine

(☑03 20 74 96 99; www.philippeolivier.fr; 3 rue du Curé St-Étienne; ⊙2.30-7.15pm Mon, from 10am Tue-Thu, from 9am Fri & Sat; Ⓜ Rihour) This shop near place de Gaulle is an excellent source for local cheeses.

ℹ Information

International Currency Exchange (Gare Lille-Europe; ⊙7.30am-8pm Mon-Sat, from 10am Sun; Ⓜ Gare Lille-Europe) Currency exchange in Gare Lille-Europe, in Hall 3.

Tourist Office (☑03 59 57 94 00; www.lilletourism.com; place Rihour; ⊙9am-6pm Mon-Sat, 10am-noon & 2-5pm Sun & holidays; Ⓜ Rihour) The tourist office occupies what's left of the Flamboyant Gothic–style Palais Rihour, built in the mid-1400s. It has free maps and an excellent map-brochure (€3) outlining walking tours of five city *quartiers*.

ℹ Getting There & Away

Even with a good map, entering Lille by car is incredibly confusing. Your best bet for getting to the city centre is to blindly follow the 'Centre Ville' signs. In the centre, parking lots are easy to find.

TOP TIP: BRADERIE DE LILLE

On the first weekend in September Lille's entire city centre – 200km of footpaths – is transformed into the Braderie de Lille, billed as the world's largest flea market. The extravaganza – with stands selling antiques, local delicacies, handicrafts and more – dates from the Middle Ages, when Lillois servants were permitted to hawk their employers' old garments for some extra cash.

The city's biggest annual event, the Braderie runs nonstop – yes, all night long – from 2pm on Saturday to 11pm on Sunday, when street sweepers emerge to tackle the mounds of mussel shells and old frites (French fries) left behind by the merrymakers. Lille's tourist office can supply you with a free map of the festivities.

Avis, **Europcar**, **Hertz** and **National-Citer** have car-hire offices in Gare Lille-Europe, while domestic rental companies such as **DLM** (☑03 20 06 18 80; www.dlm.fr; 32 place de la Gare; ⊙8am-noon & 2-6.30pm Mon-Fri, 9am-noon & 2-6pm Sat) can be found in the backstreets around Gare Lille-Flandres.

ℹ Getting Around

Lille's two speedy metro lines (1 and 2), two tramways (R and T), two Citadine shuttles (C1, which circles the city centre clockwise, and C2, which goes counterclockwise) and many urban and suburban bus lines – several of which cross into Belgium – are run by **Transpole** (www.transpole.fr). In the city centre, metros run every two to four minutes until about 12.30am. Useful metro stops include those at the train stations, Rihour (next to the tourist office), République Beaux Arts (near the Palais des Beaux-Arts), Gambetta (near the Wazemmes food market) and Gare Jean Lebas (near La Piscine).

Tickets (€1.50) are sold on buses but must be purchased *before* boarding a metro or tram. A Pass' Journée (all-day pass) costs €4 and needs to be time-stamped just once; two-/three-day passes are also available. A Pass Soirée, good for unlimited travel after 7pm, costs €2.

FLANDERS & ARTOIS

Arras

POP 43,690

An unexpected gem of a city, Arras (the final s is pronounced), the former capital of Artois, is worth seeing mainly for its exceptional ensemble of Flemish-style arcaded buildings and two subterranean WWI sites.

The city also makes a good base for visits to the Battle of the Somme Memorials.

◉ Sights & Activities

★ Grand' Place & Place des Héros
Square

Arras' two ancient market squares, the Grand' Place and the almost-adjacent, smaller Place des Héros (also known as Petite Place), are surrounded by 17th- and 18th-century Flemish-baroque houses topped by curvaceous 'Dutch' gables. Although the structures vary in decorative detail, their 345 sandstone columns form a common arcade unique in France. The squares, especially handsome at night, are about 600m northwest of the train station.

As picture-perfect as they look today, both squares were heavily damaged during WWI and most of the gorgeous facades had to be reconstructed from scratch.

Hôtel de Ville
Belfry, Cellars

(place des Héros; belfry adult/child €2.90/1.90, Boves tour adult/child €5.20/3, combined ticket adult/child €6.80/3.70; ⏱ belfry 10am-noon & 2-6pm, boves closed 3 weeks in Jan) Arras' Flemish-Gothic city hall dates from the 16th century but was completely rebuilt after WWI. For a panoramic view, hop on a lift (plus 43 stairs) to the first floor of the Unesco World Heritage-listed, 75m-high belfry, or for a truly unique perspective on Arras head into the slimy souterrains (tunnels) that fan out underneath the building. Also known as *boves* (cellars), they were turned into British command posts, hospitals and barracks during WWI.

Each spring, in a brilliant juxtaposition of underground gloom and horticultural exuberance, plants and flowers turn the tunnels into the Jardin des Boves (Cellar Gardens), designed around a different theme each year. Tours lasting 45 minutes (in English

upon request) focus on the gardens when they're there, or on the tunnels' history the rest of the year. Tours generally begin at 11am and run at least twice in the afternoon from Monday to Friday, or every 30 minutes on Saturday and Sunday.

Carrière Wellington
Historic Site

See p46.

🛏 Sleeping

Hôtel Diamant
Hotel €

(☑ 03 21 71 23 23; www.arras-hotel-diamant.com; 5 place des Héros; s €68-78, d €80-90) This small hotel feels like a cosy doll's house and has one of the city's most desirable locations. It's an excellent option if you can snag one of the six rooms overlooking the Place des Héros and the belfry. Rooms are tiny, though, and there's no lift. The hotel also rents two fully equipped apartments in the town house next door.

Ostel Les 3 Luppars
Hotel €

(☑ 03 21 60 02 03; www.ostel-les-3luppars.com; 49 Grand' Place; s/d €65/80; 🛜) Occupying the Grand' Place's only non-Flemish-style building (it's Gothic and dates from the 1400s), this hotel has a private courtyard and 42 rooms, including 10 with fine views of the square and two (28 and 29) fitted out for families. The decor and breakfast are uninspired but the atmosphere is homey. Also has a sauna (€5 per person for a half-hour).

★ La Corne d'Or
B&B €€

(☑ 03 21 58 85 94; www.lamaisondhotes.com; 1 place Guy Mollet; d incl breakfast €125-160; 🛜) Enviably secreted west of Grand' Place on a small square, this one-of-a-kind B&B occupies a magnificent 18th-century *hôtel particulier* (private mansion), where every detail is looked after. Much more than a posh B&B, it's the equivalent of staying in an art collector's residence, with five imaginatively designed suites and a wonderful little inner courtyard. Australian host Rodney is a great resource.

Hôtel de l'Univers
Hotel €€

(☑ 03 21 71 34 01; www.univers.najeti.fr; 3-5 place de la Croix Rouge; d €145-165; 🛜) Ensconced in a 16th-century former Jesuit monastery, this characterful hostelry is arrayed in a U around a quiet neoclassical courtyard. Classic draperies and bedspreads give each of the 38 rooms a touch of classic French class. That said, some rooms, including room 108, are more luminous and better laid-out than others, so ask to see a few before committing.

There's an onsite restaurant. Reserve ahead for parking in the hotel's courtyard (€10).

✕ Eating

Many places to eat are tucked away under the arches of the Grand' Place and along adjacent rue de la Taillerie, which leads to the Place des Héros (Petite Place).

★ Les Deux Frères –
Chez Zénon   Regional Cuisine €

(23 rue de la Taillerie; mains €11-14; ⊘noon-2.30pm Tue-Sat, bar 8.30am-9pm Tue-Sat) Blink and you'll miss this pocket-sized bistro with a wonderfully congenial atmosphere, a stone's throw from the Grand' Place. Chez Zénon is always packed and for good reason: fabulous-value regional dishes (think *potjevleesch* and pig intestine sausages with Maroilles cheese) taste fresh and home-cooked. The only hiccup is snagging a table; arrive at noon or 2pm. There's outdoor seating in summer.

Le Petit Rat Porteur   Brasserie €

(☑03 21 51 29 70; 11 rue de la Taillerie; mains €10-19, lunch menu €14; ⊘noon-2pm & 7-9.30pm Tue-Sat, noon-2pm Sun) This buzzing brasserie is smack in the middle of the Arras tourist trail, yet it remains a local favourite. There are lots of delightful salads to start off with, followed by spot-on regional standards such as *potjevleesch* and *waterzooi*. The menu is translated into English to play to Arras' many anglophones, who are in love with this bijou brasserie – especially the vaulted cellar.

La Cave des Saveurs   French, Flemish €€

(☑03 21 59 75 24; 36 Grand' Place; mains €13-20, menus €21-37; ⊘noon-2pm & 7-9pm Mon, Tue & Thu-Sat, noon-2pm Wed) In a vaulted brick cellar that served as a brewery before WWII, this atmospheric restaurant serves traditional French dishes as well as a few Flemish specialities such as *carbonade*.

La Faisanderie   Traditional French €€€

(☑03 21 48 20 76; www.restaurant-la-faisanderie. com; 45 Grand' Place; menus €27-48; ⊘lunch Tue, Wed & Fri-Sun, dinner Tue-Sat) This respectable restaurant occupying a heritage building on

the Grand' Place serves a range of French classics prepared with carefully chosen ingredients, but the real show stealer is its superb vaulted cellar.

Self-Catering

Open-Air Market   Market €

(place des Héros, Grand' Place & place de la Vacquerie; ⊘7am-1pm Wed & Sat) Around the *hôtel de ville*. The Saturday market is really huge.

ℹ Information

Tourist Office (☑03 21 51 26 95; www. explorearras.fr; place des Héros; ⊘9am-6.30pm Mon-Sat, 10am-1.30pm & 2.30-6.30pm Sun) Inside the *hôtel de ville*.

ℹ Getting There & Around

BICYCLE

Arras Vélo (☑06 29 71 61 91; www.arrasvelo. com; place du Théâtre; per day €10; ⊘9am-6pm) Rents electric bicycles, convenient for getting to the Vimy battlefields 12km north of town.

CAR

Avis (☑03 21 51 69 03; www.avis.fr; 6 rue Gambetta; ⊘9am-noon & 2-6pm Mon-Fri, 9am-noon & 4-6pm Sat) Half a block northwest of the train station.

Europcar (☑03 21 07 29 54; 5 rue de Douai; ⊘8.30am-noon & 2-5pm Mon-Fri, 9am-noon Sat) Half a block to the right as you exit the train station.

Place des Héros, Arras
EURASIA/GETTY IMAGES ©

BATTLE OF THE SOMME, FLANDERS & ARTOIS MEMORIALS

The First Battle of the Somme, a WWI Allied offensive waged in the villages and woodlands northeast of Amiens, was designed to relieve pressure on the beleaguered French troops at Verdun. On 1 July 1916, British, Commonwealth and French troops 'went over the top' in a massive assault along a 34km front. But German positions proved virtually unbreachable, and on the first day of the battle an astounding 21,392 British troops were killed and another 35,492 were wounded. Most casualties were infantrymen mown down by German machine guns. By the time the offensive was called off in mid-November, a total of 1.2 million lives had been lost on both sides. The British had advanced 12km, the French 8km.

The Battle of the Somme has become a symbol of the meaningless slaughter of war, and its killing fields have since become a site of pilgrimage. Each year, thousands of visitors from Australia, New Zealand, Canada and Great Britain follow the Circuit du Souvenir.

Between 2014 and 2018, a number of events will commemorate the Centenary of WWI throughout the region – it's well worth timing your trip around them.

Convenient bases to explore the area include Amiens, Arras and the rural towns of Péronne, Albert and Pozières.

⊙ Sights

Australian Corps
Memorial Park   War Memorial

(www.anzac-france.com; ⊙ vehicle access 9am-6pm Apr-Oct, 9am-4pm Nov-Mar, pedestrians 24hr) Inaugurated in 2008, this memorial commemorates the engagement of more than 100,000 Australians who served in the Australian Corps in France. It stands on the hilltop site of the Battle of Le Hamel (4 July 1916), fought and won by Australian and American troops under the command of Australian Lieutenant General John Monash. The Australian Corps Memorial is 7km northeast of Villers-Bretonneux; follow the signs to 'Monument Australien/Memorial Park'.

The memorial comprises three curvaceous walls clad in green granite; the central slab is adorned with a large bronze 'Rising Sun', which is the badge worn by members of the Australian Imperial Force.

Battle of the Somme Memorials

The German air ace Baron Manfred von Richthofen, aka the Red Baron, was shot down a bit northwest of here – Australian ground forces claimed credit but so did a Canadian pilot.

Indian & Chinese Cemetery
Cemetery

(Ayette) Towards the end of WWI, tens of thousands of Chinese labourers were recruited by the British government to perform noncombat jobs in Europe, including the gruesome task of recovering and burying Allied war dead. Some of these *travailleurs chinois* (Chinese labourers) as well as Indians who served with British forces are buried in this Commonwealth cemetery, which is 29km northeast of Albert, just off the D919 at the southern edge of the village of Ayette.

Many Chinese labourers died in the Spanish flu epidemic of 1918–19. Their gravestones are etched in Chinese and English with inscriptions such as 'a good reputation endures forever', 'a noble duty bravely done' and 'faithful unto death'. The nearby graves of Indians are marked in Hindi or Arabic. There's also the tomb of a single German.

Beaumont-Hamel Newfoundland Memorial
War Memorial

(☑ 03 22 76 70 86; www.veterans.gc.ca; Beaumont-Hamel) This evocative memorial preserves part of the Western Front in the state it was in at fighting's end. The zigzag trench system, which still fills with mud in winter, is clearly visible, as are countless shell craters and the remains of barbed-wire barriers. A path leads to an orientation table at the top of the 'Caribou mound', where a bronze caribou statue is surrounded by plants native to Newfoundland. Beaumont-Hamel is 9km north of Albert; follow the signs for 'Memorial Terreneuvien'.

The memorial to the 29th Division, to which the volunteer Royal Newfoundland Regiment belonged, stands at the entrance of the site. On 1 July 1916 this regiment stormed entrenched German positions and was nearly wiped out; until recently, a plaque at the entrance noted bluntly that 'strategic and tactical miscalculations led to a great slaughter'. Canadian students based at the Welcome Centre (☑ 03 22 76 70 86; www.veterans.gc.ca/eng/memorials; ⊘9am-5pm), which resembles a Newfoundland fisher's house, give free guided tours in French or English (except from mid-December to mid-January).

INFO: WWI SITES RESOURCES

Area tourist offices can supply you with some excellent English-language brochures, including *The Visitor's Guide to the Battlefields* and *Australians in the Somme,* as well as the free multilingual map *The Great War Remembered.* For online information, including the program of events for the WWI Centenary, see www.somme-battlefields.com and www.somme14-18.com.

La Grande Mine
Landmark

(La Boisselle) Just outside the hamlet of La Boisselle, this enormous crater looks like the site of a meteor impact. Some 100m across and 30m deep, the Lochnagar Crater Memorial (as it's officially known) was created on the morning of the first day of the First Battle of the Somme (1 July 1916) by about 25 tonnes of ammonal laid by British sappers in order to create a breach in the German lines.

La Grande Mine is 4km northeast of Albert along the D929.

Historial de la Grande Guerre
War Museum

See p48.

La Chapelette British & Indian Cemeteries
Cemetery

(Péronne) On the D1017 at the southern edge of Péronne (towards St-Quentin), this cemetery has multifaith, multilingual headstones, with a section for the fallen of units such as the 38th King George's Own Central India Horse.

Somme American Cemetery
Cemetery

See p48.

South African National Memorial & Museum
War Memorial

(www.delvillewood.com; Longueval; ⊘10am-5.30pm Tue-Sun, closed Dec & Jan) The memorial stands in the middle of shell-pocked Delville Wood, where the 1st South African Infantry Brigade fought against various units of the 4th German Army Corps in the third week of July 1916. Outnumbered, the South African troops were almost decimated but managed to hold on and fight back. The star-shaped museum is a replica of Cape Town's Castle of Good Hope. The memorial is in Longueval, about 13km east-northeast of Albert, mostly along the D20.

A wide avenue flanked by a double row of oak trees leads to the Great Arch, which precedes the rows of white headstones.

Thiepval Memorial   War Memorial
See p46.

Ulster Tower Memorial   War Memorial
(✐03 22 74 87 14; Thiepval; ☺museum 10am-5pm Tue-Sun Mar-Nov, to 6pm May-Sep) The five thousand Ulstermen who perished in the Battle of the Somme are commemorated by this mock Gothic-style tower, an exact replica of Helen's Tower at Clanboye, County Down, the place where the Ulster Division did its training. Dedicated in 1921, it has long been a Unionist pilgrimage site; a black obelisk known as the Orange Memorial to Fallen Brethren (1993) stands in an enclosure behind the tower.

It's on the D73 between Beaumont-Hamel and Thiepval; follow the signs to the 'Mémorial Irlandais'.

In a sign that historic wounds are finally healing, in 2006 the Irish Republic issued a €0.75 postage stamp showing the overwhelmingly Protestant 36th Division in action on this site, to commemorate the 90th anniversary of the Battle of the Somme.

Virtually untouched since the war, nearby Thiepval Wood can be visited on a guided tour (donation requested) at 11am and/or 3pm; call ahead for dates of scheduled group tours.

Musée Franco-Australien   War Museum
See p47.

**Australian National
War Memorial**   War Memorial
See p47.

**Vimy Ridge Canadian
National Historic Site**   War Memorial
(www.veterans.gc.ca; Vimy; ☺visitor centre 9am-5pm) Vimy Ridge, 11km north of Arras, was the scene of some of the bloodiest and toughest trench warfare of WWI, with almost two full years of attacks. Of the 66,655 Canadians who died in WWI, 3598 lost their lives in April 1917 taking this 14km-long stretch. Its highest point – site of a heavily fortified German position – was later chosen as the site of Canada's WWI memorial.

Overlooking the plain of Artois, the superbly designed white monument was built from 1925 to 1936. The peaceful, 1-sq-km park also includes two Canadian cemeteries, a monument to France's Moroccan Division (in French and Arabic) and a visitor centre staffed by bilingual Canadian students who run free guided tours.

Vimy Ridge is a very evocative site, and it's easy to see why. Whereas the French, right after the war, attempted to erase all signs of battle and return the Somme region to agriculture and normalcy, the Canadians decided that the most evocative way to remember their fallen was to preserve part of the crater-pocked battlefield exactly the way it looked when the guns fell silent. As a result, the best place to get some sense of the hell known as the Western Front is the chilling, eerie moonscape of Vimy. The zigzag trench system is clearly visible, as are countless shell craters. Because countless bodies still lie buried among the trees and craters, the entire site is treated like a graveyard.

The imposing memorial features 20 allegorical figures, carved from huge blocks of white Croatian limestone, that include a cloaked, downcast female figure representing a young Canada grieving for her fallen. The two striking columns represent Canada and France. The names of 11,285 Canadians who 'died in France but have no known graves', listed alphabetically and within each letter by rank, are inscribed around the base.

**Fromelles (Pheasant Wood) Military
Cemetery & Memorial Park**   Cemetery
(www.cwgc.org; Fromelles) In Fromelles, about 20km west of Lille, this hexagonal cemetery – the first new Commonwealth cemetery in half a century – was dedicated on 19 July 2010 following the discovery of the mass graves of 250 Australian soldiers. Just 2km northwest, the Australian Memorial Park marks the spot where, on 19 and 20 July 1916, 1917 Australians and 519 British soldiers were killed during a poorly planned offensive intended to divert German forces from the Battle of the Somme.

Another 3146 Australians and 977 British were wounded. This was 'the worst 24 hours in Australia's entire history' – in the words of Ross McMullin, writing for the Australian War Memorial (www.awm.gov.au). It seems likely that one of the soldiers on the victori-

COMMONWEALTH CEMETERIES & MEMORIALS

Almost 750,000 soldiers, airmen and sailors from Great Britain, Australia, Canada, the Indian subcontinent, Ireland, New Zealand, South Africa, the West Indies and other parts of the British Empire died during WWI on the Western Front, two-thirds of them in France. They were buried where they fell, in more than 1000 military cemeteries and 2000 civilian cemeteries that dot the landscape along a wide swath of territory – 'Flanders Fields' – running roughly from Amiens and Cambrai north via Arras and Béthune to Armentières and Ypres (Ieper) in Belgium. French and German war dead were reburied in large cemeteries after the war. American war dead of the world wars were either repatriated (61%) or reburied in large cemeteries near where they fell (39%).

The focal point of each Commonwealth cemetery, now tended by the Commonwealth War Graves Commission (www.cwgc.org), is the Cross of Sacrifice. Many of the headstones, made of Portland limestone, bear moving personal inscriptions composed by family members. Most cemeteries have a bronze Cemetery Register box that contains a visitors book, in which you can record your impressions, and a booklet with biographical details on each of the identified dead (Americans who died fighting with British forces can be spotted by their addresses). Some larger cemeteries also have a bronze plaque with historical information.

ous German side was a 27-year-old corporal in the 16th Bavarian Reserve Infantry Regiment named Adolf Hitler.

After the battle, the Germans buried many of the Australian and British dead in mass graves behind their lines. Most were reburied after the war, but eight pits containing the remains of 250 men were not found until 2008. To provide them with a dignified final resting place, the Fromelles (Pheasant Wood) Military Cemetery was established in 2010, the 94th anniversary of the catastrophic and pointless assault. DNA testing has established the identity of 109 Australians.

After the surviving Australians retreated to their pre-battle front lines, hundreds of their comrades-in-arms lay wounded in no-man's land. For three days the survivors made heroic efforts to rescue them, acts of bravery commemorated by the sculpture *Cobbers* visible in the Fromelles Memorial Park. Inaugurated in 1998, it is situated atop a row of German blockhouses 2km northwest of the new cemetery; to get there, follow the signs to the 'Mémorial Australien'.

Nearby, in what was once no-man's land between the Australian and German front lines, is the VC Corner Australian Cemetery. There are no headstones because not a single one of the 410 souls buried here was identified.

Indian Memorial   War Memorial

(www.cwgc.org; Neuve-Chapelle) The evocative Mémorial Indien (Neuve-Chapelle Memorial), vaguely Moghul in architecture, records the names of 4700 soldiers of the Indian Army who 'have no known grave'. The 15m-high column, flanked by two tigers, is topped by a lotus capital, the Imperial Crown and the Star of India. The units and the ranks of the fallen engraved on the walls evoke the pride, pomp and exploitation on which the British Empire was built.

This memorial is 20km west of Lille, in the village of Neuve-Chapelle.

- - - - - - - - - - - - - - - - - - - -

🛏 Sleeping & Eating

Although Amiens and Arras have a good range of accommodation options, a growing number of visitors choose to stay in one of the small hotels or B&Bs in the towns closer to the battlefields, including Péronne, Albert and Pozières.

★ Au Vintage   B&B €

(✉ 06 83 03 45 26, 03 22 75 63 28; www.chambres-dhotes-albert.com; 19 rue de Corbie, Albert; d incl breakfast €65-85; 🛜) This B&B is an absolute spoil from start to finish. It occupies an elegant brick mansion with two rooms and a family suite that are furnished with taste and flair. Our fave is Rubis, with its super-size bathroom. Evelyne and Jacky are delightful, cultured hosts who enjoy sharing their knowledge about the battlefields with their guests – in good English.

The B&B is on a quiet street southwest of the tourist office.

Butterworth Farm   B&B €

(📋 06 22 30 28 02, 03 22 74 04 47; www.butterworth -cottage.com; route de Bazentin, Pozières; d incl breakfast €65; 🛜) Beloved by Australians and Brits, this well-run venture is an excellent base. Well-tended, fresh guest rooms are in a converted barn, the facade of which is covered with wood panels. There's a garden, filled with flowers and herbs, for lounging in, and breakfasts are copious.

Hôtel Saint-Claude   Hotel €

(📋 03 22 79 49 49; www.hotelsaintclaude.com; 42 place Louis Daudré, Péronne; s €65-86, d €86-112; 🛜) Originally a *relais de poste* ('post inn'), the epicentral Saint-Claude makes a fine base. A breath of fresh air, it does away with old-fashioned furnishings – its dozen contemporary rooms are decorated in adventurous colours and come with up-to-date bathrooms. Downstairs there's a solid country restaurant.

La Basilique   Hotel €€

(📋 03 22 75 04 71; www.hoteldelabasilique.fr; 3 rue Gambetta, Albert; d €88-98; 🛜) This comfortable spot in the shadow of Albert's basilica looks and feels exactly the way an inn ensconced in the heart of a provincial French town should. That it has a well-priced restaurant serving *cuisine du terroir* (regional specialities made with quality ingredients from the countryside) and the tourist office is just across the street puts it over the top.

Le Tommy   Brasserie €

(📋 03 22 74 82 84; 91 route d'Albert, Pozières; mains €8-12; ⊙11am-3pm) This no-frills, slightly eccentric eatery on the main road in Pozières is ideal for a light lunch comprising a main course and dessert, or a sandwich. It also houses a small museum with WWI memorabilia and artefacts.

☞ Tours

Tourist offices (including those in Amiens, Arras, Albert and Péronne) can help book tours of battlefield sites and memorials. Respected tour companies include The Battlefields Experience (📋 03 22 76 29 60; www.thebattleofthesomme.co.uk), Western Front Tours (www.westernfronttours.com.au; ⊙mid-Mar–mid-Nov), Terres de Mémoire (📋 03 22 84 23 05;

www.terresdememoire.com), Chemins d'Histoire (📋 06 31 31 85 02; www.cheminsdhistoire.com) and True Blue Digger Tours (📋 06 01 33 46 76; www. trueblue-diggertours.com).

ℹ Information

Albert Tourist Office (📋 03 22 75 16 42; www. tourisme-paysducoquelicot.com; 6 rue Émile Zola; ⊙9am-12.30pm & 1.30-6.30pm Mon-Sat, 9am-1pm Sun) The tourist office in Albert offers abundant info and has English brochures on the battlefields. It can also help with accommodation bookings.

Péronne Tourist Office (📋 03 22 84 42 38; www.hautesomme-tourisme.com; 16 place André Audinot; ⊙10am-noon & 2-6pm Mon-Sat) Excellent English brochures on the battlefields can be picked up at Péronne's tourist office, 100m from the museum entrance.

ℹ Getting There & Away

You'll need your own transport to visit most of the Somme memorials (one exception is Villers-Bretonneux, which is accessible by train). The train station, well served from Amiens (€3.90, 10 minutes, 11 daily Monday to Friday, four to six daily weekends), is 600m south of the museum (take rue de Melbourne) and a walkable 3km south of the Australian National War Memorial. A round-trip taxi ride from Villers-Bretonneux to the memorial costs around €20.

PICARDY

Amiens

POP 137,030

One of France's most awe-inspiring Gothic cathedrals is reason enough to spend time in Amiens, the comfy, if reserved, former capital of Picardy, where Jules Verne spent the last two decades of his life. The mostly pedestrianised city centre, rebuilt after WWII, is complemented by lovely green spaces along the Somme river. Some 25,000 students give the town a youthful feel.

Amiens is an excellent base for visits to the Battle of the Somme Memorials.

◉ Sights & Activities

★ Cathédrale Notre Dame   Cathedral

(place Notre Dame; north tower adult/child €5.50/ free, audioguide €4; ⊙cathedral 8.30am-6.15pm daily, north tower afternoon only Wed-Mon) The largest Gothic cathedral in France (it's 145m long) and a Unesco World Heritage Site, this magnificent structure was begun in 1220 to house the skull of St John the Baptist. Architecture connoisseurs rave about the soaring Gothic arches (42.3m high over the transept), unity of style and immense interior, but for locals the highlight is the 17th-century statue known as the Ange Pleureur (Crying Angel), in the ambulatory directly behind the over-the-top baroque high altar.

Note that the skull of St John the Baptist is sometimes exposed – framed in gold and jewels – in the northern outer wall of the ambulatory.

The octagonal, 234m-long labyrinth on the black-and-white floor of the nave is easy to miss as the soaring vaults draw the eye upward. Plaques in the south transept arm honour American, Australian, British, Canadian and New Zealand soldiers who perished in WWI.

To get a sense of what you're seeing, it's worth hiring a one-hour audioguide, available in six languages, at the tourist office (across the street). Weather permitting, it's possible to climb the north tower; tickets are sold in the boutique to the left as you approach the west facade.

A free 45-minute light show bathes the cathedral's facade in vivid medieval colours nightly from mid-June to mid-September and December to 1 January; the photons start flying at 7pm in winter and sometime between 9.45pm (September) and 10.45pm (June) in summer.

Maison de Jules Verne   House Museum
(Home of Jules Verne; ☎ 03 22 45 45 75; www.amiens.fr/vie-quotidienne/culture/; 2 rue Charles Dubois; adult/child €7.50/4; ⊗10am-12.30pm & 2-6.30pm Mon & Wed-Fri, 2-6.30pm Tue, 11am-6.30pm Sat & Sun) Jules Verne (1828–1905) wrote many of his best-known works of brain-tingling – and eerily prescient – science fiction under the eaves of this turreted Amiens home. The

Cathédrale Notre Dame, Amiens

models, prints, posters and other items inspired by Verne's fecund imagination afford a fascinating opportunity to check out the future as he envisioned it over a century ago, when going around the world in 80 days sounded utterly fantastic. Signs are in French and English.

Musée de Picardie — Museum

(☑03 22 97 14 00; www.amiens.fr/musees; 48 rue de la République; adult/child €5.50/free; ⊙10am-noon & 2-6pm Tue-Sat, to 9pm Thu, 2-7pm Sun) Housed in a dashing Second Empire structure (1855–67) with a jaw-droppingly impressive central room, the Picardy Museum is surprisingly well endowed with archaeological exhibits, medieval art and Revolution-era ceramics.

Tour Perret — Tower

(place Alphonse Fiquet) For a long time the tallest building in western Europe, the re-inforced concrete Perret Tower (110m), facing the train station, was designed by Belgian architect Auguste Perret (who also planned postwar Le Havre) and completed in 1954. It is not open to visitors.

Hortillonnages — Boat Tour

(☑03 22 92 12 18; 54 bd Beauvillé; adult/child €5.90/4.10; ⊙2-5pm Apr-Oct) Amiens' market gardens – some 3 sq km in extent – have supplied the city with vegetables and flowers since the Middle Ages. Today, their peaceful *rieux* (waterways), home to seven working farms, more than 1000 private gardens and countless water birds, can be visited on 12-person boats with raised prows that make them look a bit like gondolas. Available later (to 6.30pm) if weather and demand allow. A not-to-be-missed experience.

🛌 Sleeping

Amiens' hotels offer excellent value for money but often fill up with businesspeople from Monday to Thursday.

Le Quatorze — B&B €

(☑03 22 47 50 85, 06 16 89 19 87; www.lequatorze.fr; 14 av de Dublin; d incl breakfast €75; 🕿) At this calm haven, in a backstreet that few know of, Amiens-born-and-bred Laure offers the perfect small B&B experience, with five snug rooms mixing modern fixtures with antique charm (original tiles, family photos, wood flooring, floral wallpapers). The B&B occupies a bourgeois town house in the *quartier anglais,* a historic neighbourhood full of superb brick mansions, a 15-minute stroll east of the train station.

Avoid room 1, which feels a tad boxy due to the cubicle shower and toilets in the corner.

Hôtel Victor Hugo — Hotel €

(☑03 22 91 57 91; www.hotel-a-amiens.com; 2 rue de l'Oratoire; d €49-65; 🕿) Just a block from the cathedral, this bargain-priced, family-run hotel has 10 simple but comfortable rooms. Best value, if you don't mind a long stair climb, are those on the sloped-ceilinged top floor (rooms 7 and 8) with rooftop views and lots of natural light. No parking.

Hôtel Le St-Louis — Hotel €

(☑03 22 91 76 03; www.amiens-hotel.fr; 24 rue des Otages; d €74-91; 🕿) The 24 rooms, some off a deck-like inner courtyard, are modern and serviceable, and double-glazing shuts out the street noise. Ask for a room on the upper floors to get more natural light.

Grand Hôtel de l'Univers — Hotel €€

(☑03 22 91 52 51; www.hotel-univers-amiens.com; 2 rue de Noyon; d €95-125; 🕿) This venerable, Best Western–affiliated hostelry has an enviable parkside location in the city's heart, only one block from the train station. Rue de Noyon is pedestrianised so you won't be bothered by noise. The 40 rooms are set around a four-storey atrium, are immaculate and very comfortable; try room 26 (€110) for its double aspect and balcony. One quibble: there's no parking.

🍴 Eating & Drinking

The St-Leu Quarter – picturesque, though not quite the 'northern Venice' it's touted to be – is lined with neon-lit riverside restaurants and pubs, many featuring warm-season terraces with views up to the cathedral. There are more places to eat across the river at place du Don.

Le T'chiot Zinc — Bistro €

(☑03 22 91 43 79; 18 rue de Noyon; menus €14-28; ⊙noon-2.30pm & 7-10pm Mon-Sat) Inviting, bistro-style decor reminiscent of the belle époque provides a fine backdrop for the tasty French and Picard cuisine, including fish dishes and *caqhuse* (pork in a cream, wine vinegar and onion sauce).

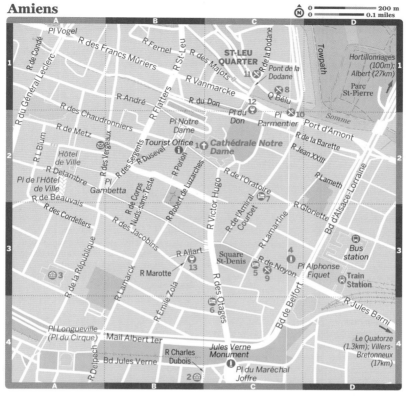

Amiens

⊙ Top Sights
1   Cathédrale Notre Dame B2

⊙ Sights
2   Maison de Jules Verne B4
3   Musée de Picardie A3
4   Tour Perret C3

🛏 Sleeping
5   Grand Hôtel de l'Univers C3
6   Hôtel Le St-Louis C4

7   Hôtel Victor Hugo C2

✴ Eating
8   Le Quai C1
9   Le T'chiot Zinc C3
10 Marché sur l'Eau C2
11 Tante Jeanne C1

⊙ Drinking & Nightlife
12 Le Rétroviseur C1
13 Marott' Street B3

Tante Jeanne   Crêperie €

(✆ 03 22 72 30 30; 1 rue de la Dodane; mains €9-16; ⊗ noon-2pm & 7-10pm Mon-Thu, 10am-2pm & 7-11pm Fri, noon-11.30pm Sat, noon-10pm Sun) Down in the Saint-Leu neighborhood, this is a good spot for an afternoon snack or a lighter meal, with crispy galettes and a variety of salads, and views from the sidewalk tables in warm weather.

Marché sur l'Eau   Food Market €

(place Parmentier; ⊗ to 12.30pm Sat, to 1pm in summer) Fruit and vegetables grown in the Hortillonnages are sold at this one-time

101

floating market, now held on dry land on Saturday mornings throughout the year. A special market is also held on the third Sunday in June, when producers don traditional outfits and bring their produce downriver in high-prowed, gondola-like boats.

Le Quai
Brasserie €€

(🖉03 22 72 10 80; www.restaurant-le-quai.com; 13 quai Bélu; mains €14-23, menus €16-24; ⊙noon-2pm & 7-10pm Mon-Thu & Sun, to 11pm Fri & Sat) With its zesty decor, recession-proof prices and lovely riverside terrace, it's no wonder Le Quai is packed to the rafters at lunchtime. The cuisine is a modern twist on French and Picard traditional recipes. If homemade *burger spécial quai* (burger with beefsteak, ham and Maroilles sauce) is on the menu, order it!

Marott' Street
Wine Bar

(🖉03 22 91 14 93; 1 rue Marotte; ⊙2.30pm-1am Mon & Sat, from noon Tue-Fri) Designed by Gustave Eiffel's architectural firm in 1892, this exquisite ex-insurance office now attracts chic, well-off 30-somethings who sip sparkling wine while suspended – on clear-glass tiles – over the wine cellar.

Le Rétroviseur
Bar, Brasserie

(🖉03 22 91 92 70; www.leretroviseur.fr; place du Don; ⊙5pm-1am Mon, noon-2am Tue-Fri, 4pm-2am Sat)

A highlight of Amiens' nightlife, Le Rétroviseur is as much a bar as a restaurant. The interior is super atmospheric but the terrace overlooking the small square is a great spot to just chill out in summer. It hosts live bands certain evenings. The eclectic menu features a few veggie options.

ℹ Information

Banks can be found around place René Goblet and rue des Trois Cailloux.

Tourist Office (🖉03 22 71 60 50; www.amiens-tourisme.com; 40 place Notre Dame; ⊙9.30am-6pm Mon-Sat, 10am-noon & 2-5pm Sun) Can supply details on the Somme memorials (including minibus tours) and cultural events.

ℹ Getting There & Around

BICYCLE

Vélo Service (Buscyclette; 🖉09 80 82 44 00; www.buscyclette.fr; 13 place Alphonse Fiquet; per day/weekend €3/7; ⊙9am-7pm Mon-Sat) A nonprofit organisation that rents bikes from the courtyard of Tour Perret, behind the main entrance.

CAR

There's free parking one or two blocks north of the Hôtel Victor Hugo, along rue Lameth, rue Cardon, rue Jean XXIII and rue de la Barette.

HEMIS/ALAMY ©

Hortillonnages gardens and the Tour Perret (p100)

ROAD TRIP ESSENTIALS

FRANCE DRIVING GUIDE 105

Driving Licence & Documents.........................105
Insurance 105
Hiring a Car 106
Bringing Your Own Vehicle............................106
Maps 107
Roads & Conditions 107
Road Rules 108
Parking 110
Fuel 110
Satellite Navigation Systems........................110
Safety 110
Radio..110

FRANCE TRAVEL GUIDE.........111

Getting There & Away 111
Air...111
Car & Motorcycle 111
Sea...111
Train...111

Directory A–Z..112
Accommodation 112
Electricity 114
Food...114
Gay & Lesbian Travellers...............................115
Internet Access 115
Money 115
Opening Hours..116
Public Holidays...116
Safe Travel...116
Telephone 117
Toilets..118
Tourist Information..118
Travellers with Disabilities 118
Visas 118

France Driving Guide

With stunning landscapes, superb highways and one of the world's most scenic and comprehensive secondary road networks, France is a road-tripper's dream come true.

DRIVING LICENCE & DOCUMENTS

Drivers must carry the following at all times:

➜ passport or an EU national ID card

➜ valid driving licence (*permis de conduire;* most foreign licences can be used in France for up to a year)

➜ car-ownership papers, known as a *carte grise* (grey card)

➜ proof of third-party liability *assurance* (insurance)

An International Driving Permit (IDP) is not required when renting a car but can be useful in the event of an accident or police stop, as it translates and vouches for the authenticity of your home licence.

INSURANCE

Third-party liability insurance (*assurance au tiers*) is compulsory for all vehicles in France, including cars brought from abroad. Normally, cars registered and insured in other European countries can circulate freely. Contact your insurance company before leaving home to make sure you're covered, and to verify whom to call in case of a breakdown or accident.

In a minor accident with no injuries, the easiest way for drivers to sort things out with their insurance companies is to fill out a *Constat Amiable d'Accident Automobile* (accident report), a standardised way of recording important details about what happened. In rental cars it's usually in the packet of documents in the glove compartment. Make sure the report includes any proof that the accident was not your fault. If it *was* your fault you may be liable for a hefty insurance deductible/excess. Don't

Road Trip Websites

AUTOMOBILE ASSOCIATIONS

RAC (www.rac.co.uk/driving-abroad/france) Info for British drivers on driving in France.

CONDITIONS & TRAFFIC

Bison Futé (www.bison-fute.equipement.gouv.fr)

Les Sociétés d'Autoroutes (www.autoroutes.fr)

ROUTE MAPPING

Mappy (www.mappy.fr)

Via Michelin (www.viamichelin.com)

Local Expert: Driving Tips

Driving tips for France from Bert Morris, research consultant for IAM (www.iam.org.uk) and former motoring policy director for the AA:

➡ First thing if you're British: watch your instinct to drive on the left. Once I was leaving a supermarket using the left-turn exit lane. I turned by instinct into the left lane of the street and nearly had a head-on collision. My golden rule: when leaving a parking lot, petrol station or motorway off-ramp, do it on the right and your instinct to stay right will kick in.

➡ French law says to give way to traffic on the right, even when you're on a main road. So I advise people to ease off on the foot whenever you get to a junction.

➡ Never go below a third of a tank, even if you think there's cheaper petrol further down the road; sometimes the next station's a long way off. My approach is, don't fret about cost; you're on holiday!

sign anything you don't fully understand. If necessary, contact the **police** (🔾17).

French-registered cars have their insurance-company details printed on a little green square affixed to the windscreen (windshield).

HIRING A CAR

To hire a car in France, you'll need to be older than 21, with an international credit card. Drivers under 25 usually must pay a surcharge.

All car-hire companies provide mandatory third-party liability insurance, but prices and conditions for collision-damage waiver insurance (CDW, or *assurance tous risques*) vary greatly from company to company. Purchasing the CDW can substantially reduce the *franchise* (deductible/excess) that you'll be liable for if the car is damaged or stolen, but car-hire companies sometimes charge exorbitant rates for this protection; if you travel frequently, sites like www.insurance4carhire.com may provide a cheaper alternative. Your credit card may also cover CDW if you use it to pay for the rental; verify conditions and details with your card issuer.

Arranging your car hire from home is usually considerably cheaper than a walk-in rental, but beware of online offers that don't include CDW or you may be liable for up to 100% of the car's value.

Be sure your car has a spare tyre (it's not uncommon for rentals to be missing these).

International car-hire companies:
Avis (www.avis.com)
Budget (www.budget.com)
Europcar (www.europcar.com)
Hertz (www.hertz.fr)
National-Citer (www.nationalcar.com)
Sixt (www.sixt.com)

French car-hire companies:
ADA (www.ada.fr)
DLM (www.dlm.fr)
France Cars (www.francecars.fr)
Locauto (www.locauto.fr)
Renault Rent (www.renault-rent.com)
Rent a Car Système (www.rentacar.fr)

Internet-based discount brokers:
Auto Europe (www.autoeurope.com)
DriveAway Holidays (driveaway.com.au)
Easycar (www.easycar.com)
Holiday Autos (www.holidayautos.co.uk)

Rental cars with automatic transmission are rare in France; book well ahead for these.

For insurance reasons, rental cars are usually prohibited on ferries, for example to Corsica.

BRINGING YOUR OWN VEHICLE

Any foreign motor vehicle entering France must display a sticker or licence plate identifying its country of registration. Right-hand-drive vehicles brought from the UK or Ireland must have deflectors affixed to the headlights to avoid dazzling oncoming traffic.

MAPS

Michelin's excellent, detailed regional driving maps are highly recommended as a companion to this book, as they will help you navigate back roads and explore alternative routes; IGN's maps are ideal for more specialised activities such as hiking and cycling. Look for both at newsagents, bookshops, airports, supermarkets, tourist offices and service stations along the autoroute.

Institut Géographique National (IGN; www.ign.fr) Publishes regional fold-out maps as well as an all-France volume, *France – Routes, Autoroutes*. Has a great variety of 1:50,000-scale hiking maps, specialised *cyclocartes* (cycling maps) and themed maps showing wine regions, museums etc.

Michelin (boutiquecartesetguides.michelin.fr) Sells excellent, tear-proof yellow-orange 1:200,000-scale regional maps tailor-made for cross-country driving, with precise coverage of smaller back roads.

ROADS & CONDITIONS

France has one of Europe's densest highway networks. There are four types of intercity roads:

Autoroutes (highway names beginning with A) Multilane divided highways, usually with tolls (*péages*). Generously outfitted with rest stops.

Routes Nationales (N, RN) National highways. Some sections have divider strips.

Routes Départementales (D) Local highways and roads.

Routes Communales (C, V) Minor rural roads.

Road Distances (KM)

	Bayonne	Bordeaux	Brest	Caen	Cahors	Calais	Chambéry	Cherbourg	Clermont-Ferrand	Dijon	Grenoble	Lille	Lyon	Marseille	Nantes	Nice	Paris	Perpignan	Strasbourg	Toulouse
Bordeaux	184																			
Brest	811	623																		
Caen	764	568	376																	
Cahors	307	218	788	661																
Calais	164	876	710	339	875															
Chambéry	860	651	120	800	523	834														
Cherbourg	835	647	399	124	743	461	923													
Clermont-Ferrand	564	358	805	566	269	717	295	689												
Dijon	807	619	867	548	378	572	273	671	279											
Grenoble	827	657	1126	806	501	863	56	929	300	302										
Lille	997	809	725	353	808	112	767	476	650	505	798									
Lyon	831	528	1018	698	439	755	103	820	171	194	110	687								
Marseille	700	651	1271	1010	521	1067	344	1132	477	506	273	999	314							
Nantes	513	326	298	292	491	593	780	317	462	656	787	609	618	975						
Nice	858	810	1429	1168	679	1225	410	1291	636	664	337	1157	473	190	1131					
Paris	771	583	596	232	582	289	565	355	424	313	571	222	462	775	384	932				
Perpignan	499	451	1070	998	320	1149	478	1094	441	640	445	1081	448	319	773	476	857			
Strasbourg	1254	1066	1079	730	847	621	496	853	584	335	551	522	488	803	867	804	490	935		
Toulouse	300	247	866	865	116	991	565	890	890	727	533	923	536	407	568	564	699	205	1022	
Tours	536	348	490	246	413	531	611	369	369	418	618	463	449	795	197	952	238	795	721	593

The last two categories, while slower, offer some of France's most enjoyable driving experiences.

Motorcyclists will find France great for touring, with high-quality roads and stunning scenery. Just make sure your wet-weather gear is up to scratch.

Note that high mountain passes, especially in the Alps, may be closed from as early as September to as late as June. Conditions are posted at the foot of each pass ('*ouvert*' on a green background means open, '*ferme*' on a red background means closed). Snow chains or studded tyres are required in wintry weather.

ROAD RULES

Enforcement of French traffic laws has been stepped up considerably in recent years. Speed cameras are increasingly common, as are radar traps and unmarked police vehicles. Fines for many infractions are given on the spot.

Speed Limits

Speed limits outside built-up areas (unless signposted otherwise):

Undivided N and D highways 90km/h (80km/h when raining)

Non-autoroute divided highways 110km/h (100km/h when raining)

Autoroutes 130km/h (110km/h when raining)

Unless otherwise signposted, a limit of 50km/h applies in *all* areas designated as built up, no matter how rural they may appear. You must slow to 50km/h the moment you come to a town entry sign; this speed limit applies until you pass a town exit sign with a diagonal bar through it.

You're expected to already know the speed limit for various types of roads; that's why most speed-limit signs begin with the word *rappel* (reminder). You can be fined for going as little as 10km over the speed limit.

Alcohol

➡ The blood-alcohol limit is 0.05% (0.5g per litre of blood) – the equivalent of two glasses of wine for a 75kg adult.

➡ Police often conduct random breathalyser tests. Penalties can be severe, including imprisonment.

Motorcycles

➡ Riders of any two-wheeled motorised vehicle must wear a helmet.

➡ No special licence is required to ride a motorbike with an engine smaller than 50cc, which is why rental scooters are often rated at 49.9cc.

➡ As of 1 January 2013, all riders of motorcycles 125cc or larger must wear high-visibility reflective clothing measuring at least 150 sq cm on their upper bodies.

Child Seats

➡ Up to age 10 (or 1.4m tall), children must use a size-appropriate child seat or booster.

➡ Children under 10 cannot ride in the front seat (unless the back is already occupied by other children under 10).

➡ A child under 13kg must travel in a backward-facing child seat.

Priority to the Right

Under the *priorité à droite* (priority to the right) rule, any car entering an intersection from a road on your right has the right of way. Don't be surprised if locals courteously cede the right of way when you're about to turn from an alley onto a highway, yet boldly assert their rights when you're the one zipping down a main road.

Priorité à droite is suspended on some main roads marked with a yellow diamond-shaped sign. The same sign with a diagonal bar through it reinstates the *priorité à droite* rule.

At roundabouts where you don't have the right of way (ie the cars already in the roundabout do), you'll see signs reading *vous n'avez pas la priorité* (you do not have right of way) or *cédez le passage* (yield/give way).

Driving Problem-Buster

I can't speak French; will that be a problem? While it's preferable to learn some French before travelling, French road signs are mostly of the 'international symbol' variety, and English is increasingly spoken among the younger generation. Our Language chapter can help you navigate some common roadside emergency situations; in a worst-case scenario, a good attitude and sign language can go a long way.

What should I do if my car breaks down? Safety first: turn on your flashers, put on a safety vest (legally required, and provided in rental-car glove compartments) and place a reflective triangle (also legally required) 30m to 100m behind your car to warn approaching motorists. Call for **emergency assistance** (☑112) or walk to the nearest orange roadside call box (placed every 2km along French *autoroutes*). If renting a vehicle, your car-hire company's service number may help expedite matters. If travelling in your own car, verify before leaving home whether your local auto club has reciprocal roadside-assistance arrangements in France.

What if I have an accident? For minor accidents you'll need to fill out a *constat amiable d'accident* (accident statement, typically provided in rental-car glove compartments) and report the accident to your insurance and/or rental-car company. If necessary, contact the **police** (☑17).

What should I do if I get stopped by the police? Show your passport (or EU national ID card), licence and proof of insurance. See our Language chapter for some handy phrases.

What's the speed limit in France and how is it enforced? Speed limits (indicated by a black-on-white number inside a red circle) range from 30km/h in small towns to 130km/h on the fastest *autoroutes*. If the motorbike police pull you over, they'll fine you on the spot or direct you to the nearest gendarmerie to pay. If you're caught by a speed camera (placed at random intervals along French highways), the ticket will be sent to your rental-car agency, which will bill your credit card, or to your home address if you're driving your own vehicle. Fines depend on how much you're over the limit.

How do French tolls work? Many French *autoroutes* charge tolls. Take a ticket from the machine upon entering the highway and pay as you exit. Some exit booths are staffed by people; others are automated and will accept only chip-and-PIN credit cards or coins.

What if I can't find anywhere to stay? During summer and holiday periods, book accommodation in advance whenever possible. Local tourist offices can sometimes help find you a bed during normal business hours. Otherwise, try your luck at national chain hotels such as Etap and Formule 1hich are typically clustered at *autoroute* exits outside urban areas.

Other Rules

➡ All passengers, including those in the back seat, must wear seat belts.

➡ Mobile phones may be used only if equipped with a hands-free kit or speakerphone.

➡ Turning right on a red light is illegal.

➡ All vehicles driven in France must carry a high-visibility safety vest, a reflective triangle, a spare set of headlight bulbs and (as of 1 July 2012) a portable, single-use breathalyser kit. Noncompliant drivers are subject to fines.

For pictures and descriptions of common French road signs, see the inside back cover.

France Playlist

Bonjour Rachid Taha and Gaetan Roussel

Coeur Vagabond Gus Viseur

La Vie en Rose Édith Piaf

Minor Swing Django Reinhardt

L'Americano Akhenaton

Flower Duet from Lakmé Léo Delibes

De Bonnes Raisons Alex Beaupain

PARKING

In city centres, most on-the-street parking places are *payant* (metered) from 9am to 7pm Monday to Saturday (sometimes with a midday break). Buy a ticket at the nearest *horodateur* (coin-fed ticket machine) and place it on your dashboard with the time stamp clearly visible. Bigger cities also have public parking garages.

FUEL

→ Diesel (*gazole* or *gasoil*) – €1.35/L; many cars in France run on diesel.

→ *Essence* (gas/petrol), or *carburant* (fuel) – €1.50/L for 95 unleaded (SP95).

→ Filling up (*faire le plein*) is most expensive at *autoroute* rest stops, cheapest at hypermarkets.

→ When renting a car, ask whether it runs on *gazole* or *essence*.

→ At the pump, diesel nozzles are generally yellow, unleaded gas nozzles green.

→ Many petrol stations close on Sunday afternoon; even in cities, staffed stations are rarely open late.

→ After-hours purchases (eg at hypermarkets' fully automatic 24-hour stations) can only be made with a credit card that has an embedded PIN chip. If you don't have a chip-and-PIN card, try to get one from your card company before leaving home; chip-and-PIN cards are also required at many toll booths and train-ticket dispensers throughout France.

SATELLITE NAVIGATION SYSTEMS

Sat-nav devices can be helpful in navigating your way around France. They're commonly available at car-rental agencies, or you can bring your own from home. Accuracy is more dependable on main highways than in small villages or on back roads; in rural areas, don't hesitate to fall back on common sense, road signs and a good Michelin map if your sat nav seems to be leading you astray.

SAFETY

Never leave anything valuable inside your car, even in the boot (trunk). Note that thieves can easily identify rental cars, as they have a distinctive number on the licence plate.

RADIO

For news, tune in to the French-language France Info (105.5MHz), the multilanguage RFI (738kHz or 89MHz in Paris) or, in northern France, the BBC World Service (648kHz) and BBC Radio 4 (198kHz). Popular national FM music stations include **NRJ** (www.nrj.fr), **Skyrock** (www.skyrock.fm) and **Nostalgie** (www.nostalgie.fr).

In many areas, Autoroute Info (107.7MHz) has round-the-clock traffic information.

France Travel Guide

GETTING THERE & AWAY

AIR

International Airports

Rental cars are available at all international airports listed here.

Paris Charles de Gaulle (CDG; www. aeroportsdeparis.fr)

Paris Orly (ORY; www.aeroportsdeparis.fr)

Aéroport de Bordeaux (www.bordeaux. aeroport.fr)

Aéroport de Lille (www.lille.aeroport.fr)

Aéroport Lyon-Saint Exupéry (www. lyonaeroports.com)

EuroAirport (Basel-Mulhouse-Freiburg; www.euroairport.com)

Aéroport Nantes Atlantique (www. nantes.aeroport.fr)

Aéroport Nice Côte d'Azur (societe. nice.aeroport.fr)

Aéroport International Strasbourg (www.strasbourg.aeroport.fr)

Aéroport Toulouse-Blagnac (www. toulouse.aeroport.fr)

CAR & MOTORCYCLE

Entering France from other parts of the EU is usually a breeze – no border checkpoints and no customs – thanks to the Schengen Agreement, signed by all of France's neighbours except the UK, the Channel Islands and Andorra. For these three, old-fashioned document and customs checks are still the norm when exiting France (as well as when entering from Andorra).

Channel Tunnel

The Channel Tunnel (Chunnel), inaugurated in 1994, is the first dry-land link between England and France since the last ice age.

High-speed **Eurotunnel Le Shuttle** (www.eurotunnel.com) trains whisk cars and motorcycles in 35 minutes from Folkestone through the Chunnel to Coquelles, 5km southwest of Calais. Shuttles run 24 hours, with up to three departures an hour during peak time. LPG and CNG tanks are not permitted; gas-powered cars and many campers and caravans have to travel by ferry.

Eurotunnel sets its fares the way budget airlines do: the earlier you book and the lower the demand for a particular crossing, the less you pay; same-day fares can cost a small fortune. Fares for a car, including up to nine passengers, start at £30.

SEA

P&O Ferries (www.poferries.com) and **DFDS Seaways** (www.dfdsseaways.co.uk) both operate regular trans-Channel car ferry service from England to France (primarily from Dover to Calais, with less frequent services from Dover to Dunkirk). **Brittany Ferries** (www.brittanyferries.com) offers additional services from Plymouth, Portsmouth and Poole to the French ports of Roscoff, St-Malo, Cherbourg and Caen.

Ferry companies typically offer discounts for advance booking and/or off-peak travel. Seasonal demand is a crucial factor (Christmas, Easter, UK and French school holidays, July and August are especially busy), as is the time of day (an early-evening ferry can cost much more than one at 4am).

For the best fares, check **Ferry Savers** (www.ferrysavers.com).

TRAIN

Rail services link France with virtually every country in Europe. The **Eurostar** (www.eurostar.com) whisks passengers from London to Paris in 2¼ hours.

You can book tickets and get train information from **Rail Europe** (www.raileurope. com). In France ticketing is handled by the national railway company **SNCF** (www. sncf.com). High-speed train travel between France and the UK, Belgium, the Netherlands, Germany and Austria is covered by **Railteam** (www.railteam.co.uk) and **TGV-Europe** (www.tgv-europe.com).

Avis (www.avis.fr), in partnership with **SNCF** (www.voyages-sncf.com/train/train -avis), has rental-car agencies in most major French railway stations. Cars booked through the SNCF website may be picked up from an SNCF representative after hours if the Avis office is closed.

DIRECTORY A–Z

ACCOMMODATION

Be it a fairy-tale château, a boutique hideaway or floating pod on a lake, France has accommodation to suit every taste, mood and pocket.

Categories

Budget covers everything from hostels to small, simple family-run places; midrange means a few extra creature comforts such as satellite TV and free wi-fi; and top-end places stretch from luxury five-star palaces with air conditioning, pools and restaurants to boutique-chic chalets in the Alps.

Costs

Accommodation costs vary wildly between seasons and regions: what will buy you a night in a romantic chambre d'hôte (B&B) in the countryside may only get you a dorm bed in a major city or high-profile ski resort.

Reservations

Midrange, top-end and many budget hotels require a credit card to secure a reservation. Tourist offices can often advise on availabil-ity and reserve for you, sometimes charging a small fee.

Seasons

➡ In ski resorts, high season is Christmas, New Year and the February–March school holidays.

➡ On the coast, high season is summer, particularly August.

➡ Hotels in inland cities often charge low-season rates in summer.

➡ Rates often drop outside the high season – in some cases by as much as 50%.

➡ In business-oriented hotels in cities, rooms are most expensive from Monday to Thursday and cheaper over the weekend.

➡ In the Alps, hotels usually close between seasons, from around May to mid-June and from mid-September to early December; many addresses in Corsica only open April to October.

B&Bs

For charm, it's hard to beat privately run chambres d'hôte (B&Bs), available throughout rural France. By law a chambre d'hôte must have no more than five rooms and breakfast must be included in the price; some hosts prepare home-cooked evening meals (table d'hôte) for an extra charge of €20 to €30. Pick up lists of chambres d'hôte at local tourist offices, or consult the following websites:

Bienvenue à la Ferme (www.bienvenue -a-la-ferme.com) Farmstays.

Chambres d'hôtes de Charme (www. guidesdecharme.com) Boutique B&Bs.

Chambres d'Hôtes France (www. chambresdhotesfrance.com)

en France (www.bbfrance.com) B&Bs and gîtes (self-catering cottages).

Fleurs de Soleil (www.fleursdesoleil.fr) Stylish maisons d'hôte, mainly in rural France.

Gîtes de France (www.gites-de-france.com) France's primary umbrella organisation for B&Bs and gîtes. Search for properties by region,

---

Practicalities

Time France uses the 24-hour clock and is on Central European Time, which is one hour ahead of GMT/UTC. During daylight-saving time, from the last Sunday in March to the last Sunday in October, France is two hours ahead of GMT/UTC.

TV & DVD TV is Secam; DVDs are zone 2; videos work on the PAL system.

Weights & Measures France uses the metric system.

Sleeping Price Ranges

The following price ranges refer to a double room with private bathroom in high season (breakfast is not included, except at B&Bs).

€	less than €80
€€	€80–180
€€€	more than €180

theme (with kids, by the sea, gourmet, etc), activity (fishing, wine tasting etc) or facilities (pool, dishwasher, fireplace, baby equipment etc).

Guides de Charme (www.guidesdecharme.com) Upmarket B&Bs.

Samedi Midi Éditions (www.samedimidi.com) *Chambres d'hôte* organised by location or theme.

Camping

Camping is extremely popular in France. There are thousands of well-equipped campgrounds, many considerately placed by rivers, lakes and the sea. Gîtes de France and Bienvenue à la Ferme coordinate camping on farms.

➡ Most campgrounds open March or April to late September or October; popular spots fill up fast in summer, when it's wise to book ahead.

➡ Economisers should look out for local, good-value but no-frills *campings municipaux* (municipal campgrounds).

➡ Many campgrounds rent mobile homes with mod cons like heating, kitchen and TV.

➡ Camping 'wild' in nondesignated spots (*camping sauvage*) is illegal in France.

➡ Campsite offices often close during the day.

Websites with campsite listings searchable by location, theme and facilities:

Camping en France (www.camping.fr)

Camping France (www.campingfrance.com)

Guide du Camping (www.guideducamping.com)

HPA Guide (http://camping.hpaguide.com)

Hostels

Hostels in France range from spartan rooms to hip hang-outs with perks aplenty.

➡ In university towns, *foyers d'étudiant* (student dormitories) are sometimes converted for use by travellers during summer.

➡ A dorm bed in an *auberge de jeunesse* (youth hostel) costs from €10.50 to €28 depending on location, amenities and facilities; sheets are always included, breakfast more often than not.

➡ Hostels by the sea or in the mountains sometimes offer seasonal outdoor activities.

➡ French hostels are 100% nonsmoking.

Hotels

We have tried to feature well-situated, independent hotels that offer good value, a warm welcome, at least a bit of charm and a palpable sense of place.

➡ Hotels in France are rated with one to five stars, although the ratings are based on highly objective criteria (eg the size of the entry hall), not the quality of the service, the decor or cleanliness.

➡ French hotels rarely include breakfast in their rates. Unless specified otherwise, prices quoted don't include breakfast, which costs around €7/10/20 in a budget/midrange/top-end hotel.

➡ A double room generally has one double bed (sometimes two singles pushed together!); a room with twin beds (*deux lits*) is usually more expensive, as is a room with a bathtub instead of a shower.

➡ Feather pillows are practically nonexistent in France, even in top-end hotels.

➡ All hotel restaurant terraces allow smoking; if you are sensitive to smoke sit inside or carry a respirator.

Chain Hotels

Chain hotels stretch from nondescript establishments near the *autoroute* (motorway, highway) to central four-star hotels with character. Most conform to certain standards of decor, service and facilities (air-conditioning, free wi-fi, 24-hour check-in etc), and offer competitive rates as well as last-minute, weekend and/or online deals.

Book Your Stay Online

For more accommodation reviews by Lonely Planet authors, check out http://hotels.lonelyplanet.com. You'll find independent reviews, as well as recommendations on the best places to stay. Best of all, you can book online.

FRANCE TRAVEL GUIDE **ACCOMMODATION**

Countrywide biggies:

B&B Hôtels (www.hotel-bb.com) Cheap motel-style digs.

Best Western (www.bestwestern.com) Independent two- to four-star hotels, each with its own local character.

Campanile (www.campanile.com) Good-value hotels geared up for families.

Citôtel (www.citotel.com) Independent two- and three-star hotels.

Contact Hôtel (www.contact-hotel.com) Inexpensive two- and three-star hotels.

Etap (www.etaphotel.com) Ubiquitous chain.

Formule 1 (www.hotelformule1.com) Non-descript roadside cheapie.

Ibis (www.ibishotel.com) Midrange pick.

Inter-Hotel (www.inter-hotel.fr) Two- and three-star hotels, some quite charming.

Kyriad (www.kyriad.com) Comfortable midrange choices.

Novotel (www.novotel.com) Family-friendly.

Première Classe (www.premiereclasse.com) Motel-style accommodation.

Sofitel (www.sofitel.com) Range of top-end hotels in major French cities.

ELECTRICITY

European two-pin plugs are standard. France has 230V at 50Hz AC (you may need a transformer for 110V electrical appliances).

230V/50Hz

FOOD

Food-happy France has a seemingly end-less variety of eateries; categories listed here are found throughout the country: The Eating & Sleeping sections of this guide include phone numbers for places that require reservations (typically higher-end bistros or family-run enterprises such as *tables d'hôte*).

Auberge Country inn serving traditional fare, often attached to a B&B or small hotel.

Ferme auberge Working farm that cooks up meals – only dinner usually – from local farm products.

Bistro (also spelt *bistrot*) Anything from a pub or bar with snacks and light meals to a small, fully fledged restaurant.

Brasserie Much like a cafe except it serves full meals, drinks and coffee from morning until 11pm or later. Typical fare includes *choucroute* (sauerkraut) and *moules frites* (mussels and fries).

Restaurant Born in Paris in the 18th century, restaurants today serve lunch and dinner five or six days a week.

Cafe Basic light snacks as well as drinks.

Crêperie (also *galetterie*) Casual address specialising in sweet crêpes and savoury *galettes* (buckwheat crêpes).

Salon de Thé Trendy tearoom often serving light lunches (quiche, salads, cakes, tarts, pies and pastries) as well as black and herbal teas.

Table d'hôte (literally 'host's table') Some of the most charming B&Bs serve *table d'hôte* too, a delicious homemade meal of set courses with little or no choice.

Eating Price Ranges

The following price ranges refer to a two-course set menu (ie entrée plus main course or main course plus dessert), with tax and service charge included in the price.

€   less than €20

€€   €20–40

€€€   more than €40

GAY & LESBIAN TRAVELLERS

The rainbow flag flies high in France, a country that left its closet long before many of its European neighbours. *Laissez-faire* perfectly sums up France's liberal attitude towards homosexuality and people's private lives in general. Paris, Bordeaux, Lille, Lyon, Montpellier and Toulouse are among the many cities with thriving gay and lesbian scenes. Attitudes towards homosexuality tend to be more conservative in the countryside and villages. France's lesbian scene is less public than its gay male counterpart.

Publications

Damron (www.damron.com) Publishes English-language travel guides, including the *Damron Women's Traveller* for lesbians and the *Damron Men's Travel Guide* for gays.

Spartacus International Gay Guide (www.spartacusworld.com) A male-only guide with more than 70 pages devoted to France, almost half of which cover Paris. iPhone app too.

Websites

France Queer Resources Directory (www.france.qrd.org) Gay and lesbian directory.

French Government Tourist Office (www.us.franceguide.com/special-interests/gay-friendly) Information about 'the gay-friendly destination par excellence'.

Gay France (www.gay-france.net) Insider tips on gay life in France.

Gayscape (www.gayscape.com) Hundreds of links to gay- and lesbian-related sites.

Gayvox (www.gayvox.com/guide3) Online travel guide to France, with listings by region.

Tasse de Thé (www.tassedethe.com) A *webzine lesbien* with lots of useful links.

INTERNET ACCESS

➡ Wireless (wi-fi) access points can be found at major airports, in many hotels and at some cafes.

➡ Some tourist offices and numerous cafes and bars tout wi-fi hot spots that let laptop owners hook up for free.

➡ To search for free wi-fi hot spots in France, visit www.hotspot-locations.co.uk or www.free-hotspot.com.

➡ Internet cafes are becoming less rife, but at least one can still be found in most large towns and cities. Prices range from €2 to €6 per hour.

➡ If accessing dial-up ISPs with your laptop, you'll need a telephone-plug adaptor, available at large supermarkets.

MONEY

ATMs

Known as *distributeurs automatiques de billets* (DAB) or *points d'argent* in French, ATMs are the cheapest and most convenient way to get money. Those connected to international networks are ubiquitous and usually offer an excellent exchange rate.

Cash

You always get a better exchange rate in-country, but if arriving in France by air or late at night, you may want to bring enough euros to take a taxi to a hotel.

Credit & Debit Cards

➡ Credit and debit cards, accepted almost everywhere in France, are convenient and relatively secure and usually offer a better exchange rate than travellers cheques or cash exchanges.

➡ Credit cards issued in France have embedded chips – you have to type in a PIN to make a purchase.

➡ Visa, MasterCard and Amex can be used in shops and supermarkets and for train travel, car hire and motorway tolls, though some places (eg 24-hour petrol stations, some autoroute toll machines) only take French-style credit cards with chips and PINs.

➡ Don't assume that you can pay for a meal or a budget hotel with a credit card – enquire first.

➡ Cash advances are a supremely convenient way to stay stocked up with euros, but getting cash with a credit card involves both fees (sometimes US$10 or more) and interest – ask your credit-card issuer for details. Debit-card fees are usually much less.

Moneychangers

➡ In Paris and major cities, *bureaux de change* (exchange bureaus) are open longer hours, give faster and easier service and often have better rates than banks.

➡ Some post-office branches exchange travellers cheques and banknotes; most won't take US$100 bills.

Tipping Guide

By law, restaurant and bar prices are *service compris* (include a 15% service charge), so there is no need to leave a *pourboire* (tip). If you were extremely satisfied with the service, however, you can – as many locals do – leave a small 'extra' tip for your waiter or waitress.

bars	round to nearest euro
hotel cleaning staff	€1-1.50 per day
hotel porters	€1-1.50 per bag
restaurants	5-10%
taxis	10-15%
toilet attendants	€0.20-0.50
tour guides	€1-2 per person

OPENING HOURS

Below are standard hours for various types of business in France (note that these can fluctuate by an hour either way in some cases). For individual business listings in this book, we've only included opening hours where they differ significantly from these standards:

banks	9am-noon & 2-5pm Mon-Fri or Tue-Sat
bars	7pm-1am Mon-Sat
cafes	7am or 8am-10pm or 11pm Mon-Sat
nightclubs	10pm-3am, 4am or 5am Thu-Sat
post offices	8.30am or 9am-5pm or 6pm Mon-Fri, 8am-noon Sat
restaurants	lunch noon-2.30pm, dinner 7-11pm six days a week
shops	9am or 10am-7pm Mon-Sat (often with lunch break noon-1.30pm)
supermarkets	8.30am-7pm Mon-Sat, 8.30am-12.30pm Sun

PUBLIC HOLIDAYS

The following *jours fériés* (public holidays) are observed in France:

New Year's Day (Jour de l'An) 1 January.

Easter Sunday and Monday (Pâques and lundi de Pâques) Late March/April.

May Day (Fête du Travail) 1 May.

Victoire 1945 8 May – commemorates the Allied victory in Europe that ended WWII.

Ascension Thursday (Ascension) May – celebrated on the 40th day after Easter.

Pentecost/Whit Sunday and Whit Monday (Pentecôte and lundi de Pentecôte) Mid-May to mid-June – celebrated on the seventh Sunday after Easter.

Bastille Day/National Day (Fête Nationale) 14 July – *the* national holiday.

Assumption Day (Assomption) 15 August.

All Saints' Day (Toussaint) 1 November.

Remembrance Day (L'onze novembre) 11 November – marks the WWI armistice.

Christmas (Noël) 25 December.

SAFE TRAVEL

France is generally a safe place to travel, though crime has risen substantially in recent years. Property crime is much more common than physical violence; it's extremely unlikely that you will be assaulted while walking down the street. Always check your government's travel advisory warnings.

Hunting is traditional and commonplace throughout rural France, and the season runs from September to February. If you see signs reading 'chasseurs' or 'chasse gardée' strung up or tacked to trees, think twice about wandering into the area.

Natural Dangers

➡ There are powerful tides and strong under-tows at many places along the Atlantic coast, from the Spanish border north to Brittany and Normandy.

➡ Only swim in zones de baignade surveillée (beaches monitored by life guards).

➡ Be aware of tide times and the high-tide mark if walking on a beach.

➡ Thunderstorms in the mountains and the hot southern plains can be extremely sudden and violent.

➡ Check the weather report before setting out on a long walk and be prepared for sudden temperature drops if you're heading into the high country of the Alps or Pyrenees.

➡ Avalanches pose a significant danger in the Alps.

Theft

There's no need to travel in fear, but it is worth taking a few simple precautions against theft.

➡ Break-ins to parked cars are not uncommon. Never leave anything valuable inside your car, even in the boot (trunk).

➡ Aggressive theft from cars stopped at red lights is occasionally a problem, especially in Marseille and Nice. As a precaution, lock your car doors and roll up the windows in major urban areas.

➡ Pickpocketing and bag snatching (eg in dense crowds and public places) are prevalent in big cities, particularly Paris. Be especially vigilant for bag-snatchers at outdoor cafes and beaches.

TELEPHONE

Mobile Phones

➡ French mobile-phone numbers begin with ✆06 or ✆07.

➡ France uses GSM 900/1800, which is compatible with the rest of Europe and Australia but not with the North American GSM 1900 or the totally different system in Japan (though some North Americans have tri-band phones that work in France).

➡ Check with your service provider about roaming charges – dialling a mobile phone from a fixed-line phone or another mobile can be incredibly expensive.

➡ It may be cheaper to buy your own French SIM card – and locals you meet are much more likely to ring you if your number is French.

➡ If you already have a compatible phone, you can slip in a SIM card (€20 to €30) and rev it up with prepaid credit, though this is likely to run out fast as domestic prepaid calls cost about €0.50 per minute.

➡ Recharge cards are sold at most tabacs and newsagents.

➡ SIMs are available at the ubiquitous outlets run by France's three mobile-phone companies, **Bouygues** (www.bouyguestelecom.fr), **Orange** (www.orange.com) and **SFR** (www.sfr.com).

Phone Codes

Calling France from abroad Dial your country's international access code, then ✆33 (France's country code), then the 10-digit local number without the initial zero.

Calling internationally from France Dial ✆00 (the international access code), the indicatif (country code), the area code (without the initial zero if there is one) and the local number. Some country codes are posted in public telephones.

Directory enquiries For national service des renseignements (directory enquiries) dial ✆11 87 12 (€1.46 per call, plus €0.45 per minute), or use the service for free online at www.118712.fr.

Emergency numbers Can be dialled from public phones without a phonecard.

Hotel calls Hotels, gîtes, hostels and chambres d'hôte are free to meter their calls as they like. The surcharge is usually around €0.30 per minute but can be higher.

International directory enquiries For numbers outside France, dial ✆11 87 00 (€2 to €3 per call).

Phonecards

➡ For explanations in English and other languages on how to use a public telephone, push the button engraved with a two-flags icon.

➡ For both international and domestic calling, most public phones operate using either a credit card or two kinds of *télécartes* (phonecards): *cartes à puce* (cards with a magnetic chip) issued by Orange (formerly France Télécom) and sold at post offices for €8 or €15; and *cartes à code* (cards where you dial a free access number and then the card's scratch-off code), sold at *tabacs*, newsagents and post offices.

➡ Phonecards with codes offer *much* better international rates than Orange chip cards or Country Direct services (for which you are billed at home by your long-distance carrier).

➡ The shop you buy a phonecard from should be able to tell you which type is best for the country you want to call. Using phonecards from a home phone is much cheaper that using them from public phones or mobile phones.

TOILETS

Public toilets around France are signposted WC or *toilettes*. These range from spiffy 24-hour mechanical self-cleaning toilets costing around €0.50 to hole-in-the-floor *toilettes à la turque* (squat toilets) at older establishments and motorway stops. In the most basic places you may need to supply your own paper.

The French are more blasé about unisex toilets than elsewhere, so save your blushes when tiptoeing past the urinals to reach the ladies' loo.

TOURIST INFORMATION

Almost every city, town, village and hamlet has a clearly signposted *office de tourisme* (government-run tourist office) or *syndicat d'initiative* (tourist office run by local merchants). Both can supply you with local maps as well as details on accommodation, restaurants and activities such as walking, cycling or wine tasting. Useful websites:

French Government Tourist Office (www.franceguide.com) The low-down on sights, activities, transport and special-interest holidays in all of France's regions. Brochures can be downloaded online. There are links to country-specific websites.

Réseau National des Destinations Départementales (www.fncdt.net) Listing of CRT (regional tourist board) websites.

TRAVELLERS WITH DISABILITIES

While France presents evident challenges for *handicapés* (people with disabilities) – namely cobblestone, cafe-lined streets that are a nightmare to navigate in a wheelchair, a lack of curb ramps, older public facilities and many budget hotels without lifts – you can still enjoy travelling here with a little careful planning.

Whether you are looking for wheelchair-friendly accommodation, sights, attractions or restaurants, these associations and agencies can help:

Association des Paralysés de France (APF; www.apf.asso.fr) National organisation for people with disabilities, with offices throughout France.

Tourisme et Handicaps (www.tourisme-handicaps.org) Issues the 'Tourisme et Handicap' label to tourist sites, restaurants and hotels that comply with strict accessibility and usability standards. Different symbols indicate the sort of access afforded to people with physical, mental, hearing and/or visual disabilities.

VISAS

For up-to-date details on visa requirements, see the website of the **Ministère des Affaires Étrangères** (Ministry of Foreign Affairs; www.diplomatie.gouv.fr/en) and click 'Coming to France'. Visas are not required for EU nationals or citizens of Iceland, Norway and Switzerland, and are required only for stays greater than 90 days for citizens of Australia, the USA, Canada, Hong Kong, Israel, Japan, Malaysia, New Zealand, Singapore, South Korea and many Latin American countries.

Language

The sounds used in spoken French can almost all be found in English. There are a couple of exceptions: nasal vowels (represented in our pronunciation guides by o or u followed by an almost inaudible nasal consonant sound m, n or ng), the 'funny' u (ew in our guides) and the deep-in-the-throat r. Bearing these few points in mind and reading our pronunciation guides below as if they were English, you'll be understood just fine.

BASICS

Hello.	Bonjour.	bon·zhoor
Goodbye.	Au revoir.	o·rer·vwa
Yes./No.	Oui./Non.	wee/non
Excuse me.	Excusez-moi.	ek·skew·zay·mwa
Sorry.	Pardon.	par·don
Please.	S'il vous plaît.	seel voo play
Thank you.	Merci.	mair·see

You're welcome.
De rien.   der ree·en

Do you speak English?
Parlez-vous anglais?   par·lay·voo ong·glay

I don't understand.
Je ne comprends pas.   zher ner kom·pron pa

How much is this?
C'est combien?   say kom·byun

ACCOMMODATION

Do you have any rooms available?
Est-ce que vous avez   es·ker voo za·vay
des chambres libres?   day shom·brer lee·brer

How much is it per night/person?
Quel est le prix   kel ay ler pree
par nuit/personne?   par nwee/per·son

DIRECTIONS

Can you show me (on the map)?
Pouvez-vous m'indiquer   poo·vay·voo mun·dee·kay
(sur la carte)?   (sewr la kart)

Where's ...?
Où est ...?   oo ay ...

EATING & DRINKING

What would you recommend?
Qu'est-ce que vous   kes·ker voo
conseillez?   kon·say·yay

I'd like ..., please.
Je voudrais ...,   zher voo·dray ...
s'il vous plaît.   seel voo play

I'm a vegetarian.
Je suis végétarien/   zher swee vay·zhay·ta·ryun/
végétarienne.   vay·zhay·ta·ryen (m/f)

Please bring the bill.
Apportez-moi   a·por·tay·mwa
l'addition,   la·dee·syon
s'il vous plaît.   seel voo play

EMERGENCIES

Help!
Au secours!   o skoor

I'm lost.
Je suis perdu/perdue.   zhe swee·pair·dew (m/f)

I'm ill.
Je suis malade.   zher swee ma·lad

Want More?

For in-depth language information and handy phrases, check out Lonely Planet's *French Phrasebook*. You'll find it at **shop.lonelyplanet.com**, or you can buy Lonely Planet's iPhone phrasebooks at the Apple App Store.

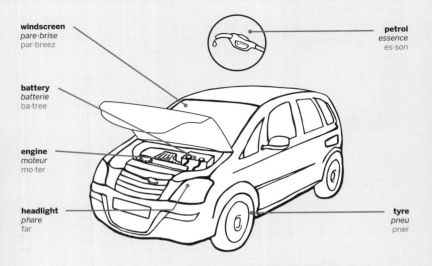

windscreen
pare-brise
par·breez

petrol
essence
es·son

battery
batterie
ba·tree

engine
moteur
mo·ter

headlight
phare
far

tyre
pneu
pner

Signs

Cédez la Priorité	Give Way
Sens Interdit	No Entry
Entrée	Entrance
Péage	Toll
Sens Unique	One Way
Sortie	Exit

Call the police!
Appelez la police!   a·play la po·lees

Call a doctor!
Appelez un médecin!   a·play un mayd·sun

ON THE ROAD

I'd like to hire a/an ...	*Je voudrais louer ...*	zher voo·dray loo·way ...
4WD	*un quatre-quatre*	un kat·kat
automatic/ manual	*une automatique/ manuel*	ewn o·to·ma·teek/ ma·nwel
motorbike	*une moto*	ewn mo·to

How much is it daily/weekly?
Quel est le tarif par jour/semaine?   kel ay ler ta·reef par zhoor/ser·men

Does that include insurance?
Est-ce que l'assurance est comprise?   es·ker la·sew·rons ay kom·preez

Does that include mileage?
Est-ce que le kilométrage est compris?   es·ker ler kee·lo·may·trazh ay kom·pree

What's the speed limit?
Quelle est la vitesse maximale permise?   kel ay la vee·tes mak·see·mal per·meez

Is this the road to ...?
C'est la route pour ...?   say la root poor ...

Can I park here?
Est-ce que je peux stationner ici?   es·ker zher per sta·syo·nay ee·see

Where's a service station?
Où est-ce qu'il y a une station-service?   oo es·keel ya ewn sta·syon·ser·vees

Please fill it up.
Le plein, s'il vous plaît.   ler plun seel voo play

I'd like (20) litres.
Je voudrais (vingt) litres.   zher voo·dray (vung) lee·trer

Please check the oil/water.
Contrôlez l'huile/l'eau, s'il vous plaît.   kon·tro·lay lweel/lo seel voo play

I need a mechanic.
J'ai besoin d'un mécanicien.   zhay ber·zwun dun may·ka·nee·syun

The car/motorbike has broken down.
La voiture/moto est tombée en panne.   la vwa·tewr/mo·to ay tom·bay on pan

I had an accident.
J'ai eu un accident.   zhay ew un ak·see·don

BEHIND THE SCENES

SEND US YOUR FEEDBACK

We love to hear from travellers – your comments help make our books better. We read every word, and we guarantee that your feedback goes straight to the authors. Visit **lonelyplanet. com/contact** to submit your updates and suggestions.

Note: We may edit, reproduce and incorporate your comments in Lonely Planet products such as guidebooks, websites and digital products, so let us know if you don't want your comments reproduced or your name acknowledged. For a copy of our privacy policy visit lonelyplanet.com/privacy.

ACKNOWLEDGMENTS

Climate map data adapted from Peel MC, Finlayson BL & McMahon TA (2007) 'Updated World Map of the Köppen-Geiger Climate Classification', *Hydrology and Earth System Sciences*, 11, 163344.

Cover photographs: (front) Veulettes-sur-Mer, Herve Hughes/Alamy; (back) Étretat, Huang Zheng/Shutterstock

THIS BOOK

This 1st edition of *Normandy & D-Day Beaches Road Trips* was researched and written by Oliver Berry, Stuart Butler, Jean-Bernard Carillet, Gregor Clark and Daniel Robinson. This guidebook was produced by the following:

Product Editors Elin Berglund, Anne Mason

Senior Cartographer Valentina Kremenchutskaya

Book Designer Virginia Moreno

Assisting Editors Kate James, Katie O'Connell

Cover Researcher Brendan Dempsey

Thanks to Shahara Ahmed, Sasha Baskett, James Hardy, Katherine Marsh, Campbell McKenzie, Darren O'Connell, Martine Power, Angela Tinson, Tony Wheeler

OUR STORY

A beat-up old car, a few dollars in the pocket and a sense of adventure. In 1972 that's all Tony and Maureen Wheeler needed for the trip of a lifetime – across Europe and Asia overland to Australia. It took several months, and at the end – broke but inspired – they sat at their kitchen table writing and stapling together their first travel guide, *Across Asia on the Cheap*. Within a week they'd sold 1500 copies. Lonely Planet was born.

Today, Lonely Planet has offices in Melbourne, London and Oakland, with more than 600 staff and writers. We share Tony's belief that 'a great guidebook should do three things: inform, educate and amuse'.

INDEX

A

abbeys, *see also* churches & cathedrals
  Abbatiale de la Ste-Trinité 60
  Abbatiale St-Ouen 29
  Abbaye-aux-Dames 72
  Abbaye-aux-Hommes 72-3, **74**
accommodation 13, 113
air travel 13, 111
Amiens 40, 46-47, 98-101, **101**
area codes 117-18
Arras 45-6
Arromanches-les-Bains 20-1, 70-2, **71**
art, *see* museums & galleries
Artois 92-3
ATMs 115

B

Battle of Normandy 67-72, **69**
Battle of the Somme 94-97, **94**
Bayeux 21, 64-8, **66**, **22**
Bayeux Tapestry 64-5
beaches
  Dieppe 58

000 Map pages
000 Photo pages

Fécamp 60
  Omaha Beach 23-4, 68
  Sword Beach 19-20
  Utah Beach 24, 71, **23**
Bénédictine 60-1
boat travel 111
border crossings 111
Braderie de Lille 91
bureaux de change 115-17
business hours 116

C

Caen 19, 71-5, **73**
Calvados 63-80
Camembert 37
Cap Fagnet 30, 60
car hire 12, 106
car insurance 105-6
car travel, *see* driving
Cassel 92-3
cell phones 13
Château de Caen 72
Château Gaillard 40, 63
churches & cathedrals
  Cathédrale Notre Dame (Amiens) 98, **99**
  Cathédrale Notre Dame (Bayeux) 65-6, **64**
  Cathédrale Notre Dame (Rouen) 40, 54
  Église Jeanne d'Arc 54
  Église Ste-Catherine 77-8
  Église St-Joseph 62
  Église St-Maclou 54

Clairière de l'Armistice 48
climate 12
Commonwealth War Graves Commission 97
costs 13, 112, 113, 114
Côte d'Albâtre 59-62
credit cards 115
currency 12

D

dangers 117, *see* safety
D-Day 17-25, 64
D-Day beaches 8-9, 17-25, 67-72, **6-7**, **69**
de Gaulle, Charles 85
Deauville 32, 74-6
Dieppe 29-30, 58-9
disabilities, travellers with 118
Distillerie Christian Drouin 38
driving 105-10, 111
  car hire 12, 106
  fuel 12
  insurance 105-6
  licences 105
  maps 107
  music 110
  parking 10, 11, 110
  road distances 107
  road rules 108-9
  safety 107-8, 109, 110
  satellite navigation systems 110

speed limits 109
tolls 109
websites 12, 13, 105

E

electricity 114
emergencies 12
Étretat 30, 61-2, **31**
Eure 63

F

Fécamp 30, 60-1, **61**
Flanders 43-9, 82, 92-3
food 13
  cheese 36-41
  costs 13
  Lille 11
  Norman cuisine 38
  Paris 10
French language 119-20
fuel 12

G

gas 12
gay travellers 115
Giverny 29
Gold Beach 20
GPS 110
Grandes Randonnée
  (GR21) 59
Gros Horloge 54, **55**

H

Historial de la Grande
  Guerre 48
holidays 116
Honfleur 31-2, 38, 76-9, **79**, **81**
Hortillonnages 100, **103**

I

insurance 105-6
internet access 13

J

Juno Beach 20, 70

L

La Boisselle 46
language 119-20
Le Domaine Saint
  Hippolyte 38
Le Havre 30-1, 62-3
Les Andelys 40, 63
lesbian travellers 115
Lille 11, 44, 82-91, **84**, **86**, **11**
L'Illustration Café (Lille)
  90, **90**
Livarot 37-8
Longues-sur-Mer 21, 71, **22**

M

maps 107
measures 112
Mémorial-Un Musée pour
  la Paix 19
mobile phones 13
Monet, Claude 32, 27-33
money 13, 113, 114, 115, 116
motorcycles, see driving
music 110
museums & galleries
  Château-Musée 58
  Cité de la Mer 58
  Juno Beach Centre 71
  La Piscine Musée d'Art et
    d'Industrie 83
  Les Maisons Satie 77
  Les Pêcheries 60
  Maison Natale de Charles
    de Gaulle 85
  Musée d'Art et d'Histoire
    Baron Gérard 65
  Musée d'Art Moderne, d'Art
    Contemporain et d'Art
    Brut - LaM 83
  Musée de la Céramique 54
  Musée de la Marine 77

Musée de l'Hospice
  Comtesse 85-6
Musée de Normandie 72
Musée de Picardie 100
Musée des Beaux-Arts
  (Caen) 72
Musée des Beaux-Arts
  (Rouen) 54
Musée d'Ethnographie
  et d'Art Populaire
  Normand 78
Musée du Camembert 37
Musée du Débarquement 70
Musée Eugène Boudin 77
Musée Le Secq des
  Tournelles 54
Musée Malraux 62
Musée Mémorial de la
  Bataille de Normandie 65
Musée Villa Montabello 74
Overlord Museum 70
Palais des Beaux Arts
  (Lille) 83, **83**
museum passes 77, 87

N

navigation systems 110
Neufchâtel-en-Brey 39-40
Newfoundland Memorial 46
Normandy 8-9, 27-33, 52-81,
  6-7
Normandy American
  Cemetary & Memorial 16

O

Omaha Beach 23-4, 68
opening hours 116
Ouistreham 19-20

P

Palais des Beaux Arts (Lille)
  83, **83**
Paris 10
parking 10, 11, 110
Péronne 48

petrol 12
phonecards 118
Picardy 98-86
Place des Héros 92, **93**
Place du Général de
  Gaulle (Lille) **88-89**
Place du Vieux Marché 54, **58**
Pointe du Hoc 24
Pont de Normandie 63
Pont L'Évêque 38
Pourville 30
Pourville-sur-Mer 59
public holidays 116

R

radio 110
road rules 106, 108-9,
  see also driving
Rouen 29, 40, 52-8, **53**, **39**

S

safety 107-8, 109, 110, 116-17
satellite navigation
  systems 110
Seine-Maritime 52-80
Somme 82-103
Battle of the Somme
  memorials 94-97, **94**
Somme American
  Cemetery 48
speed limits 109
St-Valery-en-Caux 30, 59
Sword Beach 19-20

T

telephone services 13
theft 117
Thiepval 46
Thiepval memorial 46, **47**

time 112
tipping 13
toilets 118
tolls 109
tourist information 118
Tour Perret 100, **103**
tours
  Battle of Normandy 67
  D-Day beaches 68
  distilleries 60-1
  Lille walking tour 85-6
  Wellington Quarry 92-3
train travel 111-12
transport 13, 111-12
  see also driving
  Lille 11
  Paris 10
Trouville 32, 74-6
TV 112

U

Utah Beach 24, 71, **23**

V

vacations 116
Verne, Jules 99
Villers-Bretonneux 47-8
Vimy Ridge 44-5
visas 12

W

walking tours
  Lille 85, 86, **86**
war memorials &
  cemeteries 97
  Australian Corps Memorial
    Park 94
  Australian National
    War Memorial 96

Bayeux War Cemetery 65
Beaumont-Hamel New-
  foundland Memorial 94
Bény-sur-Mer Canadian
  War Cemetery 71
Dieppe Canadian War
  Cemetery 58
Fromelles (Pheasant
  Wood) Military Cemetery
  & Memorial Park 96-7
Historial de la Grande
  Guerre 95-6
Indian & Chinese
  cemeteries 94
Indian Memorial 97
La Chapelette British &
  Indian Cemeteries 95
Le Mémorial-Un Musée
  pour la Paix 72-3
Lochnagar Crater
  Memorial 95
Mémorial des Reporters 65
Memorial du 19 Août
  1942 59
Normandy American
  Cemetery & Memorial 68
Somme American
  Cemetery 95
South African National
  Memorial & Museum 95-6
Thiepval Memorial 96
Ulster Tower Memorial 96
Vimy Ridge Canadian
  National Historic Site 96
weather 12
websites 10, 11, 13, 105
weights 112
wifi 13
William the Conqueror 64-5
WWI 43-9
WWII 17-25

000 Map pages
000 Photo pages

Jean-Bernard Carillet As a Paris-based (and Metz-born) journalist and photographer, I was delighted to rediscover my own turf while researching this book. I couldn't resist the temptation of exploring Burgundy and Beaujolais, if only to sample some of the best wines in the world. I confess a penchant for the Meursault whites (in Burgundy) and the Fleurie reds (in Beaujolais).

Daniel Robinson Daniel has been writing guidebooks and articles about France since shortly after the end of the Jurassic period. His favourite leisure activities range from walking the Grand Balcon Sud trail above Chamonix to trying to interpret the Bayeux Tapestry's naughty margin vignettes. Brought up in the United States and Israel, he holds degrees from Princeton and Tel Aviv University. His travel writing has appeared in various newspapers and magazines, including the *New York Times*, and has been translated into 10 languages.

Gregor Clark My first epic French road trip came on Bastille Day at age 20. Nearly broke and hitchhiking towards my next fruit-picking job, I landed a 400km lift from a lost tourist and proceeded to spend the night winding through the fireworks-lit streets of every little village in Haute-Provence. To this day, I love nothing better than aimlessly wandering France's back roads in search of hidden villages and unexpected treasures. I contribute regularly to Lonely Planet's European and South American guidebooks.

Read more about Gregor at: lonelyplanet.com/members/gregorclark

OUR WRITERS

Oliver Berry My first trip to France was a family holiday to Provence at the age of two, and I've been back many times since while working on Lonely Planet's bestselling *France* guide. I've covered nearly every corner of L'Hexagone on my travels, but I have an especially soft spot for Corsica and the Pyrenees. When not in France, I can usually be found wandering the beaches and clifftops of my home county, Cornwall. I'm also a regular contributor to many other websites, newspapers and magazines, including *Lonely Planet Traveller*. Check out my latest travels at www.oliverberry.com.

Read more about Oliver at: lonelyplanet.com/members/oliverberry

Stuart Butler My first encounters with southwest France came on family holidays. When I was older I spent every summer surfing off the beaches of the southwest until one day I found myself so hooked on the region that I was unable to leave – I've been here ever since. When not writing for Lonely Planet I hunt for uncharted surf on remote coastlines. The results of these trips appear frequently in the world's surf media. My website is www.stuartbutlerjournalist.com.

Read more about Stuart at: lonelyplanet.com/members/stuartbutler

 MORE WRITERS

Published by Lonely Planet Publications Pty Ltd
ABN 36 005 607 983
1st edition – June 2015
ISBN 978 1 74360 707 7
© Lonely Planet 2015   Photographs © as indicated 2015
10 9 8 7 6 5 4 3 2 1
Printed in China

0 kilometres   20

0 miles   20

Apostolos
Andreas

Dipkarpaz
(Rizokarpaso)

Aigialousa
(Yenierenkoy)

Trikomo (Iskele)

NORTH CYPRUS

Famagusta
(Gazimağusa/
Ammochostos)

North Cyprus
Pages 128–157

Agia Napa

Larnaka

South Nicosia
Pages 116–127

Southern Cyprus
Pages 64–87

CYPRUS

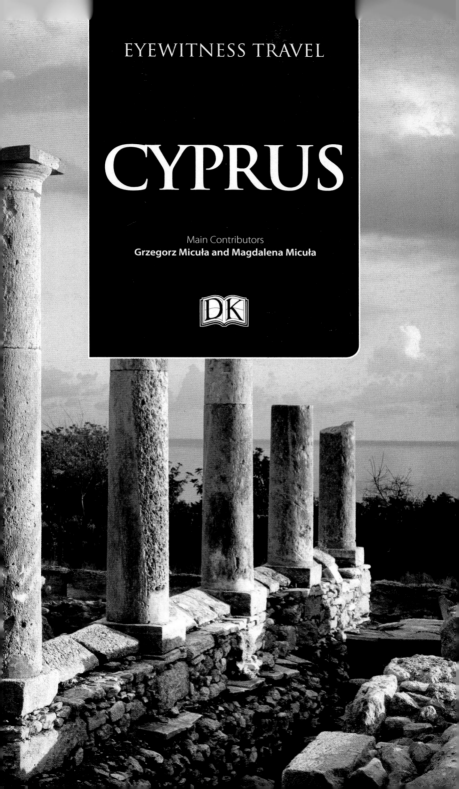

EYEWITNESS TRAVEL

CYPRUS

Main Contributors
Grzegorz Micuła and Magdalena Micuła

DK

Produced by Hachette Livre Polska sp. z o.o., Warsaw, Poland

Senior Graphic Designer
Paweł Pasternak

Editors
Agnieszka Majle, Robert G. Pasieczny

Main Contributors
Elżbieta Makowiecka, Grzegorz Micuła, Magdalena Micuła

Cartographers
Magdalena Polak, Michał Zielkiewicz

Photographer
Dorota and Mariusz Jarymowicz, Krzysztof Kur

Illustrators
Michał Burkiewicz, Paweł Marczak, Bohdan Wróblewski

Typesetting and Layout
Elżbieta Dudzińska, Paweł Kamiński, Grzegorz Wilk

Printed and bound in China

First published in Great Britain in 2006
by Dorling Kindersley Limited
80 Strand, London WC2R 0RL

16 17 18 19 10 9 8 7 6 5 4 3 2 1

Reprinted with revisions 2008, 2010, 2012, 2014, 2016

Copyright © 2006, 2016 Dorling Kindersley Limited, London
A Penguin Random House Company

ISBN: 978-0-24120-928-8

MIX
Paper from
responsible sources
FSC™ C018179
www.fsc.org

Front cover main image: Pafos, Akamas Peninsula, Akamas Natural Park

◄ Sanctuary of Apollo Ylatis, near Kourion

Contents

Introducing Cyprus

Discovering Cyprus **8**

Cypriot saint Agios Mamas, the Byzantine Museum in Pafos

Putting Cyprus
on the Map **14**

A Portrait of Cyprus **16**

Cyprus Through
the Year **26**

The History of Cyprus **30**

Beach in the bustling resort of Agia Napa in southeast Cyprus

Ruins of the Sanctuary of Apollo Ylatis, near Kourion

Cyprus Region by Region

Cyprus at a Glance **42**

West Cyprus **44**

Picturesque Kyrenia harbour, one of the most beautiful in Cyprus

Southern Cyprus **64**

Troodos Mountains **88**

Central Cyprus **106**

South Nicosia **116**

North Cyprus **128**

Travellers' Needs

Where to Stay **160**

Where to Eat and Drink **166**

Shopping in Cyprus **178**

Entertainment in Cyprus **182**

Outdoor Activities **184**

Survival Guide

Practical Information **190**

Travel Information **200**

Index **204**

Acknowledgments **212**

Phrase Book **213**

Popular Cypriot dessert *mahallepi* – a creamy pudding

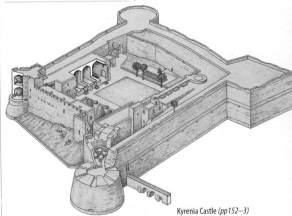
Kyrenia Castle *(pp152–3)*

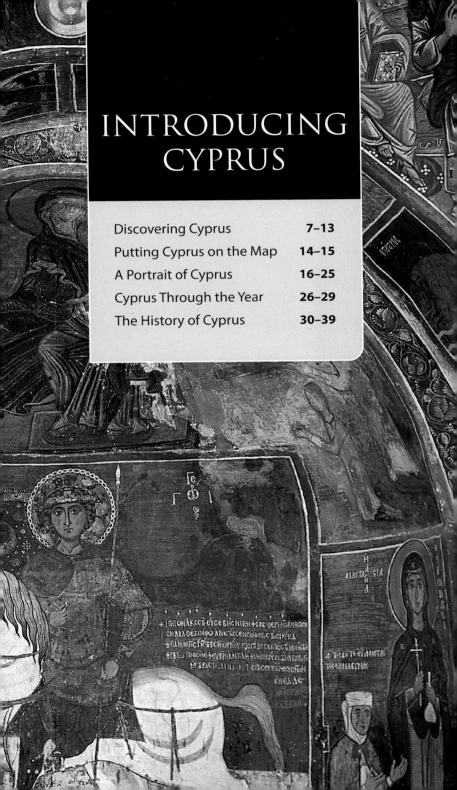

INTRODUCING CYPRUS

Discovering Cyprus   7–13

Putting Cyprus on the Map   14–15

A Portrait of Cyprus   16–25

Cyprus Through the Year   26–29

The History of Cyprus   30–39

DISCOVERING CYPRUS

The following itineraries cover the highlights of Cyprus, and are of varying lengths: mix and match these to create your ideal Cypriot holiday. First are a couple of two-day tours of the island's most walkable towns, Nicosia and Pafos. Next, a three-day driving tour of the UNESCO World Heritage-listed frescoed churches of the Troodos mountains. Of the week-long itineraries, one covers West Cyprus – essentially the hinterland of Pafos – with its hill villages, pristine beaches, country monasteries and chapels, and natural beauty spots. The other is end-to-end North Cyprus, taking in its many monuments, towns and beaches.

Agios Neofytos Monastery
Founded by the hermit monk Neofytos in the 12th century, the *enkleistra* (hermitage) was carved out the mountain by Neofytos himself. The monastery contains fine Byzantine frescoes dating from the 12th to 15th centuries.

A Week in West Cyprus

- Squeeze through the frescoed, cut-from-living-rock *encleistra* of Agios Neofytos monastery.

- Contemplate the sensual, water-sculpted sides of the unspoilt Avakas Gorge.

- Learn about sea-turtle nesting at the Lara Bay hatchery station.

- Discover the elegant stone-built villages of the Akamas peninsula.

- Sample Cyprus' cleanest sea, the supposed bathing spot of the goddess Aphrodite, at Chrysochou Bay.

- Marvel at intricately painted archaic amphorae in the Marion-Arsinoe Archaeological Museum.

- View the cedar groves of Cedar Valley.

- Pick up a bottle of the monks' own wine at the Chrysorrogiatissa monastery.

- Purchase fine lacework and woven wall-hangings in Fyti.

Avakas Gorge
This deep ravine of towering limestone cliffs, with the river Avgas runing through it, is popular with both rock climbers and hikers.

◀ Detail of the interior of Asinou Church in the Troodos mountains

Kyrenia Castle
Built on the site of a Roman fort by the Venetians, the castle affords magnificent views of the harbour below.

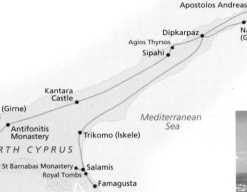

Apostolos Andreas

Dipkarpaz

Nangomi (Golden) Beach

Agios Thyrsos

Sipahi

Kantara Castle

Kyrenia (Girne)

Kyrenia (Girne) beaches

Mediterranean Sea

Bellapais

Antifonitis Monastery

uffavento Castle

Trikomo (İskele)

NORTH CYPRUS

Nicosia (efkoşa)

St Barnabas Monastery

Royal Tombs

Salamis

Famagusta

LARNAKA

Larnaka Bay

Tremithos

Bellapais Abbey
These romantic ruins date back to the 13th century, when the Gothic abbey housed Augustinian monks fleeing Jerusalem.

A Week in North Cyprus

- From Kyrenia's imposing castle, gaze over the picturesque port.
- Savour Lusignan Gothic style at Bellapais abbey.
- Visit the royal apartments of St Hilarion Castle.
- Study the north's best-preserved Byzantine frescoes in site at the Panagia Theotokos church, Trikomo.
- Walk on the stunning geometric mosaic flooring at Agia Trias basilica in Sipahi.
- Stretch out on Golden Beach (Nangomi), the island's longest and wildest, on the Karpasia peninsula.
- Explore the colonnades, Roman theatre, mosaics and baths of ancient Salamis.
- Peruse the Gothic architecture of old Famagusta, especially Lala Mustafa Pasha mosque.

0 kilometres   25

0 miles   25

Key

—— A Week in West Cyprus

—— A Week in North Cyprus

Two Days in Pafos (Paphos)

Pafos (pp52–7) offers ancient sites, worthwhile museums, a well-loved shore promenade and a lively bazaar.

- **Arriving** Pafos (PFO) airport lies 15 km (9 miles) to the southeast; take a bus, taxi or hire car to/from town.

Day 1
Morning Your first stop is the Roman mosaics in **Kato (Lower) Pafos** (pp56–7), then stroll along the harbourfront to the old fort for views from its roof, or head north to the restored Roman odeon, then east across Apostolou Pavlou to the **Agia Solomoni catacombs** (pp54–5), with their sacred pool. From there, thread through the Kato Pafos back streets to medieval **Agia Kyriaki church** (p54), before stopping for lunch.

Afternoon Take a swim at one of the pocket **beaches** (p55) along the municipal promenade leading east from the old port. Then change direction to follow the shoreline walkway north for an hour to the subterranean **Tombs of the Kings** (p54), off the road to Coral Bay.

Day 2
Morning Explore the **Agora** (p52), the covered bazaar, and the lanes between Agora and Kanari streets in Ktima, best on Saturday when there's a street

The stone church of Agia Kyriaki, built in the 12th century and still in use today

produce market. Downhill at the base of the escarpment is the **Mehmet Bey Ebubekir Hamam** (p52), with panels detailing the old public baths of Cyprus. Have lunch at a traditional bazaar taverna on Votsi Street.

Afternoon Continue into Moutallos, with its time-warped 1960s houses and the **Grand mosque** (p52). Return to the centre of town to visit the **Byzantine and Ethnographic museums** (both p53). From the nearby municipal gardens, it's a short bus ride southeast to the **Archaeological Museum** (p55). Finish the day with a traditional meze.

Two Days in Nicosia (Lefkoşa)

Old, walled Nicosia has experienced a revival, with numerous restaurants and boutiques lining its pedestrianized streets.

- **Arriving** Larnaka airport is 45 km (27 miles) southeast of Nicosia, with bus services to the edge of the city and ample hire-car facilities.

Day 1
Morning Allow 2 to 3 hours for the **Cyprus Museum** (pp126–7), one of the Mediterranean's great collections of ancient art, with special distinction in Bronze Age, Geometric and archaic artifacts. Follow this with lunch at one of the city's growing number of quality new restaurants, just southeast.

Afternoon Enter the old walled town via Plateia Solomou and head east across Ledra Ave for the excellent **Leventis Museum** (p125). From here, stroll north past the ornate **churches of Tripiotis and Faneromeni** (p126) and the **Araplar Mosque** (p126), before turning east towards the **Municipal Arts Centre** (p122), aka "the Powerhouse", as it used to be an old Electricity Authority building. Admire the exhibits, then head south for a peek

The Gothic façade of Selimiye Camii mosque (Aya Sofya Cathedral)

inside the **Omar mosque** (p123) before dining at one of the old quarter's traditional tavernas.

Day 2
Morning Enter old Greek Cypriot Nicosia from its far eastern corner, into Chrysaliniotissa, with its tottering Ottoman-era houses. Explore the **Chrysaliniotissa church** (p124) from c.1450, then meander southwest to reach the Municipal Cultural Centre in **Famagusta Gate** (p124), home to superb Byzantine art rescued from desecrated churches in North Cyprus. If time permits, peek inside the nearby **Hadjigeorgakis Kornesios House** (p123) with its ethnographic displays. Then go to the **Ledra Street checkpoint** (p125) between the two sectors of Nicosia – don't forget your passport. Have lunch at one of the restaurants around the **Selimiye Mosque** (pp132–3), after admiring this Gothic place of worship inside and out.

Afternoon West of the mosque, the craft shops of the well-restored Ottoman **Büyük Han** (p132) beckon. Nearby, the **Mevlevi Tekke** (p134) museum unveils the former monastery of the Whirling Dervishes. From here, stroll southwest to the central mosque of **Arabahmet district** (p135), North Nicosia's answer to Chrysaliniotissa. Finally, head back to the Ledra–Lokmacı crossing for a night on the town in livelier South Nicosia.

Painted Churches of the Troodos

This itinerary explores the frescoes and murals of churches in and around the Troodos mountains, most of which are on the UNESCO World Cultural Heritage list. Stay overnight in Agros , Kakopetria, or Kalopanagiotis to minimize driving.

- **Duration** This is a three-day tour.
- **Transport** A car is necessary for this itinerary.

The beautifully painted interior of Panagia Forviotissa (tis Asinou)

Day 1

Morning Take the E110 road up from the A6 motorway at Limassol to Kalo Chorio, bearing right for the small **Chapel of St Mamas** *(p115)* in Louvaras village. Continue uphill on the E110 to Potamitissa village for Pelendri village and its grander 14th-century church of **Timios Stavros** *(p102)*. Retrace your route to Potamitissa, continuing east to **Agros** *(p115)* for lunch.

Afternoon Head north via Chandria to Lagoudera and the **Panagia tou Araka** *(pp104–5)*, with its superb late-12th-century frescoes. If time and daylight permit, head one valley east, via Platanistassa village where the key-keeper lives, to visit remote **Stavros tou Agiasmati** *(p105)* church and more vivid frescoes. Return to Agros for the night.

Day 2

Morning Return to the ridge road at Chandria, then head west via Karvounas junction, Troodos resort and Prodromos, descending to Pedoulas and the late 15th-century **Church of the Archangel Michael** *(p93)*. Continue to Moutoullas village and the oldest painted church in these mountains, **Panagia tou Moutoulla** *(p93)*. Arrive at the scenic **Kalopanagiotis** village *(p93)* further down the valley in time for a spot of lunch.

Afternoon Cross the river to take in the rambling **Agios Ioannis Lambadistis monastery** *(pp92–3)*, the frescoes in its triple church recently restored by students from London's Courtauld Institute, and the excellent icon museum adjacent. Retrace your tyre treads to Pedoulas and the useful link road east to **Kakopetria** *(p103)*, a good place to spend the night.

Day 3

Morning Start the day with a pilgrimage to **Agios Nikolaos tis Stegis** *(pp102–3)* on Kakopetria's outskirts. Next, head to the nearby village of Galata, where you'll be shepherded around three churches, including **Panagia tis Podithou** *(p103)*, with frescoes by master Simeon Axenti. Stop here for some lunch.

Afternoon Drive north towards Nicosia on the fast B9 road, turning off at Koutrafas for access to **Panagia Forviotissa (tis Asinou)** *(p104)*, perhaps the finest of the UNESCO-listed churches, with frescoes of similar date to Agios Nikolaos tis Stegis. Proceed from here to Nicosia, pausing en route at Vyzakia to admire the Venetian-style frescoes in its **Church of the Archangel Michael** *(p104)*.

The UNESCO-listed ancient church of Panagia tis Podithou

A Week in North Cyprus

- **Arrival/departure** Ercan airport, northeast of Lefkoşa (North Nicosia), or Larnaka airport in the south for a greater selection of flights.

- **Transport** This tour is best undertaken with a hire car.

Day 1: Kyrenia and Bellapais
Kyrenia (Girne) (pp150–53) has long been the crown jewel of Cypriot tourism. The huge castle with its two museums, and the medieval Venetian port, are in-town highlights; after lunch, head up to **Bellapais village** (p149), graced by an exquisite Lusignan-era abbey. Bellapais and adjacent villages have a variety of restaurants for dinner. Spend the night in Bellapais or Kyrenia proper.

Day 2: Vouni and Soloi
Still using Kyrenia or Bellapais as a base, head west, then southwest via Morphou to the ancient sites of **Soloi** (pp156–7), with its mosaic-floored basilica, and the enigmatic hilltop citadel of **Vouni** (p157). Have a swim and some lunch at one of the tavernas nearby at Yedidalga or Yeşilırmak before returning to Kyrenia or Bellapais.

Day 3: Castles and Kyrenia Beaches
Climb up from the Kyrenia area to the fairy-tale Byzantine-Lusignan **St Hilarion Castle** (p149), best viewed in the early morning. Return to sea level and drive east for a swim or – if nesting season – a spot of turtle-watching at **Algadi beach**. Contact the Society for Protection of Turtles (www.cyprusturtles.org) for more information. Afterwards, drive up the good road to Beşparmak pass and take the track west from there to **Buffavento Castle** (p148) in time to take in the dramatic sunset views.

Day 4: Into the Karpasia (Karpas) Peninsula
Head east from the Kyrenia area, leaving the coast road briefly to take in the damaged but still worthwhile 12th-century frescoed monastery of **Antifonitis** (p148). Continue east to Kaplıca and the sharp climb up to **Kantara Castle** (p144), the gateway of Karpasia. Once on the peninsula trunk road, pause at **Sipahi village** (p145), where vast mosaics cover the Agias Trias basilica floor. After a restorative lunch near **Agios Thyrsos** (p145), there's time for a swim nearby before reaching abundant accommodation just outside **Dipkarpaz** (p145), your base for the next couple of nights.

Day 5: Exploring the Karpasia Peninsula
After taking in the half-ruined Levantine-fantasy church of **Agios Philon** (p145), with its flanking palm trees, pack a picnic and take the peninsula trunk road beyond Dipkarpaz to the northeastern-most cape of Cyprus, the cave-riddled **Kastros** (p145). On the return journey, stop to pay your respects at the rambling **Apostolos Andreas monastery** (p145), and spread your towel and picnic lunch at **Nangomi (Golden) Beach** (p145), the island's longest, and another haven for nesting sea turtles. Meander back to Dipkarpaz, dining at one of the excellent fish tavernas outside the village.

Day 6: Salamis and Around
With an early start, a southwesterly drive out of

Salamis, the largest archaeological site on Cyprus

Dipkarpaz brings you to Trikomo (İskele) and its **Panagia Thetokos** church (p144), sheltering the only intact Byzantine frescoes in North Cyprus. Further along the main coastal road, the sprawling site of ancient **Salamis** (pp138–9), and the beach fringing it, demand a few hours of your time until lunch. Nearby, the Bronze Age **Royal Tombs** (p136), and the **St Barnabas monastery** (p137) with its catacomb and museum, will fill the afternoon. Overnight at a beachfront hotel.

Day 7: Famagusta
Spend the day in the walled city of **Famagusta** (pp140–43), admiring the **Citadel** (p142), the façade of the **Lala Mustafa Pasha mosque** (p140) (originally a Lusignan Gothic cathedral) and the **churches of the Knights Templar and Hospitaller** (p141), before a late lunch in the *medrese* next to the mosque. Drive back to Ercan airport, or cross back into Southern Cyprus for Larnaka airport.

The formidable ruins of Bellapais abbey

A Week in West Cyprus

- **Arrival/departure** Pafos (PFO) airport.
- **Transport** A car is needed for this itinerary.

Day 1–2: Pafos
See the Two Days in Pafos itinerary on p10.

Day 3: Around Pafos
Pause in Empa for its imposing **Panagia Chryseleoussa** *(p51)*, sporting expressive, if damaged, 15th-century frescoes. Next, continue inland to **Agios Neofytos monastery** *(p51)*, where the eponymous saint dwelt in the intriguing, rock-cut *enkleistra*. After lunch, stop in **Geroskipou** *(p50)* village to admire the six-domed, vividly frescoed **Agia Paraskevi** *(p50)* church. Its frescoes – of similar date to those at Empa – were recently consolidated. Continue along the B6 highway to the ancient site and museum of **Palaipafos (Old Pafos)** *(pp48–9)*, a powerful city-state in ancient times. Undergoing continuing excavations here is the **Sanctuary of Aphrodite** *(p49)*. Finally, continue southeast to **Petra tou Romiou** *(p48)* for a late swim, and admire the sunset over this noted beauty spot. Then, return to modern Kouklia village next to Palaipafos for supper at one of its many tavernas, and overnight in Pafos.

Day 4: Safari to the Akamas Peninsula
Take the initially paved coast road beyond Coral Bay to the mouth of the **Avakas Gorge** *(p58)*, whose spectacular narrows take just over 2 hours return to hike from the parking area. Have lunch at one of the nearby snack bars before forging north on a much rougher track to **Lara** *(p58)* and its two flanking beaches – the northerly one is idyllic and has a sea-turtle research and protection station. After a swim, backtrack slightly to the narrow but paved track up to **Ineia** *(p58)* and other Akamas

The arched Venetian bridge of Roudia

peninsula villages, spending the night in **Drouseia** or **Kathikas** *(both p58)* after tastings at one (or more) of the local wineries.

Day 5: Chrysochou Bay
From Drouseia or Kathikas, descend the fast ridge road to the **Polis** *(p62)* area and enjoy a swim at one of the best beaches in West Cyprus. A 15-minute walk from town is one of the peninsula's marked nature trails from the **Baths of Aphrodite** *(p59)*, with fine views of Chrysochou Bay and Cape Arnaoutis. Spend the night on the resort strip here between Polis and the Baths of Aphrodite.

Day 6: Polis and Beyond
Stroll the tiny old town of Polis, stopping at diminutive **Agios**

Agios Neofytos monastery, located in what once was a secluded valley

Andronikos *(p62)* church to view its fine frescoes, then take in the excellent **Marion-Arsinoe Archaeological Museum** *(p62)*. (Keys to Agios Andronikos are available here if the church is unattended.) Afterwards, your course lies northwest along a rugged, wild coast to **Pomos** *(p47)* with its fish tavernas and pocket beaches, detouring halfway at **Gialia** *(p47)* to explore a 12th-century Georgian monastery excavated in 2005–07. Spend the night at **Lysos** *(p47)*, in the foothills above Polis.

Day 7: The Pafos Forest
From Lysos, head east into the wild, forested **Tilliria** *(p92)* region, via **Stavros tis Psokas** *(p92)* forestry station and the famous cedar groves of **Cedar Valley** *(p92)*, before veering southwest to **Panagia** *(p63)*, birthplace of Archbishop-President Makarios III *(see p39)*. Just 2 km south, the **Chrysorrogiatissa monastery** *(pp62–3)* has exceptional woodwork and offers quaffable products from its very own Monte Royia winery; there are more wineries in the area, such as Vouni Panagia. After a late lunch here, search out the historic medieval **bridge of Roudia** *(p63)*, built by the Venetians, before heading north to **Fyti** *(p47)*, famous for its lacework and woven wall-hangings. From here it's a scenic drive back to Lysos.

Putting Cyprus on the Map

Situated in the eastern Mediterranean Sea, Cyprus is its third largest island
(after Sicily and Sardinia), covering an area of 9,250 sq km (3,571 sq miles)
with a 720-km- (447-mile-) long coastline. Divided since the 1974 war into
the Greek Cypriot-governed Republic of Cyprus in the south and the Turkish-
sponsored Turkish Republic of North Cyprus in the north, both regions share
Nicosia as a capital. The rocky Pentadaktylos mountain range runs along
the north, while the central part of the island is dominated by the mighty
massif of the Troodos mountains. The wildest and least accessible areas are
the Akamas and Karpasia (Karpas) peninsulas.

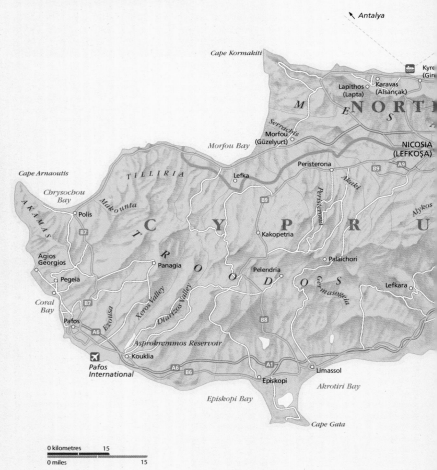

↗ Taşucu

Cape Apostolos
Andreas

Aigialousa
(Yenierenköy)

(Dipkarpaz)
(Rizokarpaso)

KARPASIA

Galateia
(Mehmetcik)

Akanthou
(Tatlısu)

Trikomo
(İskele)

C Y P R U S

Kythrea
(Değirmenlik)

Lefkonoiko
(Gecitkale)

O R

Pediaios

Famagusta Bay

Nicosia
International

Gialias

I

A

Tymvou
(Kırklar)

Vatili (Vadili)

Lysi

Famagusta
(Gazimagusa/
Ammochostos)

Paralimni

S

A2

A3

B3

Xylofagou

Agia Napa

Cape Gkreko

Aradippou

Larnaka

A5

Larnaka Bay

Larnaka
International

B5

Key

━━━ Motorway

━━━ Main road

━━━ Minor road

━━━ Border

Europe

North
Sea

SWEDEN

ESTONIA

LATVIA

LITHUANIA

RUSSIAN
FEDERATION

REP. OF
IRELAND

UNITED
KINGDOM

DENMARK

NETH.

BELGIUM

GERMANY

POLAND

BELARUS

CZECH
REPUBLIC

SLOVAKIA

UKRAINE

Atlantic
Ocean

FRANCE

SWITZ.

AUSTRIA

SLOV.

HUNGARY

CROATIA

BOSNIA
HERZ.

SERBIA

ROMANIA

MOLD

ITALY

MONTEN.

KOS.

MAC.

BULGARIA

Black Sea

SPAIN

ALBANIA

GREECE

TURKEY

PORTUGAL

MOROCCO

ALGERIA

TUNISIA

Mediterranean
Sea

CYPRUS

LEBANON

SYRIA

ISRAEL

For map symbols see back flap

A PORTRAIT OF CYPRUS

The legendary birthplace of Aphrodite, Cyprus enjoys a hot, Mediterranean climate moderated by sea breezes. Visitors bask in the sun on its many beaches, but within an hour's drive can find themselves in the mountains, enjoying the shade of cool herb- and resin-scented cedar woods, villages set amid orchards and peaceful vineyards, as though time stands still here.

Cyprus is an idyllic destination for romantics, with so many old castles, ancient ruins and secluded mountain monasteries to explore. The exploration of these historic sights is enhanced by plentiful sunshine – over 300 days of it a year. Cyprus also has a great number of scenic beaches, and the warm waters encourage bathing and relaxation.

Tucked away in the shady valleys are monasteries with ancient icons of the Virgin, one of which was supposedly painted by St Luke. The tiny churches, many of which are listed as UNESCO World Heritage Sites, hide unique frescoes – some of the most magnificent masterpieces of Byzantine art.

In the Pafos district, valleys overgrown with pine and cedar forests provide a home to the moufflon – a shy mountain sheep. Its image can be seen on Roman mosaics in Pafos.

Cypriot meadows are at their loveliest in springtime, when covered with motley carpets of colourful flowers: anemones, cyclamens, hyacinths, irises, peonies, poppies and tulips, among others. Orchid-lovers will find over 50 species of these beautiful flowers growing in the sparsely populated regions of the island – in the Akamas peninsula, in the Troodos mountains and on the Pentadaktylos mountain range. The island lies on a route for bird migration. Thousands of birds, including

A symbol of Cyprus – a carob tree against the backdrop of a sapphire-blue sea

◄ Anchored catamaran along the coastline at Konnos beach, Protaras

Beautifully preserved ruins of the Gothic Bellapais abbey, built during the Lusignan era

flamingos, cormorants and swans, can be seen wintering on the salt lakes at Larnaka and Akrotiri.

Historic Divisions

The winds of history have repeatedly ravaged this beautiful island. Cyprus has been ruled in turns by Egyptians, Phoenicians, Persians, Romans, Byzantines, Crusaders, Franks, Venetians, Turks and the British. Each of these cultures has left its mark on the architecture, style, cuisine, language and the mentality of the island's inhabitants.

Above all, the island has been shaped by the conflict between the Greeks and the Turks. The Greeks first arrived over 3,000 years ago. The Turks began to settle here following the conquest of the island by Sultan Selim II in 1571.

People and Society

Cypriot society has been composed of two completely separate cultures since the division of the island in 1974 into the Turkish-occupied North and the Greek-speaking Republic of Cyprus in the south. Greek Cypriot society

has always been highly traditional, particularly among country people. This is partly due to the power of the Orthodox Church. Life proceeds at a slow pace in the villages, centering around traditional coffee shops where men spend hours playing backgammon and discussing politics.

An Orthodox priest out shopping

Village women excel in sewing and embroidery. There has been gradual change, however, with many villages becoming deserted as their residents move to towns, where life is generally easier and the standard of living higher, but this decline is slowly being reversed; old houses are frequently bought by artists, often foreigners, in search of tranquillity. In Fikardou, two abandoned houses have been turned into a museum of village life, and awarded the Europa Nostra medal for the preservation of architectural heritage. Overall, the Republic of Cyprus is highly urbanized with a modern economy supported by the abundance of local businesses, hotels and restaurants. Life in the cities of Larnaka, Nicosia, Pafos and Limassol proceeds at a speedy pace.

In the Turkish North, life proceeds at a far gentler pace, partly due to the international boycott that has afflicted tourism and hampered development since 1974. The North is quite separate from southern Cyprus in both atmosphere and landscape. It is far less affluent and more sparsely populated, and Islam is the main religion.

The Cape Gkreko area – one of the most beautiful areas in Cyprus

A lace-maker at work

hosts and historic sights. Following the Turkish invasion of Cyprus and the displacement of tens of thousands of its people, it seemed that the island would never recover. Over 40 years on, the southern part of the island has seen great prosperity. After the 1974 invasion, hundreds of thousands of refugees from the North found new homes and began new lives. Since then, national income has increased severalfold. The economy is flourishing, based on tourism, maritime trade and financial services, despite the island being hit hard in the Eurozone crisis of 2013. The same cannot be said of the northern part of the island, where the standard of living is much lower, caused by the isolation of North Cyprus.

Modern-day Cyprus

The Republic of Cyprus lives off tourism. Its towns are bustling and – like the beaches – full of tourists. Tourist zones have been established in Limassol, Larnaka and Pafos, and around Agia Napa.

This small island provides everything for the holiday-maker, from beautiful scenery to delicious food, excellent hotels, gracious

Bustling Ledra Street in South Nicosia, dotted with restaurants and boutiques

Landscape and Wildlife

The Cypriot landscape is surprisingly varied. Besides high mountains covered with pine and cedar forests, and the rugged crags of Kyrenia, the central part of the island is occupied by the fertile plain of Mesaoria. The crowded beaches of Limassol, Pafos and Agia Napa contrast with the less developed coastal regions of the Karpasia (Karpas) and Akamas peninsulas. In spring, the hills and meadows are covered with colourful flowers. The forests are the habitat of the moufflon – mountain sheep – while the Karpasia peninsula is home to wild donkeys.

A flock of goats grazing freely – a typical sight in the Cypriot landscape

The Coast

Besides beautiful sandy and pebble beaches, the coastline features oddly shaped rocks jutting out of the sea and rugged cliffs, which descend steeply into the water. The northern part of Famagusta Bay and the Karpasia and Akamas peninsulas contain virtually empty sandy beaches where loggerheads and green turtles come to lay their eggs. The exposed Jurassic rocks near Coral Bay, northwest of Pafos, are being destroyed by erosion.

Lizards, particularly the ubiquitous sand lizard, can be seen almost everywhere. The largest Cypriot lizard, Agama (*Agama stellio cypriaca*), can reach up to 30 cm (12 in) in length.

Rocky coastlines are created wherever mountain ranges reach the sea. The rocky coast near Petra tou Romiou (Rock of Aphrodite) is being worn away over time by erosion.

Rock Formations

The Troodos mountains, in the central part of Cyprus, are formed of magma rock containing rich deposits of copper and asbestos. The Kyrenia mountains (the Pentadaktylos range), running to the Karpasia peninsula in the northeast part of the island, are made of hard, dense limestone. The lime soils in the southern part of the island, near Limassol, are ideally suited for the growing of vines.

Sandy coastlines are found at Agia Napa, Famagusta Bay and the Karpasia peninsula, but the loveliest beaches are on the Akamas peninsula.

Salt lakes – near Larnaka and on the Akrotiri peninsula – are a haven for pink flamingos, wild ducks and the Cyprus warbler (*Sylvia melanthorax*).

Copper mine at Skouriotissa

Mountains

The island features two mountain ranges, separated by the fertile Mesaoria plain. The volcanic Troodos massif in central Cyprus, dominated by Mount Olympus at 1,951 m (6,258 ft) above sea level, is covered with pine and cedar forests. The constant mountain streams in the Troodos mountains even have waterfalls. Spring and autumn bring hikers to the cool forests and rugged valleys, while winter brings out skiers. The Kyrenia mountains (the Pentadaktylos or "Five-Finger" range) in North Cyprus rise a short distance inland from the coast. The highest peak is Mount Kyparissovouno, at 1,024 m (3,360 ft).

The Troodos mountains are largely forested but vines are grown on the southern slopes and apple and cherry orchards abound in the valleys.

Mountain streams flow year-round, bringing cooling water to lower ground.

In springtime wild flowers carpet the hillsides and meadows of the island with a colourful, fragrant display.

The Cypriot moufflon is a spry mountain sheep, living wild in the forests of Pafos, in the western part of the island.

Other Regions

The island's interior is occupied by the vast, fertile Mesaoria plain, given mainly to grain cultivation. The northern area around Morfou (Güzelyurt) is full of citrus groves, and to the south, in the region of Larnaka, runs a range of white semi-desert mountains stretching for kilometres. The sun-drenched region of Limassol, with its limestone soil, is a patchwork of vineyards, which yield grapes for the production of the sweet Commandaria wine.

The Akamas peninsula is a remote region in the west of Cyprus. It features the island's most beautiful wild, sandy beaches (see pp59–61).

Donkeys can be seen in the Karpasia peninsula. These ageing domesticated animals have been turned loose by their owners.

Pelicans with wing-spans up to 2.5 m (8 ft) visit the island's salt lakes. Some stop for a few days, others remain longer. These huge birds can also be seen at the harbours of Pafos, Limassol and Agia Napa, where they are a tourist attraction.

The Karpasia peninsula is a long, narrow strip of land jutting into the sea. Its main attractions are its wild environment and historical sights (see pp144–5).

Cypriot Architecture

The long and rich history of Cyprus is reflected in its architecture, and some true gems can be glimpsed amid the ocean of nondescript modern development. The island has a number of Neolithic settlements, as well as Bronze Age burial chambers, ruins of ancient buildings (including vast Byzantine basilicas), medieval castles, churches and monasteries. From the Ottoman era, relics include mosques and caravanserais. The British left behind colonial buildings. In villages, particularly in the mountains, people today still live in old stone houses.

Brightly painted houses in Lefkara village, a beautiful example of traditional Cypriot architecture

Ancient Architecture

The Greeks, Phoenicians, Romans and Byzantines who once ruled over Cyprus left behind numerous ancient buildings. Archaeologists have uncovered the ruins of ancient Kourion, Amathous, Kition, Soloi, Salamis and Pafos with temples, theatres, basilicas, bathhouses and palaces. These ancient ruins include fragments of the old defence walls, sports stadiums, gymnasiums, and necropolises. Some Roman theatres are still in use today for shows and festivals.

The palaestra in Salamis (see pp138–9) is surrounded by colonnades and statues. It was devoted to the training of athletes and to staging sporting competitions.

Kourion, a beautiful, prosperous city, was destroyed by an earthquake in the 4th century AD (see pp70–71).

Medieval Architecture

During the 300 years when Cyprus was ruled by the Crusaders and the Lusignans, many churches were built, including the opulent cathedrals in Famagusta and Nicosia. Added to these were charming village churches and chapels, Gothic monasteries and castles. The Venetians, who ruled the island for over 80 years, created the magnificent ring of defence walls around Nicosia and Famagusta, whose mighty fortifications held back the Ottoman army for almost a year.

Angeloktisi Church in Kiti is one of a number of small stone churches on the island whose modest exteriors often hide magnificent Byzantine mosaics or splendid frescoes (see p80).

This beautifully carved capital crowns the surviving column of a medieval palace in South Nicosia.

Bellapais, with its ruins of a Gothic abbey, enchants visitors with its imposing architecture (see p149). International music festivals are held here (see p26 and p28).

Islamic Architecture

Following the conquest of Cyprus by the army of Selim II, new structures appeared, including Turkish mosques (minarets were often added to Gothic cathedrals), bath houses, caravanserais and covered bazaars. In many villages you can still see small mosques with distinctive pointed minarets.

Büyük Han in North Nicosia is a magnificent example of an Ottoman caravanserai, with a *mescit* (prayer hall) in the courtyard *(see p132).*

The Hala Sultan Tekke *(see p81)* is the country's most sacred Muslim site. It comprises a mosque and a mausoleum with the tomb of Umm Haram, aunt of the Prophet Mohammed.

The Colonial Period

British rule on the island from the 19th to the 20th centuries marked the beginning of colonial-style architecture, including churches, government offices, courts of law, army barracks, civil servants' villas, bridges and other public buildings. The British administration also admired the Greek Classical style, and commissioned, designed and built a great number of Neo-Classical buildings.

The Faneromeni High School in South Nicosia *(see p126)* is an example of a Neo-Classical public building. When it was founded in 1852, it was seen as a connection to the students' Greek roots.

The Pierides Museum in Larnaka is a typical example of colonial architecture, with shaded balconies resting on slender supports *(see p82).* Its flat roof and wooden shutters complement the image of a colonial residence.

Modern Architecture

Following independence in 1960, the architectural style of Cypriot buildings, particularly of public buildings such as town halls, offices, banks and hotels, became more modern and functional. Most of these buildings were erected in Nicosia and in Limassol, which has since become the international business capital of Cyprus. The majority of modern buildings lack architectural merit.

Limassol's modern architecture is largely limited to functional office buildings constructed of glass, concrete and steel, located in the eastern business district of town.

Traditional Homes

For centuries, Cypriot village houses, particularly in the mountains, were built of stone, offering the benefit of staying cool in summer and warm in winter. While some new homes imitate the traditional style, most are built of breeze blocks and reinforced cement.

A modern stone building reminiscent of a traditional village home

Christianity and the Greek Orthodox Church

Christianity gained an early foothold in Cyprus, when saints Barnabas and Paul introduced the religion to the island in the 1st century AD. For 500 years the Church remained relatively unified. However, subsequent divisions led to the emergence of many parallel Christian creeds. The Great Schism of 1054 marked the split between East and West, resulting in the emergence of the Orthodox and Roman Catholic Churches. One of the groups of the Eastern Orthodox Church is the Greek Orthodox Church, and the majority of Greek Cypriots are devoutly Orthodox. Most of the churches in the south are still consecrated and can be visited; in the North, most have been converted into mosques or museums.

Byzantine frescoes, some of the most splendid in existence, decorate the walls of small churches in the Troodos mountains. Ten of them feature on UNESCO's World Heritage List.

The late Father Kallinikos from St Barbara's Monastery *(Agia Varvara)* was regarded as one of the greatest icon painters of recent times. His sought-after icons are sold at the monastery *(see p80)*.

Neo-Byzantine churches are topped by a grooved cupola with a prominent cross. They have distinctive arched windows and portals.

Saint Nicholas

Saints' days are celebrated by placing an icon of the saint on a small ornamental table covered with a lace cloth.

Saint Barnabas and Saint Paul

Two saints are associated with Cyprus – Barnabas (a citizen of Salamis, and patron saint of the island), and Paul. Together, they spread Christianity to Cyprus in AD 45. Paul was captured and tied to a pillar to be flogged. It is said that the saint caused his torturer to go blind. Witnessing this miracle, the Roman governor of Cyprus, Sergius Paulus, was converted to Christianity. Barnabas was stoned to death in AD 61.

St Paul's Pillar in Kato Pafos

Icons with images of Christ or the saints, depicted in traditional Byzantine style, play a major role in the Orthodox Church. They are painted on wood, according to strictly defined rules.

The Royal Doors are found in the central part of an iconostasis. They symbolize the passage from the earthly to the spiritual world. The priest passes through them during the service.

The Iconostasis is a "wall of icons" that separates the faithful from the sanctuary.

Royal Doors

Monasticism

Cypriot monasteries, some of them hundreds of years old, are scattered among the mountains. These religious communities of bearded monks live in accordance with a strict regime. Built on inaccessible crags or in shadowy green valleys, they were established in the mountains to be closer to God and further from the temptations of this world. The monasteries hide an extraordinary wealth of frescoes, intricate decorations and magnificent iconostases. The best known of the Cypriot monasteries is Kykkos – the Royal Monastery *(see pp94–5)* which is a place of pilgrimage for the island's inhabitants.

Divine Liturgy

This is a liturgy celebrated in commemoration of the Last Supper. In the Greek Orthodox Church the service lasts longer than in the Catholic Church and there is no organ, only a choir. The service consists of two parts: the "catechumen liturgy", during which psalms and the Gospel are read; and the "liturgy of the faithful" – the main Eucharist when all worshippers (even children) receive Holy Communion in the form of bread and wine.

Icons on either side of the Royal Doors depict Mary and Jesus. The second from the right usually depicts the patron saint of the church.

Two monks in the courtyard of Kykkos Monastery

CYPRUS THROUGH THE YEAR

Cypriots hold strongly to their traditions, which are manifested in the celebration of numerous religious festivals. The Orthodox Church, to which most Greek Cypriots belong, has a great influence on their lives. Besides local village fairs and public holidays, the festivities include athletic events and even beauty contests. Added to this, every village has its own *paniyiri* – the patron saint's day celebration – the

equivalent of church fairs, when the villagers celebrate them with copious food, drink, dancing and song.

In North Cyprus, the main Muslim feasts include Şeker Bayramı, which ends the 40 days of Ramadan; Kurban Bayramı, which is held to commemorate Abraham's willingness to sacrifice his son (rams are slaughtered and roasted on a bonfire); and Mevlud, the birthday of Mohammed.

Olive trees flowering in the spring

Spring

This is the most beautiful season on the island. The slopes of the hills begin to turn green and the meadows are carpeted with a profusion of colourful flowers, though in places it is still possible to ski. The main religious festival held in spring is Easter.

March
International Skiing Competition *(mid-Mar)*, Troodos. Since 1969, competitive ski races have been held on the slopes of Mount Olympus *(see p96)*.
Evangelismós, Feast of the Annunciation *(25 Mar)*. Traditional folk fairs are held in many places around the island, such as the villages of Kalavasos *(see p78)*, and in Nicosia *(see pp116–27)*.
Easter *(varies – Mar to May)*. A

week before Easter, the icon of St Lazarus is paraded through Larnaka. In all towns on Maundy Thursday, icons are covered with veils, and on Good Friday

Winners of the May Cyprus International Rally in Limassol

the image of Christ adorned with flowers is carried through the streets. On Easter Saturday, icons are unveiled and in the evening an effigy of Judas is burned. Easter Day is celebrated with parties. Orthodox Easter is based on the Julian calendar, and may occur up to five weeks after Easter in the West.

April
Wild Flower Festival *(Mar & Apr)*. This celebration of nature's blooms is held every Saturday and Sunday in many towns throughout southern Cyprus. **International Spring Concerts** *(Apr & May)*, Bellapais. Performances by musical ensembles, singers and choirs are held in the Gothic abbey *(see p149)*.

May
Anthistiria Flower Festival *(mid-May)*, Pafos, Limassol. The return of spring is celebrated with joyful processions and shows based on Greek mythology.
Orange Festival *(mid-May)*, (Morfou) Güzelyurt *(see p156)*. Held annually since 1977 in celebration of the orange harvest, there are two weeks of parades, folk concerts and art exhibitions.
Cyprus International Rally *(May)*. Three-day international car rally, starting and ending in Limassol *(see pp72–5)*.
Chamber Music Festival *(May–Jun)*, Nicosia *(see pp116–27)* and Pafos *(see pp52–5)*. Top international orchestras and ensembles travel from far and wide to perform here.

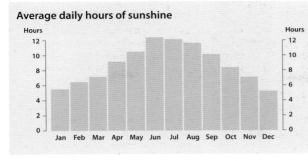

Average daily hours of sunshine

Hours

Average Hours of Sunshine
In June and July, the amount of sunshine reaches nearly 13 hours per day. These months mark the peak holiday season. December, January and February have the fewest hours of sunshine, but the winter sun is pleasant and warm.

Locals at the Wild Flower Festival in Larnaka

Summer

Summer is rich in cultural events, especially art festivals, fairs and music concerts. Tourist resorts, hotels and attractions vie with one another to organize attractive cultural events for their guests. There are numerous

The popular Limanaki Beach in Agia Napa, Southern Cyprus

folk fairs held in the mountain villages, particularly in August. This is also the hottest and sunniest time of the year.

June
St Leontios' Day *(mid-Jun)*, Pervolia village. Traditional religious fair.
Pancyprian Choirs Festival *(late Jun)*, Kato Pafos *(see pp56–7)*. During this festival, choirs perform in the ancient Roman Odeon.
Pentecost-Kataklysmos Fair (Festival of the Flood); *7 weeks after Easter*. Coinciding with Pentecost, this is celebrated over several days with processions and sprinkling each other with water to symbolize cleansing.

July
International Music Festival *(Jun–Jul)*, Famagusta *(see pp140–43)*.
Ancient Greek Drama Festival *(Jul)*, Limassol, Kourion *(see pp70–71)*, Pafos ancient Odeon *(see pp56–7)*, Nicosia and other locations. Theatre festival with Greek dramas.
Xarkis Festival *(mid-Jul)*, Lofou village *(see pp98–9)*. Concerts and workshops are held to celebrate the Cypriot tradition.
Fengaros Music Festival *(Jul–Aug)*, Kato Drys village near Lefkara *(see p79)*. Many international bands perform at this three-day celebration of various forms of music.

August
Pomos Jazz Festival *(early Aug)*, Pomos, a 15-minute drive from

Polis *(see p62)*. A two-day jazz music event with local and international bands held at the Paradise Bar.
Assumption of the Virgin Mary *(15 Aug)*. Traditional fairs in Kykkos *(see pp94–5)* and Chrysorrogiastissa monasteries and in the Chrysospiliotissa church *(see p110)* in Deftera.
Commandaria Festival *(late Aug)*. Food, wine, music and theatre at Kalo Chorio north of Limassol to mark the beginning of the grape harvest.
Dionysia *(late Aug)*, Stroumbi near Pafos. Cypriot and Greek dances and music. An all-night party with local wine and food.

Pomegranate from the environs of Larnaka

Public Holidays in South Cyprus

New Year's Day (1 Jan)
Fóta Epiphany (6 Jan)
Green Monday (varies)
Greece Independence Day (25 Mar)
Good Friday (varies)
Easter Monday (varies)
Pentecost-Kataklysmos (varies)
Greek Cypriot National Day (1 Apr)
Labour Day (1 May)
Assumption (15 Aug)
Cyprus Independence Day (1 Oct)
Ochi Day (28 Oct)
Christmas Eve (24 Dec)
Christmas Day (25 Dec)
Boxing Day (26 Dec)

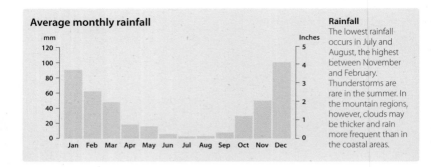

Average monthly rainfall

Rainfall
The lowest rainfall occurs in July and August, the highest between November and February. Thunderstorms are rare in the summer. In the mountain regions, however, clouds may be thicker and rain more frequent than in the coastal areas.

Autumn

After the summer heat, autumn brings cooler weather. With the end of the peak holiday season many resorts slow down. The Cypriots celebrate successful harvests, with particular prominence given to the grape-gathering festivals. Many towns and villages hold local fairs. The Wine Festival in Limassol attracts hordes of visitors.

Troodos mountains in their autumn colours

September

Wine Festival *(early Sep)*, Limassol *(see pp72–5)*. Wine-tasting and dancing in the Municipal Gardens.

Aphrodite Opera Festival *(Sep)*, Pafos *(see pp52–5)*. One of the main cultural festivals, with a cast that includes major international singers.

Agia Napa International Festival *(mid-Sep)*, Agia Napa *(see p86)*. This beautiful seaside resort becomes a gathering place for folk musicians and

Autumn harvest of grapes in the wine-growing village of Vasa

dancers, theatre groups, opera ensembles, traditional and modern singers, and magicians.

Elevation of the Holy Cross *(14 Sep)*. One of the oldest religious feasts in the Greek Orthodox Church calendar. Traditionally, men tucked basil leaves behind their ears on this day.

International North Cyprus Music Festival *(Sep–Oct)*, Bellapais *(see p149)*, and **Ta Kypria International Festival** *(Sep-Oct)*, in various locations. Both of these festivals feature performances by international artists: musical virtuosos in the first one, while drama, dance and other forms of art are the major attractions in the second event.

Participant in the Elevation of the Holy Cross

October

Afamia Grape and Wine Festival *(early Oct)*, held in Koilani village *(see p98)* in the Limassol region.

Agios Ioannis Lampadistis *(early Oct)*, Kalopanagiotis *(see p93)*. Traditional folk festival combined with a fair.

International Dog Show *(mid-Oct)*, Pafos *(see pp52–5)*; with the Kennel Club.

Agios Loukas *(mid-Oct)*. Traditional village fairs in Korakou, Koilani *(see p98)* and Aradippou.

Turkish National Day *(29 Oct)*.

November

Feast of Archangels Gabriel and Michael *(mid-Nov)*. Festival and fair in the St Michael monastery southwest of Nicosia *(see p110)*, in the village of Analiontas.

Cultural Winter *(Nov– Mar)*, Agia Napa *(see p86)*. A cycle of concerts, shows and exhibitions organized by the Agia Napa Municipality and Cyprus Tourism Organization.

TRNC Foundation Day *(15 Nov)*. Celebrating the foundation, in 1983, of the Turkish Republic of Northern Cyprus, which is recognized only by Turkey.

St Andrew's Day *(30 Nov)*. Many pilgrims from southern Cyprus visit the monastery of St Andrew *(see p145)*.

Average monthly temperature

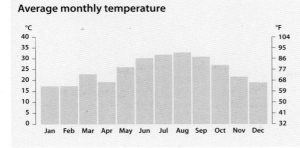

Temperature
In the summer, temperatures may reach up to 40° C (104° F). Many people enjoy visiting the island out of the high season. Only the higher sections of the Troodos mountains, which are covered with snow in winter, record temperatures below freezing.

Winter

The winters in Cyprus are mild, and the days are usually sunny. At times winter brings rain, but snow is limited to the upper reaches of the Troodos mountains. Many cultural events are organized by local authorities at this time. Christmas is traditionally celebrated within the family circle.

December

Winter Solstice *(22 Dec)*. The Solstice is observed at Amathous *(see p78)*, the Sanctuary of Apollo *(see p68)*, the Sanctuary of Aphrodite *(see pp48-9)* and Agios Tychonas in Limassol *(see pp72–5)*.
Christmas *(25 Dec)*. All over Cyprus family celebrations are held after attending church.
Carols Evening *(25 Dec)*. This occurs in the central square in Agia Napa *(see p86)*. Events include carol singing, rides in Santa's sleigh and food markets with traditional Cypriot dishes.

Welcoming the New Year *(31 Dec)*, in all towns. In Agia Napa *(see p86)*, free wine is served in the town's main square.

January

New Year (Agios Vassilios) *(1 Jan)*, formally celebrated with the exchange of presents.
Fóta, the Epiphany *(6 Jan)*. Greek Orthodox churches hold processions and bless water. In coastal towns and villages, young men compete with each other to retrieve a crucifix hurled into the water.
St Neofytos' Day *(late Jan)*. A traditional fair held in the Agios Neofytos monastery *(see p51)* near Pafos.
Şeker Bayramı (Sugar Festival) *(varies)*, North Cyprus. A religious feast and a family occasion marking the end of Ramadan, the annual Muslim fast.

February

Carnival, Limassol *(see pp72–5)*. Ten days of wild revelry preceding Lent end with **Green Monday**, which in Limassol features parades and fancy-dress balls.

Salt excavation from the salt lake near Larnaka

Presentation of Jesus to the Temple *(mid-Feb)*. Traditional fair in the Chrysorrogiatissa monastery *(see p62)*, in the Pafos district.
Kite-flying Competition *(late Feb)*, Deryneia *(see p87)*.

Public Holidays in North Cyprus

New Year's Day (1 Jan)
Children's Day (23 Apr)
Labour Day (1 May)
Youth and Sports Day (19 May)
Peace and Freedom Day (20 Jul)
Social Resistance Day (1 Aug)
Victory Day (30 Aug)
Turkish National Day (29 Oct)
TRNC Foundation Day (15 Nov)
Şeker Bayramı (varies)
Kurban Bayramı (varies)
Birth of the Prophet Mohammed (varies)

Winter sports on the slopes of the Troodos mountains

THE HISTORY OF CYPRUS

Lying at the crossroads of the eastern Mediterranean, Cyprus has long been a prize coveted by surrounding lands: Egypt and Aegia, Persia and Greece, Rome and Byzantium, and finally Venice and Turkey. Its rich copper deposits ensured the island's continuing worth to the prehistoric world. In fact the word copper derives from the ancient Greek name for the island – *Kypros*.

The location of Cyprus, at the point where the Eastern and Western civilizations met, determined its history to a large extent. Many rulers tried to conquer the island that occupied such a strategic position. Cyprus has been ruled in turn by the Egyptians, Mycenaeans, Phoenicians, Assyrians, Persians, Ptolemies, Romans, Byzantines, Crusaders, Franks, Venetians, Turks and British.

Stone Age

Not much is known about the earliest inhabitants, who lived in coastal caves and did not leave much trace of their habitation. Recent evidence from archaeological discoveries at Aetokremmos (Eagle Cliff), however, indicates that Cyprus has been inhabited since at least 8000 BC. The settlements of Petra tou Limnitis and Tenta existed here in the Neolithic era (late Stone Age), around 7000–6000 BC.

The first permanent settlements appeared in the 6th millennium BC. These early settlers are thought to have come from Asia Minor. They built round or oval huts of broken stone, covered with branches and clay. A settlement of this type was discovered in the area of Choirokotia. The inhabitants engaged in primitive farming, livestock rearing (one species of sheep was domesticated at that time) and fishing. The scarce flint stones and obsidian were used to make tools, and vessels were gouged out of limestone. Burial practices included weighing down the bodies with stones, in the belief that this would stop the dead disturbing the living.

From this period until around 4500 BC there is a gap in information about the activities on the island. Archaeologists have discovered traces of settlements in the vicinity of Çatalköy (Agios Epikitotos), in the North, and Sotira in the South, where they found early "combed pottery" – the oldest ceramics in Cyprus. This pottery was produced by dragging a comb-like tool over the wet vessel to create straight or wavy lines.

After 4000 BC the Chalcolithic era ushered in the first small-scale use of metal – copper – in addition to the widespread use of stone.

8000 BC	5000 BC	4000 BC	3500 BC	3000 BC

c.6000 BC Choirokotia is Cyprus' earliest known settlement

5250 BC Existence of monochromatic and linear-pattern painted ceramics

After 4000 BC Chalcolithic settlements start to emerge in the western part of the island

c.8000 BC evidence of Neolithic-era (Stone Age) human habitation

Howling Man from Pierides Museum in Larnaka (5500–5000 BC)

3400–2300 BC The earliest copper mines are established; copper vessels and steatite (soapstone) images of female idols are produced

◄ Richard the Lionheart, who conquered Cyprus in 1191

Neolithic settlement of Tenta

The Copper and Bronze Ages

The transitional period between the Stone and Bronze ages was known as the Chalcolithic era (after the Greek words for copper and stone: *chalkos* and *lithos*); it saw the small-scale use of copper for tools and implements. Most Chalcolithic villages were established in the previously unsettled western part of Cyprus. Figurines of limestone fertility goddesses from Lempa and cruciform figurines in picrolite (blue-green stone) from Yala indicate the growing cult of fertility.

The Troodos mountains contained large deposits of copper, and thanks to this the power of Cyprus began to increase in the third millennium BC. Cyprus became the largest producer and exporter of copper in the Mediterranean basin. The technology of bronze-smelting had by then spread throughout the entire Mediterranean basin. Copper, the main component of bronze, became the source of the island's wealth.

Trade with Egypt and the Middle East developed during this period. Along with vessels of fanciful, often zoomorphic shapes, human figurines and statuettes of bulls associated with the cult of fertility

were produced. By the start of the second millennium BC, there were towns trading in copper. The most important of these was the eastern harbour town of Alasia (modern-day Egkomi). At that time, cultural influences brought by settling Egyptian and Phoenician merchants intensified.

Flourishing trade necessitated the development of writing. The oldest text found in Cyprus is a Minoan incised clay tablet from the ruins of Alasia (16th century BC), a form of writing which came about through links with the Minoan civilization of Crete.

During the 16th and 15th centuries BC, the most important towns were Kition (modern-day Larnaka) and Egkomi-Alasia. Despite diverse influences (from Egypt, Mesopotamia, Phoenicia and Persia), it was Greek culture that would dominate.

Choirokotia, one of the earliest settlements

c.2500 BC Early Bronze Age, with the earliest bronze smelting occuring in Mesaoria

2000–58 BC The island is ruled by Mycenaeans, Egyptians, Phoenicians, Assyrians and Persians

Statuette of an idol, 1900 BC

2500 BC	2350 BC	2200 BC	2050 BC	1900 BC	1750 BC

c.2500 BC Red polished ceramics spread across the island; growth of the cult of fertility (its symbol a bull)

Ceramic pot from Vounous, 2500–1900 BC

1900–1650 BC Middle Bronze Age; settlements appear in the south and east of the island, as a result of overseas trade

Around the 12th century BC, marauders known as the "sea peoples" invaded Cyprus, destroying Kition and Alasia. They settled in Maa (Paleo-kastro) in the west of the island, among other places. But with the mass arrival of Mycenaeans in the 11th century BC, balance was restored. The Greek language, customs and culture were widely adopted, and a flourishing cult of Aphrodite developed. The Temple of Aphrodite in Palaipafos rose in status and soon became the main shrine of the goddess in the ancient Greek world. Mycenaean culture left a permanent imprint on the future development of Cypriot culture.

Ruins of Phoenician-populated Kition

Around 1050 BC, an earthquake devastated Cyprus, heralding the island's Dark Ages. Kition and Alasia were reduced to rubble, and their inhabitants relocated to Salamis.

Female figurine from the Temple of Aphrodite

Iron Age

The first millennium BC ushered in the Iron Age throughout the entire Mediterranean area, although it in no way diminished the demand for copper from Cyprus. During this time, Cyprus was divided into kingdoms, ruled by local kings. The most important were Salamis, Marion, Lapithos, Soli, Pafos, Tamassos and Kourion. By the 9th century BC the wealth of Cyprus lured Phoenicians from nearby Tyre, who established a colony at Kition. The joint influences from the Phoenicians, Mycenaeans and the Cypriots fuelled this era of outstanding cultural achievement, with the building of new towns and the development of metallurgy.

In and around the 8th century BC Amathous (east of modern-day Limassol) began to develop, and Kition (modern-day Larnaka) became a major trading hub and the centre of the cult of the Phoenician goddess, Astarte.

Archaic Era

In about 700 BC, Cyprus fell into the hands of the Assyrian kings, who did not wish to rule but merely demanded payment of tributes. This period saw the creation of Ionian-influenced limestone statues, pottery decorated with images of people and animals, and votive terracotta figurines.

Amathous, one of the oldest Cypriot towns

c.1400 BC Mycenaean merchants and craftsmen begin to settle on the island

12th century BC Invasion by the "sea peoples"

Gold jewellery 1650–1150 BC

1600 BC	1450 BC	1300 BC	1150 BC	1000 BC	850 BC

16th century BC The earliest Cypro-Minoan writing on a tablet found in the ruins of Alasia

c.1050 BC A violent earthquake destroys Cypriot towns, including Alasia and Kition

c.1000 BC Phoenicians arrive from Tyre and settle on the southern plains

Sarcophagus from Pierides Museum in Larnaka

Classical Period

In the early 6th century BC, Cyprus was ruled by Egyptians, but their influence on local art was negligible. The most distinctive architectural features of the period are the subterranean burial chambers, resembling houses, unearthed in Tamassos. In 546 BC, Egypt was conquered by the Persians, under whose control Cyprus fell. The small Cypriot kingdoms were forced to pay tributes to the Persians and to supply battleships in the event of war. Cyprus became a battleground for the Greek-Persian Wars.

Although the kingdoms were not at first involved in the Persian Wars (499–449 BC), strife akin to civil war erupted. Some kingdoms declared themselves on the side of the Greeks, while others supported the Persians (especially the Phoenician inhabitants of Kition and Amathous, as well as Marion, Kourion and Salamis). In the decisive battle at Salamis (480 BC), insurgents were defeated and the leader, Onesilos, was killed. The Persians went on to conquer

Marble statue of Apollo from Lyra, 2nd century AD

other kingdoms. These included Palaipafos and Soloi (in 498 BC). Having quashed the revolt, the pro-Persian king of Marion built a palace to watch over Soloi.

By the start of the 5th century BC, Cyprus had ten kingdoms, the existing ones having been joined by Kyrenia, Idalion, Amathous and Kition, while Soloi submitted to the rule of the king of Marion. The Athenian general Kimon, who was sent to the island, failed to conquer Cyprus, despite a few minor victories, and was killed during the siege of Kition.

Despite the difficult political situation, the influence of Greek culture on Cyprus grew considerably. This was especially noticeable in sculpture; hitherto the portrayal of gods and men had been stiff, endowed with an obligatory "archaic smile", and now it became more naturalistic.

Hellenistic Era

When Alexander the Great attacked the Persian Empire in 325 BC, the Cypriot kingdoms welcomed him as a liberator, providing him with a fleet of battleships for his victorious siege of Tyre. The weakening of Phoenicia resulted in greater revenues from the copper trade for Cyprus. But the favourable situation did not last. After Alexander's death in 323 BC, Cyprus became a battleground for his successors – the victor was the Greek-Egyptian Ptolemy I Solter. Kition, Kyrenia, Lapithos and Marion were destroyed and Nicocreon,

800 BC Phoenicians settle in Kition	**570 BC** Egyptians assume control of Cyprus		**294 BC** Island falls under the control of the Egyptian Ptolemys
	546 BC Start of Persian rule		
		Jug (5th century BC)	

700 BC **600 BC** **500 BC** **400 BC** **300 BC**

8th century BC Assyrians leave control of the island to Cypriot kings, demanding only an annual tribute

c.500 BC Ionian cities revolt against the Persians

381 BC Evagoras, King of Salamis, leads revolt against the Persians

333 BC Alexander the Great occupies Cyprus

Lion from a tomb stele (5th century BC)

Ruins of Kambanopetra basilica in Salamis

the King of Salamis who refused to surrender, committed suicide. Cyprus became part of the Kingdom of Egypt, and its viceroy resided in the new capital – Nea Pafos. Cultural life was influenced by Hellenism, with the Egyptian gods joining the pantheon of deities.

Roman Rule and Christianity

In 58 BC, Cyprus was conquered by the legions of Rome. The island was given the status of a province ruled by a governor, who resided in a magnificent palace in Nea Pafos. The largest town, port and main trading centre was still Salamis, which at that time numbered over 200,000 inhabitants. The imposing ruins of Salamis bear testimony to its prosperity, while the Roman floor mosaics in Pafos are among the most interesting in the Middle East. The flourishing city of Kourion was the site of the temple and oracle of Apollo – which continued to be of religious significance. Roman rule lasted in Cyprus until the end of the 4th century AD.

Mosaic from the house of Theseus in Kato Pafos

Christianity came to Cyprus with the arrival from Palestine of the apostle Paul in AD 45. He was joined by Barnabas, who was to become the first Cypriot saint *(see p24)*. In the same year they converted the Roman governor of Cyprus, Sergius Paulus. The new religion spread slowly, until it was adopted as the state religion by Emperor Constantine. His edict of 313 granted Christianity equal status with other religions of his empire. St Helena, the mother of Constantine the Great, stopped in Cyprus on her way back from Jerusalem, where she had found fragments of the True Cross. She founded Stavrovouni monastery, which is said to house a fragment of the cross.

Saranda Kolones in Kato Pafos

Eros and Psyche
(1st century AD)

58 BC Rome annexes Cyprus

1st century BC Cyprus hit by violent earthquakes

| 200 BC | 100 BC | AD 1 | AD 100 | AD 200 | AD 300 |

AD 45 The apostles Paul and Barnabas arrive as missionaries to spread Christianity to Cyprus

313 Edict of Milan grants freedom of worship to Christians throughout the Roman Empire, including Cyprus

115–16 Jewish rebellion put down by Emperor Hadrian. Salamis destroyed

In 332 and 342, two cataclysmic earthquakes destroyed most of the Cypriot towns, including Salamis and Palaipafos, marking the end of the era.

St Hilarion Castle boasts an idyllic viewing point

Byzantine Period

The official division of the Roman realm into an Eastern and Western Empire in 395 naturally left Cyprus on the eastern side of the divide, under the Byzantine sphere of influence.

The 5th and 6th centuries were flourishing times. The centres of pagan culture linked to the cults of Aphrodite and Apollo (Pafos and Kourion) lost importance, while the role of Salamis increased. Renamed Constantia, it became the island's capital. New towns also arose, such as Famagusta and Nicosia, and vast basilicas were built.

Beginning around 647, the first of a series of pillaging raids by Arabs took place. In the course of the raids, which continued over three centuries, Constantia was sacked and many magnificent buildings were destroyed.

In 965, the fleet of the Byzantine emperor Nicephorus II Phocas rid the island of Arab pirates and Cyprus again became safe. But not for long. From the 11th century, the entire Middle East became the

Christ Pantocrator from the church of Panagiatou tou Araka

scene of new warfare. Anatolia, Syria and, above all, the Holy Land were captured by the Seljuk Turks. Byzantium was incapable of resisting the onslaught, and Crusades were organized in Europe to recover the Holy Land and other lost territories.

Crusades and Lusignan Period

The first successful recovery of the Holy Land from the Muslims took place with the capture of Jerusalem (1099). Successive crusades continued throughout most of the 12th and 13th centuries. European knights set up the Kingdom of Jerusalem, but surrounded as it was by Turkish emirates, it was unable to survive. Further crusades were launched but mainly suffered defeats. The Sultan Saladin conquered nearly the entire Kingdom of Jerusalem in 1187. The next crusade was organized in 1190. One of its leaders was

Pendant from the early Byzantine period

488 Following the discovery of the tomb of St Barnabas, Emperor Zenon confirms the independence of the Cypriot Church

688 Emperor Justinian II and Caliph Abd al-Malik sign a treaty dividing control of the island

| 300 | 450 | 600 | 750 | 9 |

395 Partition of the Roman Empire; Cyprus becomes part of the Eastern Roman Empire

David in the Lion's Den, a 7th-century AD relief

Richard I (the Lionheart), King of England, whose ships were forced onto Cyprus by a storm. The local prince, Isaac Komnenos, who had proclaimed himself King of Cyprus, plundered the ships and tried to imprison the sister and fiancée of Richard. In reprisal, Richard smashed the Komnenos artillery on the Mesaoria plain and chased his enemy, capturing him in Kantara Castle.

As spoils of war, Cyprus passed from hand to hand. Richard turned it over to the Knights Templar, and they in turn sold the island to the knight Guy de Lusignan, who started the Cyprian Lusignan Dynasty and introduced the feudal system to Cyprus. A period of prosperity for the nobility ensued, partly due to trade with Genoa and Venice, although local Cypriots experienced terrible poverty. Magnificent cathedrals and churches were built, and small churches in the Troodos mountains were decorated with splendid frescoes. The state was weakened by a devastating raid by the increasingly powerful Genoese in 1372, who captured Famagusta. Finally, the widow of James, the last Lusignan king, ceded Cyprus to the Venetians in 1489.

A costume from Venetian times

Venetian Rule

Venetian rule over Cyprus lasted less than a century. The island was a frontier fortress, intended to defend the Venetian domains in the eastern Mediterranean from the Ottoman Empire. The most formidable fortifications around ports and towns date from this period (including Kyrenia and Famagusta). Still, these were no match for the overwhelming power of the Ottoman Empire. When the Ottoman army of Sultan Selim II landed on Cyprus in 1570, one town after another fell to the invaders. Nicosia was able to defend itself for just a few weeks; when it fell, the Turks slaughtered 20,000 people. The defence of Famagusta lasted longer – 10 months – and was one of the greatest battles of its time. The Venetian defenders did not survive to see the arrival of the relief army, and were forced to capitulate. The Ottoman commander, Lala Mustafa Pasha, reneged on his promises of clemency and ordered the garrison to be slaughtered, and its leader Bragadino to be skinned alive.

A 16th-century map of Cyprus

Seal of King Henry II Lusignan

965 Victory of Emperor Phokas II over the Arabs. Cyprus returns to the Byzantine Empire

1191 Richard the Lionheart conquers Cyprus and sells the island to the Knights Templar

1192 Knights Templar hand over Cyprus to Guy, exiled king of Jerusalem. Guy de Lusignan becomes the first king of the new Lusignan dynasty

1372 Genoese raid, capturing of Famagusta

1489 Queen Caterina Cornaro cedes the weakened island to the Venetians

1489–1571 Venetian rule

1050   1200   1350   1500

The Ottoman Era

This was the start of 300 years of Turkish rule. The conquerors destroyed most of the monasteries and churches, turning others into mosques. They abolished the hated feudal system, and divided land among the peasants. The Orthodox clergy were allowed to adopt some Catholic churches and monasteries, and later the archbishop was recognized as the Greek community's representative.

The Turks brought their compatriots to settle on the island, and quashed the regular rebellions. In 1821, after the beginning of the Greek War of Independence, the Ottoman governor ordered the execution of the popular Archbishop Kyprianos and many other members of the Orthodox clergy.

In the mid-19th century, Great Britain came to play an increasingly important role

Selimiye Mosque in North Nicosia

in the Middle East. In exchange for military aid in its war with Russia, the Ottoman Empire handed over occupation and administrative rights of Cyprus to Britain in perpetuity in 1878, though the island continued to be an Ottoman possession.

British Rule

Cyprus' strategic location was vital in defending the sea routes to India and in safeguarding British interests in the Middle East. During their rule, the British introduced the English justice system, reduced crime and built roads and waterworks. Following the outbreak of World War I, when Turkey declared itself on the side of Germany, Britain annexed Cyprus.

After World War II, Greek Cypriots pressed for *enosis* (unification with Greece), which was

Hoisting of the British flag in Cyprus

Hadjigeorgakis Kornesios mansion, South Nicosia

1570 Cyprus invaded by Ottoman Turks		**1754** The sultan confirms the Orthodox archbishop as a spokesman for the Greek Cypriots	*The hanging of Archbishop Kyprianos*	
1600	**1650**	**1700**	**1750**	**1800**
1571–1878 Ottoman era	**1660** Ottoman authorities recognize the legitimacy of the Archbishop's office with the Greeks		**1779** Establishment of the dragoman (intercessor between the Turks and the Greeks)	**1821** Bloody suppression of the Greek national uprising by the Turks

Büyük Han in North Nicosia

strongly opposed by the Turkish minority. Rising tensions led to the establishment of the organization EOKA (National Organization of Cypriot Fighters) in 1954 by Archbishop Makarios and Greek general George Grivas. Its aim was to free Cyprus from British control. In 1958, Turkish Cypriots founded the Turkish Resistance Organisation (TNT), which provided a counterbalance to EOKA.

Archbishop Makarios, first president of the Republic of Cyprus

The 1955–9 EOKA liberation struggle led the British to grant independence to Cyprus. A constitution was drafted that, among other things, excluded *enosis* and *taksim* (partition of Cyprus between Turkey and Greece, favoured by Turkish Cypriots). Britain, Greece and Turkey signed a treaty that obliged them to ensure Cyprus' independence. Archbishop Makarios, who had been interned by the British, returned to Cyprus in triumph and was elected President of the Republic of Cyprus. Independence was officially declared on 16 August 1960.

Independent Cyprus

In December 1963, animosity between Greek and Turkish Cypriots erupted into warfare. The Greek-Cypriot army intervened and the Turkish air force bombarded Tylliria. In 1964, United Nations troops arrived to restore peace between the warring parties, however the mission failed and troops remain to this day.

On 15 July 1974 a coup d'état, encouraged by Athens and staged by rebel units of the Cypriot National Guard (led by Greek army officers), ousted Makarios. This provided the Turkish government in Ankara with a pretext to send troops to Cyprus. After a short battle, the invading army controlled the north, and the resettlement of the population began. The "Green Line" buffer zone still divides the Turkish-occupied North from the South, and continues to be patrolled by UN troops.

In November 1983 the Turks declared the Turkish Republic of Northern Cyprus (TRNC), which is recognized only by Turkey. In April 2004 a referendum preceding Cyprus' entry into the European Union failed to unify the island. The leaders, President of the Republic of Cyprus Nico Anastasiades and President of the TRNC Mustafa Akıncı, make repeated attempts at reunification by participating in frequent rounds of talks.

Referendum on the reunification of Cyprus (2004)

General George Grivas

1850	1900	1950	2000	2050

78 Great Britain takes ...er the administration of Cyprus

1925 Cyprus becomes a British colony

1950 Makarios is elected Archbishop

1960 (16 August) Proclamation of independence. Archbishop Makarios III becomes President of the Republic of Cyprus

1914 Outbreak of World War I; Great Britain annexes Cyprus

1963–4 Fighting erupts between Greek and Turkish Cypriots; UN troops arrive

1974 Coup d'état against President Makarios. Turkish invasion of North Cyprus

1983 TRNC is declared

2013 Eurozone crisis

2010 Festivals mark 50 years of independence

2008 Southern Cyprus adopts the euro

2004 Referendum on reunification

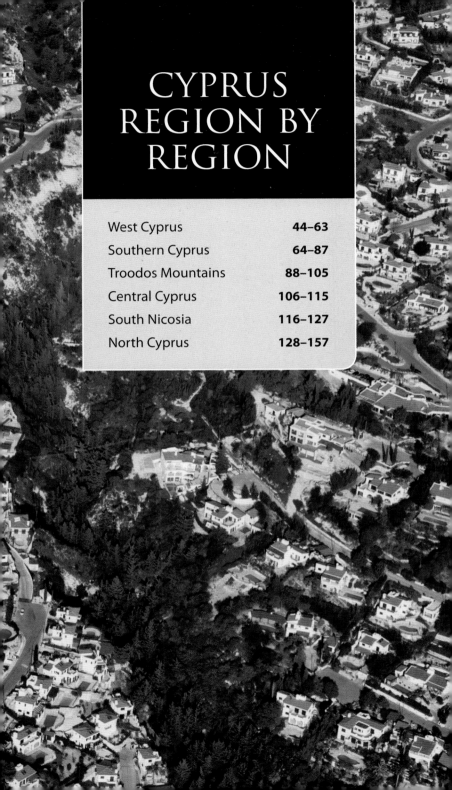

CYPRUS REGION BY REGION

West Cyprus   44–63

Southern Cyprus   64–87

Troodos Mountains   88–105

Central Cyprus   106–115

South Nicosia   116–127

North Cyprus   128–157

Cyprus at a Glance

Cyprus has a wide variety of historic sights. Visitors can find everything from Neolithic settlements and ancient towns to medieval cathedrals and small mountain churches decorated with exquisite frescoes, castles built by the Crusaders and Venetian fortresses, and modern buildings and museums. The island abounds in picturesque towns and villages, beautiful coastal areas, and scenic mountains, with diverse wildlife and friendly people.

Nicosia is the world's only divided capital city. A highlight of its southern part is the Byzantine-style Archbishop Makarios Cultural Centre, housing an impressive collection of icons *(see p122).*

Agios Nikolaos tis Stegis, a UNESCO World Heritage Site, is one of the many small churches hidden in the sheltered valleys of the Troodos mountains that feature magnificent frescoes *(see p102).*

Lapithos (Lapta)

Kyrenia (Girne)

Morfou (Güzelyurt)

Niços

SOUTH NICOSIA
(see pp116–127)

Léfka (Lefke)

Peristerona

Polis

WEST CYPRUS
(see pp44–63)

CENTRAL CYPRUS
(see pp106–115)

Agios Nikolaos tis Stegis

TROODOS MOUNTAINS
(see pp88–105)

Panagia

Troodos

Palaichori

Pelendri

Lefkar

Agios Georgios

Pegeia

Omodos

Louvarás

SOUTHERN CYPRUS
(see pp64–87)

Pafos

Monagri

Limassol (Lemesos)

Mediterranean Sea

Pafos, divided into Kato Pafos (Lower Pafos) and Ktima, is full of history. With its picturesque harbour, it is also one of the most beautiful towns in the Mediterranean *(see pp52–7).*

◀ Aerial view of rooftops in the hilltops of Cyprus

Buffavento Castle in the Kyrenia mountains was one of three castles, along with Kantara and St Hilarion, that defended Cyprus against attacks along the north coast (see p148).

Salamis was the island's most important port and trading town for almost a thousand years, and also its capital. Now it is one of the largest archaeological sites (see pp138–9).

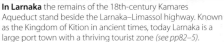

In Larnaka the remains of the 18th-century Kamares Aqueduct stand beside the Larnaka–Limassol highway. Known as the Kingdom of Kition in ancient times, today Larnaka is a large port town with a thriving tourist zone (see pp82–5).

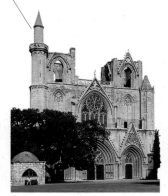

Famagusta, a city surrounded by Venetian defence walls, contains Gothic churches that have been transformed into mosques with minarets (see pp140–43).

WEST CYPRUS

West Cyprus is a varied region, made up of mountains, historical sights and a lovely coastline. It was once the most neglected part of the island, remote from the main cities and harbours. Now it is becoming a popular attraction due to its wild natural environment. Lovers of antiquities are sure to be enchanted by the Roman mosaics in Pafos, while mythology buffs can see the place where the goddess Aphrodite emerged from the sea at Petra tou Romiou.

Pafos' Hellenistic, Roman and Byzantine relics are among the most interesting on the island, especially the Roman mosaics.

The modern town is divided into a bustling tourist zone on the coast, with dozens of luxury hotels, taverns, pubs and restaurants, and Ktima – the old town of Pafos – which is only a short drive inland but a world away from the tourist zone.

This region has a slightly milder climate than the rest of the island, as witnessed by the banana plantations north of Pafos. There is practically no industry here and it has the most extensive forest areas in Cyprus, including the famous Cedar Valley inhabited by wild moufflon. The Akamas peninsula, with its rugged hills overgrown with forests, is home to many species of wild animals, and the beautiful beaches provide nesting grounds for sea turtles. This is a paradise for nature lovers and is one of the best places to hike in Cyprus. Movement around the peninsula is hindered by the lack of roads, but there are trails for use by walkers.

This is the land of Aphrodite, goddess of love, who is said to have been born in the south of the island by the rocks jutting out of the sea in the Petra tou Romiou area, which are named after her. North Akamas, on the bay of Chrysochou, is the goddess's bath, which she used after her amorous frolics with Adonis.

Boats and yachts moored in Pafos harbour on a sunny day

◄ Sunset over Petra tou Romiou beach

Exploring West Cyprus

The best place to begin exploring West Cyprus is Pafos, which has a large concentration of hotels and a developed tourist infrastructure. Here you will also find a wealth of historic relics that have made Pafos a UNESCO World Heritage Site. They range from Bronze Age dwellings (Maa Paleokastro at Coral Bay), royal tombs dating from the Hellenistic era and Roman floor mosaics to Byzantine castles and churches. Pafos forest is home to wild moufflon. Cape Lara, to the northwest of Pafos, has beautiful beaches, and further on is the Akamas peninsula.

Lempa is a favourite place with watersports enthusiasts

Getting There

The easiest way to arrive is by air to the international airport southeast of Pafos, where a motorway links the town with Limassol, offering easy access to the southwest coast. It is also possible to get from Limassol via a parallel road running along the coast and over the southern slopes of the Troodos mountains. However, the mountain roads are not of the best quality, and driving around the Akamas peninsula is best done in a four-wheel-drive vehicle.

Sights at a Glance

1. Petra tou Romiou
2. Palaipafos
3. Geroskipou
4. *Pafos pp52–7*
5. Lempa
6. Agios Neofytos
7. Coral Bay
8. Pegeia
9. Agios Georgios
10. Lara
11. Baths of Aphrodite
12. Akamas Peninsula
13. Polis
14. Marion
15. Panagia Chrysorrogiatissa
16. Xeros Valley
17. Diarizos Valley

Walking in the Akamas Peninsula pp60–61

For hotels and restaurants in this region see p162 and pp170–71

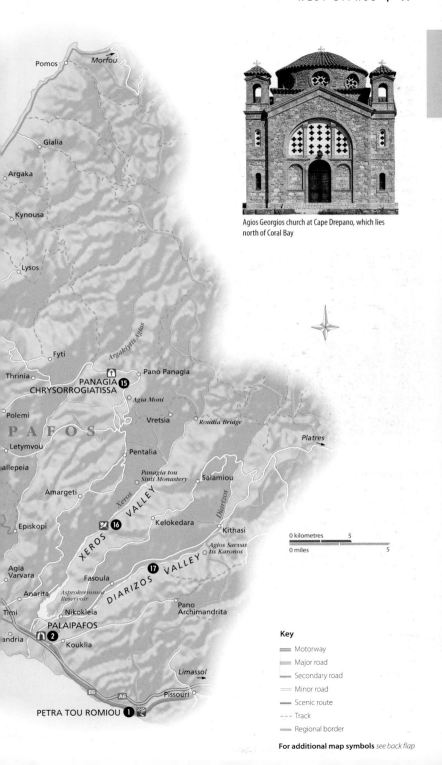

Pomos

Morfou

Gialia

Argaka

Kynousa

Lysos

Fyti

Argakiytis Agias

Thrinia

Pano Panagia

PANAGIA
CHRYSORROGIATISSA 15

Agia Moni

Polemi

Vretsia

Roudia Bridge

Platres

PAFOS

Letymvou

Pentalia

Salamiou

allepeia

*Panagia tou
Sinti Monastery*

Amargeti

Kelokedara

Xeros VALLEY

Diarizos

Episkopi

Kithasi

*Agios Savvas
tis Karonos*

Agia
Varvara

XEROS

16

Fasoula

DIARIZOS VALLEY

17

Anarita

*Asprokremmos
Reservoir*

Pano
Archimandrita

Timi

Nikokleia

andria

PALAIPAFOS

2

Kouklia

Limassol

PETRA TOU ROMIOU 1

B6   A6

Pissouri

Agios Georgios church at Cape Drepano, which lies
north of Coral Bay

0 kilometres   5

0 miles   5

Key

▬▬ Motorway

▬▬ Major road

— Secondary road

═══ Minor road

— Scenic route

--- Track

▬▬ Regional border

For additional map symbols *see back flap*

Petra tou Romiou, the legendary birthplace of Aphrodite

❶ Petra tou Romiou

Road Map B4. 25 km (16 miles) southeast of Pafos.

The area between Pafos and Limassol includes what is probably the most beautiful stretch of the Cyprus coast, dominated by limestone crags rising from the blue sea. At Petra tou Romiou there are three huge, white limestone rocks known collectively as the **Rock of Aphrodite**. In Greek mythology it was here that Aphrodite, goddess of love, beauty and fertility, emerged from the sea foam. She sailed to the shore on a shell towed by dolphins and rested in nearby Palaipafos, where a temple was built to her.

The location of these picturesque rocks is beautiful, with clear blue water beckoning swimmers. The large beach near the rocks is covered with fine pebbles and stones polished smooth by the action of the waves. A word of caution,

however: the road between the car park and the beach is dangerous, and you are advised to use the underground passage.

Nearby you can see trees on which infertile women tie handkerchiefs or scraps of fabric to appeal for help from Aphrodite. They are joined by others who are lonely and unlucky in love, beseeching the goddess of love to help them. A local legend says that swimming around the jutting rock at full moon will make you a year younger with each lap. Other legends lead us to believe that the amorous goddess, after a night spent in the arms of her lover, returned to this spot to regain her virginity by bathing in the sea.

On the slope of the hill above the Rock of Aphrodite, the Cyprus Tourism Organization has built a cafeteria where you can eat while taking in the beautiful view over Petra tou Romiou. Meaning "Rock of Romios", the name Petra tou

Romiou also commemorates the legendary Greek hero Digenis Akritas, also known as Romios. He lived during the Byzantine era and, during an Arab raid by Saracen corsairs on Cyprus, hurled huge boulders into the sea to destroy the Arab ships. According to legend, the rocks here are the stones thrown by Romios.

Environs

A few kilometres east of Petra tou Romiou is the small resort community of **Pissouri**, surrounded by orchards. There is a large resort here, and some smaller hotels, as well as a long, sandy beach. Nearby are two golf courses: Secret Valley and Aphrodite Hills.

❷ Palaipafos

Road Map A4. In Kouklia village, 14 km (9 miles) southeast of Pafos, by the Pafos–Limassol road. 🚌 632 from Ktima Pafos. **Tel** 264 32155. **Open** 8:30am–7:30pm daily (to 5pm early Sep–mid-Apr). 🏛

Just north of the large village of Kouklia are the ruins of the famous Palaipafos (Old Pafos), which was the oldest and most powerful city-state on the island in ancient times. According to tradition, it was founded by Agaperon – a hero of the Trojan Wars and the son of the King of Tegeia in Greek Arcadia. Palaipafos was also the site of the **Temple of Aphrodite**, the most important shrine of the goddess in the ancient world, but now only of specialist interest. Archaeological evidence points

Aphrodite

The cult of Aphrodite arrived in Cyprus from the East; she was already worshipped in Syria and Palestine as Ishtar and Astarte. She was also worshipped by the Romans as Venus. In Greek mythology Aphrodite was the goddess of love, beauty and fertility who rose from the sea foam off the shore of Cyprus. She was married to Hephaestus, but took many lovers, including Ares and Adonis. She was the mother of Eros, Hermaphrodite, Priap and Aeneas, among others. The main centres for her cult of worship were Pafos and Amathous. The myrtle plant is dedicated to her, as is the dove.

Marble statue of Aphrodite from Soloi

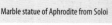

to the existence of a much older town on this site, dating back to the Bronze Age. Legend says that Pygmalion, a local king and also a brilliant sculptor, carved many statues, including one of an extraordinarily beautiful woman with whom he fell madly in love. Aphrodite, moved by his love, turned the cold statue into a living woman. Their union produced a son, Pafos, who gave the town its name.

The most famous figure of Pafos was Kinyras, ruler of the city and great priest of Aphrodite, who introduced many religious ceremonies and gave rise to the dynasty that ruled the city for centuries.

A large **centre of worship** devoted to Aphrodite was established here in the 12th century BC, at the end of the Bronze Age. Its foundations and fragments of the walls remain. The sanctuary was destroyed during an earthquake and rebuilt in the 1st century, during Roman times. Here the goddess was represented by a black stone shaped as a cone, symbolizing fertility. For centuries, crowds of pilgrims flocked to Pafos from all over the ancient world. Adorned with flowers, the pilgrims walked into the temple where they were met by the temple courtesans. Aphrodite was worshipped through ritual sexual intercourse between the pilgrims and Aphrodite's priestesses – young Cypriot women who were obliged to

The small stone church of Agios Constantinos and Eleni near Kouklia

Panagia Chrysopolitissa inscription

offer their virginity to the goddess by giving themselves to a pilgrim man within the temple area. These orgiastic rites were mainly held in the spring, and elements have survived in the form of the spring flower festival – the Anthistiria.

Palaipafos was not always peaceful. It took part in the rebellion of the Ionian cities against the Persians. In 498 BC, the Persians laid siege to the city and, following a fierce battle, forced entry by scaling the ramparts, the remains of which can still be seen. In 325 BC, following a devastating earthquake that destroyed Palaipafos, its last king, Nikikles, moved the city to Nea Pafos (present day Kato Pafos), but Aphrodite's sanctuary retained its importance until the end of the 4th century, when Emperor Theodosius banned pagan cults within

the empire. The sanctuary is now a site of excavations by Swiss archaeologists.

Standing on the hill is a Gothic structure known as the **Lusignan Court**, built in the times of the Crusaders and subsequently remodelled by the Turks. It is built on a square floor plan, and leading on to a square yard is an old tower gate. The rooms in the east wing contain a museum that exhibits locally discovered ceramics, stone idols, bronze articles and the black stone worshipped by followers of Aphrodite. On the ground floor there is an impressive Gothic hall with cross vaulting.

In the nearby Roman villa, known as the **House of Leda**, archaeologists have uncovered a 2nd-century AD floor mosaic of the Spartan queen Leda with Zeus in the guise of a swan.

Adjacent to the sanctuary is the small 12th-century church of **Panagia Chrysopolitissa**, which was built over the ruins of an early Byzantine basilica. It is dedicated to the early Christian Madonna, whose cult derives directly from Aphrodite, the pagan goddess of love. As part of a tradition stemming from Cypriot folklore, women came here to light candles to the Virgin Mary – Giver of Mother's Milk. This church contains interesting 14th-century frescoes, and some of the colourful mosaics that covered the floor of the basilica have been preserved.

Ruins of the Sanctuary of Aphrodite

Folk Art Museum in Geroskipou

❸ Geroskipou

Road Map A4. 3 km (1.8 miles) southeast of Pafos. 📟 601, 606, 612, 613, 631, 632, 633, 634, 636. 🎪 Agia Paraskevi (Jul).

The name Geroskipou means "sacred garden" *(hieros kipos)* in Greek. This testifies to the fact that this former village (now a suburban district bordering Pafos) was built on the site of a forest dedicated to Aphrodite. To this day, it is notable for its many flowers and fruit trees, especially citrus and pomegranate trees – symbols of the goddess.

The main street is lined with workshops producing the local delicacy – *loukoumi* (Cyprus delight). Made from water, sugar and citrus juice, thickened through evaporation, the resulting jelly is cut into cubes and coated with icing sugar. The workshops are open to visitors, who can view the production process and, while there, also buy other sweets including sugar-coated almonds and delicious halva – made of nuts, honey and sesame seeds. The tree-shaded main square of the town is surrounded by colourful shops selling baskets, ceramics and the celebrated *loukoumi;* there are also numerous cafés serving coffee and pastries.

Standing at the southern end of the market square is **Agia Paraskevi**, one of the most interesting Byzantine churches on the island. Built in the 9th century, this stone church features five domes arranged in the shape of a cross. The sixth one surmounts the reliquary,

located under the 19th-century belfry. Originally, the church was a single-nave structure. Its interior is decorated with beautiful 15th-century murals depicting scenes from the New Testament, including the lives of Jesus and Mary, and the Crucifixion. The frescoes were restored in the 1970s.

The vault of the central dome has been decorated with the painting of the *Praying Madonna*. The three images opposite the south entrance – the *Last Supper*, the *Washing of the Feet* and the *Betrayal* – can be dated from the Lusignan period, due to the style of armour worn by the knights portrayed. Opposite are the *Birth and Presentation of the Virgin*, the *Entry into Jerusalem* and the *Raising of Lazarus*.

Another attraction, close to the market square, is the 19th-century historic house once home of the British Consul, Andreas Zamboulakis. Now

The historic stone church of Agia Paraskevi in Geroskipou

the building houses the **Folk Art Museum**, containing a collection of local folk costumes, textiles, embroidery and toys, as well as decorated gourds, furniture and domestic items.

🏠 **Agia Paraskevi Church**
Tel 26 961 859. **Open** Apr–Oct: 8am–1pm, 2–5pm Mon–Sat; Nov– Mar: 8am–1pm, 2–4pm Mon–Sat.

🏛 **Folk Art Museum**
Leondiou. **Tel** 26 306 216. **Open** summer: 9am–5pm daily; winter: 8:30am–4pm daily. 🅿

❹ Pafos

See pp52–7.

Reconstructed Chalcolithic houses in Lempa's Experimental Village

❺ Lempa

Road Map A4. 4 km (2½ miles) north of Pafos. 📟 607, 642 from Ktima Pafos.

Set among citrus groves between the villages of Chlorakas and Kissonerga just a short distance from the sea, Lempa is home to the **Cyprus College of Art**. The artists, craftsmen and students here have studios in restored village houses. The road to the college is lined with sculptures. The independent pottery workshops are worth visiting.

Lempa was home to the earliest islanders, who settled here more than 5,500 years ago. West of the village centre you can see the **Lempa Experimental Village** – a partially reconstructed settlement dating from the Chalcolithic (Bronze) era (3500 BC). British archaeologists have rebuilt four complete houses from that era. The cylindrical clay dwellings are covered with makeshift roofs.

Agios Neofytos monastery, founded in the 12th century

▥ Cyprus College of Art
Tel 99 452 757. **W** artcyprus.org

▯ Lempa Experimental Village
Open dawn–dusk daily.

Environs
In the centre of the nearby village of Empa, 2 km (1 mile) southeast of Lempa, is the 12th-century monastery church of **Panagia Chryseleoussa**. Inside it are the remains of frescoes that were initially destroyed by an earthquake in the mid-1900s, and later damaged by a bad restoration job.

❻ Agios Neofytos

Road Map A4. 9 km (5 ½ miles) north of Pafos 🚌 604. **Open** 9am–1pm, 2–6pm daily (to 4pm Nov–Mar). 🎫 🎫 24 Jan & 28 Sep. **W** stneophytos.org.cy

This monastery was founded in the 12th century by a monk named Neofytos, one of the main saints of the Cypriot church. He was a hermit and an ascetic, author of philosophical treatises and hymns, who spent dozens of years here. Some of his manuscripts survive, including the *Ritual Ordinance*, a handbook of monastic life, and an essay on the acquisition of Cyprus by the Crusaders.

The future saint dug three cells in the steep limestone rock with his bare hands. The murals covering the walls are reputed to have been painted by Neofytos himself. This, the oldest part of the monastery, is called the *enkleistra* (hermitage). In two of the caves, murals depict the final days of the life of Christ – the *Last Supper*, *Judas' Betrayal* and the *Deposition from the Cross*, featuring Joseph of Arimathea whose face is thought to be a portrait of the saint. The dome, hewn from the soft rock, features the *Ascension*.

A pottery woman

The cell of the saint has bookshelves, benches and a desk at which St Neofytos used to work, all carved in the rock, as well as his sarcophagus, presided over by an image of the *Resurrection*.

The main buildings, which are still inhabited by monks, include an inner courtyard, a small garden with an aviary, and a *katholikon* – the monastery church with a terrace dedicated to the Virgin Mary.

❼ Coral Bay

Road Map A4. 10 km (6 miles) north of Pafos. 🚌 615, 616.

This fine sandy beach between two promontories has a tropical air. All summer long it is covered by rows of sunbeds for hire. It offers soft sand and safe swimming for families, and there is a wide choice of watersports. There are many restaurants, hotels and bars, including a beach bar, as well as a campsite for more thrifty visitors. Live pop concerts are held here on summer evenings. This beach is popular with young Cypriots, especially on summer weekends.

On the northern headland archaeologists discovered **Maa Paleokastro** – a fortified Achaian settlement dating from the Bronze Age. The site now houses the **Museum of the Mycenean Colonization of Cyprus**.

Environs
Opposite the village of Chlorakas on the road to Pafos is the **Church of St George**, which commemorates the landing of General George Grivas at this spot in 1954. The local museum has a boat that was used by EOKA fighters for weapons smuggling.

Several kilometres inland lies the Mavrokolympos reservoir. Above the car park are the **Adonis Baths**, whose main attraction is a 10-m- (32-ft-) high waterfall. The road running along the Mavrokolympos river leads to more waterfalls.

The region also features numerous vineyards and banana plantations.

The picturesque crescent-shaped Coral Bay

❹ Pafos

Pafos is the name given to the twin towns of Pano Pafos (Upper Pafos, known as the Old Town or Ktima by locals) and Nea Pafos or Kato Pafos (Lower Pafos) *(see pp56–7)*. During the Byzantine era, when coastal towns were threatened by Arab raids, the town was moved inland to its present hilltop location. This is now the modern regional centre of trade, administration and culture, while the lower town is the site of fine Roman ruins and the majority of tourist facilities.

Exploring Pafos

Ktima's major historic buildings and interesting sights, except for the Archaeological Museum, are within walking distance of one another. The main shopping street is Makarios Avenue, where you will find a wide choice of jewellery, clothing and footwear. Within the Old Town, the Agora is a colourful bazaar selling food, leather goods, art and handbags. After strolling along the streets of the Old Town it is worth stopping for a rest in the green district, to the south of town, near the acropolis and the Byzantine and Ethnographic Museums. The eastern part of town contains wide avenues lined with classical public buildings, schools and libraries. The western part is a maze of narrow streets and traditional architecture.

🄲 Grand Mosque (Cami Kebir) Namik Kemil.

The Grand Mosque is a relic of the past Turkish presence in this area. Standing in the Mouttalos district, it had been the Byzantine church of Agia Sofia before being turned into a mosque.

The façade of Agios Kendeas church, built around 1930

🄼 Agora

Agoras.

In the centre of the Old Town is an ornamental covered market hall building, dating from the early 20th century. Fresh fruits, vegetables, fish and meat produced in the Pafos region are sold at this municipal market.

🄽 Mehmet Bey Ebubekir Hamam (Turkish Baths)

Militiathou, next to the covered bazaar (Agora).

Among the trees south of the Agora are the Turkish baths. Originally this dome-covered stone structure was probably a church. After serving as the Turkish baths, some of the rooms were used to house the municipal museum, but when this moved to new premises, the building stood empty. A period of neglect followed, but the building has been restored to its former glory. It now houses a coffee shop.

🄰 Agios Kendeas

Leoforos Archiepiskopou Makariou III.
Built in 1930, the exterior is not particularly exciting, but the interior is worth a visit. Here you will find a carved wooden iconostasis, a bishop's throne and many 19th-century icons.

🄼 Town Hall

Plateia 28 Octovriou.
The single-storey Neo-Classical building standing on the edge of the Municipal Gardens, redolent of ancient Greek architecture, houses the Town Hall and Registry Office, a popular wedding venue. Opposite, behind the slender Ionian column in the middle of the square, is the one-storey municipal library.

The Neo-Classical Town Hall and Registry Office of Pafos

🄰 Agios Theodoros (St Theodore's Cathedral)

Andrea Ioannou.
Built in 1896, Agios Theodoros is the oldest church in Ktima and is as important for the Orthodox community as St John's Cathedral (Agios Ioannis) in Nicosia.

Close to the square stands a column commemorating the victims of the Ottoman slaughter of 1821 that claimed the lives of the Bishop of Pafos, Chrysanthos, and other members of the Greek clergy.

A lovely café at the Pafos market, known to the locals as the Agora

Display in the Ethnographic Museum

🏛 Geological Exhibition

Ayios Theodoros 2. **Open** 9am–4pm Mon–Sat (summer).

One of a few places on the island where you can learn about the geology of Cyprus, this is a small private collection of rocks and minerals. On display are sedimentary rocks with fossils; volcanic rocks from the Troodos mountains and the Akamas peninsula; and metallic minerals, particularly copper and asbestos which have been mined here for millennia.

🏛 Bishop's Palace and Byzantine Museum

Andrea Ioannou 5. **Tel** 26 931 393. **Open** 9am–3pm Mon–Fri, 9am–1pm Sat. 🖼

This beautiful Byzantine-style building is the residence of the Bishop of Pafos and the most important ecclesiastical building after Agios Theodoros. It was built in 1910 by Iaskos, the Bishop of Pafos. Bishop Chrysostomos subsequently extended the palace, furnishing it with beautiful

The Dormition of the Virgin Mary, Byzantine Museum

arcades and allocating part of it to the Byzantine Museum. The museum houses a collection of icons, including the oldest on the island – the 9th-century *Agia Marina*, and the 12th-century *Panagia Eloussa* from the Agios Savras monastery. There are also religious books, including a 1472 Bible and a collection of documents produced by Turkish sultans.

🏛 Ethnographic Museum

Exo Vrysis 1. **Tel** 26 932 010. **Open** 10am–5:30pm Mon–Sat, 10am–1:30pm Sun. 🖼

This privately run museum houses collections of coins, folk costumes, kitchen utensils, baskets, ceramics, axes, amphorae and carriages. In the sunken garden is a wood-burning stove from an old bakery and an authentic 3rd-century stone sarcophagus.

Pafos Town Centre

① Grand Mosque
② Agora
③ Loutra (Turkish Baths)
④ Agios Kendeas
⑤ Town Hall
⑥ Agios Theodoros
  (St Theodore's Cathedral)
⑦ Geological Exhibition
⑧ Bishop's Palace and
  Byzantine Museum
⑨ Ethnographic Museum

0 metres   200
0 yards   200

🏛 Tombs of the Kings

Leoforos Tafon ton Vasileon. 🚌 615.
Tel 26 306 295. **Open** summer:
8:30am–7:30pm daily; winter:
8:30am–5:30pm daily. 🌐

The necropolis is a fascinating system of caves and rock tombs dating from the Hellenistic and Roman eras (the 3rd century BC to 3rd century AD). Situated north of Kato Pafos, beyond the old city walls and close to the sea, it consists of imposing tombs carved in soft sandstone.

Eight tomb complexes have been opened for viewing; the most interesting are numbers 3, 4 and 8. Stone steps lead to underground vaults. Some tombs are surrounded by peristyles of Doric columns, beyond which you can spot burial niches. Others have been decorated with murals.

The architectural style of many tombs, particularly those in the northern section, reveals the Egyptian influence; they were inspired by the Ptolemy tombs in Alexandria. One funerary custom that has been documented is that on the anniversary of the death, relatives of the deceased would gather around the tomb for a ceremonial meal, depositing the leftovers by the actual sepulchre. Similar customs prevail to this day in some Greek Orthodox communities.

Over the following centuries the tombs were systematically

The 12th-century stone church of Agia Kyriaki

plundered. One of the more notorious looters was the American consul from Larnaka, Luigi Palma de Cesnola (1832–1904), who plundered many sites in Cyprus, including Kourion. The tombs were built when there were no longer kings on Cyprus, and they were probably used to bury prominent citizens of Pafos, civil servants and army officers; nevertheless, due to their opulence they became known as the Tombs of the Kings.

During times of persecution they were used by Christians as hiding places. Later the site was used as a quarry. The place has a unique atmosphere, best experienced in the morning.

Inscription on one of the stones in Agia Kyriaki

🏛 Agia Kyriaki

Odos Pafias Afroditis.
Open daily.

The 12th-century stone church of Agia Kyriaki, with a later small belfry and dome, is also known as Panagia Chrysopolitissa (Our Lady of the Golden City). It was built on the ruins of an earlier seven-aisled Christian Byzantine basilica, the largest in Cyprus. A bishop's palace also stood nearby. Both buildings were destroyed by the Arabs, but the parts that have survived include 4th-century religious floor mosaics. The road to Agia Kyriaki

leads along a special platform built over the archaeological digs, from where you can see several single columns. One of them has been dubbed "St Paul's Pillar". The apostle came to Cyprus to preach Christianity, but was captured and led before the Roman governor, Sergius Paulus, who sentenced him to flogging. St Paul blinded his accuser, Elymas, thus convincing Sergius of his innocence to such an extent that the governor converted to Christianity.

Agia Kyriaki is used jointly by the Catholic and Anglican communities. The beautiful church standing nearby, built on a rock which forms part of the Kato Pafos defence walls, is called Panagia Theoskepasti – "guarded by God". It is apocryphally told that during a scourging Arab attack a miraculous cloud enveloped the church, concealing it from the enemy.

🏛 Catacombs of Agia Solomoni and Fabrica Hill

Leoforos Apostolou Palou, Kato Pafos. **Open** dawn–dusk.

Inside a former tomb is a subterranean church dedicated to Solomoni, a Jewess, whose seven children were tortured in her presence, and regarded by the Cypriots as a saint.

In Roman times the site was probably occupied by a synagogue, and earlier on by a pagan shrine. Steep steps lead down to the sunken sanctuary. The adjacent cave

The Tombs of the Kings necropolis

For hotels and restaurants in this region see p162 and pp170–71

contains a tank with what is believed to be miraculous water. Similar catacombs on the opposite side of the street are called Agios Lambrianos.

Beyond Agia Solomoni, to the right, is the limestone Fabrica Hill containing carved underground chambers. They were created during Hellenistic and Roman times but their purpose is unknown.

On the southern slope of the hill, Australian archaeologists have unearthed a Hellenic amphitheatre hewn out of the living rock. Nearby are two small cave churches, Agios Agapitikos and Agios Misitikos. Tradition has it that when dust collected from the floor of Agios Agapitikos is placed in someone's house, it has the power to awaken their love (*agapi* means "love"), while dust collected from Agios Misitikos will awaken hate *(misos)*.

Fabric-festooned tree near the Catacombs of Agia Solomoni

A relief from the Hellenistic era, Archaeological Museum

🏛 Archaeological Museum

Leoforos Georgiou Griva Digeni 43. **Tel** 26 955 801. **Open** 8am–4pm daily. 🖼 💻 📷 🏠

Housed in a small modern building outside the city centre, along the road leading to Geroskipou, this is one of the more interesting archaeological museums in Cyprus. The collection includes historic relics spanning thousands of years from the Neolithic era through the Bronze Age, Hellenistic, Roman, Byzantine and medieval periods, and up until the 18th century AD.

Particularly interesting are the Chalcolithic (copper age) figurines. There are steatite idols, a skeleton from Lempa, a 3rd-century AD mummy of a girl and an array of Hellenic ceramics, jewellery and glass. There are also ancient sarcophagi, sculptures, a coin collection, clay pots used for hot water and a set of Roman surgical instruments – evidence of the high standard of ancient medicine. There are also numerous exhibits from Kato Pafos and from Kouklia, site of the ancient city-kingdom Paliapafos and the Sanctuary of Aphrodite. The Archaeological Museum is one of the destinations featured on the Aphrodite Cultural Route, an initiative by the Cyprus Tourist Organisation (CTO) that aims to guide visitors to key places of interest associated with the goddess. A booklet with useful information on the route is available from CTO offices.

🏖 Beaches

Pafos itself has only a few small beaches in front of hotels; these offer excellent conditions for watersports. A pleasant municipal beach is situated by Leoforos Poseidonos, at the centre of Kato Pafos, close to the Municipal Gardens. Somewhat out of the way, to the north of the archaeological zone, lies the sandy-pebbly Faros Beach.

Good pebble beaches can be found north of Pafos. About 8 km (5 miles) along the coast is a small beach in the bay of Kissonerga fringed by banana plantations. The loveliest, most popular sandy beach is situated at Coral Bay, 10 km (6 miles) north of town *(see p51)*. All the usual beach facilities are offered here, together with most popular watersports.

There are several beaches to the east, including Alikes, Latsi Vrysoudia, and Pahyammos. A beautiful place for bathing is the beach near the Petra tou Romiou, covered with smooth stones. The water here is crystal clear and the environs truly enchanting. Facilities include a restaurant, toilets and a shower near the car park. Come either early in the morning for some quiet reflection or in the evening to enjoy the beautiful sunset.

Coral Bay beach, Paphos, Cyprus

Kato Pafos

The most accessible and inspiring archaeological park on the island, the ruins at Kato (Lower) Pafos were unearthed in 1962, shedding new light on Cyprus under the Roman Empire. In ancient times, this was the capital of Cyprus. Now a UNESCO World Heritage Site, the remains found here span over 2,000 years. The lavish mosaics found on the floors of four Roman villas indicate that this was a place of ostentatious wealth.

★ House of Dionysos
Some 2,000 sq m (21,500 sq ft) of magnificent mosaics can be viewed from wooden platforms.

House of Aion
This villa, with its interesting mosaics, was destroyed by an earthquake. It takes its name from the god Aion, whose image was once to the left of the entrance.

House of Theseus
The palace of the Roman governor contains a set of interesting mosaics portraying the myth of Theseus and Ariadne. The opulent villa discovered underneath dates from the Hellenistic era.

Medieval Castle
The medieval Lusignan castle remodelled by the Ottomans now houses a museum; its flat roof affords a lovely view over the town and the harbour.

KEY

① **The East Tower** was a defence structure, guarding the town against attacks by Arab pirates in the early Middle Ages.

② **Panagia Limeniotissa**, the Byzantine basilica of Our Lady the Protectress of Harbours, was destroyed in the 7th century by Arab raids.

③ **The Hellenic theatre** is located near the Agora.

0 metres	25
0 yards	25

Lighthouse
The small white lighthouse on top of the hill is not related to the Roman ruins below.

★ **Roman Odeon**
This partly restored small music theatre, built of stone blocks, stands on a hillside overlooking the rest of the site. Summer concerts are held here.

Saranda Kolones
This castle, built by the Lusignans, was destroyed by an earthquake in 1222. It takes its name from the 40 columns found among its ruins.

Plan of Kato Pafos

Key

- 🔲 Building
- ⬜ Road
- Footpath
- —— Wall

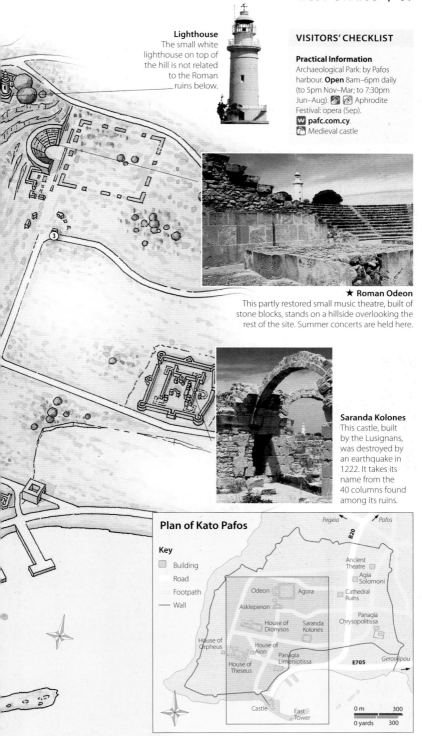

Pegeia   Pafos   B20

Ancient Theatre

Agia Solomoni

Odeon   Agora

Cathedral Ruins

Asklepieion

Panagia Chrysopolitissa

House of Dionysos   Saranda Kolones

House of Orpheus

House of Aion

Panagia Limeniotissa   E705   Geroskipou

House of Theseus

Castle   East Tower

0 m   300
0 yards   300

Tree-lined avenue in the village of Pegeia

❽ Pegeia

Road Map A3. 19 km (12 miles) north of Pafos. 🚌 607, 616.

This small, picturesque hillside village, 5 km (3 miles) inland from Coral Bay, is the last sizeable settlement before entering the wilderness of Akamas. Pegeia, meaning "springs", was founded during the Byzantine era. It is famous for its abundant spring water – a great blessing in sun-parched Cyprus.

Soak up the village atmosphere in the pretty cobbled central square with its fountains, and try a bottle of the local Vasilikon wine.

Environs

On the hilltops to the north of Pegeia, at an altitude of some 600 m (1,970 ft), are the villages of the Laona region – **Ineia**, **Drouseia**, **Arodes** and **Kathikas**. Their lofty perches offer sweeping views of the surrounding area. In Ineia you can visit the Ineia Folk Art Museum; the local school in Kathikas houses the Laona information centre.

❾ Agios Georgios

Road Map A3. 🚌 616.

During Roman times **Cape Drepano**, north of Coral Bay, was the site of a late Roman and early Byzantine town and harbour. The remains of a 6th-century early-Christian basilica have been unearthed here, revealing some well-preserved floor mosaics of sea creatures, a semi-circular bishop's throne and several columns.

The coastal cliffs contain several caves that served as hiding places for the local population during enemy raids. Atop one craggy section is the picturesque **Church of St George** (Agios Georgios) built in the Byzantine style in 1928. St George, its patron saint, champions animals and those who are unlucky in love.

Close by there are some tavernas and fishermen's cottages. The location affords a lovely view over the fishing harbour below, and of the nearby island of Geronisos with its remains of a Neolithic settlement. There are also remains of a small temple that was used during Greek and Roman times.

Environs

North of Agios Georgios is the stunning **Avakas Gorge**. This deep ravine has steep craggy banks, a dozen or so metres high, and the river Avgas runs through the base of it. Avakas Gorge is an environmentally protected area.

The picturesque Church of St George

❿ Lara

Road Map A3.

This sandy crescent is home to two of the most attractive beaches in west Cyprus. To the south lies nearly 2 km (1 mile) of uncrowded sand, while to the north there is a shallow bay with a half-moon stretch of fine white sand frequented by sea turtles.

This is one of the few remaining Mediterranean nesting grounds for the rare green and loggerhead varieties. During breeding season (June to September) staff from the Lara Turtle Conservation Project close access to the beach. However, they arrange occasional night-time walks along the beach, when you can see the turtles struggling ashore.

Although marine animals, sea turtles lay their eggs on dry land, crawling out onto beaches during summer nights to do this. Females lay about 100 eggs at a time, which they bury up in the sand up to half a metre (one and a half feet) deep. After laying, the eggs are carefully removed to a protected area on the beach where they are safe from dogs, foxes and other predators.

After seven weeks the eggs hatch and the hatchlings head immediately for the water. Turtles reach maturity at about the age of 20, and the females return to lay eggs on the same beach where they were born.

The sandy beach at Lara Bay – a nesting ground for rare sea turtles

⓫ Baths of Aphrodite

Road Map A3. 8 km (5 miles) west of Polis, towards Akamas peninsula.
🚌 622, 644.

A path from the car park leads to the Baths of Aphrodite – a pool in a grotto shaded by overgrown fig trees. According to legend it was here that Aphrodite met her lover Adonis, who stopped by the spring to quench his thirst. It is said that bathing in this spot restores youth, but sadly people are no longer allowed in the water.

Walking trails lead from the front of the Cyprus Tourism Organization (CTO) pavilion through the Akamas peninsula. The trails of Aphrodite, Adonis or Smigies will take you to the most interesting corners of the northwestern tip *(see pp60–61)*. Detailed descriptions of the trails can be found in the Nature Trails of the Akamas brochure published by the CTO.

Situated a few kilometres further west is another magnificent spring, the Fontana Amorosa (Fountain of Love). It was once believed that whoever took a sip of water from the spring would fall in love with the very first person they encountered afterwards.

Environs

On the way to the Baths of Aphrodite you will pass Latsi (also known as Latchi), a small

Akamas peninsula – the westernmost point of Cyprus

town with a fishing harbour. It was once a sponge-divers' harbour, and is now also the base for pleasure boats that offer tourist cruises along the Akamas peninsula. Latsi has numerous *pensions* and hotels; the harbour features several restaurants, where you can get tasty and inexpensive fish and seafood dishes. The town has pebble and coarse sand beaches.

⓬ Akamas Peninsula

Road Map A3. 18 km (11 miles) north of Agios Georgios.

Spring flowers

Stretching north of Agios Georgios and Pegeia is the wilderness of the Akamas peninsula. The hillsides and headlands form the island's last undeveloped frontier, a region of spectacular, rugged scenery, sandy coves, clear water and hillsides covered with thick woodlands of pine and juniper. Its name comes from the legendary Akamas, son of Theseus, who arrived here on his triumphant return from the Trojan War and founded the town of Akamatis. Archaeologists are still searching for this site.

The peninsula's westward plain has rocks jutting out of the arid landscape, which is overgrown with tangles of trees and bushes.

In the valleys and ravines the vegetation is lush due to more abundant water. The shoreline is characterized by steep cliffs dropping vertically into the sea, particularly around **Chrysochou Bay**.

Nowadays this area is practically deserted, inhabited only by wild animals and herds of goats, but this was not always so. In ancient times, the region had Greek towns, and later Roman and Byzantine towns, that bustled with life. On **Cape Drepano** you can see the ruins of a Roman harbour and a Byzantine basilica; in **Meleti Forest** you can visit the ruins of a Byzantine church and tombs carved in rocks; and in the **Agios Konon region** archaeologists have discovered an ancient settlement. The Roman settlement, which once stood on the shores of Tyoni Bay, is now submerged in water.

The only way to travel around the wild countryside of Akamas is by a four-wheel-drive vehicle or by a cruise along the coast from **Latsi**.

The westernmost point of the peninsula, and of the entire island, is **Cape Arnaoutis**, where you can see an unmanned lighthouse and the wreck of a ship that ran aground. The cape is a magnet for divers, who will find vertical crags and caves where octopuses hide; fantastic arch-shaped rocks; or even come eye-to-eye with a barracuda.

The Baths of Aphrodite

Walking in the Akamas Peninsula

This is the wildest region of Cyprus, practically uninhabited and covered with forests. Its rich flora (over 500 species, including scores of orchid varieties) and fauna, the diverse geological features, the beautiful coastline and the legends and myths associated with this fascinating country make it a paradise for ramblers and nature lovers. The shortage of surfaced roads means that many places on the peninsula can be reached only on foot.

Locator Map

Bays
A challenging section of the Aphrodite trail hugs the peninsula's wild coastline. Here you'll find the most beautiful coves and deserted beaches.

Roads
Some sections of the trails run along dirt tracks; the best way to travel here is in a four-wheel-drive vehicle.

Caves
Water has carved many caves and rock niches in the lime rocks of the peninsula. These provide shelter for animals.

Rocks
Rocks, carved in fantastic shapes by wind and water, are a distinctive feature of the peninsula's landscape.

Baths of Aphrodite

Akamas

428 m

Neo Chorio
A stone church has survived here. There are plenty of places to stay in the village, as well as a few restaurants. To the south is the Petratis Gorge, famous for its bat grotto.

0 kilometres 2
0 miles 1

Lizards
Lizards, particularly the wall lizard, are common on the island. You may be lucky enough to encounter the Agana, the largest Cypriot lizard (30 cm/12 in long).

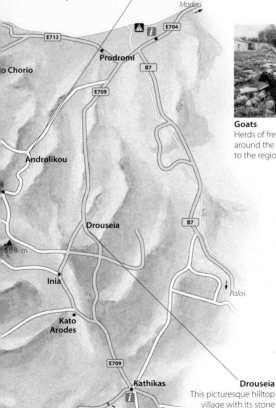

Goats
Herds of free-ranging goats wander around the peninsula, presenting a threat to the region's natural environment.

Morfou

E713
E704
Prodromi
B7
o Chorio
E709
Androlikou
Drouseia
B7
668 m
Inia
Pafos
Kato Arodes
E709
Kathikas
E711
682 m
E709
Pegeia
Pafos

Key
═══ Main road
─── Other road
••• 1. Aphrodite trail (7.5 km/4½ miles)
••• 2. Adonis trail (7.5 km/4½ miles)
••• 3. Smigies trail (7.5 km/4½ miles)
••• 4. Pissouromouttis trail (3 km/1.8 miles)
〰 5. Kathikas trail (2 km/1.2 miles)
     River

Drouseia
This picturesque hilltop village with its stone houses is increasingly popular among the expatriate community. There is a taverna and accommodation here.

For additional map symbols see back flap

The 16th-century church of Agios Andronikos in Polis

⑬ Polis

Road Map A3. 35 km (22 miles) north of Pafos. 🚌 645. 🏛 1,890. ℹ Vasileos Stasioikou 2, 26 322 468.

This small town, known as Polis Chrysochou (Town of the Golden Land), stands on the site of the ancient city-state of Marion, surrounded by extensive orange groves. Polis provides an excellent base for exploring the Akamas peninsula and the wilderness of Tilliria. In the centre of Polis is the 16th-century **Agios Andronikos** church, featuring some fine frescoes. Under Ottoman rule the church was turned into a mosque. The interior of the **Agios Rafael**, a Byzantine-style church, is decorated with colourful frescoes.

Polis is one of the most attractive and fastest-growing seaside resorts of Cyprus. Popular with both backpackers and families, it offers a range of apartment complexes and a handful of small hotels, along with several campsites, including one on the beach.

Environs
Close to the town are some of the most beautiful beaches on the island, including a sand and-pebble beach stretching eastwards along Chrysochou Bay, a 15-minute walk from Polis. There are also picturesque villages and interesting churches, including the 16th-century Agia Aikaterini and 15th-century Panagia Chorteni.

⑭ Marion

Road Map A3.

Founded in the 7th century BC by Greeks, the city-state of Marion was a major trading centre during the Classical and Hellenistic eras. It owed its rapid development to the nearby copper mines. In 315 BC Marion was destroyed by the Egyptian king, Ptolemy I Soter. His son, Ptolemy II, rebuilt Marion under the name Arsinoe, but the town never regained its former powerful status in terms of trading.

Up until now archaeologists have managed to unearth only a small portion of the ancient town, including a burial ground dating from the Hellenistic period. An interesting collection of artifacts discovered at the site can be seen in the **Marion-Arsinoe Archaeological Museum**. Of special note are the amphorae decorated with images of people, animals and birds, as well as with geometric patterns. Growing nearby to the museum is an olive tree, which is over 600 years old, and still bears fruit.

Carved decoration above the entrance to Agios Andronikos in Polis

🏛 Marion-Arsinoe Archaeological Museum
Polis. Leoforos Makariou III. **Tel** 26 322 955. **Open** 8am–2pm Mon, 8am–3pm Tue, Thu & Fri, 8am–5pm Wed, 9am–3pm Sat. 🖼

⑮ Panagia Chrysorrogiatissa

Road Map A3. 40 km (25 miles) northeast of Pafos, take a right turn before the village of Stroumpi. 1.5 km (1 mile) south of Pano Panagia. **Tel** 26 722 457. **Open** summer: 9:30am–12:30pm, 1:30–6:30pm daily; winter: 10am–12:30pm, 1:30–4pm daily. Donations welcome. 🖼 15 Aug.

In a beautiful setting 830 m (2,723 ft) above the sea, the Chrysorrogiatissa monastery is dedicated to "Our Lady of the Golden Pomegranate". It features an unusual triangular cloister built of reddish stone.

The monastery was founded in 1152 by Ignatius, who came across an icon with the image of the Virgin Mary. The Virgin appeared and told him to build a monastery. The icon is kept in a special casket. It was supposedly painted by St Luke the Evangelist. Several other icons are also stored here, the most famous being an 18th-century image of Mary and Jesus covered with a cloak. Other

Entrance to the historic Panagia Chrysorrogiatissa monastery

objects include old Bibles, sculptures, manuscripts and crosses. A small Byzantine museum sits on the premises.

Environs

The **Agia Moni** church, about 2 km (1.2 miles) from the monastery, is one of the oldest on the island. Dedicated to St Nicholas, it was built in the 4th century on the site of an old pagan temple of the goddess Hera.

Nearby **Pano Panagia** is the birthplace of Archbishop Makarios III, the statesman and politician, who was born here on 13 August 1913. In 1960 the Archbishop was elected president of the republic. He died on 3 August 1977 and was buried at Throni near Kykkos, overlooking his village.

🏛 Makarios' Family Home
Pano Panagia. **Open** daily (key available from info centre). Donations welcome.

Tomb of Archbishop Makarios at Throni above Pano Panagia

⑯ Xeros Valley

Road Map B4.

The Xeros river flows from the western slopes of the Troodos mountains through this scenic valley. The river initially flows through Pafos Forest and Cedar Valley *(see p92)*, which is the main home of the cedars of the local *cedrus brevifilia* species. The area, which has been declared a nature reserve, is also home to the moufflon.

A car is needed to explore the valley. Following the old road from Pafos, turn left in the village of Timi, opposite the airport, to reach **Asprokremmos** reservoir, a mecca for anglers, as it is fed by the Xeros river. The valley of Xeros (which in Greek

means "dry") was devastated by the tragic earthquake of 1953. At the heart of the valley, away from the main roads, is the abandoned stone **Panagia tou Sinti** monastery. It can be reached via local roads from the village of Pentalia or Agia Marina. Further on, the road leads through hillside villages and vineyards.

Beyond the village of Vretsia the road steadily deteriorates, but after driving for a few more kilometres you can cross the Xeros river near the historic Venetian **bridge of Roudia**. The deserted village of **Peravasa** marks the start of the road leading south, towards the scenic Diarizos river valley.

⑰ Diarizos Valley

Road Map B3.

Greener and better irrigated than the arid Xeros valley, the Diarizos valley is studded with medieval churches, farming villages and arched Venetian bridges. The clear-flowing river trickles southwest and, like the Xeros, feeds the Asprokremmos reservoir.

The village of **Nikokleia**, near Kouklia *(see p48)*, is an ancient settlement named in honour of King Nikokles, who transferred his capital to what is now Kato Pafos. The village is scenically located on the banks of the river. The old church contains

Sheep in the Diarizos Valley

fascinating icons. On the opposite side of the river, near the village of Souskiou, archaeologists unearthed a Chalcolithic settlement. In it they found pendants and figurines, as well as statues and ancient tombs. In the village of Agios Georgios are rock tombs.

Further northeast are the remains of a former monastery, **Agios Savvas tis Karonos**, built in the early 12th century and restored by the Venetians.

Above Kithasi the road climbs upwards and the views become increasingly beautiful. On the left side of the road is the restored church of **Agios Antonios**. The church in Praitori houses 16th-century icons. Above the village, the road climbs towards the resort of **Platres** and the peaks of the Troodos mountains.

The arid Xeros valley, a scenic, rugged nature reserve

SOUTHERN CYPRUS

The southern region of Cyprus features Neolithic settlements and ancient towns, medieval castles and monasteries, and the island's most beautiful beaches, around Agia Napa. Other attractions include charming hilltop villages and the ports of Limassol and Larnaka. The region is full of reminders of famous past visitors to Cyprus, including Zeno of Kition, Saint Helena, Richard the Lionheart and Leonardo da Vinci.

The coast from Pissouri to Protaras is famous for its beautiful scenery and historic sites. It has the largest ports on the island and many crowded beaches, but just a short distance inland life flows at a gentle, lazy pace.

This southern region was the site of powerful city-states, including Kition (present-day Larnaka), Kourion – of which only magnificent ruins are left – and Amathous.

Among the oldest traces of man on Cyprus are the Neolithic settlements around Choirokoitia and Kalavasos. There are reminders of subsequent settlers, too. There was a Phoenician presence at Kition; there are temples and stadia attesting to the Greek presence;

and villas and theatres from the Romans. The Byzantine legacy includes mosaics in vast basilicas, churches with beautiful murals, and monasteries – including the mountain-top Stavrovouni monastery and the cat-filled St Nicholas monastery on the Akrotiri peninsula.

The medieval castle in Limassol was used by the Crusaders; Richard the Lionheart married Berengaria of Navarre and crowned her Queen of England here; and from the Gothic castle in Kolossi knights oversaw the production of wine and sugar cane. A reminder of the Arab raids is the tomb of the Prophet's aunt at the Hala Sultan Tekke, on the shores of the salt lake near Larnaka. The lake itself attracts flamingoes, swans and pelicans.

Scenic village of Kato Lefkara

◀ The popular Nissi beach in Agia Napa

Exploring Southern Cyprus

The best-preserved ancient town in Southern Cyprus is the Greco-Roman Kourion, with a beautifully located theatre, interesting mosaics, baths, a Byzantine stadium and the nearby Sanctuary of Apollo Ylatis. The best beaches for swimming and sunbathing are in Agia Napa and Protaras, with their enchanting clear water and lovely sandy beaches. They also offer the greatest number of attractions for young people. When exploring this part of the island be sure to visit Lefkara, a charming Cypriot village where women produce beautiful lace by hand and men make silver jewellery. Nature lovers often head for the salt lakes around Limassol and Larnaka, and are rewarded with the sight of hundreds of birds.

Stavrovouni monastery, founded by St Helena, mother of Constantine the Great

Sights at a Glance

1. Cape Aspro
2. Sanctuary of Apollo Ylatis
3. *Kourion pp70–81*
4. Kolossi
5. Agios Nikolaos ton Gaton (St Nicholas of the Cats)
6. Akrotiri Peninsula
7. *Limassol (Lemesos) pp72–7*
8. Amathous
9. Agios Georgios Alamanos
10. Kalavasos
11. Choirokoitia
12. Agios Minas
13. Lefkara
14. Pyrga
15. Stavrovouni Monastery
16. Kiti
17. Hala Sultan Tekke
18. *Larnaka pp82–5*
19. Kellia
20. Agia Napa
21. Cape Gkreko
22. Protaras

Doorway of Panagia Chrysopolitissa church in Larnaka

Getting There

Most visitors to Cyprus arrive by air, and the biggest airport in the southern part of the island is outside Larnaka, serving a number of international flights. Motorways provide fast and safe travel links with Limassol and Agia Napa, as well as with Nicosia and Pafos. Alternatively, you can travel to Limassol by ship from Piraeus (Greece), Egypt, Israel, and Lebanon. Most of the historic sites of Limassol and Larnaka are best explored on foot. Public transport in the form of buses and taxis between major cities is good, but to reach smaller or more distant places a rental car is the best option for exploring Southern Cyprus.

The craggy coastline of Cape Gkreko

Key

- Motorway
- Major road
- Minor road
- Scenic route
- Track
- Regional border
- Green Line

For additional map symbols see back flap

❶ Cape Aspro

Road Map B4. 4 km (2½ miles) south of Pissouri.

Cape Aspro is the highest point along the virtually deserted coast that stretches from Kourion to Pafos. Most of the coast along this, the southernmost point of the island (excluding the Akrotiri Peninsula), is as flat as a pancake. Towering over the cape is the **Trachonas Hill**, which affords magnificent views over Episkopi Bay, the southern slopes of the Troodos mountains, the small town of Pissouri and the monastery church Moni Prophitis Ilias.

The area around **Pissouri** is famous for its orchards and vineyards; the fertile lime soil yields abundant crops of sweet grapes. The modern amphitheatre, which was built in 2000 with seating for a thousand people, affords a beautiful view over the sea and the southern coast. During the summer, plays and concerts are staged here.

The town of Pissouri has some good accommodation options, ranging from little inns to luxurious hotels; there are also several rustic tavernas that offer typical local cuisine.

The rugged coastal cliffs rise to a height of 180 m (590 ft). They can be seen very clearly from the air, as planes usually approach Pafos airport from this direction. To the east of Cape Aspro is the pleasant and clean sandy-pebbly Pissouri beach with its clear, blue water.

Ruins of the Sanctuary of Apollo Ylatis near Kourion

❷ Sanctuary of Apollo Ylatis

Road Map B4. 3 km (2 miles) west of Kourion. **Tel** 25 934 250. **Open** 8:30am–7:30pm daily (to 5pm winter). ♿

In ancient times the Sanctuary of Apollo Ylatis (also known as Hylates) was an important shrine. Stone fragments and toppled columns mark the site of this 7th-century BC shrine to the sun god Apollo in his role as "Ylatis", or god of the woods and forests. The present ruins date from early Roman times. It was in use until the 4th century AD, when Emperor Theodosius the Great declared a battle against pagans.

The sanctuary was surrounded by a holy garden, containing laurel trees, myrtle and palms, and was home to deer. When pilgrims arrived through the Curium and Pafian gates, they placed votive offerings by the residence of the Great Priests, which were then sent to the treasury. When the treasury became full, the priests stored the offerings (tavissae) in a nearby holy well. This hiding place was discovered centuries later by archaeologists, and the ancient offerings can be seen at the Kourion Archaeological Museum at Episkopi and in the Cyprus Museum in Nicosia.

Close by were baths and a *palaestra* (gymnasium), surrounded by a colonnaded portico and used as a venue for wrestling. Standing in one corner of the *palaestra* is a fragment of a large clay jug, which was used for storing water for the athletes. The remaining buildings of the complex include storehouses and pilgrims' dormitories.

The former pilgrims' inn marked the start of the holy procession route leading to the sanctuary. At the heart of the sanctuary there was a small temple with a pillared portico, devoted to Apollo. As reported by the ancient geographer Strabo, any unauthorized person who touched the altar was hurled from it to the sea, to placate Apollo. The front of the temple, with its two columns, a fragment of the wall and tympanum, has been partially reconstructed.

Earthquakes, the spread of Christianity and Arab raids all played a role in destroying the sanctuary, and now all that remains are the romantic ruins.

Some 500 m (546 yards) east of the sanctuary is a large, well-preserved Roman stadium that could hold 6,000 spectators. Pentathlon events – consisting of running, long jump, discus- and javelin-throwing, and wrestling – were staged here. The athletes appeared naked, and only men were allowed to watch. In the 4th century the stadium was closed, regarded as a symbol of paganism.

The craggy coast of Cape Aspro

❸ Kourion

See pp70–71.

❹ Kolossi

Road Map B4. 14 km (9 miles) west of Limassol. 🚌 17. **Tel** 25 934 907. **Open** 8:30am–7:30pm daily (to 5pm winter). 🐾

The best-preserved medieval castle in Cyprus is situated south of the village of Kolossi. In 1210 the land passed to the hands of the Knights of St John of Jerusalem, who built a castle here to be used as the Grand Master's headquarters.

At the turn of the 14th and 15th centuries the castle was sacked several times by the Genoese and Muslims.

Kolossi Castle in its present shape was built in 1454 by the Grand Master, Louis de Magnac. It is a three-storey structure, laid out on a square plan, 23 m (75 ft) high with walls over 2.5 m (8 ft) thick. Entry is via a drawbridge, with the entrance further guarded by a machicolation above the gate, which permitted the pouring of boiling water, oil or melted tar over attackers.

The entrance led to the dining room, whose walls were once covered with paintings. You can still see a scene of the Crucifixion with Louis de Magnac's coat of arms underneath. The adjacent room used to be the castle kitchen; stores were kept on the lower floor, and above were the living quarters; you can see stone fireplaces and windows. A narrow staircase leads to the flat roof surrounded by battlements. From here it was possible to supervise the work on the plantations and in the vineyards, and to spot enemy ships in the

The medieval Kolossi Castle, used by the Knights of Jerusalem

distance. Next to the castle is a large vaulted stone building, once a sugar refinery. To the north are the remains of a mill, formerly used for grinding the sugar, and the small 13th-century church of St Eustace, used as the castle chapel by the Knights Templar and the Knights of St John of Jerusalem.

❺ Agios Nikolaos ton Gaton (St Nicholas of the Cats)

Road Map B4. Cape Gata, 12 km (7½ miles) from the centre of Limassol. **Tel** 25 952 621. **Open** 8am–5pm daily.

The monastery of Agios Nikolaos ton Gaton stands on the Akrotiri peninsula, between the salt lake and the military airport. According to tradition it was founded by St Helena, mother of Constantine the Great, who visited Cyprus while returning from the Holy Land. Appalled by the plague of snakes, she sent a ship full of cats to the island to deal with them. The monks fed the cats and rallied them to fight by the

ringing of the bell. Another reference to the cats is the naming of the nearby Cape Gata – the Cape of Cats.

The monastery was founded in 325, but the buildings we see now are the result of remodelling that occurred during the 14th century. At the heart of the monastery is an old church with Gothic walls and Latin coats of arms above the entrance. Candles inside the dark church illuminate the gilded iconostasis and the elongated faces on the icons, which appear to come to life.

A small section of the salt lake on the Akrotiri peninsula

❻ Akrotiri Peninsula

Road Map B4. 🚌 22.

Akrotiri is the southernmost point of Cyprus. Most of the peninsula is occupied by a sovereign British base – Akrotiri-Episkopi, which includes an air force base and a radio communications station. This base, along with a second one at Ohekelia, is a relic of the island's colonial past, when Cyprus was governed by the British.

The central part of the peninsula is occupied by a salt lake (one of the two on the island), a vantage point for watching water birds including swans, flamingoes and pelicans. Running along the east coast is the wide beach known as Lady's Mile, which was named after a mare used by an English army officer for his regular morning ride.

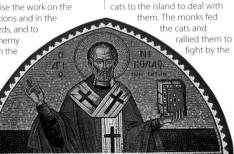

Image of St Nicholas of the Cats

❸ Kourion

Ancient Kourion (or Curium) was a major centre of cultural, political and religious life. It was home to the centuries-old site of the Sanctuary of Apollo and later the seat of a Christian bishop. Perched on a bluff, the town was founded in the 12th century BC by Mycenaean Greeks, and was a large centre in the days of the Ptolemies and the Romans. Its trump card was its defensive location, and the control it wielded over the surrounding fertile land. Kourion was destroyed by two catastrophic earthquakes in the early 4th century.

Achilles' House
This takes its name from the 4th-century mosaic discovered inside the colonnade.

Baptistry and Bishop's Palace
Adjacent to the basilica and close to the bishop's palace was a large baptistry. Its remains include floor mosaics and some columns.

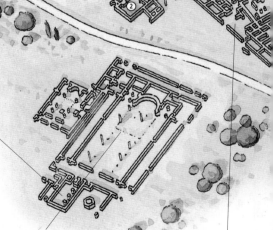

Basilica
The impressive triple-aisle building, erected in the 5th century AD on the site of a pagan temple, was destroyed by Arabs.

Nymphaeum
This imposing complex of stone fountains was built close to the public baths, on the spot where the aqueduct brought water to the city of Kourion.

For hotels and restaurants in this region see pp162–3 and pp171–3

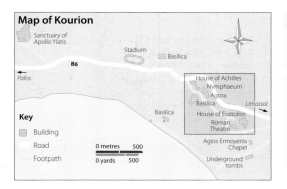

Map of Kourion

Sanctuary of Apollo Ylatis

Stadium

Basilica

B6

Pafos

Basilica

House of Achilles
Nymphaeum
Agora
Basilica
House of Eustolios
Roman Theatre

Limassol

Agios Ermoyenis Chapel

Underground tombs

Key

☐ Building

Road

Footpath

| 0 metres | 500 |
| 0 yards | 500 |

VISITORS' CHECKLIST

Practical Information
Road Map B4. Kourion
Archaeological Museum:
19 km (12 miles) west of
Limassol. 🚌 16 from Limassol.
Tel 25 934 250. **Open** 8:30am–
7:30pm daily (to 5pm winter).
🚻 Sanctuary of Apollo
Ylatis: 3 km (2 miles) west
of Kourion. **Tel** 25 934 250.
Open 8:30am–7:30pm daily
(to 5pm winter). 🚻

Roman Theatre
The theatre, built in the 2nd century BC, enjoys a magnificent location overlooking the sea as well as boasting excellent acoustics.

Baths
These baths form part of the House of Eustolios, a late 4th-century AD private residence. The best mosaic depicts Ktissis as a woman holding a Roman measure, a personification of architectural art.

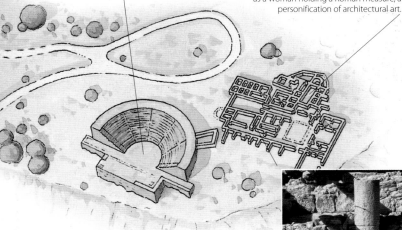

House of Eustolios
Built in the early Christian period, this house had some 30 rooms arranged around a colonnaded courtyard with mosaic floors. The inscription by the entrance reads: "Step in and bring happiness to this house".

KEY

① **The House of the Gladiators** was so named after the discovery of two mosaics depicting gladiator fights.

② **Public baths**

🅐 Limassol (Lemesos)

Limassol is a major centre of trade, business and tourism, and has the biggest harbour in southern Cyprus. It is probably the most fun-filled city on Cyprus in terms of the number of fairs and festivals held here. The year starts with a riotous carnival; May marks the Flower Festival; and September brings the famous Wine Festival. Hotels, restaurants and nightclubs are clustered mainly along the beach.

Strolling along the seaside promenade

Exploring Limassol

It is best to start from the medieval castle, the town's most interesting historic site. Nearby is the Carob Museum, where visitors can learn about this important Cypriot export. A covered bazaar and a mosque are also close by.

The area has many restaurants with Cypriot and international cuisine, bars and cafés. From here it is not far to the new Limassol Marina, the latest tourist attraction in the town. You can enjoy an extended walk along the seaside promenade, passing the Orthodox Agia Napa cathedral. Just inland from here, is the main shopping street, Aiou

Andreou, which runs parallel to the coast.

🏛 Central Market
Saripolou, in the old district near the town hall. **Open** 6am–2pm Mon–Sat.

The Central Market, housed in an arcaded building dating from the British era in the early 20th century, is a great place to shop for handmade reed baskets, olive oil, *loukoumia* (Cyprus delight) and other Cypriot delicacies, as well as fruits, vegetables, cheeses and meats. The stone market hall, its roof supported by metal pillars, is of particular note, featuring two arched gates with Doric columns. The market is surrounded by restaurants and cafés serving local and international cuisine. The stone-paved front square is used as a venue for shows and fairs.

🏛 Cyprus Handicraft Centre
Themidos 25. **Tel** 25 305 118. **Open** 7:30am–2:30pm Mon–Fri (also 3–6pm Thu except Jul–Aug).

At this centre you can buy locally made gifts and souvenirs, including jewellery, lace, ceramics, mosaics and wood carvings produced by Cypriot craftspeople using traditional methods.

All stock is government-vetted and the fixed prices offer a good gauge of how much visitors should spend on products elsewhere.

🏛 Town Hall
Archiepiskopou Kyprianou.
Ⓦ limassolmunicipal.com.cy

The town hall is situated in the centre of Limassol, on a narrow street opposite the post office and near Agia Napa Cathedral. It was built to a design by the German architect Benjamin Gunzburg, based on the ancient Greek style of civic architecture.

🏛 Agios Andronikos Church
Agiou Andreou. 🕑 6:30pm (summer), 4:30pm (winter) Sat; prayers Sun (times vary).

The Church of Agios Andronikos and Athanosis (in Greek *athanosis* means immortality) was built in the 1870s in Neo-Byzantine style. For a while it served as the town's cathedral. The church is accessible only from the waterfront. It is separated from the sea by the promenade, near the Agia Napa Cathedral.

Town Hall, dating from colonial times

Seaside Promenade

Perfect for an evening stroll, Limassol's palm-fringed promenade stretches for nearly 3 km (2 miles) along the shoreline, starting at the old harbour and continuing eastward towards St Catherine's Church. It is lined with well-kept greenery and benches, from where you can admire the seascape and watch the ships awaiting entry to the harbour.

🏛 Agia Napa Cathedral
Genethliou Mitella.

On the fringe of Limassol's old quarter, this vast Byzantine-style structure was built in the early 20th century on the ruins of a Byzantine church. It was consecrated in 1906,

Colourful stalls of fruit and vegetables at the Central Market

The Orthodox cathedral of Agia Napa

and today it serves as Limassol's Orthodox cathedral.

This large stone church, sporting a twin-tower façade, is covered with a dome resting on a tambour over the intersection of the nave with the transept.

The cathedral was consecrated with the veil of St Veronica, with the imprinted image of Christ's face (the *veraikon*).

C Grand Mosque

Genethliou Mitella. **Open** times vary. Donations welcome.

The area around the harbour and castle was once inhabited mainly by Turks, and there are some remaining Turkish inscriptions and street names. The Grand Mosque – Cami Kebir – is still used by the handful of Turkish Cypriots in the city, and by Muslim visitors. The city's largest mosque is squeezed between old buildings behind the Turkish Bazaar.

Limassol Castle
See pp76–7.

Carob Museum
Vasilissis 1, by Limassol Castle. **Tel** 25 342 123. **Open** daily (times vary so call ahead). **w** antisfoundation.org

This museum is located in a renovated former mill close to the medieval castle, in an area that is known for its art exhibitions and stylish cafés.

The Carob Museum shows how the carob is harvested, what it is used for and its relevance to the island's economy. The carob can be used in the production of honey, sweets and chocolate. Derivatives are also used for making paper,

The Grand Mosque with its distinctive pointed minaret

photographic filmplates and medicines. Historic machinery used to store and process the fruit is displayed alongside utensils and useful information.

Rialto Theatre
Andrea Drousioti 19, Heroes Square. **Tel** 77 777 745.

Located at the centre of Heroes Square, the Rialto Theatre hosts film shows, plays, dance and music performances. It serves as the venue for a number of events held throughout the year such as the European Dance Festival, the International Short Film Festival of Cyprus, and concerts featuring international musicians. During summer, the Cyprus Rialto World Music Festival takes place outside the building.

Limassol Town Centre

① Central Market
② Cyprus Handicraft Centre
③ Town Hall
④ Agios Andronikos Church
⑤ Seaside Promenade
⑥ Agia Napa Cathedral
⑦ Grand Mosque
⑧ Limassol Castle
⑨ Carob Museum
⑩ Rialto Theatre

0 metres 400
0 yards 400

For key to symbols *see back flap*

Artifacts in the Archaeological Museum

Further Afield

Outside the city centre are a number of sights worth visiting, including St Catherine's Catholic Church, the Municipal Gardens and mini-zoo, the District Archaeological Museum and Folk Art Museum, as well as a theatre, municipal art gallery and – among the best of the local attractions – the wineries. Stretching beyond the municipal beach to the east is the extensive tourist zone, with dozens of hotels, tavernas, pubs, restaurants, souvenir shops and clubs.

⛪ St Catherine's Catholic Church

28 Oktovriou 259. **Tel** 25 362 946.
⛪ 6:30pm daily (English & Greek);
8am (Greek), 9:30am (Greek), 11am
(Latin) & 6:30pm (English) Sun.

This twin-tower church stands opposite the beach, near the end of Limassol's palm-lined promenade. Consecrated in 1879, it is one of several Catholic churches in this part of the island.

🏛 District Archaeological Museum

At the junction of Kanningos and Vyronos, next to the Municipal Gardens. **Tel** 25 305 157. **Open** 8am–4pm Mon–Fri. ♿

At the entrance to this museum is a mosaic depicting the bath of Eros and Aphrodite. The museum's collection includes artifacts found in excavations of the ancient city-states of Kourion and Amathous, as well as Neolithic tools and jewellery.

The highlights of the collection are the statue of the Egyptian god Bes – the god of harvest depicted in the guise of a dwarf; the statue of Hathor, Egyptian goddess of heaven, music and dance; the statue of Zeus discovered at Amathous; and the head of Zeus from Fasoula, carved from limestone. Other exhibits include collections of glass and terracotta artifacts.

🏛 Municipal Gardens and Mini-Zoo

28 Oktovriou, on the seafront.
Open summer: 9am–7pm; winter: 9am–4pm. ♿

The charming Municipal Gardens contain ponds and fountains. Shaded by trees, they are full of exotic greenery and flowers. The gardens include an amphitheatre and a small zoo and aviary. The zoo, following a redesign, looks more like a park than a traditional zoo. It consists of farm animals from Cyprus. In early September the Municipal Gardens become the venue for the famous Wine Festival. As well as grape-trampling and folk dances, the crowds are treated to free wine from local producers.

🏛 Folk Art Museum

Agiou Andreou 253. **Tel** 25 362 303.
Open 8:30am–2:30pm daily. ♿
The Folk Art museum is housed in an attractive historic building dating from 1924. Arranged over six rooms is a good collection of 19th- and 20th-century Cypriot folk art.

The exhibition includes country tools, domestic utensils, wooden chests, traditional folk costumes, jewellery, tapestries and handcrafted products such as net curtains, bedding and bedspreads, which were traditionally stored in *sentoukia* – decorative trunks used as a bride's dowry.

Costume from the Folk Art Museum

🏛 Cyprus Wine Museum

Pafos St 42, Erimi. **Tel** 25 873 808.
Open 9am–5pm daily.
🌐 cypruswinemuseum.com
Wine-growing is a long-established tradition in Limassol, which is dotted with vineyards and wineries. The popular sweet dessert wine, Commandaria, is produced in 14 villages in the area. The wine museum offers an ideal opportunity for visitors to learn about the history of Cyprus wine. It is located in Erimi, which initiated the cultivation of grapes and wine production in Europe over 5,500 years ago.

Housed in a restored inn that served as a meeting point for wine merchants from the villages of Limassol and Pafos, the museum exhibits old photographs, documents and audio-visual presentations as well as ancient jars and vases,

The leafy, pleasantly shaded Municipal Gardens

For hotels and restaurants in this region see pp162–3 and pp171–3

medieval drinking vessels and instruments that were used in the wine-making process. There is also a good collection of the different Commandaria wines produced in Cyprus.

Pattichion Theatre

Agias Zonis. **Tel** 25 343 341.

Musicals, drama and ballet productions are staged at the Pattichion, the oldest theatre in Limassol. The theatre was purchased by the Nicos and Despina Pattichi Foundation, then rebuilt and reopened in 1986. It is sponsored by the Limassol Municipality.

The theatre holds up to 760 people; backstage there are dressing rooms for 80 artists. The Pattichion theatre has hosted the Vienna Philharmonic Orchestra, the Athens Chamber Music Ensemble, the Vivaldi Orchestra from Moscow and Jazz Art Ballet from Paris.

Municipal Art Gallery

28 Oktovriou 103. **Tel** 25 586 212. **Open** 7:30am–2:30pm Mon–Fri.

The Municipal Art Gallery houses works by Cypriot painters, including early artists such as Diamantis, Kashialos (whose famous work *Chariot Drawn by Two Donkeys* is displayed), Kanthos and Frangoudis. Contemporary painters are also represented. The gallery, designed by Benjamin Gunzburg (who also designed the Town Hall), was built in the 1930s.

Lady's Mile beach and the new harbour in Limassol

Fasouri Watermania Waterpark

Near Trahoni village, Limassol–Pafos Road. **Tel** 25 714 235. **Open** May–Oct: 10am–5pm daily (to 6pm Jun–Aug). **fasouri-watermania.com**

This popular water park has many water attractions including swimming pools, slides and artificial waves. Great for families and kids of all ages.

New Port

4 km (2½ miles) west of city centre. **Tel** 25 819 200. 30.

The New Port in Limassol is the largest in Cyprus. It was enlarged after 1974, when Famagusta port fell under Turkish occupation. Besides the commercial port, it includes a terminal for passenger ferries as well as cruise ships.

The old harbour, situated near Limassol castle, is now used by fishing boats and pleasure craft. The modern yachting marina at the St Raphael resort, is situated around 12 km (7½ miles) east of the city centre, in the tourist zone, near Amathous.

Beaches

Although long and wide, the municipal beach in Limassol is not among the island's most attractive beaches; it is covered with compressed soil and pebbles, and is located near a busy street.

Better beaches can be found further afield. Beyond the new harbour, in the eastern part of the Akrotiri peninsula, is Lady's Mile – a long and relatively quiet sandy beach (see p69). To the west, about 17 km (10½ miles) from the city centre, Kourion beach enjoys a lovely location at the foot of the hill where ancient Kourion once stood. You can reach it by public transport from Limassol. Avdimou beach, a further 12 km (7½ miles) along, has nice sand and a pleasant restaurant, although no shade.

The most pleasant sandy beach is found near Pissouri, some 44 km (27 miles) from Limassol. Here you can hire a deck chair and an umbrella, and nearby are several pleasant tavernas and restaurants.

The pre-war building of the Municipal Art Gallery

King Richard the Lionheart

The English king, famed for his courage, was passing near Cyprus on his way to the Crusades when a storm blew one of his ships, carrying his sister and fiancée, to the shore. The ruler of Cyprus, the Byzantine Prince Isaac Komnenos, imprisoned both princesses and the crew. The outraged Richard the Lionheart landed with his army on the island, smashed the Komnenos army, imprisoned Komnenos and occupied Cyprus. In May 1191, in the chapel of Limassol Castle, he married Princess Berengaria. Soon afterwards he sold the island to the Knights Templar.

English king Richard the Lionheart

Limassol Castle

This stronghold at the centre of the Old Town, near the harbour, was built by the Lusignan princes on foundations erected by the Byzantines. Later Venetian, Ottoman and British occupiers strengthened its defences. In 1191 the castle chapel was the venue for the wedding of Richard the Lionheart to Princess Berengaria of Navarre. The Ottomans later rebuilt the castle as a prison. During World War II it served as British army headquarters. Nowadays it houses the Medieval Museum.

Castle Roof
The flat, stone roof of Limassol Castle was once used by its defenders. Today visitors come here to admire the panoramic view – the best in town.

The Reliefs
The section of the museum devoted to Byzantine art houses not only numerous beautiful reliefs and mosaics from the oldest Christian basilicas, but also a number of religious icons.

Grape Press
This grape press is among the stone artifacts in the castle gardens.

Knights' Hall
The first-floor hall, in the south wing of Limassol Castle, houses two suits of armour and a collection of rare antique coins.

Main Hall
The Main Hall houses a large collection of Byzantine, Gothic and Renaissance sculptures, carvings and reliefs. Among them are carved images of the Lusignan kings from the portal of Agia Sofia Cathedral.

Main Lobby
Leading to the most opulent room, the lobby houses sculptures and coats of arms as well as photographs of Gothic and Renaissance architecture.

Fragment of a Portal
This fragment from Agia Napa Cathedral forms part of the medieval stonemasonry exhibits in the museum collection.

Sarcophagi Chamber
A chamber hidden in the shadowy recesses of the castle contains a collection of sarcophagi and tombstones.

Main Entrance
The castle is entered through a small bastion located on the east side of the castle.

The ruins of ancient Amathous, scenically located along the coast

❽ Amathous

Road Map C4. 12 km (7½ miles) east of Limassol city centre. ⬛ 30. **Open** 8am–5pm daily (to 6pm Apr, May, Sep & Oct; to 7:30pm Jun–Aug). 🖼

Located on a high hill east of Limassol are the stone remains of the ancient port of Amathous. Named after its legendary founder Amathus, son of Aerias and king of Pafos, this once major commercial centre was founded between the 10th and 8th centuries BC.

Amathous was the first of the island's city-states. Over the centuries it was inhabited by Greeks, Phoenicians, Egyptians and Jews.

After the arrival of Christianity on Cyprus, St Tychon founded a church here and became the first bishop of Amathous. He became the patron saint of the town.

The town existed until the 7th century AD when, together with other coastal centres, it was destroyed in Arab raids.

In later times the site was used as a quarry; huge stones were transported to Egypt for use in the construction of the Suez Canal. The American consul (and amateur archaeologist) Luigi Palma di Cesnola destroyed large areas of the city while treasure-hunting.

The best-preserved part is the agora (marketplace), with a dozen remaining columns. In the north section are parts of the aqueduct system and the site of a bath house. Standing on top of the hill was the acropolis, with temples to Aphrodite and Hercules, the remains of which can still be seen. Close by, archaeologists have unearthed the ruins of an early Christian, 5th-century Byzantine basilica. Fragments of powerful defence walls can be seen on the opposite side of the road.

The coastal part of the town collapsed during an earthquake. Its ruins stretch a great distance into the sea.

Large stone vessel from Amathous

❾ Agios Georgios Alamanos

Road Map C4.

The buildings of the Agios Georgios Alamanos monastery can be seen from the Nicosia–Limassol motorway. Although the monastery, just like the new Byzantine-style church, is not of great architectural merit, it is interesting to watch the local monks painting icons.

In the nearby village of Pentakomo, on the opposite side of the motorway, are surviving stone houses. Close to the church is a pleasant café, where there are occasional concerts and plays.

❿ Kalavasos

Road Map C4. 40 km (25 miles) from Larnaka, 1.5 km (1 mile) from exit 15 on the motorway. ⬛ 95 from Limassol, 401 from Larnaka.

Up until the 1970s the inhabitants of this village were involved in mining copper ore from the neighbouring mountains. A symbol of this industrial past is the local steam engine, which was once used here. The Cyprus Agrotourism Company has restored some of the houses for the use of tourists.

Environs
Close by archaeologists have unearthed the Neolithic settlement of **Tenta**. Smaller than the neighbouring Choirokoitia, part of it is covered by a huge tent. The settlement, which was encircled by a defensive wall, featured a roundhouse and beehive huts built from clay and stone.

The nearby village of **Tochni** is one of the most popular agrotourism sites in Cyprus. Situated in a valley, amid olive trees and vineyards, the peaceful village is built around a small church. Picturesque narrow alleys lead to stone houses.

The Neolithic settlement of Tenta

⓫ Choirokoitia

Road Map C4. 40 km (25 miles) from
Limassol, 1.5 km (1 mile) from exit
14 on the motorway. 🚌 401, 402,
403 from Larnaka. **Tel** 24 322 710.
Open Apr, May, Sep & Oct: 8am–6pm
daily; Jun–Aug: 8am–7:30pm daily;
Nov–Mar: 8am–5pm daily. 🚫

In the village of Choirokoitia,
close to the motorway that runs
between Limassol and Nicosia,
archaeologists discovered the
ruins of a large Neolithic
settlement surrounded by a
stone wall. One of the oldest
settlements in Cyprus, it existed
as early as 6800 BC.

It was sited on the slope of a
hill, close to the river Maroni. Its
inhabitants, who numbered
close to 2,000 at the peak of its
development, lived in beehive
huts built of stone and clay.
Many of the houses unearthed
by archaeologists contained
under-floor graves with gifts
and personal effects. The
dead were laid to rest in an
embryonic position, with heavy
stones placed on their chests to
prevent them from returning
to the world of the living.

The population of
Choirokoitia formed a well-
organized farming community.
They cultivated the fertile local
soil, hunted, bred goats, spun
and weaved, and produced clay
figurines and other objects. The
artifacts uncovered at this site
include flint sickle blades, stone
vases and primitive triangular
fertility gods. The women wore
beautiful necklaces made of
shells or imported red cornelian.

The foundations of several
dozens of houses have been
unearthed. Some of these have
been reconstructed, providing
a glimpse into how the earliest
Cypriots lived. Many of the items
found here are exhibited in the
Cyprus Museum in Nicosia.

The settlement was
abandoned suddenly, and then
repopulated around 4500 BC.
These later inhabitants
introduced clay pots, some of
which have been unearthed.
The Choirokoitia archaeological
site has been declared a
UNESCO World Cultural and
Natural Heritage Site.

Lefkara's Lace and Silverware Museum

⓬ Agios Minas

Road Map C4. Close to Lefkara.
Tel 24 342 952. **Open** May–Sep: 8am–
noon, 3–5pm daily; Oct–Apr: 8am–
noon, 2–5pm daily.

Agios Minas, a small monastery
located in a scenic mountain
setting, was founded in the 15th
century and renovated in the
mid-18th century. Subsequently
abandoned, it was taken by a
convent in 1965. The nuns are
involved in painting icons,
growing flowers and fruit, and
keeping bees. They sell the
delicious honey.

The 15th-century convent
church, which was built by the
Dominicans, features wall
frescoes depicting St George
slaying the dragon and the
martyrdom of St Minas.

Environs
The nearby village of **Vavla** has
lovely stone houses, some of
which are being renovated for
use by tourists.

⓭ Lefkara

Road Map C4. 40 km
(25 miles) from Larnaka.
🚌 405 from Larnaka.

This village, set amid
picturesque white
limestone hills (*lefka ori*
means white hills), is
famous for the lace-
making skills of its
womenfolk. In the Middle
Ages, Lefkara was a health
resort visited by Venetian
ladies. While staying here
they busied themselves
with embroidery, which
they taught the local
women. One story tells
of Leonardo da Vinci
supposedly coming to
the island in 1481 to
order an altar cloth for Milan
cathedral. The lace patterns
are predominantly geometric,
with crosses or diamonds
and occasionally flowers,
birds or butterflies. While the
women busy themselves
with embroidery, the local
men produce jewellery and
other objects from silver
and gold.

The village buildings, with
their yellow walls and red roofs,
stand in attractive contrast with
the natural surroundings. At the
centre of Lefkara is the
16th-century Church of the
Holy Cross containing a carved
and gilded wood iconostasis
and a precious sacred relic –
a fragment of the True Cross
on which Christ was crucified.
The beautiful stone Patsalos
building houses the **Lace and
Silverware Museum**.

🏛 **Lace and Silverware Museum**
Pano Lefkara. **Tel** 24 342 326.
Open 9:30am–5pm daily. 🚫

Reconstructed houses at Choirokoitia archaeological site

⑭ Pyrga

Road Map D3. 35 km (22 miles) from Larnaka. 🚌 455 from Larnaka.

This village is home to the Gothic **Chapel of St Catherine**, also known as the "Chapelle Royal". Erected by the Lusignan king Janus for his wife Charlotte de Bourbon, the chapel is built of volcanic rock on a square floorplan. It has three doors and, on the altar wall, three Gothic windows. The interior features fragments of the original frescoes. These depict the *Crucifixion*, with King Janus and Queen Charlotte by the cross; the *Raising of Lazarus*; the *Last Supper*; and the Lusignan coats of arms.

Close by is the Marini river on whose banks in 1426 the Egyptian Mamelukes smashed the Cypriot army, capturing King Janus and taking him prisoner to Cairo. The king regained his freedom two years later, after a ransom was paid.

Environs
The village of **Kornos**, to the west, is famous for its oversized ceramic products, such as storage jars.

Gothic chapel of St Catherine in Pyrga

⑮ Stavrovouni Monastery

Road Map D3. 40 km (25 miles) from Larnaka, 9 km (5½ miles) from motorway. **Tel** 22 533 630. **Open** Apr–Aug: 8am–noon, 3–6pm daily; Sep–Mar: 7–11am, 2–5pm daily. 🚫 No women allowed 🎉 14 Sep.

Stavrovouni (Mountain of the Cross) monastery was built on a steep, 750-m (2,460-ft)

Agia Varvara (monastery of St Barbara) at the foot of Stavrovouni

mountain. In ancient times the mountain was called Olympus, and it was the site of a temple to Aphrodite. According to tradition, the monastery was founded in 327 by St Helena, mother of Constantine the Great. On her journey back from the Holy Land, where she found the True Cross of Christ, she stopped in Cyprus and left behind fragments of the precious relic. These can be seen in a large silver reliquary in the shape of a cross. Over the following centuries the monastery fell prey to enemy raids and earthquakes. In 1821, during the Greek independence uprising, it was burned to the ground by the Ottoman governor of Cyprus. The present monastery is the result of 19th-century restoration. The small **church** contains a lovely iconostasis and a wooden cross dating from 1476, carved with

scenes from the life of Jesus. Around the church are the monks' cells and other monastic quarters. The monastery houses a collection of monks' skulls, with the name of the deceased written on each forehead.

Today the monks produce exquisite cheeses and sultanas, and also keep honey bees.

At the foot of Stavrovouni is the **monastery of St Barbara** (Agia Varvara), known for the local monks' icon painting. Their most celebrated artist was Father Kallinikos *(see p24)*.

⑯ Kiti

Road Map D4. 7 km (4½ miles) southwest of Larnaka. **Open** church: 7am–6:45pm daily (from 9:30am Sun).

The **Panagia Angeloktisti** ("Built by Angels") church, in the northwestern end of the village of Kiti, consists of three parts. The first is the 14th-century Latin chapel with the coats of arms of knights above the entrance. The second part is the 11th-century dome-covered church, built on the ruins of an early Byzantine basilica, whose apse has been

The Stavrovouni monastery towering over the district

incorporated into the present building. The 6th-century apse mosaic is the church's main attraction. It depicts Mary holding the Christ Child, flanked by the Archangels Michael and Gabriel, with peacock-feather wings.

The third part of the church is a small 12th-century chapel dedicated to Saints Cosmas and Damian (patron saints of medicine) and decorated with 15th-century murals.

Environs
The 15th-century watchtower, 1 km (half a mile) from Kiti lighthouse, features a statue of a lion – the symbol of the Venetian Republic.

Panagia Angeloktisti church in the village of Kiti

⓱ Hala Sultan Tekke

Road Map D3. 5 km (3 miles) southwest of Larnaka. **Open** 8am–5pm daily (to 6pm Apr, May, Sep & Oct; to 7:30pm Jun–Aug).

On the shores of a salt lake, surrounded by cypress, palm and olive trees, the Hala Sultan Tekke is a major Muslim sanctuary. It includes an octagonal 1816 mosque built by the Ottoman governor of Cyprus, and a mausoleum with the tomb of Umm Haram.

Umm Haram, paternal aunt of the Prophet Mohammed, was killed after falling off a mule while accompanying her husband in a pillage raid on Kition in 649. The mosque has a modest interior and the mausoleum contains several sarcophagi covered with green cloths. After Mecca, Medina and Jerusalem, the Hala Sultan Tekke is among the holiest sites for Muslims.

To the west of the car park, archaeological excavations continue, unearthing a late-

Mosque and Hala Sultan Tekke mausoleum on the shores of the Salt Lake

Bronze Age town. Many items found here originated from Egypt and the Middle East.

Environs
The salt lake, close to the mosque, is one of two such lakes in Cyprus. In winter and early spring it provides a gathering point for thousands of flamingoes, swans, pelicans and other migrating water birds. The lake lies below sea level and in winter is filled with water seeping from the sea through the lime rocks. In summer it dries out, leaving a thick deposit of salt. Until the 1980s it yielded 3–5,000 tons of salt annually.

According to legend, the salt lake was created after Lazarus landed on this shore. Hungry and thirsty, he asked a local woman in the vineyard for a handful of fruit. She tersely refused to give him anything, so the saint, in revenge, turned her vineyard into a salt lake.

⓲ Larnaka
See pp82–5.

⓳ Kellia

Road Map D3. 5 km (3 miles) north of Larnaka. 442 from Larnaka.

Standing to the west of Kellia, formerly a Turkish Cypriot village that derives its name from the cells of early Christian hermits who once made this their home, is the small **Church of St Anthony** (Agios Andonios), where cells are carved into the rocks.

It was first built in the 11th century, but the subsequent remodelling works have all but obliterated its original shape. The layout resembles a cross inscribed into a square, with the three aisles terminating in an apse and a 15th-century narthex.

Restoration efforts have revealed some beautiful murals. The most interesting of them is the *Crucifixion*, painted on the southeast pillar, one of the oldest paintings on the island. Other notable paintings are on the pillars and on the west wall of the church, including the *Assumption of the Virgin Mary*, *Judas' Betrayal* and *Abraham's Sacrifice*.

Zeno of Kition (Kitium)

Born in 334 BC, this Greek thinker founded the Stoic school of philosophy (named after Stoa Poikale – the Painted Colonnade on the Athenian agora where he taught). Zeno's philosophy embraced logic, epistemology, physics and ethics. The Stoics postulated that a life governed by reason and the harnessing of desires was of the highest virtue, leading to happiness. Stoicism left a deep mark on the philosophy and ethics of the Hellenic and Roman eras.

Bust of Zeno of Kition

⑱ Larnaka

Larnaka stands on the site of ancient Kition. It takes its name from the Greek *larnax*, meaning "sarcophagus" (there were many ancient and medieval tombs in the district). The city has an international airport, a port, several interesting museums and a seaside promenade lined with numerous cafés and restaurants. The tourist zone has luxurious hotels, tavernas, nightclubs and souvenir shops.

Larnaka's seaside promenade lined with palm trees

Exploring Larnaka

The best place to begin is ancient Kition, followed by the Archaeological and Pierides Museums. From here continue with the church of St Lazarus (Agios Lazaros) and the Byzantine Museum, then proceed towards the sea, visiting the Turkish fort and mosque. The seaside promenade leads to the marina and beach.

🏛 Kition

500m (550 yards) NE of Archaeological Museum. **Open** 8am–2:30pm Mon–Fri (to 5pm Wed).

The ancient city of Kition (Kitium) lies in the northern part of Larnaka. According to tradition it was founded by Kittim, grandson of Noah. Archaeological excavations indicate, however, that the town was founded in the 13th century BC. Soon afterwards the Mycenaeans landed on the island; they reinforced the city walls and built a temple. The Phoenicians, who conquered the city in the 9th century BC, turned the temple into a shrine to the goddess Astarte. Kition was a major trade centre for copper, which was excavated in mines near Tamassos.

🏛 Mycenaean Site

Leoforos Archiepiskopou Kyprianou. The main archaeological site (dubbed Area II) is near the cemetery for foreigners. There are wooden platforms from where you can view the dig. The defence walls dating from the late Bronze era were later strengthened by the Mycenaeans, who added fortifications built of stone and clay bricks.

🏛 Acropolis

Leontiou Kimonos. Situated on top of Bamboula hill (immediately behind the Archaeological Museum) was the acropolis, which had its own defence walls. In the late 1800s the hill was plundered by British soldiers, who used the rubble to cover malaria-breeding swamps. In the 1960s archaeologists stumbled upon ancient tombs filled with ceramics and jewellery, as well as alabaster sculptures and stone fragments.

A figurine from Pierides Museum

🏛 Archaeological Museum

Kalograion. **Tel** 24 304 169. **Open** 8am–4pm Mon–Fri, 9am–4pm Sat. 🅿

The Archaeological Museum displays vases, sculptures and cult statues from Larnaka and the surrounding area. It has a collection of ceramics (mostly Mycenaean), votive terracotta figurines and glass objects from Roman times. There is also an interesting exhibition of Cypriot-Minoan inscriptions, as yet undeciphered. There are also sculptures in the garden.

Interior staircase of Larnaka's Pierides Museum

🏛 Pierides Museum

Zinonos Kitieos 4. **Tel** 24 145 375. **Open** 9am–4pm Mon–Thu, 9am–1pm Fri & Sat. 🅿
🔲 pieridesfoundation.com.cy

This museum contains the largest private collection in Cyprus. Comprising some 2,500 relics assembled by five generations of the Pierides family, the collection spans from the Neolithic era to medieval times. It was started in 1839 by Cypriot archaeologist Demetrios Pierides, who committed part of his fortune to the preservation

Excavations of the ancient city of Kition

Museum of Natural History in the municipal park

of artifacts pillaged from ancient tombs by treasure-hunters such as the American consul in Larnaka, Luigi Palma di Cesnola.

The most precious objects include Neolithic stone idols and 3,000-year-old ceramic vessels. There are also terracotta figurines dating from the archaic era; miniature war chariots and cavalry soldiers; amphorae and goblets in geometric and archaic styles decorated with images of fish and birds; and Hellenic statues. Of particular note is the striking astronaut-like figure jumping on springs, painted on an archaic ceramic vessel. Other exhibits include weaponry and a set of historical maps of Cyprus and of the eastern Mediterranean.

In the rooms at the back of the building is a collection of handicrafts, including jewellery, embroidery, everyday items and richly carved furniture. There are also works by the primitive artist Michael Kashialos, who was murdered by the Turks in his studio in 1974.

⏳ Museum of Natural History
Leoforos Grigori Afxentiou.
Tel 24 652 569.
Open 9am–4pm Mon–Fri,
10am–1pm Sat.

Located in the municipal park, this small building houses a diverse collection of exhibits illustrating the natural environment of Cyprus.

Fountain in front of the town hall

Arranged across eight rooms displays show specimens of plants, insects and animals (from both land and sea), many of which are now rare in the wild.

There are also interesting geological exhibits. Besides the collection of copper minerals – the main source of the island's wealth since ancient times– you can see minerals belonging to the asbestos group. The large open mines from which these minerals came are located near Amiantos, on the southeastern slopes of the Troodos mountains. Other exhibits include fossils from the island's limestone.

Larnaka Town Centre

1. Kition
2. Mycenaean Site
3. Acropolis
4. Archaeological Museum
5. Pierides Museum
6. Museum of Natural History
7. Agios Lazaros Church
8. Agia Faneromeni
9. Büyük Cami
10. Larnaka Fort and Medieval Museum
11. Beaches

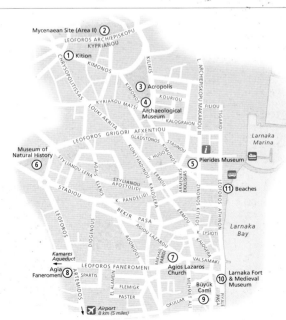

0 metres 400
0 yards 400

St Lazarus Church dating from the 10th century

⬆ Agios Lazaros Church

Plateia Agiou Lazarou. **Tel** 24 652 498.
Open 8am–12:30pm, 2–6:30pm daily
(to 5:30pm Sep–Mar).

The Church of St Lazarus (Agios Lazaros) stands in the southern part of Old Larnaka. It was constructed in the early 10th century on the site of a church dating from 900, which was built to house the saint's tomb.

Its architectural style reveals the influence of both Eastern and Western trends. Following its retrieval from the hands of the Turks in 1589, the church was used by Roman Catholic and Orthodox communities for 200 years, as evidenced by inscriptions on the portico. The interior is built around four vast pillars supporting a roof with three small domes. Its main features are the Rococo pulpit, around 300 years old, and a small icon depicting Lazarus emerging from his tomb. The icon dates from the 17th century and can be seen in the magnificently

Icon from the
Byzantine Museum

carved iconostasis. The image is reverently paraded through the church at Easter. On the right side of the central nave is a large gilded reliquary containing the skull of the saint. The crypt houses several stone sarcophagi. One of them supposedly housed the relics of St Lazarus. The tomb bore the Greek inscription: "Lazarus, friend of Jesus".

The graves in the courtyard are mainly of British consuls, civil servants and merchants.

Larnaka has other notable places of worship, including the metropolitan cathedral, Agios Chrysostrios, built in 1853; Agios Ioannis, featuring a beautiful iconostasis from the beginning of the 17th century; and the Roman Catholic church Terra Santa. Also of note is the 19th-century Zahuri Mosque, with its double dome and truncated minaret.

▥ Byzantine Museum

Plateia Agiou Lazarou.
Tel 24 652 498. **Open** 8:30am–12:30pm, 3–5:30pm Mon–Sat. **Closed** Wed & Sat pm.

Entry to this museum is from the courtyard of Agios Lazaros church. The collection consists of icons and other objects associated with the Orthodox religion, including chasubles and Bibles. A previous, extensive collection

vanished during the turbulent period between 1964 and 1974. It was kept in the fort, which fell into the hands of the Turks. When it was regained by the Greeks, many items had vanished.

⬆ Agia Faneromeni

At the junction of Leoforos Faneromeni and Artemidos.

This subterranean chapel is a two-chambered cave hewn into the rock. Its structure suggests a pagan tomb, probably dating from the Phoenician era. The chapel was famed for its magical properties. The sick would circle it twice, leaving behind anything from a scrap of clothing to a lock of hair in the hope that they were also leaving behind their illnesses. Girls whose boyfriends were far away would come here to pray for their safe return.

▦ Pattichion Municipal Theatre

Leoforos Artemidos.

The open-air amphitheatre, used for staging events during the July Festival, is situated opposite the Zeno of Kition Stadium, close to the Agia Faneromeni chapel.

☪ Büyük Cami

Leoforus Athenon. **Open** daily.

Standing beyond the fort, at the border between the Greek and Turkish districts, is the Grand Mosque (Büyük Cami). Originally the Church of the Holy Cross, this building now serves Muslim visitors mostly from the Middle East. Modest attire is required, and before entering you must remove your shoes. For a small fee you can climb the narrow, steep stairs that lead to the top of the minaret. From here there is a

Saint Lazarus

Lazarus, brother of Martha and Mary, was resurrected by Jesus four days after his death at Bethany. He moved to Cyprus, becoming Bishop of Kition. After his final death he was buried here; his tomb was discovered in 890. Emperor Leo VI helped to build St Lazarus church, in exchange for which some of the saint's relict were transferred to Constantinople, from where they were stolen in 1204. Today they are in Marseille Cathedral.

Painting showing the resurrection of Lazarus

lovely panoramic view of Larnaka and the nearby salt lake. Stretching beyond the fort, right up to the fishing harbour, is a large district that once belonged to the Turks. Its streets still bear Turkish names, but it is now inhabited by Greek Cypriot refugees from the area around Famagusta and the Karpasia peninsula.

The imposing mid-18th-century aqueduct

A variety of yachts moored in Larnaka marina

🚢 Larnaka Harbours

The southern part of town has a small but picturesque fishing harbour. Larnaka marina is situated several hundred metres to the north of the coastal promenade, beyond a small beach. Only boat crews are allowed entry, but you can stroll along the breakwater. Beyond the marina there are cargo and passenger terminals; the passenger terminal is the second largest in Cyprus.

🏛 Larnaka Fort and Medieval Museum

On the seashore, by the south end of the coastal promenade. **Tel** 24 304 576. **Open** 8am–5pm Mon–Fri (to 7:30pm Jun–Aug).

The fort in Larnaka was built by the Ottomans around 1625 on the site of a medieval castle which had been destroyed by Mamelukes two centuries previously. When ships sailed into the harbour (which no longer exists), they were welcomed by a gun salute fired from the castle.

During the Byzantine period, the fort was used as a police headquarters, prison and execution site. In 1833, it was partially destroyed by a lightning strike. The fort now houses a small Medieval Museum with arms and armour dating from Turkish times, and treasure troves unearthed in Kition and at the Hala Sultan Tekke. The crenellated wall, with guns and cannons, is now a viewing platform. In summer the castle yard hosts concerts, occasional plays and other cultural events.

🏖 Beaches

The sandy municipal beach by the Finikoudes promenade, in the neighbourhood of the marina, owes its popularity to a double row of shade-giving palm trees. There are some good beach bars such as the award-winning Kastella. Another municipal beach is situated to the south of the fishing harbour. Although the beach itself is small, it is popular with locals due to its watersports facilities and the numerous restaurants and cafés in the vicinity.

A cannon at Larnaka's Fort

The best sandy public beach in the area is located some 10 km (6 miles) east of the city and is run by the Cyprus Tourism Organization. About 10 km (6 miles) south of Larnaka, near Kiti, there is a rocky cove with patches of sand; this area is undeveloped and relatively free of people.

A bit further from Finikoudes is Mackenzie beach with water-sports facilities, restaurants, beach bars and cafés. Weekends get crowded and there are concerts at night feature local and international artists.

🏛 Aqueduct (Kamares)

3 km (2 miles) from Larnaka.

On the outskirts of Larnaka, by the road leading to Limassol, are the remains of an aqueduct that once supplied the town with water taken from the Thrimitus river. The aqueduct was built in 1745 by the Ottoman governor, Elhey Bekir Pasha, and functioned until 1930. Some 75 spans of the structure still stand; they are illuminated at night.

The popular Finikoudes beach on a pleasant, sunny day

Octagonal fountain in the courtyard of Agia Napa monastery

⑳ Agia Napa

Road Map E3. 🚌 201 Agia Napa Circle Line. 🏔 3,200. 🛈 Leoforos Kryou Nerou 12, 23 721 796. 📅 Kataklysmos.

Until the 1970s, Agia Napa was a quiet fishing village with a scenic harbour. However, following the Turkish occupation of Varosha – the Greek Cypriot neighbourhood of Famagusta – Agia Napa assumed the role of Cyprus' prime bathing resort. Now a teeming holiday resort especially popular with British, German, Russian and Scandinavian young people, the town centre has scores of hotels, nightclubs and cafés that have given Agia Napa its reputation as the second most entertaining playground in the Mediterranean, after Ibiza.

An interesting historic relic of Agia Napa is the 16th-century Venetian **Monastery of Agia Napa**, enclosed by a high wall. According to legend, in the 16th century a hunter's dog led him to a spring in the woods where he found a sacred icon of the Virgin that had been lost 700 years earlier. (A church had been built here as early as the 8th century, hacked into the solid rock and named Agia Napa – Holy Virgin of the Forest). The spring was thus believed to have healing powers and the monastery of Agia Napa was built on the site. Soon after, Cyprus fell to the Ottomans and the Venetian monks fled, but villagers continued to use the

Fountain detail, Agia Napa monastery

beautiful **monastery church**. The only church on the island with a free-standing belfry, it is built partly underground in a natural grotto. The route to its gloomy, mysterious interior leads through an entrance crowned with an arch and a rosette. Inside is a complex maze of grottoes, niches and shrines. Between April and December, the church celebrates Anglican Mass every Sunday at 11am and Roman Catholic Mass at 5pm.

At the centre of the monastery's arcaded **courtyard** is an octagonal Renaissance fountain decorated with marble reliefs and topped with a dome resting on four columns. Nearby, water supplied by a Roman aqueduct flows from the carved marble head of a wild boar.

The monastery was restored in the 1970s and now houses the **World Council of Churches Ecumenical Conference Centre**.

The **Thalassa Museum of the Sea** in Agia Napa is designed

to show the impact of the sea on the history of the island. It features a replica of the "Kyrenia Ship" dating from the time of Alexander the Great, which sank off the coast of Kyrenia some 2,300 years ago.

The majority of the museum's exhibits come from the private collection of naturalist George Tomaritis. They include a range of preserved marine fauna as well as a collection of shells and maritime exhibits.

Beautiful sandy beaches can be found in the surrounding area. One of them is **Nissi Beach**, with its small island. Neighbouring **Makronissos Beach** is linked to the town centre by bicycle routes. Nearby, on a craggy peninsula, are 19 Hellenistic tombs hacked into the rock. Two kilometres (1 mile) west is a sandy beach, **Agia Thekla**, with a small chapel and an old church in a rock cave.

🏛 **Thalassa Museum of the Sea**
Leoforos Kryou Nerou. **Tel** 23 816 366. **Open** summer: 9am–1pm Mon, 9am–5pm Tue–Sat, 3–7pm Sun; winter: 9am–1pm Mon, 9am–5pm Tue–Sat, closed Sun. 🚫
🌐 pieridesfoundation.com.cy

㉑ Cape Gkreko

Road Map E3. 🚌 101 from Famagusta and Paralimni.

This headland at the southeastern tip of Cyprus rises in a steep crag above the sea. The neighbouring coves with their clear water are a paradise for scuba divers and snorkellers. The entire area, with its limestone rock formations, is a **protected nature reserve**.

Popular sandy beach in Agia Napa

The rugged coast of Cape Gkreko with its limestone cliffs

Archaeologists discovered the remains of two **temples**: the Hellenic temple of Aphrodite, and the Roman temple of Diana. The cape is surrounded by underwater **shipwrecks**, including a Genoese ship once filled with looted treasure, which sank in the 15th century.

Walking along the shore towards Protaras you will come across a rock bridge over a small bay protruding inland, a Roman quarry, and a little further on, the **Agii Anargyri Church** above a grotto hidden in a craggy cliff underneath. The area affords magnificent views over Konnos Bay and the clifftop hotel.

㉒ Protaras

Road Map E3. 101 from Famagusta and Paralimni. Leoforos Protaras Cape Gkreko 356, 23 832 865.

Protaras is a conglomeration of hotels, restaurants, tavernas, bars, cafés and watersports centres, and an excellent place to spend a holiday. In summer, its beautiful sandy beaches such as Fig Tree, which was named one of Europe's best beaches, and the magical Konnos Bay attract crowds of tourists for watersports and cruises on one of the local pleasure boats.

The area is dominated by a rocky hill with the picturesque **Chapel of Prophitis Elias** (the Prophet Elijah) affording a magnificent panoramic view of Protaras and nearby Varosha.

Further north are more beaches including Pernera, Minas and Agia Triada, with a small church, situated in a coastal cove. Near the latter, close to the roundabout on the road to Paralimni, is **Ocean Aquarium**, with crocodiles, penguins and other marine life.

🐠 **Ocean Aquarium**
Paralimni, Protaras Ave. **Tel** 23 741 111. **Open** 10am–6pm daily.
W protarasaquarium.com

Environs
The area encompassing Agia Napa, Paralimni and the tourist region of Protaras is known as **Kokkinohoria** (red villages) due to its red soil, which is rich in iron and produces the famous Cyprus potato. The scenery is dominated by windmills that drive pumps, which draw water from deep underground.

After 1974, the village of **Paralimni** became the district's administrative centre. Close to the occupied, northern part of Cyprus, it received many refugees after the invasion and now its population numbers about 11,000.

The village skyline is dominated by three churches. The oldest of these is Panagia (Virgin Mary) dating from the 18th century and lined with porcelain tiles typical of the period. It also houses a small Byzantine museum. Paralimni is famous for delicacies such as smoked pork (*pasta*) and pork sausages (*loukanika*).

The neighbouring farming village of **Deryneia** perches atop a hill, right by the "Green Line". From here there

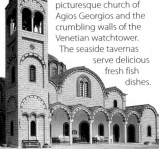

Statue of a diver in Protaras

are views of Varosha's abandoned houses, the former tourist district of Famagusta now resembling a ghost town, and the Gothic Cathedral of St Nicholas, which has been turned into a mosque.

Deryneia has three pretty churches–15th-century Agia Marina, 17th-century Agios Georgios and the church of the Panagia.

The village of **Liopetri** is famous for the potatoes that are grown here, as well as the woven baskets used to collect them. You can still see local basket-weavers at work.

The 15th-century village church of Agios Andronikos has a carved iconostasis with beautiful icons and paintings in the apses.

The Akhyronas barn is Cyprus' national memorial. It was here that four EOKA fighters were killed in a battle with the British in 1958.

Potamos Liopetriou, to the south, is the most beautiful fishing village in Cyprus, situated on the shores of a long bay, next to the picturesque church of Agios Georgios and the crumbling walls of the Venetian watchtower. The seaside tavernas serve delicious fresh fish dishes.

The 18th-century Panagia church in Paralimni

TROODOS MOUNTAINS

Stretching some 120 km (75 miles) over southwestern Cyprus, the Troodos mountain region is truly astonishing and completely different from the rest of the sun-baked island. In winter and early spring, the peaks are often capped with snow, and the forests fill the cool air with the scent of pine and cedar. The mountain villages and monasteries hidden in the forests seem a world away from the crowded coastal areas, even during the peak holiday season.

The shady valleys and lofty peaks of the Troodos mountains have long been a refuge for people in search of calm and tranquillity, including the monks who came here looking for a place where they could be closer to God and further from temptation.

Mount Olympus, the island's highest peak at 1,950 m (6,400 ft), rises above the other mountains in the mighty massif, crowned with the distinctive radar domes of the British army. In winter, its slopes swarm with skiers eager to enjoy a sport that is rare in this part of Europe.

The southern slopes are perfectly suited to growing the grapes used to produce the island's famous wine, the sweet Commandaria, as well as other varieties.

Almost half of the 144 species of plants unique to Cyprus grow in the Troodos region. The Troodos geopark, located in the central part of the island, has been declared a nature reserve.

Travelling through the Troodos mountains brings visitors into contact with quiet, friendly villages, where the local people produce sweets of fruit and nuts soaked in grape juice *(soujouko)*, as well as wine and flavourful goat's cheese *(halloumi)*.

No trip to the region is complete without seeing the Byzantine painted churches. The austere architecture of these Orthodox sanctuaries, within remote valleys and glens, hides a wealth of amazingly rich murals (commonly referred to as frescoes) depicting scenes from the Bible.

A church hidden in the mountains – a distinctive feature of the region

◀ The royal Kykkos Monastery in the Troodos mountains

Exploring the Troodos Mountains

Among the highlights of a visit to the Troodos mountains are the many painted churches, some dating from the Byzantine period. Ten of these isolated churches have been listed as UNESCO World Cultural Heritage Sites. The tomb of Archbishop Makarios, the first president of Cyprus, lies near Kykkos Monastery at Throni. The Commandaria region's 14 villages have produced the famous Cypriot dessert wine since the 12th century. The true treasures of the Troodos mountains are their waterfalls hidden among lush greenery – unusual in the eastern Mediterranean.

Theotokos Archangelos Church, one of the many small churches in the region

Sights at a Glance

1. Tilliria
2. Cedar Valley
3. *Kykkos pp94–5*
4. Agios Ioannis Lampadistis
5. Panagia tou Moutoulla
6. Pedoulas
7. Mt Olympus (Chionistra)
8. Troodos
9. Trooditissa
10. Platres
11. Omodos
12. Potamiou
13. Vouni
14. Koilani
15. Lofou
16. Monagri
17. Timios Stavros
18. Pelendri
19. Agios Nikolaos tis Stegis
20. Kakopetria
21. Panagia tis Podithou
22. Panagia Forviotissa
23. Panagia tou Araka
24. Stavros tou Agiasmati

0 kilometres   5

0 miles   5

Winding roads and arid landscape typical of the region

Getting There

From Larnaka airport, follow the motorway signs toward the Troodos mountains, and then take the B8 road. The B9 road from Nicosia passes through Kakopetria. The best route from Pafos is along the scenic Diarizos Valley. Leave the motorway at Mandria and turn towards Nikoklea. The mountain roads are of good quality, but winding and steep in places.

Morfou

Astromeritis

Nicosia

B9

Nikitari • Vyzakia •

22 PANAGIA FORVIOTISSA

Evrychou

L E F K O S Í A

Adhelfi Forest

Xyliatos •

rakies •

21 PANAGIA TIS PODITHOU

Kapoura •

Kalopanagiotis •

4 AGIOS IOANNIS LAMPADISTIS

NAGIA TOU OUTOULLA 5

20 KAKOPETRIA

24 STAVROS TOU AGIASMATI

6 PEDOULAS

19 AGIOS NIKOLAOS TIS STEGIS

Kourdali •

Saranti •

Marathassa

Spilia •

23 PANAGIA TOU ARAKA

Prodromos •

Mt Adhelfi 1612m △

Chandria •

Platanistasa •

B9

MOUNT OLYMPUS 7

Kyperounta •

Alona •

Kaminaria •

8 TROODOS

Pano Amiantos •

Agridia •

Pitsillia

9

Troodos

Agros •

TROODITISSA

Fini •

PELENDRI 18

PLATRES 10

L E M E S O S

17 TIMIOS STAVROS

Pera Pedi •

11 OMODOS

14 KOILANI

Trimiklini •

POTAMIOU

Silikou •

12

13 VOUNI

B8

Laneia •

Malia

15 LOFOU

16 MONAGRI

Agios Therapon •

Panagia tis Amasgou

↓ Limassol

Key

— Secondary road
··· Minor road
— Scenic route
– – Track
— Regional border
■·■ Green Line
△ Summit

For additional map symbols *see back flap*

❶ Tilliria

Road Map B3.

Tilliria is a desolate region east of Polis, on the northwestern slopes of the Troodos mountains. Its forested hills extend behind the former monastery, Stavros tis Psokas, in the direction of the Turkish enclave of Kokkina, Pyrgos, Kato and the sea. This region has never been inhabited, although people came here to work the long-since defunct copper ore mines. It is ideal for experienced hikers.

In ancient times, Cyprus was overgrown with dense forests, which were cut down to build ships and fire the furnaces in the copper-smelting plants.

Under British rule of the island, action was taken to restore the former character of the Cypriot forests. The extensive Pafos Forest was created in the western region of the Troodos mountains.

The wooded hills of the remote Tilliria region – a hiker's paradise

❷ Cedar Valley

Road Map B3.

This valley, set in the midst of the forest backwoods, contains most of the island's trees of the local *cedrus brevifolia* variety, different from the better known Lebanese cedar. The valley is a nature reserve, and with a bit of luck visitors will see the moufflon – a wild Cypriot sheep. In the early 20th century, when the British declared these animals a protected species, only 15 of them remained in the wild;

now the forests of Cyprus are home to over 1,500 of them. The male displays powerful, curled horns. The moufflon is a symbol of Cyprus and appears on its coins.

Environs
Standing in the midst of the Pafos Forest is the abandoned 19th-century monastery of **Stavros tis Psokas**, now used by the Forestry Commission. It contains a restaurant, several guest rooms and a campsite. The locals claim it to be the coolest place on the island. Close to the campsite is an enclosure containing moufflon.

The Forestry Commission building is the starting point for hiking trails to the nearby peaks of Tripylos and Zaharou. Starting from the car park by the spring and the junction with the road leading towards the sea, you can walk or drive to Mount Tripylos – one of the highest peaks in the district at 1,362 m (4,468 ft), which offers a magnificent panorama of the Pafos and Tilliria hills.

❸ Kykkos

See pp94–5.

❹ Agios Ioannis Lampadistis

Road Map B3. Kalopanagiotis.
Tel 22 952 580. **Open** 9am–12:30pm, 2–5pm daily (Nov–Apr: 9am–noon, 1–4pm). Donations welcome.

The monastery of St John of Lampadou (ancient Lambas) is one of the most interesting in Cyprus and has been awarded

Kalopanagiotis village, scenically located on a mountain slope

UNESCO World Heritage status. The old monastery complex includes three churches covered with one vast roof. The oldest one, dedicated to St Irakleidios, dates from the 11th century and is decorated with over 30 12th- and 15th-century frescoes illustrating key events in the life of Jesus. The painting on the dome depicts Christ Pantocrator. Others show the Sacrifice of Abraham, the Entry into Jerusalem and the Ascension. The 15th-century series of paintings seen on the vaults, arches and walls depicts various scenes from the New Testament.

The second church, of **Agios Ioannis (St John) Lampadistis**, dating from the 11th century, is dedicated to the saint who was born in Lampadou. He renounced marriage in favour of the monastic life, went blind, died at the age of 22, and was canonised soon afterwards. His tomb is inside the church and the niche above contains a silver reliquary with the saint's skull. The church interior is

Monastery buildings of Agios Ioannis Lampadistis

decorated with 12th-century paintings. The richly gilded iconostasis dates from the 16th century. The narthex (portico) common to both churches, which was added in the 15th century, includes a cycle of paintings depicting the miracles of Christ.

The **Latin chapel**, added in the second half of the 15th century, is decorated with 24 magnificent Byzantine wall paintings with Greek texts written in about 1500.

Environs

The mountain village of **Kalopanagiotis** is scenically located in the Setrachos Valley. It has existed since medieval times and has retained its traditional architecture, cobbled streets, and many churches and chapels. The village is now a small spa resort with therapeutic sulphur springs (with beneficial properties for rheumatic conditions and gastric ailments). It is also known for its beautifully carved breadbaskets called *sanidha*. Kalopanagiotis is believed to be descended from ancient Lambas, which produced the local saints, Ioannis and Irakleidios. Nearby is an arched medieval bridge.

❺ Panagia tou Moutoulla

Road Map B3. 3 km (1.8 miles) from Pedoulas. Moutoullas. **Open** vary. Donations welcome.

The village of Moutoulla, situated in a valley below Pedoulas, is renowned for its mineral water spring and its tiny church of **Our Lady of Moutoulla** (Panagia tou Moutoulla) built in 1280.

This is the oldest of the Troodos mountain painted churches. Its most interesting features are the pitched roof and finely carved entrance door. Beyond these doors is another set of equally beautiful doors (wood carving has been a local speciality for centuries). Above them is the image of *Christ Enthroned*, flanked by *Adam and Eve*, and *Hell and Paradise*, with a procession of

Panoramic view of Pedoulas in the Marathassa valley

saints marching into Heaven. The cycle of paintings inside the church, illustrating key events in the life of Jesus and Mary, are similar to the wall paintings in the nearby Church of the Archangel Michael. The most distinctive of these faded paintings include *Mary with the Christ Child* in a cradle, and *St Christopher and St George Fighting the Dragon* with the head of a woman in a crown. There is also a portrait of the church founder, Ioannis Moutoullas, with his wife Irene.

Remains of a wall painting in Panagia tou Moutoulla

❻ Pedoulas

Road Map B3. 🚌 190.

This sizeable village is located in the upper part of the Marathassa valley. The Setrachos River that drains it flows down towards Morfou Bay. Pedoulas is famed for its surrounding orchards, gentle climate, bracing air and bottled spring water, which you can buy in most shops in Cyprus. The most beautiful season

here is spring, when the houses are completely enveloped by a sea of flowering cherry trees.

The most significant site in the village is the **Church of the Archangel Michael** (Archangelos Michail), dating from 1474. It is one of ten mountain churches listed as UNESCO World Cultural Heritage Sites, due to its magnificent interior wall paintings.

The paintings are unusually realistic. The north side of the tiny reading room is decorated with a painting of the Archangel Michael.

The renovated paintings are notable for their realistic images, including the *Sacrifice of Abraham*, the *Baptism in the Jordan River*, the *Kiss of Judas* and the *Betrayal of Christ in the Garden of Gethsemane*. The apse, usually decorated with an image of Christ Pantocrator, includes the Praying Mary (*Virgin Orans*) and the *Ascension*. Seen above the north entrance is the figure of the founder, Basil Chamados, handing a model of the church to the Archangel Michael.

Environs

The neighbouring village of Prodromos, which numbers only 150 inhabitants, is perched on top of a mountain range at an elevation of 1,400 m (4,593 ft). It is the highest village in Cyprus, and also, thanks to its decent accommodation facilities, a good base for starting to explore the Marathassa valley.

● Kykkos

This is the largest, most imposing and wealthiest of all the monasteries in Cyprus. Built in the middle of magnificent mountains and forests, away from human habitation, its most precious treasure is the icon of the Most Merciful Virgin, claimed to have been painted by St Luke and credited with the power to bring rain. The holy image is kept in the monastery museum.

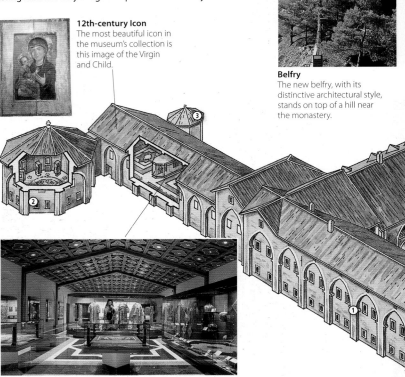

Belfry
The new belfry, with its distinctive architectural style, stands on top of a hill near the monastery.

12th-century Icon
The most beautiful icon in the museum's collection is this image of the Virgin and Child.

★ Museum's Main Hall
The monastery museum contains some important treasures: gold and silver liturgical vessels, holy books, and embroidered vestments, as well as beautiful and precious icons.

KEY

① **The main wing** of the monastery is home to the monks' cells.

② **The rotunda** has a darkened room housing the museum's most precious exhibits – the ancient, beautiful icons.

③ **A collection of manuscripts, documents and books**

General View
The hills surrounding Kykkos afford memorable views over the small monastery church and belfry, flanked by one-storey buildings with red roof tiles.

Small Courtyard
The church courtyard leads to the monastery buildings that used to house the museum.

VISITORS' CHECKLIST

Practical Information
Road map B3. Monastery, church & museum: **Tel** 22 942 736.
Open Jun–Oct: 10am–6pm daily; Nov–May: 10am–4pm daily.
📇 ✉ 🌐 **kykkos.org.cy**

★ **Royal Doors**
Inside the church is a richly decorated iconostasis incorporating the Royal Doors.

Church Entrance
The *katholicon*, or monastery church, is entered via a doorway decorated with lovely mosaics.

Main Monastery Entrance
The small but wonderfully decorated entance is covered in beautiful mosaics.

Main Courtyard
The cloisters running along the edge of the main courtyard are decorated with mosaics depicting the history of Kykkos Monastery.

❼ Mount Olympus (Chionistra)

Road Map B3. 45 km (28 miles) north of Limassol. 🚌 bus from Nicosia in the summer.

Chionistra, the traditional name of Olympus, means "the snowy one". The slopes of the 1,950-m (6,400-ft) mountain are covered with umbrella-shaped pine trees interspersed with cedars and junipers. The most beautiful season here is spring, when wildflowers are in bloom. In good weather the view from the top extends as far as the coast of Turkey.

In winter the mountain is covered with a layer of snow up to 3 m (nearly 10 ft) deep, making Mount Olympus popular with downhill skiers. The ski runs on the southern slopes of Sun Valley are short and easy, while the northern runs are much longer and considerably more difficult. There are also two cross-country trails. Equipment hire and lessons are available.

The nearest hotel and restaurant facilities are in Troodos and Platres.

Ski Station
Open Jan–Mar. 🅦 cyprusski.com

Umbrella pines on the slopes of Mount Olympus

❽ Troodos

Road Map B3. 🚌 64 from Limassol. 🏨 15. 🛈 25 421 316. **Open** 8:15am–3:45pm Mon–Fri (2nd week of month: to 3pm Mon–Fri, 9am–2pm Sat). 🅦 mytroodos.com

This small resort offers a few restaurants, souvenir shops and tourist car parks. In the summer there are horse and donkey rides,

The iconostasis in Trooditissa church with the miraculous icon of Mary

while hikers have a choice of several trails. The **Visitor Centre of the Troodos National Forest Park** has a collection of local natural specimens. There is also a walk along a 300-m- (984-ft-) long botanical-geological trail and a short film about the natural environment of Troodos.

Hidden in the forest a few kilometres south is the former residence of the British governor of Cyprus, now the summer villa of the president of the Republic of Cyprus. The overseer who helped to build it in 1880 was Arthur Rimbaud, the famous French poet.

❾ Trooditissa

Road Map B3. 8 km (5 miles) northwest of Platres. **Closed** to the public.

This monastery, originally founded in 1250, is surrounded by pine forests on the southern slopes of the Troodos mountains, a few kilometres west of Platres. During the Iconoclastic Wars of the 8th century, a monk brought an icon of the Virgin Mary which, according to tradition, was painted by St Luke. The icon remained hidden in a cave until 990, when it was discovered, thanks to the miraculous light emanating from it.

The present **monastery church** dates from 1731. Its carved wooden

iconostasis is covered with gold leaf. The miracle-working icon – the magnificent image of the Panagia, Queen of Heaven – is to the left of the Royal Doors, covered with a curtain of silver and gold.

The monastery, whose austere regime is similar to that of Stavrovouni (see p80), is home to a dozen or so monks.

Environs
The nearby village of **Fini** (Foini) is renowned for its traditional handicrafts, now limited to pottery studios and a workshop producing distinctive Cypriot chairs.

The private **Pilavakion Museum**, run by Theofanis Pilavakis, displays vast ceramic jugs for storing olive oil. Adjacent to Iliovasilema bar is a small shop producing the local delicacy – loukoumi (Cyprus delight) that is different from the versions made in Lefkara and Geroskipou.

Between Fini and the monastery, on a small stream running through a deep ravine where British soldiers practise climbing skills, is the picturesque **Chantara waterfall**.

Panoramic view of Fini, known for handicrafts

For hotels and restaurants in this region see p164 and pp173–4

⑩ Platres

Road Map B3. 37 km (23 miles) northwest of Limassol. 🚌 62 from Limassol. 🏨 350. ℹ️ 25 421 316.

The most famous mountain resort in Cyprus, Platres lies on a steep bank above the Kyros stream. The location and surrounding forests give it an excellent climate, making it a favourite holiday spot for Limassol and Nicosia residents.

Several colonial-style villas serve as reminders of British rule, and the few hotels and restaurants have all been designed in the same style. The town centre consists of a single street with a post office and a square next to the tourist information office, from where buses depart for Limassol (*see p73*).

Platres is the starting point for several nature trails. One of them is "Caledonia", which passes by the magnificent Caledonia waterfall and ends at Psilo Dendro in Platres. The other trail, "Persefoni", passing through the black pine forest offers amazing views.

⑪ Omodos

Road Map B4. 8 km (5 miles) southwest of Platres. 🏨 300. 🚌 40 from Limassol.

Scattered over the southern slopes of the Troodos mountains are the Krassochoria vine-growing villages, of which Omodos is one. Established in the 11th century, the settlement is famous for its

Courtyard of the Timiou Stavrou Monastery, in Omodos

production of wine, as well as for specialized *papilla* lace-making.

Timiou Stavrou monastery (Monastery of the Holy Cross) stands in the centre of the village. Built around 1150, it acquired its present shape in the 19th century. Timber-roofed monastic buildings surround the three-hall basilica, which contains a carved wooden iconostasis dating from 1813. According to legend, St Helena (mother of Emperor Constantine) left here a piece of the rope with which Christ was tied to the cross. The venerated relic is kept in a vast silver cross-shaped reliquary. Another holy relic, St Philip's skull, is kept in a silver casket.

There are no more monks in the village. The shops and stalls sell local *papilla* lace, silver

Famous Omodos *papilla* lace

jewellery, wine, honey and the ring-shaped *arkatena* bread typical of this village.

Environs

Vasa, a few kilometres southwest of Omodos, is a pleasant village. The Knights Hospitaller of St John, from the Kolossi commandery, were drawn to the village to escape the unbearable summer heat. The knights stayed in the monastery which once stood here. Its 14th- century church, **Agios Georgios**, survives to this day together with its interesting frescoes. The small church museum in Vasa has religious icons and liturgical objects rescued from various abandoned churches.

Vasa has pretty stone houses with red-tiled roofs and a spring flowing with pure mineral water. The village and the surrounding area offer several good restaurants where you can get simple Cypriot dishes.

The Cypriot poet Dimitris Lipertis (1866–1937) has associations with Vasa. The house in which he lived has been made into a small museum.

The nearby archaeological site has yielded several Roman tombs, and the artifacts found in them – including amphorae and jewellery – can be viewed in Nicosia at the Cyprus Museum.

🏛️ **Timiou Stavrou Monastery**
Omodos. **Open** sunrise to sunset daily.

Kingdom of Alashia

For more than 100 years scientists have been searching for the mysterious Kingdom of Alashia. According to texts preserved on clay tablets in el-Amama, its kings corresponded with the Egyptian pharaohs. Analysis of the texts has established that the copper-rich kingdom was situated at the foot of the Troodos mountains, close to present-day Alassa, where equipment for smelting and processing copper has been discovered.

Tablet from el-Amarna describing Alashia

The Donkey Sanctuary west of Vouni

⑫ Potamiou

Road Map B4. 3.5 km (2 miles) south of Omodos.

This backwoods hamlet, reached via Omodos or Kissousa, is on an architectural par with the neighbouring village of Vouni. In summer its red-roofed stone houses vanish from view, swamped by creeping vines. The pride of the village is its small 16th-century church, Agia Marina, and the ruins of a Byzantine church standing near the Khapotami stream.

⑬ Vouni

Road Map B4. 4 km (2½ miles) south of Koilani.

In the mid-1990s this extraordinarily picturesque, partly deserted village was declared a legally protected historical site. Turned into an open-air museum, its life now centres around a handful of *kafeneia* (local cafés) and restaurants. As you walk along the cobbled streets, take note of the signboards of the cafés and restaurants. Most of them are beautifully hand-painted.

One of the main attractions is the **Vouni Donkey Sanctuary**, to the west of the village, which is run by the charitable foundation "Friends of the Cyprus Donkey". Mary and Patrick Skinner founded the sanctuary in 1994 with just six donkeys; today they care for about 120 elderly, sick and abandoned animals. During the grape-harvest season, strong and healthy animals are hired out to the local farmers to help them collect the grapes.

✉ **Vouni Donkey Sanctuary**
Vouni. **Tel** 25 945 488.
Ⓦ donkeysanctuarycyprus.org

⑭ Koilani

Road Map B4.

Another tiny mountain village built on lime soil, Koilani has excellent conditions for growing grape vines and fruit trees. The scenic location, surrounded by lush vineyards, makes up for its shortage of historic sites.

A small two-room **museum** set up behind the Neo-Byzantine church of Panagia Eloussa houses a collection of icons and other religious objects gathered from old churches in the area. For a period during the 17th century, the Limassol archbishopric was based in Koilani.

Close to the village in the valley of the Kyros stream, on the site of a former monastery, is the 12th-century domed **chapel of Agia Mavris**, which was subsequently extended. Its interior, including the domed vault, is decorated with rather unsophisticated wall paintings.

Men whiling away the afternoon in the centre of Koilani

⑮ Lofou

Road Map B4. 26 km (16 miles) northwest of Limassol.

This gorgeous village lies hidden amid the vineyards that cover the hillsides of the Commandaria region. The south-facing slopes and the abundance of water from the nearby Kourris and Kyros rivers produce local grapes that are large and sweet.

Lofou village spreads atop a limestone hill (*lofos* means hill). Its buildings represent the traditional stone-and-timber architecture typical of Cyprus mountain villages.

The Wines of Cyprus

"The sweetness of your love is like Cyprus wine", wrote Mark Antony, offering Cyprus to Cleopatra as a wedding present. To this day various wines, including the sweet Commandaria, are produced on the island and continue to receive international acclaim. Although wines made from known grape varieties, such as Cabernet Sauvignon and Shiraz, are available here, it is worth trying some of the island's indigenous varieties.
Maratheftiko, an ancient grape variety grown here, produces full-bodied red wines with rich aromas and flavours.
Another indigenous variety, Xinisteri, is used to make floral- and fruity-flavoured white wines.

Wine barrels in Koilani

Towering above the village is the white silhouette of the **Church of the Annunciation**, with a tall, slender belfry. The present church was built in the late 19th century. Inside, among many beautiful icons, is a 16th-century image of the Mother of God.

References to Lofou appear in records dating from the Lusignan period, when it was called Loffu, but the village is probably much older, existing already in the Byzantine era.

Lofou can be reached from the north, via Pera Pedi village, or by a rough track (suitable only for four-wheel-drive vehicles) from Monagri, to the east.

Environs

The attractions of **Silikou** village, situated north of Lofou, include an olive press museum and some interesting examples of 14th-century frescoes in the Timios Stavros church.

⑯ Monagri

Road map B4. 21 km (13 miles) northwest of Limassol.

Rising above the vine covered hills and the Kouris valley are the walls of the **Archangelos monastery**. Built in the 10th century on the ruins of an ancient temple, the monastery was rebuilt in the mid-18th century after a tragic fire. The monastery church features a number of lovely wall paintings, some of them by Filaretos – the creator of the magnificent paintings adorning the cathedral church of John the Theologian (Agios Ioannis) in Nicosia. There are also reminders of Ottoman times, when the new rulers converted the church into a mosque, including the geometric *mihrab* decorations, unique in

View of the hilltop Lofou village

Cyprus. The two Corinthian columns that support the portico probably date from the Roman era. The church has a carved, painted iconostasis.

Environs

A few kilometres downstream from Monagri, on the west bank of the river, is the 12th-century convent church of **Panagia tis Amasgou**, one of several Byzantine churches in the Kouris valley, near Limassol. It features beautiful but unrestored frescoes, created between the 12th and 16th centuries. These can be viewed, thanks to the generosity of the resident nuns.

The **Kouris dam**, down the river, is one of the largest structures of its kind in Cyprus. The reservoir collects rainwater used for domestic supplies and for irrigating fields and vineyards.

Situated along the main road leading from Limassol to the Troodos mountains is **Trimiklini** village. Hidden behind its church is a charming, tiny old stone chapel in a cemetery.

On the east side of the road, amid vineyards, lies another vine-growing village, **Laneia** (Lania). Its well-preserved and lovingly maintained old houses are set along narrow winding streets. Standing in the village centre is a white church with a tall belfry and next to it are two pretty cafés. Laneia and its surrounding villages are home to local artists.

🏛 **Archangelos Monastery**
Monagri. **Tel** 25 362 756.
Open by prior arrangement.

🏛 **Panagia tis Amasgou**
Tel as above. **Open** as above.

Neo-Classical school building in Lofou

⓱ Timios Stavros

Road Map B3. 8 km (5 miles) southwest of Agros. **Open** times vary. Donations welcome.

The design of Timios Stavros (Holy Cross) church is different from that of other Cypriot churches. Standing on the lakeshore, at the southern end of the village, this three-aisled edifice was built on a square plan and topped with a slender dome on four columns.

Opposite the entrance are the portraits of the church's founders, as well as their coats-of-arms, and the figure of the apostle Doubting Thomas. The painting to the right depicts the lineage of Jesus. The series of 14 preserved paintings above the pulpit illustrates the life of Mary, including the *Nativity* and the *Presentation of Jesus at the Temple*, with figures dressed in Lusignan-period costumes.

The iconostasis includes a silver reliquary containing fragments of the True Cross, for which the church is named.

⓲ Pelendri

Road Map B3. 8 km (5 miles) southwest of Agros, 32 km (20 miles) from Limassol. 🚌 60, 66 from Limassol.

In the Middle Ages, this village on the southern slopes of the

Fragment of a painting in Timios Stavros church

Troodos mountains was the seat of Jean de Lusignan, son of Hugo V (the Franconian King of Cyprus).

At the centre of the village is the **Panagia Katholiki** church, dating from the early 16th century, which has Italian-Byzantine-style paintings.

It is worth taking the nature trail **Moni-Fylagra** that starts from the Trimiklini-Pelendri road, passes through pine forests and ends at the Fylagra river.

⓳ Agios Nikolaos tis Stegis

Road Map B3. 3 km (2 miles) southwest of Kakopetria. **Tel** 22 922 583. **Open** 9am–4pm Tue–Sat, 11am–4pm Sun. Donations welcome.

This stone church, built in the form of a cross, supports a double roof, giving it the name St Nicholas of the Roof. The oldest section of the building dates from the 11th century; the dome and narthex were added a hundred years later, and in the 15th century the entire structure was covered with a huge ridge roof. This outer roof was designed to protect the building from snow, which falls here occasionally.

The church once served as the chapel of a monastery, no longer in existence. Inside, you can

see some of the oldest wall paintings anywhere in the Troodos mountain churches. Painted over a period of about 500 years, between the 11th and the 15th centuries, they demonstrate the evolution of Orthodox religious art, making this church an excellent place to study the development of Byzantine wall painting.

Along with paintings from the early Byzantine period, known as "hieratic" or "monastic" styles influenced by the art of Syria and Cappadocia, you can also see typical Komnenos and Paleologos art styles. During the Komnenos dynasty (1081–1180), the Byzantine style, which had been rigid and highly formalized up to that point, began to move towards realism and emotional expression in the figures and in their settings.

The artists who created the wall paintings during the Paleologos dynasty continued to display similar attention to the emotional and aesthetic qualities of their art.

Paintings inside the church illustrate scenes from the New Testament. Among the earliest paintings here are the *Entry to Jerusalem*, and the warrior saints George and Theodore brandishing their panoply of arms. The ceiling of the main vault depicts the **Transfiguration of the Lord** on Mount Tabor and the **Raising of Lazarus** from

Interior of Timios Stavros church

◀ Mountain village in Troodos

the dead, conveying the startling impression the events made on the disciples of Jesus and the relatives of Lazarus.

The **Crucifixion** in the north transept shows the Sun and Moon personified weeping over the fate of the dying Jesus. A painting of the **Resurrection**, depicts the women coming to visit the grave and being informed of Christ's resurrection by an angel at the empty tomb. The painting dates from the Lusignan period.

The **Nativity** in the south transept vault shows the Virgin Mary breastfeeding the Christ Child. Painted around it is an idyllic scene with pipe-playing shepherds and animals. Adjacent is a shocking 12th-century painting of the 40 **Martyrs of Sebaste** – Roman soldiers who adopted Christianity and were killed for it – being pushed by soldiers into the freezing waters of an Anatolian lake. In the dome vault is an image of **Christ Pantocrator**.

Agios Nikolaos tis Stegis, featuring magnificent wall paintings

name "Accursed Rocks" from the rocks which, during an earthquake, once killed a great number of people.

The surrounding district has several intriguing churches and chapels, including the **Archangelos** church which dates from 1514, covered with a ridge roof. It is decorated with paintings depicting the life of Jesus. The paintings in the **Agios Georgios** church are influenced by folk tradition.

❷❶ Panagia tis Podithou

Road Map B3. Panagia tis Podithou: Galata. **Open** collect key from café on the village square. **Tel** 22 922 394. Donations welcome.

Dating from 1502, this church is also known as Panagia Elousa (Our Lady of Mercy). Originally, it was a monastery church dedicated to St Eleanor. Later, it belonged to the Venetian family of Coro. The wall paintings that decorate the church date from the Venetian period. Created by Simeon Axenti, their style betrays both Byzantine and Italian influences. They are an example of the strong influence that Western art exerted at that time on Cypriot decorative art. The poignant **Crucifixion** is particularly interesting, painted within a triangle and revealing Italian influences. Mary

Magdalene can be seen at the foot of the cross, her hair loose, alongside a Roman soldier and the two crucified thieves. The **Communion of the Apostles** in the apse is flanked by the figures of two kings: Solomon and David. The painting in the narthex depicts **Our Lady the Queen of Heaven**; painted below it is the image of the church's founder – Dimitrios Coro – with his wife.

It is worth spending some time visiting the early 16th-century church **Agios Sozomenos**, with its cycle of folk-style wall paintings created in 1513, also by Simeon Axenti. Take a closer look at the painting depicting St George fighting the dragon, whose tail is entwined around the hind legs of the knight's horse, as well as the image of St Mamas riding a lion while carrying a lamb in his arms. The nearby church of **Agia Paraskevi** features the remains of some 1514 wall paintings, probably created by a disciple of Axenti.

A picturesque narrow street in old Kakopetria

❷❿ Kakopetria

Road Map B3. 80 km (50 miles) from Nicosia.

This old village in the Solea region, in the valley of the Kargotis river, displays interesting stone architecture. At an elevation of 600 m (1,968 ft), its climate is mild enough to allow the cultivation of grapes. Besides wine, Kakopetria was once renowned for its production of silk. Now it is a weekend retreat for Nicosia residents. The village derives its

The charming church of Panagia tis Podithou

Fresco in Panagia Forviotissa church

㉒ Panagia Forviotissa (Panagia tis Asinou)

Road Map B3. 5 km (3 miles) southwest of Nikitari village. **Tel** 99 830 329. **Open** 9:30am–1pm, 2–4pm Mon–Sat, 10am–4pm Sun & public hols. Donations welcome.

Beyond the village of Nikitari, the road climbing towards the Troodos mountains leads through a dark forest and into a valley overgrown with pine trees. Here, on a wooded hillside, stands the small 12th-century church of Panagia Forviotissa, also known as Panagia tis Asinou. With its red tiled roof, this church dedicated to Our Lady of the Meadows is listed as a UNESCO World Cultural Heritage Site.

The church was founded in 1206 by Nikiforos Maistros, a high-ranking Byzantine official, portrayed in the paintings inside. At first glance the building, with its rough stone walls and simple ridge roof, does not resemble a church. However, this humble one-room structure hides a number of genuine treasures. There are frescoes dating from the 12th to the 16th centuries, which were restored in the 1960s and 1970s.

The wall and ceiling decorations are among the finest examples of Byzantine frescoes, starting with the Christ Pantocrator (Ruler of the World) on the vault of the narthex. There are also figures of the apostles, saints, prophets and martyrs. The following frescoes date from 1105: the *Baptism in the Jordan River*, the *Raising of Lazarus*, the *Last Supper*, the

Crucifixion and the *Resurrection*. They were painted by artists from Constantinople who represented the Komnenos style.

Altogether there are over 100 frescoes here, illustrating various religious themes. It is worth taking a closer look at the extraordinarily realistic painting covering the westernmost recess of the vault – the *Forty Martyrs of Sebaste*. Next to this are the *Pentecost* and the *Raising of Lazarus*.

The cycle of paintings in the nave illustrates the life of Jesus, from the Nativity to the Crucifixion and Resurrection. Seen in the apse is the *Communion of the Apostles*; Jesus offers the Eucharist to his disciples, with Judas standing aside.

The best paintings include the *Dormition of the Virgin*, above the west entrance, and the terrifying vision of the *Last Judgment*. Above the south entrance is a portrait of the founder, Nikiforos Maistros, presenting a model of the church to Christ.

The narthex offers further surprises. The moufflon and two hunting dogs on the arch of the door herald the arrival of the Renaissance; Byzantine iconography did not employ animals. Here, too, is another image of the church founders, praying to the Virgin and Child, with Christ Pantocrator surrounded by the Apostles. Between 1965 and 1976, the frescoes underwent a process

of meticulous cleaning and restoration, under the supervision of Harvard University Byzantine art experts.

Environs
The village of **Vyzakia**, some 6 km (4 miles) down the valley from Panagia Forviotissa, is worth visiting to see the small, wooden-roofed Byzantine **Church of the Archangel Michael** with its frescoes depicting the life and the martyrdom of Jesus. Dating from the early 16th century, these wall paintings reveal a strong Venetian influence.

The little 12th-century church of Panagia Forviotissa

㉓ Panagia tou Araka

Road Map C3. Lagoudera. **Tel** 99 557 369. **Open** 9am–noon, 2–5pm daily. Donations welcome. Feast of the Birth of the Virgin (6–7 Sep).

The 12th-century church of Panagia tou Araka stands between the villages of Lagoudera and Saranti. Its interior is decorated with some of the island's most beautiful frescoes, painted in 1192 by Leon Authentou, who arrived from Constantinople and worked in

Panagia tou Araka Church, surrounded by mountains

Christ Pantocrator fresco in the Church of Panagia tou Araka

the aristocratic Komnenos style. This church contains some of the most interesting examples of pure Byzantine art in Cyprus.

The most magnificent of the paintings depicts Christ Pantocrator in a blue robe, surrounded by images of angels and prophets. In the apse are images of 12 early Christian saints, including St Barnabas, the patron saint of Cyprus. Above them is the Virgin Mary enthroned, with the Child Jesus on her knees, flanked by the Archangels Gabriel and Michael.

Relief from Panagia tou Araka

Another interesting fresco is the *Birth*, showing the Infant Jesus being bathed, watched by angels, shepherds, a flock of sheep and a white donkey.

The small, richly carved and gilded iconostasis contains only four icons. On the right is a larger-than-life painting of the Madonna of the Passion (*Panagia Arakiotissa*), to whom the church is dedicated.

Environs

The mountain hamlet of **Spilia** has a splendidly preserved oil press housed in a stone building. In the central square are monuments commemorating the EOKA combatants who fought the British, blowing themselves up in a nearby hideout used to produce bombs. Some 2 km (1.2 miles) to the north of Spilia, in the village of **Kourdali**, is a three-aisle basilica, **Koimisis tis Panagias**,

which once belonged to a former monastery. Inside, the Italian-Byzantine wall paintings depict figures dressed in Venetian clothes. The Virgin, fainting at the foot of the cross, wears a dress with exposed shoulders. Other interesting paintings here include: *Doubting Thomas*, the *Praying Virgin (Virgin Orans)* and the *Dormition of the Blessed Virgin*. The best times to visit are 14–15 August, which are local feast days.

Another site worth visiting is the diminutive **Church of Timiou Stavrou** in **Agia Eirini**, which contains more paintings depicting the life and death of Jesus. It also has a deisis – an image of the Mother of God and John the Baptist sitting on both sides of Christ, who holds in his hand the prophecy pronouncing him the Messiah and adjudicator on the Day of the Last Judgment. An attractive local walk leads along the Madhari ridge to the top of **Mount Adhelfi**, at 1,612 m (5,288 ft). From here there is a stunning panoramic view over the Troodos mountain region.

㉔ Stavros tou Agiasmati

Road map C3. 6 km (3½ miles) north of Platanistasa. **Open** times vary; collect key from custodian in the coffee shop. Donations welcome. 13 & 14 Sep.

A rough road leads to this small church, in an isolated setting on the mountainside of Madhari. Originally built as the chapel for an older monastery, its low

main door was designed to prevent Arab and Turkish invaders from entering on horseback, a common way of desecrating churches.

Inside Stavros tou Agiasmati is the island's most complete cycle of paintings illustrating the Gospel. Some parts refer to the Old Testament. Another cycle of paintings illustrates the story of the Holy Cross. Together they form a fine assemblage of 15th-century frescoes.

The church's interior is divided into two horizontal zones of paintings: the lower zone displays life-size figures of the saints while the upper zone has 24 scenes from the New Testament.

Behind the iconostasis, the apse features a magnificent image of the Virgin uniting Heaven and Earth. Some of the paintings depict scenes not known anywhere else, like the fresco of the *Last Supper* in which only Christ is present; or the *Raising of Lazarus* in which a group of Jews is clearly offended by the smell of the resurrected Lazarus. The fresco of *Peter's Denial* includes a shockingly large image of a rooster. One of the niches in the north wall features a series of ten paintings that illustrate the discovery of the Holy Cross by St Helena, the mother of the Emperor Constantine. The frescoes are partly the work of Philip Goul, a Lebanese artist who is characterized by his spare yet profound style.

Standing in the north wall niche is a magnificently decorated cross, which gives Stavros tou Agiasmati (Church of the Holy Cross) its name.

Stavros tou Agiasmati church, in its remote mountainside location

CENTRAL CYPRUS

With the exception of the divided city of Nicosia, the heartland of Cyprus remains surprisingly unexplored by visitors. The plains are covered with colourful carpets of cultivated fields, crisscrossed by roads that link the small villages. They descend radially towards Nicosia *(see pp116–35)*, whose suburbs sprawl across the Pentadaktylos range. The eastern part of the Troodos mountains – the Pitsillia area is – incorporated in this region.

The vast plain on Mesaoria (meaning "the land between mountains") is a gently undulating area dotted with small towns and old-fashioned villages. The watchtowers and fences occasionally seen from the road are reminders of the "Green Line" – the buffer zone border. The defunct airport to the west of Nicosia once provided international service.

Central Cyprus is the island's least developed region from a tourist's point of view. It is almost devoid of hotels and restaurants, although here and there you can find a small agrotourism farm or a *kafeneion* – a local café. Tourists usually visit this region on their way to the beautiful Troodos mountains, or to the bustling seaside resorts in the south.

The most interesting historical sites of central Cyprus are the ruins of ancient Tamassos and Idalion. Tamassos, which was established around 4000 BC, grew rich thanks to the copper ore deposits discovered nearby. Today, items made of this metal are among the most popular souvenirs from this region.

Also of interest are the convent of Agios Irakleidios, the unusual subterranean Church of Panagia Chrysospiliotissa and Machairas monastery on the northeastern slopes of the Troodos mountains, in the Pitsillia area. Nearby are the mountain villages of Fikardou, Lazanias and Gourri, and further south the town of Agros, which is famous for its roses.

Roadside vineyard in central Cyprus

◀ Panagia tou Machaira monastery and church, Troodos

Exploring Central Cyprus

Central Cyprus, stretching south of Nicosia and covering the Pitsillia area of the eastern Troodos mountains, has limited facilities for visitors. Nevertheless, when travelling to the Troodos mountains or Nicosia it is worth exploring this region, especially the ruins of ancient Tamassos, the centre of the copper-producing area since the Bronze Age. Peristerona, home to one of the most beautiful Byzantine churches in Cyprus, as well as a fine mosque, is well worth a visit. Life proceeds slowly in the picturesque villages, with their bougainvillea-clad houses.

The lively Dali municipality, near ancient Idalion

0 kilometres   5
0 miles   5

Getting There

Central Cyprus is easily accessible. From Larnaka airport the A2 motorway runs inland towards Nicosia. From the main port in Limassol, a motorway follows the coastline and branches off as the A1 road towards Nicosia. The route from Pafos airport leads through the mountains. The road is good, and you can combine the journey with a tour of the Troodos mountains.

For hotels and restaurants in this region see p164 and pp174–5

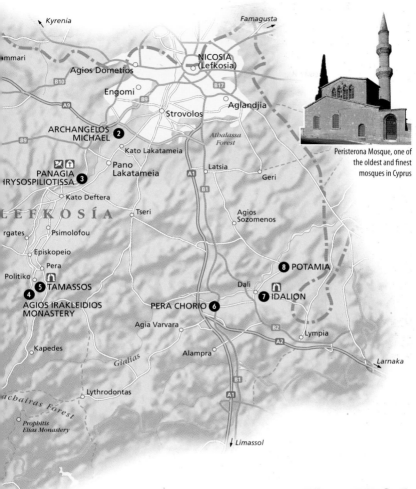

Peristerona Mosque, one of
the oldest and finest
mosques in Cyprus

Sights at a Glance

1. Peristerona
2. Archangelos Michael
3. Panagia Chrysospiliotissa
4. Agios Irakleidios Monastery
5. Tamassos
6. Perachorio
7. Idalion
8. Potamia
9. Machairas
10. Palaichori
11. Agros
12. Louvaras

The gleaming Royal Doors in
Archangelos Michael church

For additional map symbols *see back flap*

Key

- ═══ Motorway
- ▬▬ Major road
- ── Secondary road
- ┅┅┅ Minor road
- ── Scenic route
- ─ ─ Track
- ─ Regional border
- ▬▪ Green Line

❶ Peristerona

Road Map C3. 27 km (17 miles) west of Nicosia, along the road to Troodos.

Peristerona is the centre of Cyprus' watermelon-growing district. The village straddles a river that is usually dry, and features the beautiful five-domed **Church of St Barnabas and St Hilarion**, whose tall slender belfry is topped with a cross. This is a prime example of early- 10th-century Byzantine architecture. The domes, resting on tall tambours with conical tips, are arranged in the shape of a cross. (A similar five-domed structure, the Agia Paraskevi church, can be seen near Pafos, in the village of Geroskipou, *see p50*.) The proprietor of the neighbouring café holds the key to the church; it is worth gaining entry.

The narthex, which houses a vast chest depicting the siege of a castle, provides a view of the nave, which is separated by arches from the side aisles. The remains of the 16th-century wall paintings illustrate the life of King David, and there is also a vast reading room. The gilded iconostasis, beautifully carved in wood, dates from 1549.

The nearby **mosque**, one of the oldest and most magnificent anywhere on the island, was built on a square floor plan. Its tall, arched, tracery-laden windows indicate that this was once a Gothic church. Now the mosque stands empty, with pigeons nesting inside. The proximity of the church belfry and the mosque's minaret are reminders of a time when both communities – Greeks and

Fresco from the Archangelos Michael church

Turks – coexisted peacefully here in the village. Today, Peristerona is inhabited only by Greek Cypriots, while their Turkish Cypriot neighbours have moved north, beyond the demarcation line several kilometres away.

Environs
The Mesaoria plain lies between the Pentadaktylos mountain range to the north and the Troodos massif to the south. The village of Orounta, a few kilometres south of Peristerona, is home to the **Church of Agios Nikolaos**, part of the long deserted monastery here. Similar to other villages scattered on the north slopes of the Troodos mountains, such as Agia Marina, Xyliatos and Vyzakia, this area is home to small mountain churches, as well as numerous taverns and *kafenia* (coffee shops) where you can savour Cypriot *mezédhes* (a platter of hot and cold dishes) or relax over a cup of Cyprus coffee.

❷ Archangelos Michael

Road Map C3. On the outskirts of south Nicosia.

The Byzantine church of the Archangel Michael on the bank of the Pediaios river was built by Archbishop Nikiforos, whose tomb can be seen in the northern section of the building. It was rebuilt in 1636 and again in 1713, when it was bought by Kykkos Monastery. The austere edifice, constructed from a yellowish stone with small windows and a simple portico, is covered with a shallow white dome resting on a tall tambour.

The church interior has a lovely wooden iconostasis and frescoes depicting, among others, the Archangel Michael. The frescoes are more lively than some of their rivals. Their colours were brightened by restoration in 1980 and include a range of Gospel and Old Testament scenes.

Environs
To the north is a complex of playing fields and a market site; next to these is the church of Panagia Makedonitissa. Nearby is a military cemetery. On the opposite side of the river, at the end of Athalassa Avenue is Athalassa forest, the largest wooded area in the vicinity of Nicosia. It features pine, cedar and eucalyptus trees. There is also a reservoir where permit holders are allowed to fish. All this makes it a pleasant place during high summer.

❸ Panagia Chrysospiliotissa

Road Map C3. 12 km (8 miles) southwest of Nicosia.

This rarely visited subterranean church, situated near the village of Kato Deftera, is dedicated to Our Lady of the Golden Grotto. Originally a series of ancient catacombs, these were converted

The five-domed Church of St Barnabas and St Hilarion, in Peristerona

into a church in the early Christian era. The interior of Panagia Chrysospiliotissa was once covered with beautiful frescoes, which are now severely damaged.

An apse, nave, narthex and a series of vestries are carved into the sandstone. This underground church is considered one of the earliest examples of a Levantine-style Christian monastery. This type of monastery, although rare in Cyprus, was common in the region that covers present-day Israel, Jordan, Lebanon and parts of Syria. On 15 August every year, a festival is held here to celebrate the monastery's name day.

Agios Irakleidios monastery buildings

Inside the subterranean Panagia Chrysospiliotissa

❹ Agios Irakleidios Monastery

Road Map C3. 21 km (13 miles) southwest of Nicosia. **Tel** 22 623 950. **Open** 9am–noon Mon, Tue & Thu.

St Heracleidius (Agios Irakleidios) monastery stands close to the ruins of Tamassos. In the mid-1st century, in the course of their activities as missionaries on the island of Cyprus, the apostles Barnabas and Paul appointed a local man, Heracleidius, as the first Bishop of Tamassos. Bishop Heracleidius became famous for his many miracles; he was also a well-known exorcist. At the age of 60 he was killed by pagans and buried at this spot, where a small early Christian church and monastery were built. The monastery church, built in the

5th century, was repeatedly destroyed; the present building was erected in 1759.

Inside is a fresco depicting the baptism of Heracleidius administered by the apostles Paul and Barnabas, as well as beautiful geometric Byzantine mosaics and a monogram of Jesus. Relics of St Heracleidius – including his skull and forearm – are kept in a special silver reliquary.

From the side chapel to the south, a stairway descends to the catacombs, where Heracleidius spent his final years, and where he was buried.

The present buildings date from the late 18th century. The wall paintings of the period depict scenes from the life of St Heracleidius. At that time the monastery was famous for its icons, which were painted here. Now it is inhabited by a group of nuns, who breed canaries and make delicious rose-petal jam and sugar-coated almonds.

❺ Tamassos

Road Map C3. 21 km (13 miles) southwest of Nicosia. Excavation site: **Tel** 22 622 619. **Open** by appointment (**Tel** 99 218 525) Mon–Fri.

Near the village of Politiko, along the route leading to Machairas monastery, archaeologists have unearthed the remains of the

Mosaic fragment from Tamassos

ancient town of Tamassos, founded by Trakofryges of Asia Minor c.4000 BC. Around 2500 BC, rich copper deposits were discovered here, which led to the town's growth and prosperity. Temesa (an alternative name for Tamassos) is mentioned in Homer's *Odyssey*; an excerpt describes Athena's journey to Temesa in order to trade iron for copper.

Later, in about 800 BC, the town was taken over by the Phoenicians. Their king, Atmese of Tamassos, along with other Cypriot kings, paid tribute to the Assyrian rulers.

Alexander the Great gave the local copper mines as a present to King Protagoras of Salamis, in gratitude for his help during the siege of Tyre. In AD 12, the Judaean king Herod the Great leased the local copper mines; many Jews arrived on the island to supervise the excavation of this valuable commodity. Archaeological works started in 1890 and continue to this day. The major discoveries are the subterranean royal tombs dating from 650–600 BC, which have long since been looted. Two of them survive in perfect condition. Other discoveries include a citadel, the site of copper processing and the Temple of Aphrodite (or Astarte). Many items discovered here are now in London's British Museum and Nicosia's Cyprus Museum.

❻ Pera Chorio

Road Map C3. 17 km (10½ miles) south of Nicosia.

The small village of Pera Chorio is the setting of the hilltop **Church of the Holy Apostles** (Agioi Apostoloi). This domed, single-aisle building has several side chapels.

The church, in a scenic setting, conceals fragments of beautiful 12th-century frescoes, in a style similar to those in the church of Panagia Forviotissa (see p104). Experts regard these as the best examples of the Komnenos style anywhere on the island. The most interesting are the images of angels in the dome, below the damaged painting depicting Christ Pantocrator. Another interesting painting shows two shepherds conversing casually, their shoulder bags hanging from a tree, while the infant Jesus is bathed. The apse features a picture of the Virgin, flanked by St Peter and St Paul. Also depicted are saints, martyrs, emperors and demons.

Nearby is the 16th-century church of Agios Dimitrios.

The ancient Church of the Holy Apostles in Pera Chorio

❼ Idalion

Road Map D3. 20 km (12 miles) south of Nicosia. 🎭 Adonis Festival (spring).

The ancient Idalion, whose remains can be seen in the present-day municipality of Dali, was one of the oldest city-states on the island. According to legend, it was founded by King Chalcanor, a Trojan War hero.

The town is built on top of two hills; only a small portion of its ruins has so far been unearthed, including tombs along the road

A stone church in the Potamia area

to Larnaka. Idalion existed from the Bronze Age up to about 1400 BC. The town had 14 temples, including those dedicated to Aphrodite, Apollo and Athena. Archaeological excavations are still under way. The best artifacts can be seen in the Cyprus Museum in Nicosia.

The remains of Idalion had already sparked interest in the 19th century. The American consul, Luigi Palma di Cesnola, plundered thousands of tombs in this area, robbing them of all their valuable items. Local farmers also found large numbers of votive figurines of Aphrodite while working in the fields, which indicates that this was a major site of the cult of Aphrodite, the most important Cypriot goddess.

Legend tells of Aphrodite's love for Adonis, son of Zeus and Hera. Ares, the jealous god of war, turned himself into a wild boar and killed Adonis in a nearby forest. Each spring, millions of red poppies and anemones cover the area, said to spring from his blood.

Ruins of the ancient city-state of Idalion, near present-day Dali

❾ Potamia

Road Map D3.

Situated close to the Green Line, the little village of Potamia is one of the few places in the south with a small Turkish community. The village has a history of coexistence and today elects both a Greek- and a Turkish-Cypriot mayor.

Not far from the village are the ruins of the Lusignan kings' summer palace, and several Gothic churches.

Environs

The surrounding area is not of great interest, due to the many factories and industrial estates built in the immediate vicinity of Nicosia. To the southwest of the derelict village of **Agios Sozomenos** are the ruins of **Agios Mamas** church, built in the Franco-Byzantine style. This is one of the best Gothic historic sites on the island. Construction began in the early 15th century, in the Gothic style which was prevalent on the island at that time. However, it was never completed. Today visitors can see the walls of the three-apsed aisles, separated by intricate arcades, and the monumental portico.

The village of Agios Sozomenos was abandoned early in 1964, when Greek Cypriot police attacked the village inhabited by Turkish Cypriots in retaliation for the killing of two Greeks. Both sides suffered severe losses. The stone wall surrounding the village is a reminder of these events.

Cypriot Church Frescoes

The shady, forested valleys of the Troodos mountains hide small Byzantine churches; ten of these have been named UNESCO World Cultural Heritage Sites. Along with a few other churches and chapels throughout the island, they conceal frescoes representing some of the most magnificent masterpieces of Byzantine art. In keeping with Orthodox canons, the interiors are divided according to theological order. The dome symbolizes Heaven, presided over by Christ Pantocrator, the Ruler of the World, usually surrounded by archangels and prophets. Below are the main scenes from the New Testament, including the saints and fathers of the Church. The apse behind the altar features an image of the Virgin with Child. The portico usually contains the Last Judgment, painted above the exit.

Christ Pantocrator
Often painted within the dome, the Omnipotent King of the World looks down from heaven. His right hand is raised in a gesture of benediction; his left hand holds a book as a symbol of the Law.

The Life of Jesus and Mary
The life of the Holy Family has been depicted in many frescoes, as illustrations of the New Testament.

Agios Mamas
Mamas is one of the most celebrated and popular of all Cypriot saints. His name has been given to many churches throughout the island.

The Praying Virgin (Virgin Orans)
Mary raises her hands towards heaven in a pleading gesture. Her eyes are turned towards the people, urging them to trust in Christ.

The 40 Martyrs of Sebaste
In the early days of Christianity, many followers suffered death for their faith. These men, despite being subjected to freezing temperatures and then fire, held to their faith and were martyred.

The Way of the Cross
The images of the way of the cross and the Lord's Passion are among the most dramatic subjects for fresco painters.

❾ Machairas Monastery

Road Map C3. 41 km (25 miles) southwest of Nicosia. **Tel** 22 359 334 **Open** 8:30am–5:30pm daily (groups only 9am–noon Mon, Tue & Thu).

On the northern slopes of the Troodos mountains, in the area known as Pitsillia, stands one of Cyprus' most famous monasteries – Machairas (Panagia tou Machaira). The monastery rises like a fortress from the mountainside of Kionia, almost 800 m (2,625 ft) above sea level. Its name originates from the word *mahera*, which means "knife" and probably derives from the knife found next to an icon hidden in a cave. Two hermits from Palestine found the icon in the cave, and then built a church dedicated to the Virgin Mary in 1148. In 1187, Emperor Manuel Komnenos provided the funds to build a bigger church; he also exempted it from the jurisdiction of the local bishop.

The monastery buildings in their present form date from the early 20th century. The beautiful church, surrounded by cloisters, contains numerous beautiful and well-preserved icons and cult objects. A Gospel printed in Venice in 1588, is held in the treasury. The monks are extremely pious; their vows are as severe as those taken by the brothers from Mount Athos in Greece.

For Cypriots, this place is associated with EOKA commander Grigorios Afxentiou, who hid here disguised as a monk. British soldiers ambushed him in a nearby bunker. His comrades surrendered, but Afxentiou chose to fight and resisted the attacks of 60 British soldiers for several hours. Only flame-throwers could put an end to this heroic battle. On the spot where Afxentiou fell now stands a larger-than-life statue depicting the hero.

View of Palaichori village

Environs
Beyond the village of Lythrodontas, where the paved road ends, is a small monastery dedicated to the Prophet Elijah (Prophitis Elias), hidden in the Machairas Forest.

❿ Palaichori

Road Map C3.

The village of Palaichori lies in a deep valley, near the source of the Peristerona river. The village and the surrounding area feature several churches and chapels, but the most interesting of these is the **Metamorfosis tou Sotiros chapel**. Erected in the early 16th century, this small church is decorated with frescoes. On the south wall is the scene that gives the chapel its name. It shows a luminous figure of Christ, with prophets and disciples, atop Tabor Mountain at the time of the Transfiguration.

Lions are the predominant motif of the remaining paintings: in the den with Daniel, preparing to bury the body of St Mary the Beatified of Egypt and, finally, St Mamas riding a particularly elongated predator (*see p115*).

Environs
The three picturesque villages of **Fikardou**, **Gourri** and **Lazanias** at the eastern end of the Pitsillia area form a legally protected conservation zone, due to their unique traditional architecture. The largest number of typical folk buildings have survived in Fikardou, which now looks more like an open-air museum than a village. The village was declared a monument of national culture by Europa Nostra in 1987, for being the best example of rural architecture from the past few centuries. It has narrow alleys paved with stone, and neat little timber houses, two-storeys high, with wooden balconies. The old houses of Katsinioros

Courtyard of the Machairas monastery

and Achilleas Dimitri, which are some of the loveliest in the village, have been turned into a **Rural Museum** with a collection of tools and period furnishings. They include a loom, distillery equipment and an olive press.

🏛 Rural Museum
Fikardou. **Tel** 22 634 731.
Open Apr–Oct: 9am–5pm daily ; Nov–Mar: 8am–4pm daily. 🐾

⓫ Agros

Road Map C3. 🚌 66 from Limassol.

Agros is a large village lying at an altitude about 1,000 m (3,280 ft) above sea level, in the picturesque Pitsillia area. The village is famous for its delicious cold meats, particularly its sausages and hams, as well as its fruit preserves and products made of rose petals. The locally cultivated Damask rose is said to have been brought here by the father of Chris Tsolakis, in 1948. Chris now owns a small factory of rose products, making rose water, liqueur, rose wine, rose-petal jam and rose-scented candles. Rose petals are harvested in the summer months.

The charms of Agros and its environs are promoted enthusiastically by Lefkos Christodoulu, who runs the largest local hotel – Rodon.

His efforts have resulted in the creation of numerous walking trails. The neighbourhood is home to several Byzantine churches decorated with frescoes. Agros itself has no historic sights. The old monastery, which stood here until 1894, was pulled down by the villagers in a dispute with the local bishop. Agros boasts an excellent climate, reputedly good for a long lifespan.

Interior of the Chapel of St Mamas, Louvaras, with frescoes of Jesus' life

⓬ Louvaras

Road Map C4. 25 km (15½ miles) north of Limassol.

Louvaras is a small village situated among the hills. The local attraction is the **Chapel of St Mamas**, decorated with exquisite late-15th-century frescoes depicting scenes from the life of Jesus. They include

Detail of a colourful fresco from St Mamas chapel

the *Teaching in the Temple*, *Meeting with the Samaritan Woman at the Well*, and the *Resurrection*, in which the guards wear medieval suits of armour. The figures above the door, dressed in Lusignan clothes, are likely to represent the original donors.

St Mamas is one of the most popular Cypriot saints. He is portrayed on the north wall riding a lion while cradling a lamb in his arms. The scene is associated with an interesting legend. Mamas, a hermit, was ordered to pay taxes by the local governor. He refused to do so, claiming to live solely from alms. The governor lost patience and ordered Mamas to be thrown in jail. As the guards led Mamas away, a lion leapt from the bushes and attacked a lamb grazing peacefully nearby. The saint commanded the lion to stop, took the lamb into his arms and continued his journey on the back of the chastened lion. Seeing this miracle, the governor freed St Mamas, who became the patron saint of tax-evaders.

The village of Agros, scenically located among the hills

SOUTH NICOSIA

Near the centre of the island, Nicosia (Lefkosia in Greek) is Europe's only divided capital city. The numerous historic sights and traditional atmosphere of South Nicosia have been carefully preserved. The Old Town lies within imposing defence walls erected by the Venetians in the 16th century. In the evenings, the narrow streets fill with strolling crowds of Cypriots and tourists alike, who come to dine and socialize in the buzzing streets and neighbourhoods of the Old Town.

Nicosia is the business and financial centre of the Republic of Cyprus, as well as its seat of government, home to the president. It is composed of three districts: the Old Town, the modern city, and the sprawling suburbs where most families live, extending beyond the city far into the Mesaoria valley.

The charming Old Town, with its narrow streets, is surrounded by Venetian walls stretching for 4.5 km (3 miles). The walls are punctuated by 11 bastions and three gates. The Porta Giuliana (Famagusta Gate) houses a Cultural Centre. Visitors heading for the border foot-crossing to Turkish-controlled North Nicosia (near the Ledra Palace Hotel) are greeted by the grim Pafos Gate, near the demarcation line. Crossing the border is much easier these days thanks to the partial lifting of restrictions.

The Laiki Geitonia district, east of Eleftheria Square (Plateia Eleftherias), has narrow, winding alleys filled with restaurants, art galleries and boutiques set between traditional houses, typical of Cypriot urban architecture. Ledra and Onasagorou streets are prestigious pedestrian precincts with smart boutiques, restaurants and bars. One of the crossings to North Cyprus is located here. At the heart of Nicosia stands the Archbishop's Palace.

South Nicosia has a wide range of museums that are worth a visit, including the wonderful Cyprus Museum.

Rooftop view of the tightly packed Nicosia area

◀ Laiki Geitonia in the Old Town area

Exploring South Nicosia

The majority of historical sights in Nicosia are found within the mighty town walls. The main attractions, not to be missed, are the Cyprus Museum, the Archbishop's Palace and St John's Cathedral. The latter contains pristine 18th-century frescoes on Biblical themes. The Cyprus Museum holds the island's largest collection of archaeological artifacts, gathered from many sites. The bustling Ledra and Onasagorou streets and the surrounding neighbourhood provide a wide choice of food and drink options with numerous cafés, restaurants, bars and tavernas. The Cyprus Tourism Organization also offers free tours of the capital *(see p125)*.

5th-century BC figurine from the Cyprus Museum

Key

- City wall
- Pedestrianized street

Church in South Nicosia

Getting There

You can reach South Nicosia via the A2 motorway from Larnaka
international airport, or the A1 motorway from Limassol port.
The town stands against the backdrop of the Pentadaktylos
mountain range, situated on the Turkish side of the border.
A good, wide road leads through the suburbs almost
to the centre of Nicosia. You can
cross the border to North
Nicosia at the
Ledra Palace
Hotel and
Ledra Street.

A decorated shutter from the
Ethnological Museum,
Hadjigeorgakis Kornesios House

Sights at a Glance

1. The National Struggle Museum
2. Folk Art Museum
3. Archbishop Makarios Cultural Centre
4. Cathedral of St John the Theologian
5. Hadjigeorgakis Kornesios House
6. Omar Mosque
7. Panagia Chrysaliniotissa
8. Centre of Visual Arts and Research
9. Famagusta Gate
10. Constanza Bastion
11. Town Hall
12. Laiki Geitonia
13. Leventis Museum
14. Tripiotis Church
15. Bank of Cyprus Cultural Foundation
16. Araplar Mosque
17. Cyprus Museum
18. A. G. Leventis Gallery
19. State Gallery of Contemporary Art

0 metres 200
0 yards 200

For additional map symbols see back flap

Street-by-Street: South Nicosia

South Nicosia is surrounded by Venetian defence walls and bastions, and has served as the capital since the 11th century. During the Lusignan era, this was a magnificent city, home of the Royal Palace and scores of churches. Today, the area within the old walls is full of museums, sacred buildings and historical buildings, which help to recreate the atmosphere of bygone centuries. It is enjoyable to stroll along the streets of old Nicosia, stopping for coffee, or taking a shopping trip to the rebuilt district of Laiki Geitonia.

❸ Archbishop Makarios Cultural Centre
The island's largest, most precious collection of magnificent icons and mosaics is housed here.

Richly decorated
19th-century houses are the pride of the southern part of the Old Town.

← Laiki Geitonia

PATRIARCHOU GRIGORIOU

ISOKRATOUS

HADJIGEORGAKI KORNESIOU

THINON

ZIN

AGIOU

❻ Omar Mosque
A former Augustinian church was converted into a mosque in 1571, following the capture of the city by Ottomans. It is the largest mosque in southern Cyprus.

The Archbishop's Palace
was built in 1956-60 in Neo-Byzantine style.

❺ Hadjigeorgakis Kornesios House
This historic 18th-century building, a former home of the Cypriot dragoman, was awarded the Europa Nostra Prize following its restoration. Now it houses a small Ethnological Museum.

❷ Folk Art Museum
The highlight here is the collection of 19th- and early-20th-century Cypriot folk art. The textiles, ceramics, wooden artifacts and folk costumes are housed in the Old Archbishop's Palace.

Locator Map
See pp118–19

❶ The National Struggle Museum
Here are documents, photographs and weapons associated with the struggle for independence from 1955 to 1959.

Liberty Monument
on the Podocataro Bastion symbolizes the liberation of the Cypriot nation.

PLATEIA ARCHIEPISKOPOU KYPRIANOU

AGIOU IOANNOU

ERMEIOU

ADAMANTOU KORAI

IRAKLEOUS

PERSEOS

PROUSIS

THEONOS

OTHONOS

EOS

ELENIS PALEOLOGIS

LEOFOROS NIKIFOROUFOKA

❹ Cathedral of St John the Theologian
Erected by Archbishop Nikiforos, this small church contains beautiful 18th-century frescoes.

Key
— Suggested route

❶ The National Struggle Museum

Plateia Archiepiskopou Kyprianou.
Tel 22 305 878. **Open** 8:30am–2:30pm
Mon–Fri.

Housed in a building just behind the Old Archbishop's Palace is The National Struggle Museum. Its collection of photographs, documents, weapons and other objects chronicles the bloody struggle of the EOKA organization against the colonial British army from 1955 to 1959. The exhibits illustrate the fights carried out by EOKA against the British.

The collection also includes materials documenting British reprisals, including arrests, interrogations and torture. The museum is primarily intended for Cypriots and school groups.

The Folk Art Museum, housed in the Old Archbishop's Palace

❷ Folk Art Museum

Plateia Achiepiskopou Kyprianou.
Tel 22 432 578. **Open** 9:30am–4pm
Mon–Fri, 9am–1pm Sat.

Behind the cathedral is the Old Archbishop's Palace, which now houses the Folk Art Museum. On display here is a diverse array of exhibits illustrating the culture of Cyprus. Outside, the main museum attractions are the wooden water wheel, olive presses and carriages. Inside are folk costumes dating from the 19th and 20th centuries, household furnishings and other domestic implements, ceramics, textiles, Lefkara laces and silver jewellery.

Façade of The National Struggle Museum

❸ Archbishop Makarios Cultural Centre

Plateia Achiepiskopou Kyprianou.
Byzantine Museum: **Tel** 22 430 008.
Open 9am–4pm Mon–Fri, 9am–
1pm Sat. **Closed** Sat pm in Aug.
W makariosfoundation.org.cy

This cultural centre, adjacent to the New Archbishop's Palace, houses several libraries, the School of Ecclesiastical Music and the Byzantine Museum, which first opened in 1982.

Also known as the Icon Museum, the Byzantine Museum contains the largest and most valuable collection of icons in Cyprus. Around 230 icons span the 8th to the 19th centuries. Through the exhibition you can follow the changing trends in the art of icon "writing", and see the idiosyncratic images of Jesus, the Virgin Mary, the saints and the apostles. The best exhibits include the 13th-century icon by the main door, portraying the Prophet Elijah being fed by a raven, and the image of the Virgin holding the dead body of Christ – the equivalent of the Roman Catholic *Pietà*.

The reconstructed apse was rescued from the church of Agios Nikolaos tis Stegis in the Troodos mountains.

Crown exhibit from the Byzantine Museum

For several years the museum has displayed 6th-century Byzantine mosaics stolen during the 1970s from Panagia Kanakaria church in Lythrangomi in the Turkish-occupied Karpasia peninsula. Following a lengthy court battle, the Cypriot government recovered the mosaics. They depict various religious figures, including the Virgin Mary, the archangels Michael and Gabriel, and several apostles. The figure of Jesus, depicted in one of the mosaics clutching a scroll of parchment, has the appearance of a Hellenic god. All of the figures have un-naturally large eyes, a characteristic trait of early-Christian art.

In addition to mosaics and icons, the museum's collection includes ecclesiastical garments and books.

The New Archbishop's Palace was erected in 1956–60 in the Neo-Byzantine style to a design by Greek architect George Nomikos. Usually closed to visitors, it does open occasionally, when you can visit the bedroom of Archbishop Makarios, where his heart is kept.

Located near the Makarios Cultural Centre, and housed in a former power plant, is the **Municipal Arts Centre**, which serves as a venue for major art exhibitions.

❹ Cathedral of St John the Theologian

Plateia Achiepiskopou Kyprianou. **Tel** 22 432 578. **Open** 8am–noon, 2–4pm Mon–Fri, 8am–noon Sat.

The small Cathedral of St John (Agios Ioannis) dates from 1662. Built of yellow stone and covered with a barrel vault, it stands on the ruins of a medieval Benedictine monastery. Its interior is decorated with magnificent paintings depicting Biblical scenes from the life of Jesus, from birth to crucifixion, including a striking **Last Judgment** above the entrance.

The four paintings on the right wall, next to the Archbishop's throne, show the discovery of the relics of the apostle Barnabas, founder of the Cypriot church. They also show the privileges granted by Byzantine emperor Zeno to the Cypriot Church, including *autokefalia* (independence from the Patriarch of Constantinople) and the right of the Archbishop to wear purple garments during ceremonies, to use the sceptre instead of the crosier, and to sign letters with red ink. The paintings tightly covering the walls and ceiling are by the 18th-century artist Filaretos.

To the right, by the door leading to the courtyard, stands a small marble bust of Archbishop Kyprianos, who was hanged by the Turks in 1821 in retaliation for the outbreak of

Ornately decorated interior of the Hadjigeorgakis Kornesios House

Greek national insurgence. Kyprianos founded the first secondary school in Cyprus. The Pancyprian Gymnasium, regarded as the most prestigious high school in the Greek part of the island, exists to this day. Its Neo-Greek building is on the opposite side of the street.

❺ Hadjigeorgakis Kornesios House

Ethnological Museum: Patriarchou Grigoriou 20. **Tel** 22 305 316. **Open** 8:30am–3:30pm Tue–Fri, 9:30am–3:30pm Sat.

One of the town's most interesting buildings is the House of Hadjigeorgakis Kornesios, a well-preserved building from the late 18th century. Kornesios, a highly educated Greek Cypriot businessman and philanthropist, served from 1779 as a dragoman – a liaison between the Ottoman government and

the Greek Cypriot population. Despite serving the Turks for a number of years, he was arrested and executed by them.

The opulent house is decorated with Anatolian-style columns and lattice-work. The bedroom and Turkish-style drawing room lined with carpets occupy the first floor. The ground floor contains servants' quarters and a *hammam* – a Turkish bath. Part of the house holds a small ethnological exhibition.

❻ Omar Mosque (Ömeriye Cami)

Trikoupi and Plateia Tyllirias. **Open** daily, except during services. Donations welcome.

This mosque takes its name from Caliph Omar, who supposedly reached Nicosia in the course of the 7th-century Arab raids on Cyprus.

The site now occupied by this mosque was once home to a 14th-century church, which served the local Augustine monastery. The Church of St Mary drew pilgrims in great numbers from Cyprus and throughout Europe to visit the tomb of the Cypriot saint John de Montfort, a member of the Knights Templar.

Minaret of the Omar Mosque

The church was converted into a mosque after the town was captured by the Ottomans, led by Lala Mustapha Pasha, in the 16th century. On the floor of the mosque are Gothic tombstones, used by the Turks as building material.

The mosque is used by resident Muslims from Arab countries. It is open to visitors; please remove your shoes before entering. It is also possible to climb to the top of the minaret, from where there are lovely views of Nicosia.

The small, yellow-stone Cathedral of St John the Theologian

Chrysaliniotissa church, renowned for its collection of icons

❼ Panagia Chrysaliniotissa

Chrysaliniotissas.

The Chrysaliniotissa church, the capital's oldest house of worship, is dedicated to Our Lady of the Golden Flax. It stands at the centre of the district bearing the same name, right on the Green Line. It was built in c.1450 by Helen, the Greek-born wife of the Frankish king John II. The church takes its name from a miraculous icon found in a field of flax.

This L-shape building, with two domes and a slender belfry, is famous for its collection of rare icons of the Byzantine era.

Located nearby at Dimonaktos 2 is the small **Chrysaliniotissa Crafts Centre**. Various types of Cypriot art and handicrafts can be seen and purchased in this small crafts centre, which is modelled on a traditional inn.

Prior to the division of Nicosia, the opposite side of Ermou Street, called Tahtakale Cami after the mosque that stood here, was home to many Turkish Cypriots. Based on the Nicosia Master Plan, the old houses are being renovated and new occupants are moving in. Thanks to the founding of the Municipal Cultural Centre in Famagusta Gate, the district is becoming popular, with boutiques, restaurants, bars and tavernas springing up.

❽ Centre of Visual Arts and Research

Ermou Street 285. **Tel** 22 300 999.
Open summer: 9:30am–4:30pm Tue–Thu, Sat & Sun; winter: 10am–6pm Mon–Sat. 🅦 cvar.severis.org

Located opposite Famagusta Gate, the Centre of Visual Arts and Research offers visitors a peek into the history and culture of Cyprus and its neighbours through paintings, antique costumes and other exhibits. The Travelling Artists Collection has more than 1,000 artworks created by artists who visited the island during 18th–20th centuries. The Costumes Collection, featuring clothes, bed linen and embroidery, showcases the influence of other cultures on the development of Cypriot attire. There are also smaller collections of books, many of them rare and old, photographs and colonial memorabilia.

Chrysaliniotissa church detail

❾ Famagusta Gate

Leoforos Athinon. **Tel** 22 797 660.
Open 10am–1pm, 4–8pm Mon–Fri.

One of three city gates, Famagusta Gate is situated in the Caraffa bastion of the Venetian defence walls. Low-built and comprising a log tunnel ending at a wooden gate, it resembles the Venetian gate from Iraklion, in Crete. The side facing town is decorated with six Venetian coats-of-arms.

The structure was thoroughly renovated in the 1980s. Now it houses the **Municipal Cultural Centre**. The main room is used for exhibitions, concerts and theatrical performances. The smaller side room is devoted to art exhibitions.

Environs

The medieval Venetian defence walls are the most distinctive element of old Nicosia. They were erected during 1567–70 to a design by Italian architect Giulio Savorgnano. The present-day Famagusta Gate was originally called the Porta Giuliana, in honour of the architect.

The 5-km- (3-mile-) long Venetian walls contain 11 artillery bastions and three gates – the other two are called the Pafos and Kyrenia Gates, after the towns they face.

The defence walls fit in well with Nicosia's overall appearance. The bastions and the areas between them have been converted into car parks and market squares. The d'Avila bastion, near the Plateia Elefteria (Eleftheria Square), is the site of the town hall and the municipal library. The Podocataro bastion features the Liberty Monument, which depicts the goddess of Liberty clad in ancient robes, while two EOKA soldiers at her feet open prison bars from which a group of Cypriots emerges.

Famagusta Gate, housing Nicosia's Municipal Cultural Centre

Entrance to the town hall building, resting on Ionian columns

❿ Constanza Bastion

Leoforos Konstantinou Palaiologou. 🏛 Wed. Bayraktar Mosque: closed to visitors.

One 11 bastions protruding from the Venetian walls of the old quarter of Nicosia, Constanza Bastion is the site of the Bayraktar Mosque, erected to commemorate a Turkish soldier killed during the siege of Nicosia. Every Wednesday and Saturday, the area in front of the mosque turns into a colourful fruit and vegetable market.

⓫ Town Hall

Plateia Eleftheria (Eleftheria Square).

Built in the Classical Greek style, the single-storey town hall stands on the d'Avila bastion, next to the municipal library. An ornamental semicircular stairway leads to the portal, which rests on Ionian columns. **Plateia Eleftheria** (Eleftheria Square), opposite the town hall, has undergone a multi-million-euro renovation based on a design by renowned architect Zaha Hadid.

Eleftheria Square is the starting point for the two main shopping streets of old Nicosia: **Onasagorou** and **Ledra**. Both are lined with dozens of shops, tavernas, *kafenia* (coffee shops), restaurants and bars.

At the end of Ledra Street, whose name evokes the ancient town that once stood on the site of present-day Nicosia, is a checkpoint and crossing to North Nicosia, with a monument to those Greek Cypriots who went missing during the Turkish invasion. There is a small museum here.

⓬ Laiki Geitonia

The pedestrianized Laiki Geitonia (Popular Neighbourhood) is a restored section of Old Nicosia near the brooding Venetian defence walls, the town hall and Onasagorou Street.

Figurine, Leventis Museum

Clustered within a small area of narrow, winding alleys in prettily restored houses are numerous restaurants, shady cafés, handicraft workshops and souvenir shops aimed primarily at tourists. Here you will also find tourist information offices, offering free maps and brochures.

The project to rebuild and restore the Laiki Geitonia district was honoured with the prestigious Golden Apple ("Pomme d'Or") Award, granted by the World Federation of Journalists and Travel Writers in 1988.

Guided tours around South Nicosia start from outside the Cyprus Tourist Organization office located at 35 Odos Aristokyprou, in the Laiki Geitonia district. It is worth joining one of these tours, as they take visitors to many interesting sites that are normally closed to tourists.

⓭ Leventis Museum

Ippokratous 15–17, Laiki Geitonia. **Tel** 22 661 475. **Open** 10am– 4:30pm Tue–Sun.
🖥 leventismuseum.org.cy

The fascinating Leventis Museum houses a collection devoted to the history of Nicosia, from ancient times until today. Its creators have succeeded in putting together an intriguing exhibition showing the everyday life of Nicosia's residents. Of particular interest to visitors are the exhibits relating to the times of the Franks and the Venetians, including medieval manuscripts and the opulent clothes of the city's rulers. Also of note are the documents and photographs dating from the colonial era.

British-period costumes on display at Leventis Museum

⓮ Tripiotis Church

Solonos Street. **Open** 9am–5pm daily.

Dedicated to the Archangel Gabriel, Tripiotis church is the loveliest of the surviving Gothic churches in south Nicosia. This three-aisled, square edifice topped with a small dome was built in 1695 by Archbishop Germanos. Designed in the Franco-Byzantine style, it has a rich and interesting interior with Gothic windows, while the exterior has a medieval stone relief depicting lions, mermaids and sea monsters. The pride of the church is its intricately carved iconostasis, which contains several old icons covered with silver revetments. The church takes its name from the district of Nicosia in which it stands.

⓯ Bank of Cyprus Cultural Foundation

Phaneromeni 86–90. **Tel** 22 128 157.
Open 10am–7pm Mon–Sun.
🌐 boccf.org

One of Cyprus' most prominent private art collections, the George and Nefeli Giabra Pierides collection, is housed here. The Cultural Foundation is an institution that sponsors scientific research and conducts educational and cultural activities. The magnificent exhibits represent works from the early Bronze Age (2500 BC) to the end of the Middle Ages. The exhibits, numbering over 600 items, include ancient bronze and gold jewellery and Mycenaean amphorae and goblets. Also on display are terracotta figurines, anthropomorphic red-polished vases and realistic limestone Hellenic statues depicting, among others, Apollo and Hercules. Glazed ceramics dating from the Middle Ages can also be seen.

Close to the Bank of Cyprus Cultural Foundation stands the **Agia Faneromeni** church, the largest church within the city

View of the three-aisled Tripiotis church

walls, built in 1872 on the site of a former Greek Orthodox monastery. *Faneromeni* in Greek means "found through revelation". Inside is a beautiful iconostas and a marble mausoleum containing the remains of the bishops and Greek priests who were murdered by the Turks in 1821.

Adjacent to the church is the imposing Neo-Classical building of the **Faneromeni High School**.

⓰ Araplar Mosque

Odos Lefkonos.

Standing close to the Agia Faneromeni church, the Araplar Mosque (Stavros tou Missirikou) was founded in the converted 16th-century Stavros tou Missirikou church, which had been designed in the Gothic-Byzantine style.

Although the mosque is usually closed, it is sometimes possible to peek inside and see its imposing interior with the octagonal-drummed dome supported on columned arches.

⓱ Cyprus Museum

Leoforos Mouseiou 1. **Tel** 22 865 864. **Open** 8am–6pm Tue–Fri, 9am–5pm Sat, 10am–1pm Sun. 🖼
🌐 cyprusmuseum.org

Jug, Bank of Cyprus Cultural Foundation

The island's largest and best archaeological museum occupies a late-19th-century Neo-Classical building. It houses a range of exhibits illustrating the history of Cyprus, from the Neolithic era (7000 BC) to the end of Roman rule (AD 395).

The museum is arranged in chronological order. **Room 1** displays the oldest traces of mankind's presence on the island. This area exhibits objects from Khirokitia, stone bowls, primitive human and animal figures carved in andesite, limestone idols, and jewellery made of shells and cornelian (which would have been imported to Cyprus). There are also early ceramics, both without decoration and with simple geometric patterns, Bronze Age amulets and cross-shaped figurines carved in soft, grey steatite.

Room 2 contains clay bowls and vessels decorated with figurines of animals. Here you will find a miniature model of a temple and a collection of ceramic vessels and figurines. **Room 3** houses a collection of ceramics up to Roman times, including Mycenaean vases and craters dating from the 15th century BC. There is also a collection of several thousand terracotta figurines depicting smiling gods.

Room 4 holds a collection of terracotta votive figurines found in the Agis Eirini sanctuary near the Kormakitis peninsula, in the north of the island. In the sculpture gallery in **Room 5** is a statue of Zeus hurling a lightning-bolt. There is a stone head of Aphrodite, the famous marble statue of Aphrodite of

Soloi dating from the 1st century AD, and an exquisite Sleeping Eros.

Room 6 features a larger-than-life bronze statue of the Emperor Septimius Severus (c.193–211), a masterpiece of Roman sculpture. The adjoining rooms contain a bronze statue of a Horned God from Engomi at the eastern end of the island and interesting collections of coins, jewellery, seals and other small artifacts. There are also sarcophagi, inscriptions, alabaster vases and the mosaic of Leda with the Swan found in Palea Pafos (**Room 7a**).

Further rooms contain reconstructed ancient tombs, as well as items found during excavations in the Salamis area, including a marble statue of Apollo with a lyre. **Room 11** contains a reconstructed royal tomb from Salamis with the famous bronze cauldron decorated with griffons and the heads of sphinxes. **Room 12** has items found in the Royal Tombs, such as a throne decorated with ivory and a silver-encrusted sword. Other exhibits include a collection of silver and gold Byzantine vessels – part of the Lambousa Treasure.

The **Municipal Garden**, on the opposite side of the street, is a green oasis set in the town centre, providing welcome shade on hot days. Named Victoria Gardens in honour of Queen Victoria, construction of the garden started in 1901. A short distance away, in Leoforos Nechrou, stands the **Cyprus Parliament** building. Adjacent to the nearby Pafos Gate, stands the Roman Catholic **Church of the Holy Cross** and the **Apostolic Nunciature**. Nearby is a UN-controlled border crossing, linking the two parts of the city. The **Ledra Palace Hotel** is the headquarters of the UN Peacekeeping Forces in Cyprus.

⓲ A. G. Leventis Gallery

A. G. Leventis Street 5. **Tel** 22 668 838.
Open 10am–5pm Mon & Thu–Sun, 10am–10pm Wed. 🖼
Ⓦ leventisgallery.org

The latest addition to Nicosia's cultural scene, the A. G. Leventis Gallery opened in 2014. It houses more than 800 works of art by Cypriot, Greek and international artists, collected by Cypriot businessman Anastasios George Leventis. Among the prominent displays is the Paris Collection showcasing paintings by Monet, Renoir, Pissarro, Chagall and other renowned painters. The collection contains French antique furniture dating from the reigns of Louis XV and Louis XVI, Chinese porcelain and an impressive selection of historic objects. The Greek Collection has significant artworks by 19th- and 20th-century Greek artists such as Parthenis, Papaloukas, Tsarouchis and Moralis. The gallery also hosts works by prominent Cypriot artists, including Adamantios Diamantis' monumental piece, *The World of Cyprus*.

⓳ State Gallery of Contemporary Art

Corner of Leoforos Stasinou and Kritis.
Tel 22 458 228. **Open** 10am–4:45pm Mon–Fri, 10am–12:45pm Sat.

This gallery occupies a splendid building situated beyond the walls, level with the Constanza Bastion. It displays a representative collection of the best works by Cypriot artists dating from 1930 to 1980. When entering Nicosia from the south you will come across the **Cyprus Handicraft Centre**, situated in Athalassa Avenue, adjacent to St Barnabas church. Traditional Cypriot handicrafts are produced here, including embroidery, lace, woodcarvings, ceramics, metalwork, mosaics, leather and textile goods, and traditional costumes. The centre was established in order to cultivate the tradition of artistic handicrafts in Cyprus, and give employment to refugees from the North.

Bronze statue of Septimius Severus, the Cyprus Museum

Environs

In the suburban district of Strovolos, 2½ km (1½ miles) southwest of the Old Town, stands the **Presidential Palace**. It is located in an extensive park, with only its dome visible from the street. Built by the British, the palace was destroyed by fire during the riot of 1931. Rebuilt by the British governor Sir Ronald Storrs, it became his official residence. The first president of the independent Republic of Cyprus, Archbishop Makarios, had his office here and lived in the Archbishop's Palace in Old Nicosia.

Paintings on display at A. G. Leventis Gallery

NORTH CYPRUS

Inhabited and governed by the Turks, and isolated from the southern Greek side of the island since the Turkish invasion in 1974, North Cyprus has some of the most beautiful spots on the entire island. The sandy beaches along Famagusta Bay and the wild Karpasia (Karpas) peninsula attract thousands of tourists, although there are still far fewer here than in southern Cyprus. The heart of the region is North Nicosia, home to over one third of the population of North Cyprus.

Most hotels and facilities can be found on the northern side of the Pentadaktylos mountains, whose rugged peaks contrast with the azure of the sea. Kyrenia (Girne) has a charming yacht harbour, one of the most attractive in the Mediterranean, with a vast, old castle recalling the time the island was under Byzantine rule. Nearby, on the northern slopes of the Pentadaktylos range (Beşparmak), lies the most beautiful village in Cyprus – Bellapais, with the romantic ruins of a Gothic abbey. Nearby St Hilarion Castle is one of three fortresses in North Cyprus, alongside the castles of Buffavento and Kantara.

The western plains, in the vicinity of Morfou (Güzelyurt), are planted with citrus orchards. Wedged between the mountains and the blue sea are the archaeological excavation sites of Soloi and ruins of the Persian palace, located on top of Vouni Hill.

Numerous fascinating relics from the Lusignan, Venetian and Ottoman eras are enclosed by the Venetian walls of North Nicosia. Old Famagusta, full of Gothic remains, is equally interesting, with its Othello's Tower and several fascinating historic sights close by – including ancient Salamis (the island's first capital), as well as Engomi and St Barnabas monastery.

Nature lovers will be enchanted by the Karpasia peninsula, inhabited by tortoises and feral donkeys and boasting nearly 60 species of orchid.

A fruit and vegetable stall in Belediye Bazaar, in North Nicosia

◀ The walls of the historic Kantara Castle, affording impressive views of Famagusta Bay

Exploring North Cyprus

Previously, this region was fairly inaccessible, but is now visited by increasing numbers of tourists. The largest choice of hotels can be found in the regions of Kyrenia and Famagusta. The area has good main roads, and is best explored by car. Nicosia, Europe's only divided capital, is full of medieval churches, caravansarais and museums. Famagusta is equally rich in historic sights. It's old town, enclosed by a ring of Venetian walls, has a unique atmosphere. Nature lovers will be drawn to the wild Karpasia peninsula, while those interested in architecture should travel to the Kyrenia mountains, with its medieval castles and Bellapais abbey.

Window from the Church of St Mary of Carmel Mountain, in Famagusta

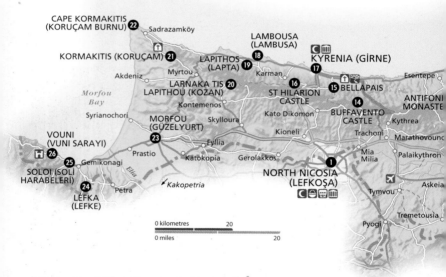

Apostolos Varnavas monastery, built near the tomb of St Barnabas

Key

— Motorway

— Major road

— Secondary road

····· Minor road

— Scenic route

– – Track

— Green Line

Getting There

There are no direct flights to Ercan (Tymvou) airport from anywhere but Turkey, and ferries sail only from Turkish ports. These include a twice-daily service from Tasucu, a three-times-a-week sailing from Mersin and a catamaran ferry from Alanya (summer only). EU passport holders may cross from the south of the island to the north via the pedestrian-only Ledra Palace and the end of Ledra Street crossing points, or via one of five vehicle crossing points (at Agios Dometios, Pergamos, Zodia, Kato Pyrgos and Strovilia). North Cyprus is best explored by car but you will need to take out inexpensive special insurance if using a car rented in the South.

The picturesque harbour of Kyrenia

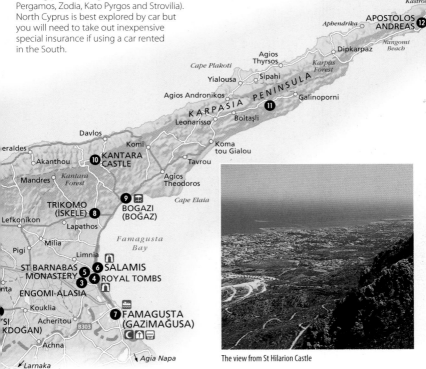
The view from St Hilarion Castle

Sights at a Glance

1. North Nicosia (Lefkoşa) pp132–5
2. Lysi (Akdoğan)
3. Engomi-Alasia
4. Royal Tombs
5. St Barnabas Monastery
6. Salamis pp138–9
7. Famagusta (Gazimağusa/Ammochostos) pp140–43
8. Trikomo (İskele)
9. Bogazi (Boğaz)
10. Kantara Castle
11. Karpasia Peninsula
12. Apostolos Andreas
13. Antifonitis Monastery
14. Buffavento Castle
15. Bellapais
16. St Hilarion Castle
17. Kyrenia (Girne) pp150–53
18. Lambousa (Lambusa)
19. Lapithos (Lapta)
20. Larnaka tis Lapithou (Kozan)
21. Kormakitis (Koruçam)
22. Cape Kormakitis (Koruçam Burnu)
23. Morfou (Güzelyurt)
24. Léfka (Lefke)
25. Soloi (Soli Harabeleri)
26. Vouni (Vuni Sarayı)

For additional map symbols see back flap

➊ North Nicosia (Lefkoşa)

Following the invasion by Turkish troops in 1974, the northern part of Nicosia became the capital of the Turkish part of the island. It is home to over half the population of North Cyprus, as well as the seat of government. It is also the administrative, business, banking and commercial centre of North Cyprus. The majority of local historic sights are found within the old Venetian walls – Gothic churches turned into mosques, bazaars, Ottoman fountains, baths and caravansarais stand among the often ugly residential buildings.

Exploring North Nicosia

The Old Town is best explored on foot. At the bus station you can board a free bus that will take you to the centre of old Lefkoşa. Do not take photographs in the vicinity of the "Green Line" that divides the city, guarded by UN and Turkish troops.

The roof terrace of the Saray Hotel in Atatürk Square (Atatürk Meydanı) provides a great view. The best place for coffee and a rest is the former caravanserai, Büyük Han.

🏛 Büyük Han

Asma Altı Sokağı. **Open** 8:30am–3:30pm daily.

The Big Inn, a former caravanserai, is one of the most interesting Ottoman buildings in Cyprus. The Turks built it shortly after the capture of Nicosia in 1572, as an inn for visiting merchants. Its architectural style is redolent of other inns of that period seen in Anatolia. Under British administration, it became Nicosia's main prison. Following its restoration, the 68 former rooms spread around the inner courtyard now house souvenir shops, art galleries, cafés and a wine bar.

Colourful fruit and vegetable stalls in Belediye Ekpazarı bazaar

The courtyard itself features a small octagonal Muslim shrine and prayer hall (*mescit*) with an ablution fountain. Büyük Han is frequently used for theatrical performances, concerts and exhibitions.

The nearby Ottoman "Gamblers' Inn" (Kumarcılar Han), in Asma Altı Square, was built in the late 17th century. Its entrance hall features two Gothic arches, since the inn was built on the ruins of a former monastery. Now it houses the North Cyprus centre for the conservation of historic sites.

Büyük Han, a former caravanserai with a Muslim shrine in the courtyard

🏛 Belediye Ekpazarı

Open 7am–5pm Mon–Fri, 7am–2pm Sat.

This covered bazaar, situated between the Bedesten and the "Green Line" that bisects old Nicosia, was the main shopping area in Ottoman times. It remains a market, where you can buy fresh meat and vegetables, as well as Turkish sweets and souvenirs. Hanging by the exit from the bazaar, on the wall of one of the houses, a plaque marks the centre of the Old Town.

🏛 Bedesten

By the Selimiye Mosque. **Closed** for restoration.

The 12th-century Byzantine Church of St George was remodelled in the 1300s in the Gothic style by the Lusignan kings. After the 16th-century occupation of Nicosia by the Turks, it was used as a warehouse, and later as a market for selling jewellery and precious metal objects. The word *bedesten* means "lockable bazaar". The north wall has an original Gothic portal, a variety of carved stonework elements and the escutcheons of the Venetian nobility.

Selimiye Camii, the former Gothic Cathedral Church of St Sophia

🄲 Selimiye Camii (Aya Sofya Cathedral)

At the centre of the Old Town, in Arasta Sokağı. **Open** 24 hours daily.

The former Cathedral Church of St Sophia (the Divine Wisdom), erected by the Lusignan kings from 1208 to 1326, is the oldest and finest example of Gothic architecture in Cyprus. Once regarded as one of the most magnificent Christian buildings in the Middle East, its unique features include the entrance portal, stone-carved window and huge columns that support the criss-cross vaulting. It was here that the Frankish rulers were crowned kings of Cyprus. This ceremony preceded a second, nominal coronation as Kings of Jerusalem, performed in St Nicholas Cathedral, in Famagusta.

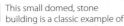

Shield above entrance to Lapidary Museum

The cathedral was destroyed, in turn, by the Genoese, the Mamelukes and several earthquakes. Following the capture of Nicosia by the Turks in 1570, the cathedral was transformed into Hagia Sophia mosque, which, in 1954, was renamed Selimiye Camii (Aya Sofya Cathedral). All images have been removed and the Gothic stone sculptures in the main portal have been chipped away. The interior has been stripped of all ornamentation and painted white. Two 50-m- (164-ft-) tall minarets, entirely out of keeping with the rest of the building, have been added on the sides of the main façade.

Other adaptations made to the interior include the addition of three *mihrabs* indicating the direction of Mecca, and carpets.

🏛 Sultan Mahmut II Library
Kirilzade Sokağı. **Open** 8am–3:30pm daily. 🏛

This small domed, stone building is a classic example of Ottoman architecture. The library was erected in 1829 by Turkish governor, Al Ruchi. It holds a collection of 1,700 books and manuscripts, including a handwritten Koran and exquisite works by Turkish and Persian calligraphers.

🏛 Lapidary Museum
Kirilzade Sokagi. **Open** 8am–3:30pm daily.
The 15th-century Venetian building at the rear of the Selimiye Mosque, near the Sultan Mahmut II Library, houses a collection of stone sculptures removed from Gothic tombs, old houses and churches.

The garden includes a Lusignan royal sarcophagus, fragments of columns, stone rosettes and Venetian winged Lions of St Mark.

C Haydarpaşa Mosque
Haydarpasa Sokağı. **Open** 8am–1pm, 2:30–5pm Mon–Fri, 8am–1pm Sat.
Originally St Catherine's Church, erected by the Lusignans in the 14th century. Their coats of arms can be seen on the south portal in carved stone.

Following the occupation of Nicosia, the Turks converted the church into Haydarpaşa Camii (Haydarpaşa Mosque), adding a disproportionate minaret. Today it houses a modern art gallery.

Haydarpaşa Mosque, originally the Gothic Church of St Catherine

North Nicosia City Centre

① Büyük Han
② Belediye Ekpazarı (bazaar)
③ Selimiye Camii (Aya Sofya Cathedral)
④ Sultan Mahmut II Library
⑤ Lapidary Museum
⑥ Haydarpaşa Mosque
⑦ Kyrenia Gate
⑧ Mevlevi Tekke
⑨ Atatürk Square
⑩ Dervish Pasha Mansion
⑪ Arabahmet Mosque (Arabahmet Camii)

0 metres 400
0 yards 400

Key
– – Green Line

🏛 Venetian Walls

Construction of the Venetian defence walls that encircle the Old Town of Nicosia was completed in 1567, three years before the Ottoman invasion. Of the 11 bastions in the walls, five are now in the northern, Turkish sector. The **Quirini** (Cephane) bastion is now the official residence of the president of the Republic of North Cyprus. The **Barbaro** (Musalla) bastion houses the National Struggle Museum set up by the army. The **Roccas** (Kaytazağa) bastion is now a park. The other two in the Turkish sector are **Mula** (Zahra) and **Loredano** (Cevizli). A sixth bastion – **Flatro** – is split across the "Green Line" between the Greek and Turkish sides.

Also on the north side is the **Kyrenia Gate**, one of the three original gates leading to the Venetian fortress.

The point at where the "no man's land" is at its narrowest is at Pafos Gate; here only a few metres separate the Greeks strolling along the street from the Turks on the bastion.

🏛 Kyrenia Gate

Girne Caddesi, by Inönü Meydanı.

The Kyrenia Gate between the Quirini and Barbaro bastions was once the main entrance to North Nicosia. It was originally named Porta del Proveditore, in honour of the Venetian engineer who supervised the fortification works. The gate walls bear inscriptions dating from the Venetian and Ottoman eras. The Turks erected the square, domed building above the gate in 1812. The street

Figures of Whirling Dervishes in Mevlevi Tekke

on either side of the gate was laid out in 1931 by the British, who took down part of the Venetian wall. Today, Kyrenia Gate houses a tourist information office.

Between the gate and the Atatürk monument are two huge iron cannons; several more have been placed along the walls. Although badly corroded, some of them still display British insignia. The cannons were cast in the late 18th century and used during the Napoleonic Wars.

🅒 Mevlevi Tekke

Girne Caddesi. **Open** 8am–3:30pm daily. 🚫

Less than 100 m (110 yards) south of Kyrenia Gate is the entrance to this small museum. It is housed in the former Muslim monastery *(tekke)* of the Mevlevi order (the Whirling Dervishes) that existed here until the middle of the 20th century. A kind of monastic brotherhood, it was founded in the 13th century in Konya by the poet Celaleddin Rumi, later known as Mevlana and revered as one of Islam's greatest mystics. Dervishes whirl to the music of a reed flute, a Levantine lute and a drum. To them, the dance represents the spiritual search for Divine Love, and provides a means of

A tombstone from Mevlevi Tekke

inducing ecstasy that frees human beings from all suffering and fear.

The museum contains figures of Whirling Dervishes accompanied by an instrumental trio sitting in the gallery. The display cabinets contain musical instruments, traditional costumes, small metal objects (such as knives), embroidery, photographs, illuminated copies of the Koran and other Turkish objects. The adjacent hall features a replica of a dervish's living quarters. Next to this is a mausoleum with sarcophagi covered with green cloth, containing the bodies of 15 religious leaders, including the last leader of the order, Selim Dede, who died in 1953. In the courtyard are several tombstones from a former cemetery that occupied this site.

🛁 Büyük Hamam

Irfan Bey Sokağı 9. **Tel** 0548 830 0881. **Open** 8am–3:30pm daily. 🚫 for a bath. 🌐 grandturkishhamam.com

This 14th-century building was originally the Church of St George. After capturing the town, the Turks converted it into baths. Steep stairs lead down through a Gothic portal to the large hall, and from there to the bathing rooms.

The baths are open to the public; you can also treat yourself to a Turkish massage. Check website for hamam opening times.

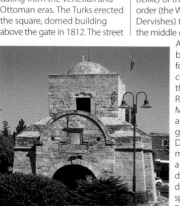

The northernmost Kyrenia Gate

For hotels and restaurants in this region see p165 and p177

🏛 Atatürk Square (Saray Square)

Atatürk Meydanı, also known as Sarayönü, was the political centre of Cyprus. On the north side of the square stood a palace inhabited, in turn, by the Frankish, Venetian and Turkish rulers, or their commissioners. In 1904, the British dismantled the 700-year-old palace complex, with its splendid throne room, opulent state rooms and cloistered courtyard.

Atatürk Meydani, the main square in the Turkish zone of Nicosia

Atatürk Square is the main square of Turkish Nicosia. The grey granite column at its centre was brought here from Salamis by the Venetians. In Venetian times, the column bore the Lion of St Mark, while its base was decorated with the coats of arms of the Venetian nobility. The Turks overturned the column; the British raised it again in 1915 and added a globe in place of the lion.

The northern end of the square features a stone platform with the British national emblem, erected here in 1953 to commemorate the coronation of Queen Elizabeth II.

Nearby are the courts of law, police headquarters, numerous banks and a post office, which was built by the British.

Dervish Pasha Mansion

🏛 Dervish Pasha Mansion

Beliğ Paşa Sokağı. **Open** 9am–1pm & 2:30–5pm Mon–Fri, 9am–1pm Sat. 🗗
This two-storey building, typical of early 19th-century Turkish architecture, was owned by Dervish Pasha, the publisher of Cyprus' first Turkish newspaper, *Zaman* (meaning "Time"). Archival copies of the paper, published since 1891, can be seen among the other exhibits here.

Following its restoration, the building has been turned into an ethnographic museum where you can see a panelled and carpet-lined drawing room, dining room, bedroom and bridal room. The exhibits include embroidery, jewellery, hookahs, lamps, ceramics and copperware.

The ground floor, intended as servants' quarters, is built of stone, while the upper floor, which was occupied by the owner, is built of brick.

🏛 Arabahmet District

Stretching southwest of Kyrenia Gate (Girne Caddesi), the Arabahmet district is full of Ottoman houses, restored partly with funding from the European Union. At the junction of Zahra and Tanzimat, close to the Mula bastion, is a somewhat neglected octagonal Ottoman fountain.

Until 1963, this district was home to residents from a variety of countries, including Greece and Armenia. There was even an Armenian church dedicated to the Virgin Mary, which was originally a Benedictine monastery. Nowadays the church stands in the closed military zone.

The **Holy Cross Church**, straddling the border, has an entrance from the Greek side. Its tower, topped with a cross, dominates the entire Arabahmet district.

The **Roccas bastion** (Kaytazağa), which overlooks the "Green Line", was turned into a municipal garden in the 1990s. This is the only place in Nicosia where the buffer zone vanishes and the inhabitants of both sides of divided Nicosia can meet each other in the Home of Cooperation. Photography, as is to be expected, is prohibited.

🕌 Arabahmet Mosque (Arabahmet Camii)

Salahi Sevket Sokağı.
Standing at the centre of the Arabahmet district is the Arabahmet Camii, covered with a vast dome. Built in the early 17th century on the site of a former Lusignan church, it was remodelled in 1845. The mosque was named after the Turkish military commander, Arab Ahmet Pasha.

The floor is paved with medieval tombstones taken from the church that formerly stood on this site. In the courtyard is a fountain and several tombs, including that of Kemal Pasha, Grand Vizier of the Ottoman Empire. The mosque holds a relic – a hair believed to come from the beard of the Prophet Mohammed – that is shown to the faithful once a year.

The Arabahmet district with its traditional Ottoman houses

❷ Lysi (Akdoğan)

Road Map D3. 23 km (14.3 miles) southeast of Tymvou (Kırklar).

A small farming village in the southeastern part of the Mesaoria plain, Lysi lies close to the "Green Line". Its most interesting historic site is the unfinished Byzantine-style church decorated with Neo-Gothic architectural elements.

Environs

Along the road to Ercan airport are the remains of Ottoman aqueducts. The surrounding area is home to several neglected Orthodox churches, including Agios Themonianos, Agios Synesios, Agios Andronikos and Moni Agiou Spyridona monastery in Tremetousha (Erdemli). The latter is guarded, and visitors should not approach it.

The unfinished Neo-Byzantine church in Lysi

❸ Engomi-Alasia

Road Map E3. **Open** summer: 8am–7pm daily; winter: 8am–3:30pm daily. 🅿️

Remains of a Bronze Age town have been found near the village of Engomi-Alasia. Archaeologists estimate that Alasia was founded in the 18th century BC. The town grew rich on trading in copper, which was excavated on the island and exported to Anatolia, Syria and Egypt.

Alasia was the capital of Cyprus and its main town – its name synonymous with the entire island. In the 12th century BC, when the Mycenaeans arrived here, the town's

Ruins near the village of Engomi, a few kilometres west of Salamis

population numbered an impressive 15,000. Following an earthquake in the 11th century BC, the town was deserted and its inhabitants moved to Salamis.

Excavation works conducted since 1896 have unearthed the ruins of a Late Bronze Age settlement, with low houses lining narrow streets.

The Alasia ruins yielded a tablet with Cypriot-Minoan writing, not yet deciphered, and the famous bronze statue of the Horned God, dating from the 12th century BC, which is now kept in the Cyprus Museum in Nicosia. Strolling around the excavation site you will come across the Horned God's sanctuary and the "House of Bronzes", where many bronze objects were discovered.

Environs

Along the road to Famagusta is the village of Engomi (Tuzla). Next to the shop is a white platform, known as the **cenotaph of Nikokreon**. It contains the remains of Nikokreon – the last king of Salamis. Refusing to surrender to the Hellenic king of Egypt, Ptolemy I, Nikokreon committed suicide by setting

fire to the royal palace. He perished, along with his entire family, in the flames that day.

❹ Royal Tombs

Road Map E3. **Open** summer: 8am–7pm daily; winter: 8am–3:30pm daily. 🅿️

The royal necropolis by the side of the road leading to St Barnabas monastery has over 100 tombs from the 7th and 8th centuries BC. Some have been given names, and others designated numbers. Almost all of the tombs are open to the east. Each one was approached by a slanting corridor known as a *dromos*, on which the most interesting artifacts were found.

Most of the tombs were looted in antiquity, but some, in particular numbers 47 and 49, contained a multitude of objects that could be useful to the royals in the next world. The most famous finds include an ivory inlaid royal bed and throne, showing clear Phoenician and Egyptian influences. The kings of Salamis were buried here with their servants and horses.

Tomb number 50, the so-called "St Catherine's prison", was built during Roman times on top of older tombs. According to legend, the Alexandrian saint, a native of Salamis, was imprisoned by her father, the Roman governor, for refusing to marry the man chosen by him. The tomb's walls bear the remnants of Christian decorations.

The site also features a small museum with plans and photographs of the tombs, and a reconstructed chariot used to carry the kings of Salamis on their final journey.

Royal Tombs from the 7th and 8th centuries BC, west of Salamis

St Barnabas monastery, built near the tomb of the apostle Barnabas

❺ St Barnabas Monastery

Road Map E3. **Open** summer: 8am–7pm daily; winter: 8am–3:30pm daily.

The monastery of St Barnabas was erected in 477 on the western end of the Constantia (Salamis) necropolis, near the spot where the apostle's grave was discovered. The construction was financed by the Byzantine emperor Zeno himself.

Two centuries later, it was demolished in one of the devastating Arab raids on Cyprus. All that remains of the original Byzantine edifice are the foundations. The present church and monastery were constructed in 1756 on the orders of Archbishop Philotheos, during Ottoman rule. The three-aisled church is covered with two flat domes resting on high drums. It now houses an **Icon Museum**.

Much more interesting, however, is the small **Archaeological Museum** occupying former monks' cells around the courtyard of the monastery. Displayed in a series of rooms are Neolithic tools and stone vessels, as well as a large number of ceramic items such as amphorae, jugs, vases and cups. Among the more curious items are a polished bronze mirror, swords, hatchets and spearheads, made of the same metal. There are also terracotta figurines of people and animals, including an unusual horse with wheels instead of hooves, and clay baby rattles shaped like boars.

Other interesting exhibits are the black-glazed ceramics imported from Attica. These are decorated with intricate motifs of animal and human figures, including lions, wild boars and hares. There is also gold jewellery, a collection of Roman glass, and a stone figure of a woman holding a poppy – probably the goddess Demeter. The Classical period is further represented by sphinxes, showing the Egyptian influence, and carved lions. A short distance

A terracotta figurine, Archaeological Museum

east of the monastery stands a small **Byzantine-style church**. This rectangular, domed chapel was erected over the tomb of the apostle Barnabas. A stone staircase leads down to two chambers hewn into the rock where, according to legend, St Barnabas was buried. The saint was killed near Salamis for preaching Christianity, and his body was cast into the sea. His disciples fished the body out, and he was buried with St Matthew's gospel on his chest, under a lonely breadfruit tree to the west of Salamis.

From 1971 until the Turkish occupation of 1974, the St Barnabas monastery was inhabited by the last three monks, the brothers Barnabas, Chariton and Stephen, who made a humble living by selling honey and painting icons.

St Barnabas

Born in Salamis, Barnabas accompanied St Paul on his missionary travels around Cyprus and Asia Minor. After parting from his master, Barnabas continued to promote Christianity on the island, for which he was killed in the year AD 57. St Mark buried the body in secret.

St Barnabas acquired fame following a miracle that occurred after his death, when he revealed the site of his burial to Anthemios, the Bishop of Salamis. The discovery of the saint's relics, and the prestige they brought, helped preserve the autonomy of the Cypriot Church.

The tomb of St Barnabas

⊙ Salamis

The former Roman Salamis, which later became Byzantine Constantia, was the island's main port and capital for a thousand years. Destroyed by the Arabs in 648, Salamis is still the largest and the most interesting archaeological excavation site on Cyprus. The unearthed relics date from the Roman and Byzantine periods. Allow a full day for a visit, including a relaxing break on the nearby beach.

Caldarium
The hot bath chamber, fitted with a central heating system, had walls decorated with abstract mosaics.

Sudatorium
The Greek-Roman baths complex included a steam bath, which was also decorated with mosaics. An underfloor heating system is in evidence.

Latrines
This semicircular colonnaded structure contained a latrine which could be used by 44 people simultaneously.

Gymnasium
A colonnade surrounded the rectangular *palaestra* of the gymnasium, which was devoted to the training of athletes.

KEY

① **Two pools** with cold water were located beyond the east portico.

② **The backstage area** housed dressing rooms for the actors.

For hotels and restaurants in this region see p164 and pp176–7

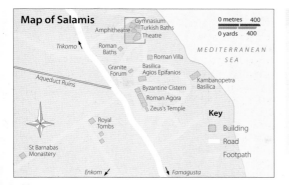

Map of Salamis

Trikomo
Amphitheatre
Gymnasium
Turkish Baths
Theatre
Roman Baths
Roman Villa
MEDITERRANEAN SEA
Granite Forum
Basilica Agios Epifanios
Aqueduct Ruins
Byzantine Cistern
Kambanopetra Basilica
Roman Agora
Zeus's Temple
Royal Tombs
St Barnabas Monastery
Enkom
Famagusta

0 metres 400
0 yards 400

Key

▢ Building
— Road
Footpath

VISITORS' CHECKLIST

Practical Information
Road map E3. 8 km (5 miles) north of Famagusta. 🚌 ℹ️ 0392 366 28 64. Archaeological site: **Open** summer: 8am–7pm daily; winter: 8am–5pm daily. 🛒 Necropolis: 1 km (0.6 mile) west of Salamis. **Tel** 0392 378 83 31. **Open** summer: 9am–7pm; winter: 9am–1pm & 2–4:45pm. 🛒

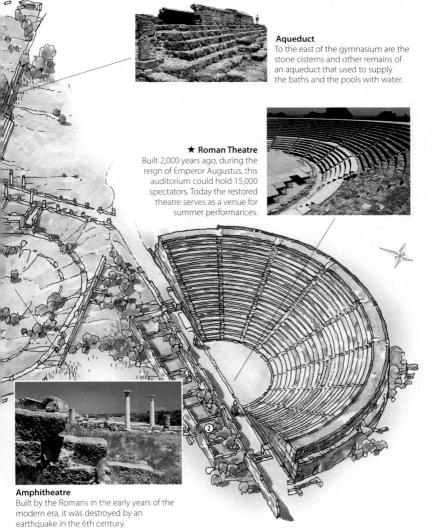

Aqueduct
To the east of the gymnasium are the stone cisterns and other remains of an aqueduct that used to supply the baths and the pools with water.

★ Roman Theatre
Built 2,000 years ago, during the reign of Emperor Augustus, this auditorium could hold 15,000 spectators. Today the restored theatre serves as a venue for summer performances.

Amphitheatre
Built by the Romans in the early years of the modern era, it was destroyed by an earthquake in the 6th century.

❼ Famagusta (Ammochostos/ Gazimağusa)

Once the world's wealthiest city, present-day Famagusta (Ammochostos in Greek and Gazimağusa in Turkish) presents a depressing sight. Yet within the mighty fortifications that kept out the Turkish army for nearly a year, and amid the many dere- lict buildings, are true gems of Gothic architecture. Former magnificent churches have been destroyed or turned into mosques. South of Famagusta, within the Venetian walls, lies the deserted Old Town of Varosha, once Cyprus' biggest resort.

Namik Kemal Square, once the site of the Venetian Palace

Exploring Famagusta

Virtually all of Famagusta's major historic sights are within the Old Town, surrounded by the Venetian fortifications. The best way to enter the city is through the Land Gate, leaving your car behind. The tourist information office is located by the gate. It is possible to explore the city by foot.

◧ Lala Mustafa Pasha Mosque

Namik Kemal Meydanı.
Open 24 hours daily.
This former cathedral was built between 1298 and 1312 to a Gothic design modelled on Reims Cathedral in France. It was here that Lusignan royalty, after their coronation in Nicosia, received the symbolic title of "King of Jerusalem".

Following the capture of the city in 1571, the victorious Turks converted the cathedral into a mosque and named it after the

commander of the besieging army – Lala Mustafa Pasha. They also added a minaret to the left tower. The building is still a functioning mosque; visitors are admitted only outside the hours of prayer.

The white interior has 12 columns to support the Gothic vaulting. There is a modest *minbar* (pulpit) in the right aisle. The façade with its unusual window and enormous rosette, basking in the light of the setting sun, is one of the most beautiful sights in Cyprus.

⬆ Agia Zoni and Agios Nikolaos

Hisar Yolu Sokağı.
Open 24 hours daily.
This small Byzantine-style church, decorated with wall paintings, dates from about the 15th century. It stands in an empty square, surrounded by a handful of palm trees. Close by is the larger Church of St Nicholas, which is partly demolished.

Gothic portal of Lala Mustafa Pasha Mosque

▦ Fountain and Jafar Pasha Baths

Naim Effendi Sokağı.
Located northwest of Namik Kemal Square, the fountain and baths were built in 1601 in Ottoman style by the Commander of the Sultan's Navy and the Ottoman Governor of Cyprus.

Jafar Pasha ordered the building of the aqueduct in order to supply the city with water. Both the aqueduct and the original town fountain have been destroyed. The current fountain was reconstructed using fragments of the original.

◧ Sinan Pasha Mosque

Abdullah Paşa Sokağı.
Closed to visitors.
The former church of saints Peter and Paul was turned into a mosque after the capture of the city by the Turks. This beautiful Gothic edifice, built of yellow stone and maintained in excellent condition, now houses the municipal library collection.

A former church turned into the Sinan Pasha Mosque

▦ Venetian Palace

Namik Kemal Meydanı
Open 24 hours daily.
Not much remains of the former palace of the Lusignan kings and Venetian governors, built during Lusignan times. The area marked by its jutting stone walls is now a car park.

On the side of Namik Kemal Square stands a triple-arched façade supported by four granite columns from Salamis. Above the central arch is the coat of arms of Giovanni Renier – the Venetian military commander of Cyprus. Between 1873 and 1876, the left section of the building was used as a prison in which Turkish poet and playwright Namik Kemal was locked up on the Sultan's order. Now it houses a museum.

Remains of the Venetian Palace

🏠 Nestorian Church
Somuncuoğlu Sokağı.
Closed to the public.

Syrian merchant Francis Lakhas built this church in 1338 for Famagusta's Syrian community. The façade is adorned with a lovely rose window. Inscrip-tions inside are in Syrian, the language of the Nestorian liturgy.

Later, the church was taken over by Greek Cypriots and renamed Agios Georgios Exorinos. The word *exorinos* means "exiler". Greeks believe that dust taken from the church floor and sprinkled in the house of an enemy will make him die or leave the island within a year.

🏠 Churches of the Knights Templar and Knights Hospitaller
Kişla Sokağı.

These two adjacent medieval churches are known as the twins. On the north façade, above the entrance, you can still see the carved stone coats of arms of the Knights Hospitaller. In the early 14th century, following the dissolution of the Knights Templar order, their monastery

Romantic ruins of the Gothic Church of St John (Latin)

and the Chapel of St Anthony were handed over to the order of St John of Jerusalem (the Knights Hospitaller). The Hospitallers' chapel, featuring a lovely rose window in the façade, now houses a theatre and an art gallery.

🏠 Church of St John (Latin)
Cafer Paşa Sokağı.
Open 8am–3:30pm daily.

Built in the late 13th century, during the reign of the French king Louis IX, the Church of St John was one of Famagusta's ealiest churches, and a splendid example of Gothic architecture. Now largely in ruins, the original north wall with the presbytery and tall Gothic windows remains standing. The capital of the surviving column is decorated with floral motifs and winged dragons.

Famagusta City Centre

① Lala Mustafa Pasha Mosque
② Agia Zoni & Agios Nikolaos
③ Fountain & Jafar
   Pasha Baths
④ Sinan Pasha Mosque
⑤ Venetian Palace
⑥ Nestorian Church
⑦ Churches of the Knights
   Templar & Knights
   Hospitaller
⑧ Church of St John (Latin)

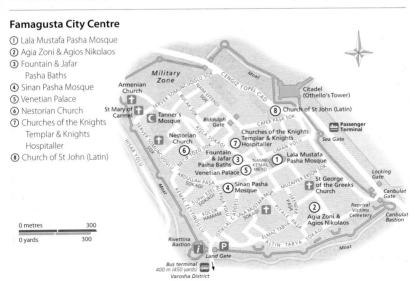

0 metres   300
0 yards   300

⛪ Agios Ioannis

Varosha (Maraş). Polat Paşa Bulvarı. 🏛

The Neo-Byzantine Church of St John stands in the Varosha (Maraş) district of Famagusta, where the Turkish army is currently stationed. It is the only part of the area that is open to the public. Entry inside the church, however, is no longer permitted. The renovated church houses a museum of icons, mostly from the 18th century, that were gathered from many destroyed Greek Orthodox churches.

The Varosha area, controlled by Turkish and UN forces, has been uninhabited for more than 40 years, ever since the expulsion of the Greek Cypriots. It is forbidden to photograph the crumbling houses or dozens of decaying beachfront hotels, dating from the 1960s.

Iconostasis in Agios Ioannis church

🏛 Canbulat Bastion

Tel 0392 366 28 64. Open summer: 8am–7pm daily, winter: 8am–3:30pm daily. 🏛

The bastion at the southeast corner of the Venetian defence walls was once called the Arsenal. Today it bears the name of the Turkish commander, Canbulat, who charged his horse at the Venetian war machine, which was studded with spinning knives, during the siege of Famagusta. Canbulat perished, cut to shreds, but his desperate attack put the machine out of action, and the Turks regard him as a hero. The bastion contains his tomb and a small museum with a collection of artifacts dating from antiquity and the Ottoman era.

🏛 Venetian City Walls

Famagusta's Old Town is encircled by huge defence walls

Ruins of the Citadel (Othello's Tower)

erected by the Venetians, who felt threatened by the Ottoman Empire's expansion into the eastern Mediterranean. The walls, 15 m (49 ft) high and up to 8 m (26 ft) thick, are reinforced with 15 bastions. The two gates leading to the town are the Land Gate and Sea Gate, which was constructed by the Venetian Nicolo Prioli. His name, coat of arms, construction date (1496) and the Lion of St Mark have been carved in the marble, brought from the ruins of Salamis.

To the right of the entrance are two marble statues of lions. Legend has it that one night the larger of the two will open its mouth, and the person who sticks his head in at that moment will win a fortune. The entrance to the Old Town from the opposite side leads over a stone bridge that spans the moat. It is defended by the massive Rivettina (Ravelin) Bastion, which the Turks call Akkule ("White Tower"). It was here that the Venetians hoisted the white flag following the 10-month siege of Famagusta

in 1571 by the Ottoman army. From the Old Town side you can see wall paintings and the coats of arms of the Venetian commanders.

The passageway features a small shrine. The restored rooms beyond the gate now house the tourist information bureau. Under the Rivettina Bastion are subterranean casemates. In 1619, a small mosque was built for the Muslim guards.

🏛 Citadel (Othello's Tower)

Cengiz Topel Caddesi (adjacent to the Sea Gate). Open summer: 8am–7pm daily, winter: 8am–3:30pm daily. 🏛

The Citadel was erected in the 12th century by the Lusignan kings, to defend Famagusta Harbour from attack. Carved in marble above the gate are Lions of St Mark (symbolizing Venice) and the name of Nicolo Foscari, who supervised the rebuilding of the fortress in 1492. This was a vast structure for its time, and it included a system of fortifications and subterranean casemates.

The Citadel is popularly known as Othello's Tower, after Shakespeare's play *Othello*, which was set largely in Famagusta. The empty interiors, Gothic rooms and gloomy casemates are now inhabited by pigeons, and the floors littered with discarded bullets and fragments of broken sculptures.

The Citadel walls afford a magnificent view over old Famagusta and the harbour.

The massive Venetian defence walls

⛪ St George of the Greeks Church

Mustafa Ersu Sokağı.
Open 24 hours daily.

Erected in the 15th century, in Gothic-Byzantine style, just a shell remains of this church. The east apse still shows the fragments of wall paintings. The steps in the nave are typical of early Christian basilicas.

The roof was brought down by Turkish bombardment in the siege of Famagusta. To this day, the walls bear pockmarks of cannonballs. Legend says that a treasure belonging to St Epifanos (Archbishop of Salamis) lies under the floor.

Abutting the church to the south is the smaller church of Agios Symeon (St Simon's).

Biddulph Gate – a remnant of a Venetian merchant's home

🏛 Biddulph Gate

Naim Effendi Sokağı.
Open 24 hours daily.

This Renaissance gate standing in a side street is a remnant of a medieval merchant's house. It was named in honour of Sir Robert Biddulph, British High Commissioner, who saved it from being pulled down in 1879. Departing from the usual custom of demolishing old structures, Biddulph pioneered the protection of Famagusta's historic sites.

Another interesting relic found along Naim Effendi Sokağı is an old, intact merchant's house, an excellent example of secular Renaissance architecture.

⛪ Churches in North Famagusta

The area at the north end of old Famagusta, around the Martinengo, San Luca and Pulacazara bastions, was previously occupied by the Turkish army. Now some of its

Ruins of St George of the Greeks church

historic sites are open to visitors. Among them is the rectangular **Church of St Mary of Carmel**, built of a yellow stone. It may be viewed only from the outside. The adjacent **Armenian Church** was built in the 16th century, when the Armenians had their bishops in Nicosia and Famagusta. The interior is covered with paintings and Armenian inscriptions. A short distance away, in the direction of the Moratto bastion and beyond the Tanner's mosque, stands the splendidly preserved medieval **Church of St Anna**, featuring an unusual belfry rising above the façade; unfortunately it is closed to visitors.

🏛 Medresa

Liman Yolu Sokağı.

The single-storey domed building to the north of the Lala Mustafa Pasa Mosque was once a college of Islamic studies, attached to an Ottoman mosque.

Coat of arms
St Mary of Carmel church

Nowadays it would be difficult to discern any particular style in it, although it is often cited as an example of classic Ottoman architecture. The two granite columns, brought from Salamis and placed in front of the building,

add to the overall impression of architectural chaos. The stone plinth opposite the entrance bears the bust of Namik Kemal, a 19th-century Turkish poet and playwright, who, on orders of the Sultan, was imprisoned in the Venetian Palace opposite. To the right are two domed Turkish tombs, one with an interesting wrought-iron gate.

After serving as a college, the former **Medresa** was later used as offices, and then as bank premises. Today the building stands empty.

🏛 Tanner's Mosque

Somuncuoğlu Sokağı.

This small, yellow limestone building was erected in the late 15th century as a church. In 1571, following the capture of Famagusta by the Turks, it was converted into a mosque.

Clay pots were built into its vaults, intended to improve the general acoustics of the building.

The mosque was later abandoned and left to decay. Since 1974 the building has been fenced off in a compound used by the Turkish army; it now serves as a depot.

Ruins of St Mary of Carmel church seen at sunset

❽ Trikomo (İskele)

Road Map E2.

This small town lies close to the base of the Karpas peninsula. At its centre, right by the roundabout, stands the tiny Dominican **Church of St James** (Agios Iakovos). Intricately carved in stone, it resembles an encrusted jewellery box. At the western end of the town stands the two-aisled, single domed **Panagia Thetokos** church, which was erected in the 12th century. The church was restored in 1804, when it was also given its marble-panelled belfry. Inside you can still see the original wall paintings dating from the 12th century.

The **Icon Museum**, opened here in 1991, houses a collection of icons removed from local Greek churches. The images are modern and of little artistic merit, yet the museum is worth visiting for its lovely interior frescoes.

🏛 **Icon Museum**
Panagia Theotokos Church.
Open 8am–3:30pm daily. 🅿

A mosque in Trikomo, a town at the base of the Karpas peninsula

❾ Bogazi (Boğaz)

Road Map E2. On the road leading to the Karpas peninsula.

At this little fishing port on Famagusta Bay you can watch the fishermen returning with their catch, and also buy fresh fish each morning. Fishing trips are available for visitors, as are lessons in scuba diving. There are beautiful long, sandy beaches in this area. A half-dozen local restaurants specialize in fish and seafood. European cuisine is also on offer at some places.

The imposing walls of Kantara Castle, overlooking Famagusta Bay

❿ Kantara Castle

Road Map E2. **Open** summer: 8am–5pm daily; winter: 8am–3.30pm daily. 🅿

Kantara Castle is the easternmost medieval fortress of North Cyprus. It lies 630 m (2,068 ft) above sea level, at the base of the Karpasia peninsula, on a spot affording views of both Famagusta Bay and the shores of Asia Minor. This was already the site of a castle in Byzantine times. It was here that the English king Richard the Lionheart finally caught up with his adversary, Byzantine governor Isaac Komnenos, in 1191 and forced him to capitulate.

The castle rooms were mostly torn down by the Venetians, but the mighty walls survive in excellent condition. The route to the castle leads through a barbican with two towers; the vast southeastern tower has a water cistern at its base, also used as a dungeon. The two adjacent former army barracks are in good condition. The southwestern wing of the castle features a secret passage that enabled the defenders to sneak out and launch a surprise attack on the besiegers. The north towers and the bastions afford magnificent views of the surrounding area.

Environs
A dozen or so kilometres (7½ miles) west of the castle, close to the sea, is the lonely Late Byzantine **Panagia Pergaminiotissa** church.

⓫ Karpasia Peninsula

Road Map E2, F1–2.
ℹ Yialoussa, 0392 374 49 84.

This long, rocky spit is the least developed part of the island, with sandy beaches on its north and south coasts, and a scattering of historic Christian churches, including the monastery of Apostolos Andreas, which is awaiting restoration, to be funded by the UN and the EU. Known as Karpaz Yarımadası (sometimes Karpas) to the Turks, this quiet

Picturesque Panagia Pergaminiotissa

peninsula has rolling hills, where wild donkeys roam, fringed by empty beaches which provide nesting grounds for sea turtles. The eastern part of the peninsula is a nature reserve, home to birds and donkeys.

The best starting point for exploring the peninsula is the fishing village of **Bogazi**. A few kilometres to the left of the main road, near the village of **Komi** (Büyükkonuk), stands a small Byzantine church with beautiful 6th-century mosaics. The church is surrounded by the ruins of a Roman town. Only the apse remains of the 5th-century Church of Panagia Kanakaria, on the edge of **Lythrangkomi** (Boltaşlı), east of **Leonarisso** (Ziyamet); the mosaics that used to decorate it can be seen in the Byzantine Museum, in Nicosia. The rest of the church dates from the 11th century, except the tamboured dome which was added in the 18th century. The church is now closed.

The last petrol station is in **Yialousa** (Yenierenköy). Further south is the village of **Sipahi** (Agia Trias) with a three-aisled early Christian basilica. Dating from the 5th century, it was discovered by archaeologists in 1957, and is noted for its handsome floor mosaics. The marble-encrusted, cruciform font in the baptistry is the biggest in the island.

Beyond the small village of **Agios Thyrsos** stands Hotel Theresa, with the best accommodation on the peninsula.

Rizokarpaso (Dipkarpaz) is the peninsula's biggest, if somewhat neglected, village. It has a population of 3,000, comprised mainly of immigrants from Anatolia. Some 3 km (2 miles) to the north are the ruins of the 5th-century church of **Agios Philon**, standing amid the ruins of the Phoenician town of Karpatia. The 10th-century basilica was later replaced by a chapel; just the south wall and the apse remain.

North of Agios Philon stands an ancient stone breakwater. A narrow road running along the coast leads to **Aphendrika**, with the ruins of an ancient harbour, a Hellenic necropolis and a fortress erected on bare rock. It also has three ruined churches: the Agios Georgios dating from the Byzantine period; the 12th-century Romanesque Panagia Chrysiotissa; and Panagia Assomatos, the best preserved of all three. On the opposite side of the peninsula is the beautiful **Nangomi Beach**.

Apostolos Andreas – the monastery of St Andrew

⑫ Apostolos Andreas

Road map F1. **Open** 24 hours daily.

Near the tip of the Karpasia peninsula stands the monastery of St Andrew (Apostolos Andreas), an irregular edifice of yellow stone with a white bell tower. According to legend, it was here that the saint's invocation caused a miraculous spring to appear, whose water cures epilepsy and ailments of the eyes, and grants pilgrims their wishes. During the Byzantine period, a fortified monastery occupied the site; some historians believe that it was here, rather than in Kantara, that Richard the Lionheart caught up with Isaac Komnenos.

In the early 20th century the monastery gained a reputation for its miracles, and became the target of mass pilgrimages. After 1974, the site was taken over by the Turkish army. Today it is once again open to visitors.

The 19th-century church has been stripped of its icons, but on the Feast of the Assumption (15 August) and St Andrew's Day (30 November), services are held for the pilgrims arriving from southern Cyprus.

In the crypt beneath the church the holy well, famed for its healing properties, still gushes the "miraculous" water. The site is regarded as holy by Greeks and Turks alike.

Environs

Less than 5 km (3 miles) from Apostolos Andreas monastery is **Zafer Burnu**, the furthest point of the Karpasia peninsula. This cave-riddled cape was a Neolithic settlement known as **Kastros**, one of the earliest places of known human habitation in Cyprus. In ancient times it was the site of a temple to the goddess aphrodite.

The offshore **Klidhes islets** (the "Keys" islets) are a haven for a variety of sea birds.

Nangomi (Golden) Beach on the Karpasia peninsula

⓭ Antifonitis Monastery

Road Map D2. 29 km (18 miles) east of Kyrenia via Agios Amvrosios (Esentepe). **Open** daily. 🖼

In a pine-covered valley on the northern slopes of the Pentadaktylos mountains, some 8 km (5 miles) south of Agios, stands the disused 12th-century monastery church of Antifonitis. This was once the most important Byzantine church in the mountains of North Cyprus. Its Greek name, meaning "He who responds", is associated with a legend about a pauper who met a wealthy man and requested a loan. When the rich man asked who would vouchsafe the loan, the pauper replied, "God will". At this moment they both heard a voice from heaven. The monastery was built on the site of this miracle.

The church was built in the 7th century; the narthex and gallery date from the Lusignan period and the loggia was added by the Venetians. The church was originally decorated with magnificent frescoes, but since 1974 these have been defaced and damaged.

⓮ Buffavento Castle

Road Map D2. **Open** summer: 8am–7pm; winter: 8am–3:30pm. 🖼

Built on the site of a Byzantine watchtower remodelled by the Lusignans, this castle perches 950 m (3,117 ft) above sea level. The date of its construction is unknown, but this mountain stronghold was captured in

Buffavento, the highest castle in Cyprus

1191 by the Frankish king Guy de Lusignan. The castle was used for years as an observation post and political prison. Under Venetian rule the castle lost its importance and was abandoned.

Steep stairs lead from the gate to the top of the tallest tower, where a magnificent view awaits. In fine weather it is possible to see Kyrenia, Nicosia and Famagusta, as well as the Troodos mountains and the coast of Turkey.

Cold winter wind blowing from Anatolia explains the name of the castle, meaning the "wind blast". In the past bonfires lit on top of the

tower served as means of communication with the garrisons stationed at St Hilarion and Kantara castles.

A marble monument by the car park commemorates the passengers and crew of a Turkish aircraft that crashed in fog in February 1988 on its approach to Ercan airport.

Environs
West of the castle, on the southern slopes of the juniper-covered mountains, stands the 12th-century Byzantine **Panagia Apsinthiotissa monastery**. It was restored in the 1960s, but after 1974 the monks were forced to abandon it. Its church is crowned with a vast dome; on its north side is a lovely original refectory.

The site is reached by turning off the Kyrenia-Nicosia highway and passing through Kato Dikomo (Aşaği Dikmen) and Vouno (Taşkent) villages.

Along the way is a giant stone flag erected by Turkish Cypriot refugees from Tochni *(see p78)* where, in the 1960s, the Greek EOKA organization murdered all the Turkish men.

The breathtaking view from Buffavento Castle

◄ View of the Old Harbour in Kyrenia

⑮ Bellapais

Road Map C2. 7 km (4.3 miles) SE
of Kyrenia. **Tel** 0392 815 75 40.
Abbey: **Open** summer: 8am–7pm;
winter: 8am–5pm.

One of the most beautiful
villages in Cyprus, Bellapais
lies amid citrus groves on
the northern slopes of the
Pentadaktylos mountains. It
features the splendidly
preserved ruins of a Gothic
abbey, to which the village owes
its name. It is thought to be
derived from the French **Abbaye
de la Paix** (Peace Abbey).

The first monks to settle here
were Augustinians from
Jerusalem, forced to flee the city
after its capture by Saladin. The
first buildings were erected in
the early 13th century, but the
main section of the abbey was
built during the reign of the
Lusignan kings Hugo III and
Hugo IV. The abbey was
destroyed by the Turks, following
their conquest of the island.

Bellapais is one of the loveliest
Gothic historic sites in the Middle
East. The oldest part of the abbey
is its well-preserved church,
built in the French Gothic style.

A spiral staircase in the
western end of the garth (the
garden close) leads to the roof,
affording a magnificent view of
the sea and the mountains. The
remaining parts include the
living quarters, the kitchen, and
the old refectory illuminated by
the light entering through the
vast windows facing the steep
crag. The garth cloisters once

Splendidly preserved ruins of Bellapais abbey

contained a carved marble
sarcophagus and a lavatory,
where the monks washed their
hands before entering the
refectory. Now they are used for
concerts during music festivals.

The English writer
Lawrence Durrell lived in
Bellapais in 1953–6,
and described the
struggles of the EOKA
fighters in his novel
Bitter Lemons. The
house in which he
lived bears a com-
memorative plaque.

Sign from Durrell's
house in Bellapais

⑯ St Hilarion Castle

Road Map C2. 7 km (4½ miles)
SW of Kyrenia. **Tel** 0533 161 276.
Open summer: 9am–6pm; winter:
9am–4:30pm.

The best-preserved mountain-
top stronghold in North Cyprus,
this magnificent castle bristles
with turrets on its walls built on
sheer rock. It was named after the
monastic saint from Palestine,

who came to Cyprus in search of
solitude, dying here in 372. The
Byzantines built the church and
monastery in his memory.

The outer defence wall was
erected by the Lusignans. The
castle played an important
role in the 1228–31
struggle for the
domination of Cyprus
between German
emperor Frederick II
of Hohenstaufen
and Jean d'Ibelin;
and in the 1373
Genoese invasion.
The lower section of the fortress
held stables. A huge gate leads
to the inner castle with a chapel
and a refectory, which in the
Lusignan period was converted
into a banqueting hall. From
here you can pass to the
belvedere and the adjoining
kitchen. An arched gate leads
to the upper castle.

The south part of the castle
has the Gothic "queen's
window", with a spectacular
view over Karmi village.

Ruins of St Hilarion Castle, on top of a steep rock

For hotels and restaurants in this region see p164 and pp176–7

⑰ Kyrenia (Girne)

Enjoying a picturesque location flanked by a range of craggy hills and the sea, Kyrenia is built around a charming harbour – the most beautiful in Cyprus – guarded by a mighty medieval castle. Its compact Old Town is full of bars, tavernas and restaurants, yet remains a tranquil place. The nearby seashore is lined with the best hotels in North Cyprus. Home to a sizeable expatriate community until 1974, there is still a small number of expats living here today.

Town hall building with its forecourt fountain

View of the Lusignan Tower in the castle (see pp152–3)

Exploring Kyrenia

Once you arrive in Kyrenia, it is best to leave your car at the car park near the town hall, and then continue exploring on foot. Most of Kyrenia's historic sights are clustered around the old harbour. The tourist information office is housed in the former customs house. The town's main attractions – the harbour, castle and small museums – can be explored in a day.

🏛 Byzantine Tower

Ziya Rizki Caddesi and Atilla Sokağı. **Open** summer: 9am–5pm daily; winter: 9am–3:30pm daily.

This massive stone defence structure, with walls several metres thick, once formed part of the town's defence walls. It now houses an art gallery selling local handicrafts, including rugs, paintings and other souvenirs. Strolling down Atilla Sokağı you will come

across a similar, but more derelict tower; also a number of Greek and Roman tombs.

🏛 Market

Canbulat Sokağı. **Open** 8am–7pm. The covered town bazaar was once a food market, but funding from the UN has allowed it to be renovated into a revitalised area with trendy restaurants and a handicraft centre. The market stands along Canbulat Street leading towards the shore.

🏛 Folk Art Museum

The old harbour. **Open** 8am–3:30pm daily.

Set in a centuries-old Venetian house midway along the harbour, the Folk Art Museum houses a small collection of traditional village costumes, household implements, furniture and tools. Also on display is a giant olive press made of olive wood.

Art gallery inside the Byzantine Tower

🏛 Town Hall

This modern building stands on a small square, just a stone's throw from the Old Town. Standing in the forecourt is a unique fountain featuring three huge birds carved in white stone.

The nearby Muslim cemetery is full of the distinctive tombs – *baldaken türbe*.

☪ Djafer Pasha Mosque (Cafer Paşa Camii)

In the Old Town, close to the castle and the harbour. **Open** 24 hours daily.

This small mosque with a stocky minaret was erected in 1589 by Djafer Pasha, commander of the Sultan's army and navy, and three times the Turkish governor of Cyprus. The founder's body rests in the small stone tomb to the right of the entrance. The simple prayer hall is lined with carpets.

About a dozen metres (40 ft) west of the mosque is the small, abandoned Chysospiliotissa church which was erected by the Lusignans in the early 14th century.

⚓ Harbour

Kyrenia's once-important harbour was heavily fortified and the safest haven along the north coast of Cyprus. In ancient times the Romans built a defence castle here; later on the Lusignans and the Venetians rebuilt it, creating a vast fortress. In the Middle Ages the harbour entrance was protected by a strong iron chain. Evidence of its former importance are the medieval stone lugs that were used to fasten the mooring lines of large ships.

Now the old harbour is devoted exclusively to yachts

For hotels and restaurants in this region see p165 and pp176–7

and pleasure boats, ready to take visitors on cruises along the coast. It is lined with an array of dining spots, particularly fish restaurants, with tables set close to the water's edge. The harbour looks particularly enchanting at night, when the calm waters reflect myriad sparkling lights.

⬆ Archangelos Church and Icon Museum

Near the harbour. **Open** 8am–3:30pm daily. 🖼

The former church of the Archangel Michael, standing on top of a hill close to the old harbour, now houses the Icon Museum.

This white edifice with its slender belfry was built in 1860. Some of its original furnishings remain, including the exquisite

The distinctive white silhouette and belfry of the Archangelos church

carved wooden iconostasis and pulpit. The walls are now hung with over 50 icons, dating from the 18th–20th centuries, that were removed from local churches. One of the oldest was painted in 1714. Other objects

VISITORS' CHECKLIST

Practical Information
Road Map C2. 🗺 14,000. ℹ
Kordon Boyu Cad, by the entrance to the old harbour, 0392 822 21 45.

Transport
🚌 Fergün, 0392 822 23 44.

on display are sacral books and a carved crosier. Outside are marble sarcophagi, dating from the Byzantine period.

During summer, Catholic Mass is celebrated in the late-Gothic **Chapel of Terra Santa**, situated further west, in Ersin Aydın Sokağı. The only other Christian place of worship in Kyrenia is the Anglican **Church of St Andrew**, which was built in 1913 close to the castle and the Muslim cemetery.

⬛ Fine Arts Museum

Open 8am–3:30pm daily. 🖼
This fine arts museum is housed in a somewhat ostentatious villa that was built in 1938 in the western part of Kyrenia. Its eclectic collection of artwork comprises a variety of unrelated exhibits, ranging from anonymous paintings (both oil and watercolour) to European porcelain, to Oriental jewellery.

Kyrenia's natural horseshoe harbour, the most beautiful in Cyprus

Kyrenia Town Map

① Byzantine Tower
② Market
③ Folk Art Museum
④ Town Hall
⑤ Djafer Pasha Mosque (Cafer Paşa Camii)
⑥ Harbour
⑦ Archangelos Church and Icon Museum

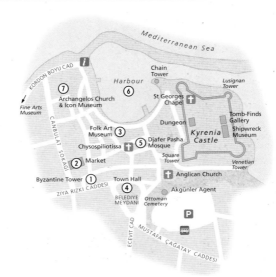

0 metres   150
0 yards   150

For keys to symbols see back flap

Kyrenia Castle and Shipwreck Museum

Kyrenia Castle was built by the Byzantines on the site of
a Roman fort and later extended by the Lusignans. The
Venetians turned it into a vast fortress occupied by the
Turks in 1570. The castle was never taken by force.

Today it houses a Tomb-Finds Gallery and a
Shipwreck Museum, with the wreck of an ancient
vessel dating from the time of Alexander the Great. The
magnificent view from the city walls encompasses the
harbour and St Hilarion Castle.

Shipwreck Museum
On display here is what
remains of a merchant
vessel that sank in a
storm some 2,300
years ago.

Amphorae
Nearly 400 clay amphorae
for storing wine were
found in the wreck of a
sailing vessel, probably
bound for Anatolia from
the Greek islands.

The Lusignan Tower
Arranged in the vaulted rooms
of the two-storey tower are
figures of medieval soldiers
standing by the guns.

The Courtyard
Surrounded by stone
walls, the courtyard
has a number of
stone balls lying
around and a quern
(millstone) of
volcanic rock.

KEY

① **The Tomb-Finds Gallery**
comprises a reconstructed late-
Neolithic dwelling and tombs from
both Kirini and Akdeniz (Agia Irini).

② **Square Tower**

③ **West Wall**

VISITORS' CHECKLIST

Practical Information
Road Map C2. Kyrenia Castle
and Shipwreck Museum:
Open summer: 9am–7pm daily;
winter: 9am–5pm daily. 🔛 The
visitors' entrance is located in the
eastern part of the old harbour.

The Venetian Tower
The southeast section of Kyrenia Castle
includes the Venetian Tower. Arranged in its
gloomy casemates are figures of resting
soldiers and Venetian gunners in action.

Defence Walls
Once powerful castle fortifications
are now severely dilapidated.

Coat of Arms
A medieval knight's stone-
carved coat of arms
is preserved in the
castle walls.

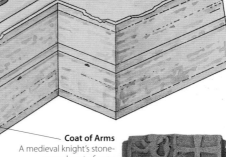

Entrance
The castle is reached via a
narrow bridge spanning
a moat, once filled with
sea water.

Lapithos (Lapta) – a popular destination for daytrips from Kyrenia

⑱ Lambousa (Lambusa)

Road Map C2. Situated on the coast, 1.5 km (1 mile) from the village of Karavas (Alsançak).

On a small, rocky peninsula near Cape Acheiropitios, Lambousa was one of several ancient Cypriot kingdoms. This cosmopolitan city-state was inhabited by the Greeks, Phoenicians, Romans and Byzantines, as well as the Hittites and Franks. The earliest inhabitants arrived in the 13th century BC. In the 8th century BC Lambousa was conquered by the Phoenicians, but its most glorious times were in the Roman and Byzantine periods.

In the course of excavation works carried out in the early 20th century, archaeologists

Fragments of ruins from the ancient city-state of Lambousa

discovered on this site a 6th-century Byzantine treasure consisting of gold and silver artifacts. Some of these are now on display in the Cyprus Museum in Nicosia (see p127), with the rest divided between the British Museum in London, the Metropolitan Museum in New York and the Dumbarton Oaks Collection in Washington, DC.

Only the eastern portion of ancient Lambousa is open to the public. It includes a dozen rock tombs and a series of vast tanks for keeping freshly caught fish alive.

⑲ Lapithos (Lapta)

Road Map C2. 18 km (11 miles) west of Kyrenia.

This picturesque village, with its isolated dwellings scattered around mountain slopes, is a popular day-trip destination from Kyrenia.

The abundant water supply made this a natural supply base for ancient Lambousa, until the threat of Arab raids in the 7th century caused the inhabitants to move to a safer site inland. The settlement was once famous for its silks and exquisite ceramics.

Lapithos was formerly inhabited by both Cypriot communities living in concord; they left behind seven churches and two mosques. In 1963–4 the local Turks were forced to

leave the village. After 1974 it was the Greeks' turn to leave.

Now, in addition to Turkish Cypriots, Lapithos' population includes settlers from Anatolia and a handful of foreigners.

Environs
Karman (Karmi) is one of the loveliest Cypriot villages, with whitewashed houses built on hillsides. The small church has a collection of icons removed from the abandoned Greek churches. Nearby is a necropolis dating from 2300–1625 BC. The village is now inhabited by a large number of British and German expatriates.

⑳ Larnaka tis Lapithou (Kozan)

Road Map C2.

This village enjoys a scenic location on the southern slopes of Selvili Dağ (Kiparissovouno), the peak of the Kyrenian range at 1,024 m (3,360 ft). It makes an excellent base for hikes and bicycle trips around the neighbouring mountains. The local church was turned into a mosque, while the nearby monastery, Panagia ton Katharon, was sacked after 1974.

Kormakitis village, the capital of the Cypriot Maronites

㉑ Kormakitis (Koruçam)

Road Map B2. 9 km (6 miles) west of Myrton (Çamlibel).

Kormakitis is the capital of the Cypriot Maronite Christian sect. In the 1960s this was a prosperous small town with a

Views from the Kormakitis peninsula

population of over 1,000. Now it has dwindled to about one-tenth of that number. Although the Maronites tried to stay impartial in the Greek-Turkish conflict, after 1974 many were forced by Turkish persecution to leave their homes and emigrate. Current residents are mostly elderly, and despite living through those difficult times, the people are unfailingly kind, cheerful and hospitable.

Daily Mass is still celebrated in the local church, **Agios Gregorios**, which is now far too large for the needs of its current congregation. To visit the church you should contact the nearby convent or go to the next-door coffeehouse to enquire about the church being opened. **Profitis Ilias**, standing close to the village, is the main Maronite monastery on the island.

Environs

Next to the village of Agia Irini(Akdeniz), which lies close to the Morfou (Güzelyurt) Bay, is an interesting archaeological site believed to date from the late Bronze era to the Archaic era. A reconstruction of a tomb that was discovered here can now be seen in the Kyrenia Castle museum.

Just off the road leading to Nicosia stands a Bronze Age shrine – the Pigadhes sanctuary. Its stone altar is decorated with geometric reliefs and crowned by a pair of bull's horns, indicating the Minoan influence.

㉒ Cape Kormakitis (Koruçam Burnu)

Road map B2.

Cape Kormakitis, called Koruçam Burnu by the Turks, is the northwesternmost part of Cyprus. In terms of landscape and wildlife, it is similar to the Karpasia and Akamas peninsulas; together they are the wildest and least accessible parts of the island. The few villages that existed in this areas have now been largely deserted. The North Cyprus authorities plan to turn this area into a nature reserve.

A rough track running among limestone hills covered with Mediterranean vegetation leads from the Maronite village of Kormakitis towards the small village of Livera (Sadrazamköy). From here, a 3.5-km (2.2-mile) unmade but serviceable road runs towards Cape Kormakitis. The cape lies in a desolate area

Waves breaking off Cape Kormakitis

of dreary rocks, a handful of deserted dwellings and an unmanned lighthouse at the very tip. The nearby rocky island of Nissi Kormakitis lies a mere 60 km (37 miles) from Cape Anamur, on the Anatolian coast of Turkey.

For centuries, the cape has been inhabited by Maronites, a Christian sect that originated in Syria and Lebanon in the 7th century. This Eastern Christian sect, whose members proclaim themselves to be Catholic and to recognize the supremacy of the Pope, arose from a dispute between Monophysites (who postulated a single, divine nature of Jesus) and Christians (who believed Jesus to be both divine and human). The Maronites took their name from the 4th- or 5th-century Syrian hermit St Maron. They arrived on Cyprus in the 12th century, with the Crusaders, whom they served during their campaigns in the Holy Land.

Endangered Sea Turtles

The legally protected green turtle (Chylonia mydas)

Both the loggerhead (Caretta caretta) and green (Chylonia mydas) species of sea turtle that nest on the beaches of Cyprus are endangered species subject to conservation programmes. Their nesting season lasts from mid-May to mid-October. The female digs a hole 30–60 cm (12–24 in) into the sand, in which she deposits her eggs. The hatchlings emerge after 55–60 days and head for the sea. Those that survive will return after 20 years to the same beach to breed. Only one in 40 turtles succeeds.

㉓ Morfou (Güzelyurt)

Road Map B3. 🎯 Orange Festival (May).

The Turkish name Güzelyurt means "beautiful place". And, indeed, the local citrus groves and picturesque bay add to the lovely scenery here.

It was close to the town that archaeologists discovered the earliest traces of human habitation in Cyprus, dating from the Neolithic and Early Bronze eras when copper was produced and exported.

The best historic site in Güzelyurt is the **church and monastery of Agios Mamas**, built during the Byzantine period on the site of a former pagan temple. In the 15th century it acquired Gothic embellishments, and in the 18th century a dome.

The interior features the throne of St Mamas, a Gothic window carved in stone, an iconostasis and a marble sarcophagus of the saint.

Until 1974 swarms of pilgrims streamed to Agios Mamas from all over Cyprus, but after the Turkish invasion it was shut and used to store icons brought here from nearby Orthodox churches. It is now an **Icon Museum**.

Other than Agios Mamas, the town has few tourist attractions. Next to the church is the **Archaeology and Natural History Museum**. Besides several exhibits of stuffed animals

Monastery buildings of Agios Mamas in Morfou

Atatürk's statue in Léfka

and birds, and a collection of ancient ceramics, the museum also houses an exhibition of Late Bronze Age objects found in the course of excavations conducted in Töumba and Skourou.

🏛 Icon Museum & Archaeology and Natural History Museum
Agios Mamas. **Open** summer: 9am–6pm daily; winter: 9am–3:30pm daily. 📷

㉔ Léfka (Lefke)

Road Map B3.

Inhabited for over 400 years by Turks, Lefke is a major centre of Islam on the island. The central square sports a huge equestrian statue of Atatürk. A few hundred metres further on stands the early 19th-century mosque of Piri Osman Pasha, built in the Cyprian style. The garden surrounding the mosque contains the tomb of Vizier Osman Pasha, who was supposedly killed by poison – a victim of a palace intrigue. His marble sarcophagus is one of the loveliest surviving works of its kind from the Ottoman period.

Lefke European University, one of five universities in North Cyprus, trains students from many countries of the Middle East and Central Asia. Along the coastline, there are a number of restaurants serving local cuisine and fresh seafood. Lefke was once the seat of Kibrisi

Logo of the university in Léfka

Şeyh Nazim, the *murshid* or spiritual leader of the Naqshbandi order of Sufism, who decides on all spiritual aspects of life of the faithful.

Environs
In the nearby coastal town of Karavostasi (Gemikonağı) is the excellent **Mardinli** restaurant, standing on a beach surrounded by a garden and orchard that provide its kitchen with fruit and vegetables. On the other side of town, between the road and the sea, stands an imposing monument to a Turkish pilot killed during the 1974 invasion.

㉕ Soloi (Soli Harabeleri)

Road Map B3. 20 km (12½ miles) west of Morfou. **Open** summer: 9am–6pm daily; winter: 9am–3:30pm daily. 📷

Soloi, a one-time city-state of Cyprus, was supposedly founded at the suggestion of the Athenian law-giver Solon, who persuaded King Philocyprus of Aepea to build a new capital close to the river Ksero. In his honour, the town was named Soloi. The reality, however, was probably quite different. As long ago as Assyrian times (c.700 BC) a town called Sillu stood on this site. It was a stronghold of Greek culture, and was the last town to fall to the Persians.

The town gave its name to the entire region of Solea, on the northern slopes of the Troodos mountains, where Cypriot copper was mined near the present-day town of Skouriotissa. The extraction and export of this metal spurred the growth of Soloi, particularly during Roman times. There was a good harbour, needed for the export of copper, and abundant water.

It was in Soloi that St Mark converted a Roman named

Auxibius to Christianity; he later became bishop of Soloi. Stones taken from the ruins of the ancient town were used by the British and the French in the building of the Suez Canal and the coastal town of Port Said. It was only in the late 1920s that Swedish archaeologists unearthed a theatre, and in 1964 a Canadian team uncovered the basilica and part of the agora (market place).

The Roman theatre was built for an audience of 4,000 people, and has been restored. During the summer it is used as a venue for shows and concerts.

Above the theatre the archaeologists uncovered remains of palaces and a temple to Athena. The famous 1st-century marble statuette of Aphrodite found nearby can now be seen in the Cyprus Museum in Nicosia *(see pp126-7)*. Lower down are the ruins of a 5th-century Byzantine basilica, destroyed in the course of the 632 Arab raid.

Displayed under a makeshift roof are some fairly well-preserved mosaics from the temple floor, featuring geometric and animal motifs. The most interesting mosaics depict water birds surrounded by dolphins. Another small medallion features a swan.

Unearthed to the north of the ruined basilica is a poorly preserved agora.

Soloi is surrounded by vast burial grounds, dating from various periods of antiquity.

Ruins of the ancient palace in Vouni

㉖ Vouni (Vuni Sarayı)

Road Map B3. 27 km (17 miles) west of Morfou. **Open** summer: 9am–6pm daily; winter: 9am–3:30pm daily.

This magnificent, somewhat mysterious palace stands atop a coastal hill, 250 m (820 ft) above sea level. The site is extraordinarily beautiful, with panoramic views over the North Cyprus coast and the Troodos mountains to the south. The palace was likely built by a pro-Persian king of Marion (a city near present-day Polis), as evidenced by its Oriental architectural details.

Mosaic from Soloi

Occupying a strategic spot, the residence was probably intended to intimidate the nearby pro-Athenian town of Soloi. Following an anti-Persian insurrection, Vouni (which means "mountain" in Greek) was taken over by the supporters of Greece.

Having occupied the palace, they rebuilt it, adding a temple to Athena, among other things. When the reversal of military fortunes resulted in the Persians returning to power, the palace was burned down in 380 BC.

Today the ruins are reached via a new, narrow and winding road. Above the car park are the scant remains of a temple to Athena, dating from the late 5th century BC. The stairs on the opposite side lead to the palace courtyard, which features a guitar-shape stone stele with a hole in it and an unfinished face of a woman, probably a goddess. The adjacent cistern was used to supply water to the luxurious baths in the northwestern portion of the palace, which reputedly had 137 rooms.

Environs

The small rocky island off the west coast, visible from Vouni palace, is **Petra tou Limniti**. This is the oldest inhabited part of Cyprus, colonized as early as the Neolithic era.

Remains of the ancient agora in Soloi

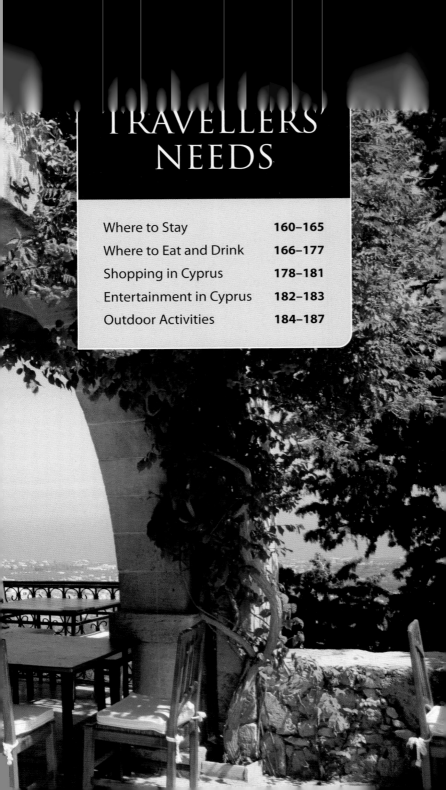

TRAVELLERS' NEEDS

Where to Stay · · · · · · · · · · · · · · · 160–165

Where to Eat and Drink · · · · · 166–177

Shopping in Cyprus · · · · · · · · · 178–181

Entertainment in Cyprus · · · · 182–183

Outdoor Activities · · · · · · · · · · 184–187

WHERE TO STAY

Cyprus has a choice of places to stay that is every bit as wide as its portfolio of visitor attractions and holiday activities, with accommodation to suit all budgets. Its climate attracts holiday-makers all through the year, and most of the hotels and guesthouses are open year round. Accommodation ranges from simple, family-run guesthouses and small apartment complexes to large resort hotels with an array of facilities for families, luxury villas with private pools and stylishly restored village houses. Hotels in the three- and four-star categories are generally more luxurious than their equivalent in other Mediterranean countries, and Cyprus has a well-deserved reputation for affordable comfort.

Pleasant guestroom with minimalist decor at Almyra Hotel, Pafos (see p162)

Package Deals

Some hotels in the popular resorts are fully booked by holiday companies, which can, at peak times, make it difficult for independent travellers to find good accommodation on arrival. Booking a holiday package (which includes flights and hotel) is often the best, and usually the cheapest, option. In low season, bargains may be found on the Internet.

Hotels

Most of the island's hotels are clustered along the coast on either side of Larnaka and Limassol, and in the resorts of Pafos, Agia Napa and Protaras. There are a few stretches of coastline that lack any accommodation options. In the Larnaka and Limassol areas some hotels are compact high-rise blocks, while many hotels in the Pafos and Agia Napa regions are low-rise resort complexes with swimming pools and play areas for children. There are also small hotels and apartment complexes in these resorts, though some are reserved by tour operators. Visitors looking for a tranquil stay can head to some of the lesser-known places inland.

All major hotels are modern, well equipped and come with air conditioning. The **Cyprus Tourism Organization (CTO)**, and the Turkish tourism ministry in the North, grade hotels from one to five stars. Those rated one or two stars are likely to be slightly shabby with few facilities. Upper-end hotels may offer a wide range of activities, from watersports, spas, tennis and golf to cabaret, traditional music and dancing, and discos.

Rates

Rates vary depending on the season, with bargains available outside the peak spring and summer months. Rates are highest during Easter (both Greek Orthodox and non-Orthodox Easter), for the two weeks around Christmas, and from June to September.

The trend for many of the larger hotels in Cyprus is to offer all-inclusive options, with fewer bed-and-breakfast, half-board or full-board choices. Smaller hotels may not include breakfast in the rate. Make sure the quoted rate includes local taxes.

Private Accommodation

It is not always easy to find accommodation in private homes and, when found, they may not always offer a high standard of comfort or facilities. They are nonetheless graded by the **CTO** to ensure they meet their minimum standards. Avoid unofficial private accommodation. The **CTO** can provide a list of small bed-and-breakfast establishments.

Lodgings in monasteries were once a popular option, but today are available only to Orthodox pilgrims.

Agrotourism

Visitors who prefer the charm of a quiet, rural village to the hustle and bustle of a tourist resort can go for agrotourism options, which are increasingly popular among couples and independent travellers. Accommodation is usually in a restored traditional house, where guests sometimes have the opportunity to participate

The outdoor swimming pool at Episkopiana Hotel (see p163)

◀ A picturesque restaurant with views over the Bellapais village in North Cyprus

Onar Holiday Village, Kyrenia *(see p165)* surrounded by mountains

in some of the traditions of the village. This is especially common in the mountains.

Village houses usually feature modern kitchens and bathrooms; some even provide swimming pools. These houses almost always have gardens with fruit trees. Basic homemade foodstuffs such as bread, fresh honey or jam can be bought from local shops, while other supplies can be brought from the larger towns nearby.

The website of the **Cyprus Agrotourism Company** can assist in finding suitable village accommodation.

Hostels and Campsites

Youth hostels in South Cyprus that once belonged to the International Youth Hostel Association are no longer in operation. The **CTO** runs five officially designated camping sites at Governor's Beach (Limassol district), Geroskipou, Pegeia and Polis (Pafos district), and in the Troodos mountains. Facilities are basic, but include showers and toilets, and a simple bar-restaurant.

Reservations

While reserving a place to stay ahead of arrival is advisable, it is not always necessary, even in the more rugged North. Some hotels, especially those in Pafos, Agia Napa and Protaras are block-booked by package holiday companies. The **CTO** can supply hotel information for travellers to book directly with hotels or via websites.

Disabled Travellers

Most of the newer and larger hotels in the South of Cyprus are wheelchair-accessible (many even have ramp facilities leading to the beach) and hotels here meet European accessibility norms. Cheaper, smaller hotels, village houses and villas are unlikely to offer wheelchair access. In the North, hotels are far less likely to be wheelchair-accessible. Contact the hotel, travel agent or tour operator well ahead of time to confirm accessibility details.

Recommended Hotels

The hotels listed on the following pages have been divided into categories that are indicative of that hotel's main feature, although it is fair to say that some establishments will fall into more than one

The bar area of the plush Hilton Cyprus, South Nicosia *(see p164)*

category. Cyprus has a large number of luxury hotels and some of the best feature here. Similarly, many hotels offer family amenities like playgrounds, babysitting and children's clubs and for this reason have been judged ideal for families. The business hotels may have a full conference centre, or may have fewer facilities but be in locations that make them ideal for meetings; for instance, closer to the airports or major towns. The rural and apartments/villa categories detail establishments in villages and for independent holidays respectively.

Many of the most interesting and remarkable options in Cyprus are not necessarily the most expensive ones, so look out for the hotels selected as a "DK Choice". These establishments have been highlighted for their excellent service and come highly recommended. This may be due to them having a stunning location, notable history, an inviting atmosphere or, quite often, just being outstanding value. Whatever the reason, the accommodation selected should offer a memorable stay.

Where to Stay

West Cyprus

CORAL BAY: Coral Beach Hotel
Family   €€   Map A4
Coral Bay Ave, Pafos, 8099
Tel *26 881 000*
W coral.com.cy
Sprawling resort offering a crafts workshop, kids' facilities, an Olympic-sized pool and a spa.

CORAL BAY: Crown Resorts Horizon
Family   €€   Map A4
Coral Bay Ave, Pafos, 8068
Tel *26 813 800*
W crownresortsgroup.com
All rooms in this complex have verandas. Children are well catered for with activities.

DK Choice

LATSI: Anassa   €€€
Luxury   Map A3
Baths of Aphrodite Rd, Neo Chorio, 8830
Tel *26 888 000*
W anassa.com.cy
Luxuriously stylish with a thalassotherapy spa, tennis courts and five sea-view restaurants, the five-star Anassa overlooks the picturesque Chrysochou Bay. Offers good facilities for kids, including special menus.

PAFOS: Lasa Heights
Rural   €   Map A4
Lasa village, 8021
Tel *26 732 777*
W lasaheights.com
Agrotourism hotel set in a 19th-century former coffee shop. En-suite rooms and a pretty courtyard.

The sleek, white-toned interior of Anassa, in Latsi

PAFOS: Smartline Hotel
Family   €   Map A4
Pari St, Kato, Pafos 8064
Tel *26 948 000*
W smartlinepaphoshotel.com
Range of amenities for families, including babysitting. Good restaurant and alfresco taverna.

PAFOS: Avanti Hotel
Family   €€   Map A4
Poseidonos Ave, 8130
Tel *26 965 555*
W avantihotel.com
Centrally located hotel with lovely landscaped gardens and a pool. Offers fun activities for kids.

PAFOS: Kissos Hotel
Modern   €€   Map A4
Queen Verenikis St, 8045
Tel *26 936 111*
W kissoshotel.com
Attractive low-rise hotel near the Tombs of the Kings. With a mini golf course and lagoon-style pool.

PAFOS: Queen's Bay Hotel
Family   €€   Map A4
Coral Bay Rd, 8102
Tel *26 946 600*
W queensbay.com.cy
Set in lavish gardens, this hotel has simple yet elegant rooms and excellent sports facilities.

PAFOS: St George
Modern   €€   Map A4
Coral Bay Rd, 8063
Tel *26 845 000*
W stgeorge-hotel.com
Luxurious yet informal hotel with minimalist rooms and stylish restaurants and bars.

PAFOS: Almyra Hotel
Modern   €€€   Map A4
12 Poseidonos Ave, 8042
Tel *26 888 700*
W almyra.com
Chic accommodation with stylish rooms. Excellent dining options.

PAFOS: Annabelle
Luxury   €€€   Map A4
Poseidon Ave, 8102
Tel *26 885 000*
W thanoshotels.com
Located on the seafront, Annabelle is a sumptuous hotel with relaxation at its heart.

PAFOS: Azia Beach
Luxury   €€€   Map A4
Akamas Rd, Chlorakas, 8061
Tel *26 845 100*
W aziaresort.com
Elegantly decorated hotel nestled among palm trees. Good health complex and spa.

Price Guide

Prices are based on one night's stay in high season for a standard double room, inclusive of service charges and taxes.

€	under €100
€€	€100 to €250
€€€	over €250

PAFOS: Elysium Beach Resort
Luxury   €€€   Map A4
Queen Verenikis St, 8107
Tel *26 844 444*
W elysium-hotel.com
Luxurious resort with a Byzantine chapel, a spa and kids' facilities.

POLIS: Bougainvillea Apartments
Apartments/Villas   €€   Map A3
Verginas St, 8820
Tel *26 812 250*
W bougainvillea.com.cy
Villas set around a pool and covered in bright bougainvillea.

POLIS: Natura Beach
Family   €€   Map A3
Papanikopoulos Ave, 8831
Tel *26 323 111*
W natura.com.cy
Eco-friendly, family-run hotel near the beach. Good restaurant.

Southern Cyprus

AGIA NAPA: Limanaki Beach Hotel
Family   €€   Map E3
1st October St, 5330
Tel *23 721 600*
W limanakibeach.com
Seafront hotel with terraces, a health suite and good restaurants.

AGIA NAPA: Grecian Bay Hotel
Luxury   €€€   Map E3
Kriou Nerou 32, 5330
Tel *23 842 000*
W grecianbay.com
Fantastic beachside hotel. Spa, lagoon pool and à la carte dining.

AGIA NAPA: Nissi Beach
Family   €€€   Map E3
Nissi Ave, Nissi Beach, 5343
Tel *23 721 021*
W nissi-beach.com
Centrally located popular hotel with great sports amenities.

LARNAKA: Boronia Hotel Apartments
Apartments/Villas   €   Map D3
Dhekelia Rd, 7040
Tel *24 646 200*
A cosy complex of 21 fully furnished apartments centered

on a pool. Located close to the beach. The in-house restaurant serves international cuisine.

LARNAKA: Flamingo Beach €€
Modern   Map D3
Piale Pasha Ave, 6028
Tel *24 828 208*
🌐 flamingobeachhotel.com
Business and leisure hotel where most rooms have beach views.

LARNAKA: The Golden Bay Beach Hotel
Family   Map D3
Dhekelia Rd, Pyla, 7080
Tel *24 645 444*
🌐 goldenbay.com.cy
A five-star hotel complex with luxury rooms and modern decor. Fantastic Greek-style taverna.

LARNAKA: Hotel-E €€
Modern   Map D3
Farou 70, Pervolia, 7560
Tel *24 747 000*
🌐 hotel-e.com
Contemporary and eco-friendly. Business suite and rooftop bar.

LARNAKA: Lordos Beach Hotel €€
Family   Map D3
Dhekelia Rd, Pyla, 7080
Tel *24 647 444*
🌐 lordosbeach.com.cy
Next to a long sandy beach. Offers pools, watersports and a spa.

LARNAKA: Palm Beach Hotel €€
Luxury   Map D3
Dhekelia Rd, Oroklini, 6303
Tel *24 846 600*
🌐 palmbeachhotel.com
Seafront five-star hotel amid pretty gardens. The restaurants serve local and international cuisines.

LEFKARA: Lefkarama €
Rural   Map C4
Pano Lefkara, 7700
Tel *24 342 154*
Housed in a traditional Cypriot stone inn, this pleasant hotel has 10 guestrooms and a restaurant.

LIMASSOL: Ajax Hotel €
Modern   Map C4
G. Neophytou & D. Nicolaou St, 3311
Tel *25 590 000*
🌐 ajaxhotel.com
Located close to the city centre and features well-equipped, good-value rooms. Chic lounge area.

LIMASSOL: Alasia Hotel €€
Modern   Map C4
6 Haidari St, 3020
Tel *25 332 000*
🌐 alasiahotel.com.cy
Boutique hotel offering charming rooms with contemporary decor. First-rate restaurant and bar.

The pool at Hill View, Pissouri overlooking the bay

LIMASSOL: Episkopiana Hotel €€
Modern   Map B4
Kremmastis Rd, Episkopi village, 3505
Tel *25 935 093*
🌐 episkopianahotel.com
Popular with business and sports travellers, with its conference suite, huge pool and football ground.

LIMASSOL: Mediterranean €€
Modern   Map C4
Amathous Ave, 3310
Tel *25 311 777*
🌐 medbeach.com
Four-star beachside complex with modern rooms. Swimming pool on a separate connected island.

LIMASSOL: Amathus Beach Hotel €€€
Luxury   Map C4
Amathous Ave, 4532
Tel *25 030 320*
🌐 amathuslimassol.com
This sumptuous resort offers well-appointed rooms, excellent restaurants and a relaxing spa.

LIMASSOL: Four Seasons €€€
Luxury   Map C4
Amathous Ave, 3313
Tel *25 858 000*
🌐 fourseasons.com.cy
One of the island's best hotels, with four gourmet restaurants, luxurious rooms and the renowned Shiseido spa.

LIMASSOL: Grand Resort €€€
Luxury   Map C4
Amathous Ave, 3724
Tel *25 634 333*
🌐 grandresort.com.cy
A seafront hotel with fine dining options, a wellness centre, a spa and poolside gardens to relax in.

LIMASSOL: Londa €€€
Luxury   Map C4
George I Ave, Potamos Yermasoyias, 4048
Tel *25 865 555*
🌐 londahotel.com
For business and leisure travellers. Ultra-stylish decor and upmarket restaurant, spa and patisserie.

LIMASSOL: St Raphael Resort €€€
Family   Map C4
Amathous Ave, 3594
Tel *25 834 200*
🌐 raphael.com.cy
An all-inclusive five-star resort with superb restaurants and many sports and health amenities.

PISSOURI: The Bunch of Grapes Inn €
Rural   Map B4
Ioannou Erotokritou 9, 4607
Tel *25 221 275*
🌐 thebunchofgrapesinn.com
Family-run inn offering apartments and a courtyard restaurant that serves a wide range of cuisines.

PISSOURI: Hill View Apartments/Villas €€
                Map B4
Stadiou 30, 4697
Tel *25 221 972*
🌐 hillview.com.cy
This superb apartment complex enjoys fantastic views. Comfortable rooms and a good restaurant.

DK Choice

PISSOURI: Columbia Beach Hotel & Resort €€€
Luxury   Map B4
Coastal Rd, Pissouri Bay, 3779
Tel *25 833 333*
🌐 columbiabeach.com
This complex comprises a resort and a five-star beach hotel with luxurious rooms. Looking out over the bay, it is designed to resemble a traditional Cypriot village. There are a range of amenities: an upmarket spa, lagoon-style swimming pools, gourmet restaurants and a chapel.

PROTARAS: Sunrise Gardens €€
Family   Map E3
Protaras Ave, 5310
Tel *23 831 466*
🌐 sunrisegardens.com.cy
Centrally located hotel with spacious rooms. The in-house restaurants offer varied cuisines.

For more information on types of hotels *see pp160–61*

Troodos Mountains

KAKOPETRIA: Makris Hotel €
Rural   Map B3
Kakopetria village, 2810
Tel *22 922 419*
Traditional hotel in a pine forest
with a swimming pool, tennis
courts and organized excursions.

KAKOPETRIA: Maritsa Lodge €
Rural   Map B3
Paleas Kakopetria 70, 2800
Tel *22 754 727*
Cosy stone-house lodge. Well
located for cycling and hiking in
the Troodos mountains.

KAKOPETRIA: The Mill Hotel €
Family   Map B3
Mylou 8, 2800
Tel *22 922 536*
w cymillhotel.com
This picturesque 17th-century
former mill boasts a fantastic
restaurant specializing in trout.

PEDOULAS: Mountain Rose €
Rural   Map B3
Filoxenias 35, 2850
Tel *22 952 727*
w mountainrosehotel.com
Experience quaint village life at
Mountain Rose. Well-equipped
rooms, a restaurant and a shop.

PLATRES: Edelweiss Hotel €
Rural   Map B3
Spyrou Kyprianou 53, 4820
Tel *25 421 335*
Simple hotel with classic decor.
Some rooms offer views over the
mountains. Sample Cypriot
cuisine at the in-house restaurant.

PLATRES: New Helvetia Hotel €
Family   Map B3
6 Helvetia St, 4820
Tel *25 421 348*
w newhelvetiahotel.com
Charming colonial-style hotel
with classic decor. Good base for
exploring nearby trails.

PLATRES: Petit Palais Hotel €
Rural   Map B3
Pano Platres village, 4825
Tel *25 421 723*
w petitpalaishotel.com
Lodge-style rooms with amazing
views of the Troodos. The two
restaurants serve local cuisine.

PLATRES: Forest Park Hotel €€
Rural   Map B3
Pano Platres, 4825
Tel *25 421 751*
w forestparkhotelcy.com
The only four-star hotel in the
area, Forest Park has a retro
charm that is reflected in the
classic decor of its rooms.

Charming colonial-style façade of New
Helvetia Hotel, Platres

DK Choice

TROODOS: Jubilee Hotel €
Rural   Map B3
Troodos Square, 1504
Tel *25 420 107*
w jubileehotel.com
Cyprus' highest hotel, close to
the runs for winter skiing, and
to hiking and cycling trails. A
perfect antidote to the beach
resorts. Offers a games room,
restaurant and playground for
the kids.

Central Cyprus

DK Choice

AGROS: Rodon Hotel €
Rural   Map C3
Rodou 1, 4860
Tel *25 521 201*
w rodonhotel.com
The Rodon is a beautifully
renovated country house with
stylish rooms and lounge areas.
It retains a rustic charm while
offering modern amenities
including two swimming pools,
a tennis court and a gymnasium.

AGROS: Vlachos Hotel €
Family   Map C3
Agros village, 4860
Tel *25 521 330*
A cosy hotel with babysitting
services and a good restaurant
serving international cuisine.

ASKAS: Evghenia's House €
Rural   Map C3
Gregori Afxentiou 77, 2752
Tel *22 642 344*
w agrotourism.com.cy
Housed in a charming 17th-
century cottage, part of the
country's agrotourism project.
An ideal base to explore the area.

**LYTHRODONTAS: Avli
Georgallidi** €
Rural   Map C3
Georgallidi Courtyard, 2565
w agrotourism.com.cy
Rustic self-catering cottages
from the 19th century. The focus
is on the natural environment.

South Nicosia

Asty Hotel €
Modern   Map C3
*12 Prince Charles, Agios
Dometios, 1300*
Tel *22 773 030*
w astyhotel.com
Close to the business district,
with modest rooms, a
gymnasium and restaurant.

Classic Hotel €
Modern   Map C3
Regenis 94, 1513
Tel *22 664 006*
w classic.com.cy
Stylish rooms, plus restaurants
and bars. Within the city walls.

Castelli €€
Luxury   Map C3
Ouzounian 38, 1504
Tel *22 712 812*
w castellihotel.com.cy
Housed in a 19th-century
mansion. Elegant rooms on offer.
Amenities for business travellers.

Cleopatra Hotel €€
Luxury   Map C3
Florinis 8, 1065
Tel *22 844 000*
w cleopatra.com.cy
Located close to attractions with
comfortable rooms, a Greek
restaurant and a health suite.

DK Choice

Holiday Inn €€
Family   Map C3
Rigenis 70, 1504
Tel *22 712 712*
w holidayinn.com
One of the few hotels located
within the city walls, the
Holiday Inn is ideal for exploring
the historic heart of Nicosia. The
hotel offers luxurious rooms, an
indoor swimming pool and spa
complex, and restaurants where
children eat for free.

Hilton Cyprus €€€
Luxury   Map C3
Archbishop Makarios III, 1516
Tel *22 377 777*
w hilton.com
The five-star Hilton is the finest
hotel in the capital, with a health

spa, gourmet dining restaurants and stylish bars. Classic yet chic decor in the guestrooms and communal areas.

North Cyprus

BELLAPAIS: Ambelia Village Hotel €
Apartments/Villas   Map C2
Bellapais
Tel *0392 815 36 55*
W cyprus-ambelia.com
Self-catering villas and studios near the village's famous abbey and tavernas. The restaurant serves traditional Cypriot as well as international dishes.

FAMAGUSTA: Portofino Hotel €
Family   Map E3
Fevzi Çakmak Blvd, Ammochostos
Tel *0392 366 43 92*
W portofinohotelcyprus.com.tr
A small traditional hotel with panoramic views from its rooftop restaurant and bar. Simple, comfortable rooms with balconies.

FAMAGUSTA: Arkin Palm Beach Hotel €€
Family   Map E3
Nadir Yolu, Deve Limani
Tel *0392 366 20 00*
W arkinpalmbeach.com
Contemporary seafront hotel great for families, with snug rooms, gardens, a spa and babysitting facilities.

FAMAGUSTA: Salamis Bay Conti Resort Hotel & Casino €€
Luxury   Map E3
Coast Rd
Tel *0392 378 82 00*
W salamisbay-conti.com
One of Famagusta's best accommodation options, with restaurants, a fitness centre, kid's club and nightly entertainment.

KYRENIA: Acapulco Resort & Convention & Spa €€
Family   Map C2
Çatalköy
Tel *0392 824 44 49*
W acapulco.com.tr
Well-furnished rooms with all modern amenities. Offers many daily activities from tennis and football to aerobics.

KYRENIA: Club Lapethos €€
Family   Map C2
Maresai Febri Çakmak Cad, Lapta
Tel *0392 821 86 69*
W lapethoshotel.com
Resort with an aqua park of pools and slides. First-class multi-cuisine restaurant.

KYRENIA: Dome Hotel €€
Family   Map C2
Kordonboyu Cad
Tel *0392 815 24 54*
W hoteldome.com
A constant near the harbour since 1937, its rooms feature classic decor. The fine-dining restaurant serves everything from healthy snacks to classic Cypriot cuisine.

KYRENIA: Merit Crystal Cove €€
Family   Map C2
Karavas
Tel *0392 650 02 00*
On a hill overlooking the beach, this opulent hotel has beautiful rooms, restaurants and bars, a health suite and a casino.

KYRENIA: Onar Holiday Village €€
Apartments/Villas   Map C2
Coast Rd
Tel *0392 815 58 50*
W onarvillage.com
This sprawling complex of villas is designed to resemble a village. Includes a swimming pool, play areas, Turkish bath and spa.

DK Choice

KYRENIA: The Colony Hotel €€€
Luxury   Map C2
Ecevit Cad
Tel *0392 815 15 18*
W thecolonycyprus.com
This colonial-style hotel is Kyrenia's most famous. Set between the North Cyprus mountains and the Mediterranean sea, the luxurious guestrooms and fine-dining restaurant ooze style. Relax in the spa and health centre or in the cocktail lounge. Located on the approach to Kyrenia harbour.

KYRENIA: Cratos Premium Hotel €€€
Luxury   Map C2
Çatalköy
Tel *0392 444 42 42*
W cratospremium.com
Plush rooms, a gourmet French restaurant, terrace bar and casino make for a welcoming stay at this stylish hotel.

KYRENIA: Savoy Ottoman Palace Hotel €€€
Luxury   Map C2
Şehit Fehmi Ercan 5
Tel *0392 444 70 00*
W savoyhotel.com.tr
One of Kyrenia's finest hotels, with deluxe rooms featuring classic Ottoman decor.

LAPITHOS: Manolya Hotel €
Rural   Map C2
Fevri Çakmak Cad
Tel *0392 821 84 98*
W manolyahotel.com
Modern hotel hugging the rocky shoreline. Rooms and the restaurant offer panoramic views. Snorkelling equipment available.

LÉFKA: Lefke Gardens Hotel €
Rural   Map B3
Lefke
Tel *0392 728 82 23*
W lefkegardenshotel.org
Housed in a period property in the centre of the village. A good base to explore the area. Rooms have traditional Cypriot decor.

NORTH NICOSIA (LEFKOŞA): Merit Hotel & Casino €€€
Modern   Map C3
Bedrettin Demirel Cad
Tel *0392 600 55 00*
W meritlefkosa.com
A five-star business hotel with contemporary rooms, conference facilities, upmarket restaurants, a health suite and a casino.

The relaxed lounge area of the Hilton Cyprus, South Nicosia

For more information on types of hotels *see pp160–61*

WHERE TO EAT AND DRINK

The range of restaurants in Cyprus is wide enough to satisfy even the most discerning gastronome. For those looking for options beyond their hotel, there are many tavernas and restaurants to choose from. Many hotels now offer an all-inclusive option. The true atmosphere that Cypriot cuisine evokes can be experienced in a traditional taverna.

Greek-style tavernas and Turkish-style restaurants (*meyhane*) guarantee an evening with a great Cypriot atmosphere, sometimes featuring folk performances and music. Smart restaurants are more likely to serve European or Asian cuisine. In general, the further one goes from the popular resorts, the more authentic the cuisine.

A traditional Cypriot taverna in Nicosia

Choosing a Restaurant

A vast selection of eating establishments exists in Cyprus. This is particularly evident in the popular resorts, where there are tavernas and restaurants on every street, serving local and international cuisine. In addition to the traditional tavernas serving Greek and Turkish dishes, there are French, Italian, Mexican, Thai, Chinese, Indian, Middle Eastern, Russian and Japanese restaurants. There are also cafés and snack bars, along with international fast-food eateries.

Many restaurants are casual, without a dress code. In terms of value, restaurants in town are usually cheaper than those found in hotels. Look out for establishments frequented by locals – these tend to serve good-value, tasty food.

On the whole, eating out in Cyprus is reasonable. Opt for a good Cyprus wine along with your lunch or dinner. It is worth trying the local varieties.

When to Eat

Breakfast is usually eaten between 7:30am and 10am.

Most budget and inexpensive hotels serve a Continental breakfast comprising tea or coffee, fruit juice, toast, white bread, jam, honey and butter. Upscale hotels usually provide guests with a self-service bar stocked with light salads, a selection of cheeses, scrambled eggs, sausages and cakes. The traditional Cypriot breakfast is also served. In North Cyprus it is customary to serve the traditional Turkish breakfast of bread, jam, white cheese and olives.

Lunch is usually eaten between noon and 2:30pm and may consist of pulses, salads, grilled meats such as *souvlakia* or

Menu boards outside a fish restaurant

kebabs and sandwiches. Dinner, is the main meal of the day eaten between 8pm and late into the night by Cypriots, although earlier by other European nationals or in hotels or international restaurants. Traditionally, an evening around the table in a Cypriot home is a social event, and can last several hours. One of the most common meals on the island consists of *souvlakia* or kebabs, usually of pork or chicken, *shieftalia* (minced meat with spices) and salads.

What to Eat

The exquisite cuisine of Cyprus is famous for the simplicity of its ingredients and ease of preparation. Traditional local recipes are an interesting blend of Greek and Middle Eastern flavours.

The most important item on a Cypriot menu is *mezédhes* – a platter of hot and cold dishes, similar to Spanish tapas or Turkish *mezze*. They are accompanied by traditional Cypriot bread baked in a plinth oven. A decent restaurant will always include grilled *halloumi* (a cheese made from goat and sheep's milk), fried courgettes and eggs, and the real delicacy, *koupepia* – stuffed vine leaves. Other specialities include hummus (chickpea dip), *tahini* (sesame sauce), *keftedes* (meat balls) and spicy *loukanika* and *pastourma* sausages.

For main courses, the Cypriot menu is dominated by lamb, pork, fish and seafood, and an array of vegetables, usually served with rice or roast potatoes.

Fish can be the most expensive item on the menu,

although in coastal locations it is generally very fresh and tasty, so well worth the cost. Chicken is usually the cheapest meat dish available.

Happily for visitors, there should be no problem choosing from the menu, as the names of dishes are translated.

Vegetarians

Cypriot cuisine is based on essentially healthy Mediterranean produce and includes many vegetarian dishes traditionally eaten in Cypriot homes during the Lenten period and other Orthodox fasts, when meat is shunned. As well as huge "village salads" (*choriatiki*) of tomatoes, cucumber, onions, peppers, lettuce, cabbage, olives and feta cheese, there is plentiful fresh fruit and a good array of grilled and fried vegetable dishes, based on aubergines (eggplant), courgettes (zucchini), artichokes, peppers and tomatoes, and lots of tasty dips based on chickpeas, fava beans and other pulses. Traditional Cypriot cheeses, especially the *halloumi* cheese is eaten fried, grilled or as it is.

All restaurants and hotels in Cyprus now also prepare vegetarian meals.

Alcohol

As far back as ancient times, Cyprus has produced good local wines, helped by the fertile soil and mild climate. In the last

15 years or so, the wine industry of the country has developed rapidly and local wineries now produce world-class wines. Wine-tasting sessions are held in wineries all over the island. There are seven Wine Routes that visitors can take and most of the wineries are included in them. Together these wineries produce nearly 40 varieties of wine, including indigenous varieties such as Xinisteri, Maratheftiko, Spourtiko and Lefkada. In some villages at the foot of the mountains visitors can sample home-made liqueurs which, in terms of quality and flavour, are often as good as branded products.

Cyprus' best-known product is the sweet dessert wine Commandaria. Nicknamed "Cypriot sun", fortified with a raisin-like flavour it makes an excellent digestive to round off a traditional Cypriot dinner and a good souvenir. The strong, dry *zivania* apéritif is classified as *eau-de-vie*.

The locally produced beers have a good flavour and are also inexpensive. When in North Cyprus try cold Efes; in the south, try KEO, the island-bottled Carlsberg or beers from other local microbreweries.

Prices

The highest prices are charged by restaurants in fashionable resorts. Set menus may be substantially cheaper than a

Enjoy cocktails in a stylish setting at Domus Lounge Bar, South Nicosia *(see p176)*

selection of à la carte items. Seafood dishes tend to be particularly expensive.

One can eat at a more reasonable cost at restaurants in town – especially those frequented by the locals. The total bill always includes VAT and usually a service charge of around 10 per cent. Most restaurants accept credit cards.

Recommended Restaurants

Restaurants recommended on the following pages have been chosen to provide a insight into the island's diverse cuisine. Cyprus has a large number of traditional tavernas and those selected offer the most authentic Cypriot dining experience. The island also has a wide choice of restaurants serving international cuisine.

Cyprus is a multicultural destination and our restaurant selection includes suggestions for those who might want something different, for example Italian, French, Chinese, Japanese, Syrian or Indian cuisine. Cyprus has a large number of fish restaurants, and restaurants with good vegetarian menus. Places marked "DK Choice" are considered to have superior quality and come highly recommended. They may have historical charm, exceptional cooking or an ounstanding location. Be sure to book ahead.

Elegant table setting at Oliveto in Pafos *(see p170)*

The Flavours of Cyprus

Cypriot food is a mixture of Greek, Turkish and Middle Eastern cooking, and features all the rich flavours typical of Mediterranean produce. Fruit such as oranges, lemons, cherries and figs are all grown locally, and the island's grapes are made into delicious wines. Vegetables, herbs and olives (to eat and for oil) grow in abundance. Meat is predominently lamb, pork and chicken, and fresh fish and seafood is plentiful along the coast. A good way to try a selection of local food is with a platter of *mezédhes* (*mezze* for short), which may comprise of up to 20 dishes.

Oregano and thyme

Cypriot fisherman preparing his catch for sale

Southern Cyprus

The cuisine of the south is inspired by the flavours of the Mediterranean area. Popular ingredients include olives and fresh herbs from the rich soils of the foothills of the Troodos mountains, and lemons from the groves found largely in the western region near Pafos. Locally made cheeses such as *anari* and *halloumi* give a distinctive taste to many dishes. Most meals start with a selection of dips made using recipes that have been handed down from generation to generation for centuries. These recipes have their roots in Greek cuisine, and are generally served with a freshly baked "village" loaf. Bread plays an important part in the diet of southern Cypriots. A flattish-domed loaf, village bread, is usually plain white but may also be flavoured with *halloumi* or olives. Main courses tend to be meat-based rather than fish. Chickens, pigs and goats are reared in most rural areas and provide meat that is usually cooked on the grill, either plain or marinated with herbs and served with the famous Cyprus potatoes grown in the red soil found in the Larnaka area. A

Pita breads
Roasted red peppers
Grilled *halloumi*
Kupepia
Taramosalata
Olives
Tzatziki
Selection of typical Cypriot *mezédhes*

Regional Dishes and Specialities

Dishes of the south include *afelia* (pork simmered in red wine with coriander) and *kleftiko*. Moussaka and *kupepia* (stuffed vine leaves) are among the dishes drawn from Greek cuisine. Dips include *taramosalata* (puréed salted mullet roe) and *tzatziki* (yoghurt, cucumber, garlic and mint). The cuisine of northern Cyprus includes dishes such as *imam bayıldı* (tomato-and onion-stuffed aubergines), *böörek* (cheese-filled pastries) and *bamya basti* (tomato and okra stew). Meat dishes include *döner* kebabs of sliced, spiced roast lamb, *iskender* or *bursa* (kebabs in a thick, spicy tomato sauce) and *adana*, a length of minced lamb bound together with red pepper flakes and cooked on a skewer.

Sweet pastries

Souvlakia are small chunks of pork, marinated in lemon juice, herbs (usually oregano) and olive oil, grilled on skewers.

Local grocer offering a wide range of fresh and dried produce

"village salad" *(choriatiki salata)*, made of lettuce, cabbage, tomatoes, cucumber, onions, pepper, olives and feta cheese is a typical accompaniment to the main course. Bananas, oranges and cherries are among the many fruits grown in this part of the island and, along with sweet cakes, generally complete a meal.

Northern Cyprus

Cuisine in North Cyprus takes its influences from the island itself and the Turkish mainland, where many of the staple dishes were inspired by Middle-Eastern and Central Asian cooking. Spices such as saffron and paprika, along with garlic, chillies and peppers, are used extensively; these ingredients give a colourful hue and a spicy kick to traditional northern

dishes. Most meals are based around meat, usually chicken or lamb, and vegetables grown on the flat plains south of the Pentadaktylos mountain range and along the coast. Many recipes come from the days of the Ottoman Empire and are characterized by their spicy

Cypriot coffee, served strong and black with pastries

tomato-, yoghurt- and cream-based sauces. Meze-style meals, usually for large groups of friends or family, are a staple on the menu too, but differ slightly from those found in the south in that they are more often inspired by Turkish cuisine. Main courses are generally served with rice, boiled potatoes and salad accompaniments, and are usually followed by sweet pastries, such as *baklava*, or milk puddings and fresh fruit, especially citrus fruits, which grow prolifically in the north of the island.

What to Drink

Cyprus offers the ideal climate and geography for growing grapes for wine-making, and production can be traced back to around 2000 BC. Of the over 40 varieties, the most famous is Commandaria, a sweet wine dating from the time of Richard the Lionheart. Maratheftiko, Xinisteri, Spourtiko, Lefkada are some of the island's indigenous grape varieties producing excellent wines. *Zivania* is a popular drink, while Brandy Sour is Cyprus' signature cocktail. Freshly squeezed fruit juices are also very good, and inexpensive. Cyprus, however, is above all the land of the coffee shop and villagers, mostly men, will spend hours over a strong Cypriot coffee, which is always served with a glass of cold water.

Scharas means "from the grill". Here, swordfish has first been marinated in lemon juice, olive oil and herbs.

Kleftiko is usually goat meat wrapped in paper and slow-cooked in a plinth oven so that the flavours are sealed in.

Giaourti kai meli (yoghurt with honey) is a popular dessert that is found everywhere, from cafés and tavernas to fancy restaurants.

Where to Eat and Drink

West Cyprus

KATHIKAS: Petradaki Tavern €
Cypriot   **Map** A3
Kato Vrisi 45, 8573
Tel *26 814 191*
This taverna is popular with both locals and tourists. A good choice of Cypriot and vegetarian dishes and delicious desserts such as *bourekia* (traditional pastry) filled with *anari* cheese and cinnamon.

**KATHIKAS: Yiannis
Tavern**   €
Cypriot   **Map** A3
Georgiou Kleanthous 11, 8573
Tel *26 633 353*   **Closed** *Thu*
A welcoming restaurant, with amiable hosts. Its lengthy menu offers classic Cypriot dishes such as *kleftiko* and *moussaka* (lamb and eggplant casserole).

DK Choice

**PAFOS: 7 St. Georges
Tavern**   €
Cypriot   **Map** A4
*Geroskipou, Anth. Georgiou M.
Savva 37, 8200*
Tel *99 655 824*
A one-of-a-kind tavern in a rural setting. The atmospheric interior is adorned with traditional Cypriot memorabilia. The menu consists of dishes prepared from fresh vegetables and fruits grown in the owner's garden. Meat is cured in-house and they even make their own breads and wines. Try the delicious *mezédhes* – it doesn't get any better.

PAFOS: Fettas Corner €
Cypriot   **Map** A4
Ioanni Agroti 33, 8047
Tel *26 937 822*
Lovely spot away from the touristy Kato Pafos. The menu here emphasises local cuisine consisting of dishes such as fried courgettes with eggs, "village salad", *souvlaki*, *sheftalia* (sausages), pork ribs and *mezédhes*.

PAFOS: Kingfisher Fish Tavern €
Seafood   **Map** A4
Tombs of the Kings Rd, 8022
Tel *26 949 459*
One of the best seafood restaurants in Pafos, this family-run eatery prepares savoury dishes from fresh, locally caught fish. Don't miss the *kavakia* (fish soup). Vegetarian and meat dishes are also available.

PAFOS: Koh-i-Noor €
Indian   **Map** A4
110 Tombs of The Kings Rd, 8042
Tel *26 965 544*
Fantastic curries and tandoori dishes on offer at this elegant, family-run restaurant in the heart of Kato Pafos. Good selection of wines.

PAFOS: Koutourou Ouzeri €
International   **Map** A4
8 25th March St, 8047
Tel *26 952 953*
Enjoy a glass of ouzo or opt for a heavier meal. Lunch features hearty portions made from seasonal produce, while small plates of Cypriot, Greek and international dishes are served at dinner.

PAFOS: Laona €
Cypriot   **Map** A4
Votsi 6, 8010
Tel *26 937 121*
A traditional taverna housed in a beautiful period mansion, hidden away down one of the old town's side streets. It specializes in oven-baked food including *kleftiko* and casserole dishes such as *afelia*.

**PAFOS: O'Neills Irish Bar
and Grill**   €
International   **Map** A4
Tombs of the Kings Rd, 8022
Tel *26 935 888*
A good selection of hearty meals along with an extensive drinks list that includes speciality Irish beers amongst others. A large flatscreen TV shows the latest sports.

**PAFOS: Pizzeria Italiana La
Sardegna Da Gino**   €
Italian   **Map** A4
70 Ap. Pavlos Ave, 8040
Tel *26 933 399*
A local favourite for years, this eatery serves delectable pizzas

Price Guide

The following price ranges cover a three-course meal for one with a half-bottle of wine, tax and services.

€	under €30
€€	€30 to €60
€€€	over €60

made from fresh ingredients and baked in wood-fire ovens. Try the lasagne too.

PAFOS: Chloe's €€
Chinese   **Map** A4
Tombs of the Kings Rd, 8102
Tel *26 934 676*
Beautifully decorated in Oriental style, with soft background music, Chloe's serves some of the finest Chinese food in Cyprus.

PAFOS: Gold Sakura €€
Japanese   **Map** A4
Agiou Antoniou St, 8041
Tel *26 947 492*
Popular Japanese restaurant just minutes from the beach. The extensive menu includes a range of sushi to choose from. Contemporary decor.

PAFOS: Muse Café Kitchen Bar €€
International   **Map** A4
Mousallas, 8027
Tel *26 941 951*
An informal alfresco-style eatery located in the centre of the old town, with panoramic views over the coast. Grills, pasta dishes and desserts make up the menu.

PAFOS: Oliveto €€
International   **Map** A4
96 Tombs of the Kings Rd, 8102
Tel *26 220 099*
Elegant restaurant with crisp white linens, specializing in stone-grilled steaks cooked by the chefs or the guests themselves. Delicious desserts and well-chosen wine list.

Traditional rustic setting at 7 St. Georges Tavern, Pafos

Outdoor seating and sea views at Vassos Psarolimano, Agia Napa

PAFOS: Ouzeri €€
Greek/Cypriot **Map** A4
12 Poseidonos Ave, 8042
Tel *26 888 700*
Housed inside Almyra Hotel, this beachfront restaurant is a good place to sample sumptuous Greek food and local delicacies, accompanied by a glass of ouzo.

PAFOS: Phuket Chinese €€
Chinese/Thai **Map** A4
44 Tombs of the Kings Rd, 8102
Tel *26 936 738*
Upmarket yet good-value restaurant with Oriental decor. Serves Chinese and Thai à la carte dishes with fine wines.

PAFOS: Risto La Piazza €€
Italian **Map** A4
Poseidon Ave, 8098
Tel *26 819 921*
One of the best Italian restaurants in Pafos, La Piazza offers tasty dishes such as penne with tomato sauce and pesto, and seabass stuffed with vegetables and king prawns. Impressive wine list.

PAFOS: Theo's Seafood Restaurant €€
Seafood **Map** A4
Apostolou Pavlou Ave, 8046
Tel *26 932 829*
Located in the harbour, this is one of the area's long-established favourites. The specials focus on fresh fish, although other Cypriot and international dishes also feature on the menu.

POLIS: Archontariki Tavern €
Cypriot **Map** A3
Makarios Ave, 8830
Tel *26 321 328*
Informal restaurant located in a traditional town house. A wide choice of Cypriot fish and seafood dishes to choose from. Alfresco dining in a quiet courtyard hidden from the road.

POMOS: Kanalli Restaurant €
Cypriot **Map** A3
Pomos Harbour, 8870
Tel *26 342 191*
Pleasant location on the harbour overlooking the coastline of Pomos. The dishes on offer are classic Cypriot and seafood delicacies. Popular with families.

Southern Cyprus

AGIA NAPA: Los Bandidos €
Mexican **Map** E3
A. Velouchioti 2, 5330
Tel *23 723 258*
Enjoy Mexican delights such as *fajitas*, chilli corn carne and margaritas at this restaurant set in an exotic garden. Be sure to try the desserts. Book ahead.

AGIA NAPA: Tony's Tavern €
Cypriot **Map** E3
Nissi Ave, 5343
Tel *23 722 515*
One of the best taverns in the district, Tony's dishes up appetizing *mezédhes*. Also, try the famous *moussaka* and *kleftiko*. The wine list includes only Cypriot wines.

AGIA NAPA: Captain Andreas €€
Seafood **Map** E3
Evagorou 33, 5340
Tel *23 722 162*
Family-owned restaurant located right on the harbour. Sample the fresh fish caught by Captain Andreas himself and cooked using locally grown lemons and herbs. Prices are calculated by weight.

AGIA NAPA: Fiji Polynesian Restaurant €€
Polynesian **Map** E3
Archbishop Makarios III 21, 5343
Tel *23 725 925*
Sample authentic Polynesian cuisine on a beautiful terrace opposite Agia Napa's central square. Leave room for cocktails and the coconut-based dessert.

AGIA NAPA: Vassos Psarolimano €€
Seafood **Map** E3
Makariou 51, 5342
Tel *23 721 884*
Lively taverna renowned for its seemingly endless fish *mezédhes* selection, along with dishes that include lobster straight from the tank.

LARNAKA: Ammos Beach Bar €€
International **Map** D3
Mackenzie Beach, 6027
Tel *24 828 844*
Inspired by world cuisine, Ammos is well known for its delicious food and cocktails. It hosts a number of musical events with world-renowned DJs and musicians.

LARNAKA: Art Café 1900 €€
International **Map** D3
Stasinou 6, 6305
Tel *24 653 027*
Housed in a building dating to 1900, hence its name, with frescoes and wooden floors. The bistro-style menu features vegetarian dishes as well as meat and fish. Good selection of beers.

LARNAKA: Captain's Table Fish Tavern €€
Seafood **Map** D3
Grigoris Afxentiou 48, Zygi, 7739
Tel *24 333 737*
Upmarket seafood restaurant located next to the old harbour. Dishes include lobster and seafood soufflé. Good wine list. Reservations recommended on weekends.

LARNAKA: Gevsis En Lefko €€
Greek **Map** D3
Piale Pasa 8, 6026
Tel *24 655 664*
Greek fare is the focus here as well as a variety of fish and seafood dishes, including fish *mezédhes*. The interior is decorated in white hues with Greek film posters adorning the walls.

LARNAKA: Loizos Koubaris Fish Tavern €€
Seafood **Map** D3
Grigoris Afxentiou 34, Zygi, 7739
Tel *24 332 450*
Located in a former fisherman's home right next to the sea, this comfortable taverna specializes in fresh fish. Try the various combinations on the *mezédhes*. Reservation recommended on weekends.

For more information on types of restaurants *see pp166–7*

The elegant dining area at Cleopatra Lebanese Restaurant, Limassol

LARNAKA: Nippon Bistro €€
Japanese   Map D3
Stadiou 120, 6020
Tel *24 400 330*
The award-winning Nippon Bistro combines trendy minimalist decor with a *maki-mono* bar, *teppanyaki* tables and a vast selection of sushi and sashimi dishes.

LIMASSOL: Agios Epiktitos Tavern €
Cypriot   Map C4
Armenochori, 4523
Tel *99 346 529*
A few minutes' drive from the city, this place serves authentic Cypriot cuisine. Eat *mezédhes*, drink wine and listen to live Greek music while enjoying scenic views of Limassol and Amathus archaeological sites.

LIMASSOL: Dino Bistro Café €
International   Map C4
Gladstonos 137, 3032
Tel *25 762 030*
A modern bistro serving food from around the world. Delicious burgers, creatively prepared salads and mouthwatering desserts feature on the menu.

LIMASSOL: Forsos Tavern €
Cypriot   Map C4
Moutayiaka, 4527
Tel *25 329 490*
One of the oldest taverns in the area, this local favourite charms guests with classic Cypriot fare. *Mezédhes* are a speciality and there are live music nights during the week. Book ahead.

LIMASSOL: Incontro Café €
International   Map C4
Archbishop Makarios III 244, 3105
Tel *25 377 519*
Stylish venue with art on the walls and comfortable sofas. The menu has salads, burgers and bistro-style sandwiches, plus there's a good wine list.

LIMASSOL: Mairkon Sikaminia €
Cypriot   Map C4
Eleftherias 26, 3042
Tel *25 365 280*
A traditional taverna in the heart of the old town, Mairkon Sikaminia serves Cypriot delicacies such as *souvlakia* and salad for lunch, and seemingly endless *mezédhes* dishes nightly.

LIMASSOL: Yiagkini €
Cypriot   Map C4
H. Michaelides 6, 3036
Tel *97 839 617*
This informal eatery serves casserole dishes such as *afelia* and grilled delights including *souvlakia, sheftalia* and grilled chicken. Lovely summer garden in the backyard.

LIMASSOL: Zen Room €
Japanese   Map C4
194 Amathous Ave, 4533
Tel *25 025 555*
With a chic dining ambience, the award-winning Zen Room features an open kitchen, a *teppanyaki* bar and exquisite Japanese food.

Diners enjoying Cypriot delicacies at Karatello Tavern, Limassol

LIMASSOL: Chesters €€
International   Map C4
194 Amathous Ave, 4044
Tel *25 025 555*
Meat delicacies – ranging from steaks to burgers – is the speciality at this atmospheric gastropub. There is also a selection of Mexican and Russian dishes. Good choice of wines and cocktails. Lovely patio outside.

LIMASSOL: Cleopatra Lebanese Restaurant €€
Lebanese   Map C4
John Kennedy St, 3106
Tel *25 586 711*
One of the best Lebanese restaurants on the island. Prides itself on using authentic age-old recipes to provide a great culinary experience. For dessert, try the delectable small pastries.

LIMASSOL: The Cookhouse €€
International   Map C4
Gladstonos 112, 3032
Tel *25 353 434*
Trendy, vibrant restaurant ideal for breakfast, brunch and lunch. Freshly made bread, salads, soups, burgers and sandwiches are some of the highlights of the menu.

LIMASSOL: Fat Fish €€
Seafood   Map C4
Georgiou Griva Digeni, 4103
Tel *25 828 181*
Visit Fat Fish to get a taste of fresh fish and seafood, cooked in Mediterranean-inspired flavours. The menu also includes meat dishes. Good wine list.

LIMASSOL: Karatello Tavern €€
Cypriot   Map C4
Vasilissis St, 3036
Tel *25 820 464*
Housed in a restored carob mill, Karatello blends traditional flavours with modern techniques. The menu includes *halloumi* cheese boiled in brine, "village salad", *souvlakia* and *sheftalia*.

Key to prices *see p170*

LIMASSOL: The Noodle House €€
Chinese   Map C4
Agiou Andreou, 3036
Tel *25 820 282*
Bright and airy restaurant in the heart of Limassol, with a kids' menu and a play area. Try the *tempura* fish and spring rolls.

**LIMASSOL: Puesta Oyster
Bar & Grill** €€
International   Map C4
42 Amathountos Ave, 3313
Tel *25 329 040*
Oysters are a speciality at this restaurant near the beach. Meat, fish, mussels, lamb rack and steaks are cooked with a Mediterranean-Asian flavour.

LIMASSOL: Ta Piatakia €€
International   Map C4
N. Mylona 7, 3095
Tel *25 745 017*
True to its name, which means "little plates" the restaurant serves small plates from across the world, such as duck with traditional walnut spoon sweets inspired by Cypriot cuisine.

DK Choice

LIMASSOL: Caprice €€€
Italian   Map C4
72 George 1st St, 4048
Tel *25 865 555*
Located inside the Londa Hotel, the luxurious Caprice has panoramic views of the coastline. Its gourmet menu of antipasti, pasta, meat, fish and vegetarian dishes promises the best of Italian cuisine with a contemporary twist. Well-chosen wine and cocktail list.

**LIMASSOL: La Maison
Fleurie** €€€
French   Map C4
Christaki Kranou 18, 4041
Tel *25 320 680*
Popular, award-winning restaurant where the menu is classic French with a modern twist. Try the succulent steak Béarnaise, *foie gras* and oysters. Good French wine list.

DK Choice

**LIMASSOL: Seasons
Oriental** €€€
Chinese   Map C4
Amathountos Ave, 3313
Tel *25 858 000*
A must-visit for the lovers of Far East cuisine, this restaurant offers creative dishes such as lobster with sliced ginger and spring onion. Dimsums are also highly recommended.

PISSOURI: Apollo Tavern €€
Cypriot   Map B4
Pissouri Bay, 4607
Tel *25 833 000*
Enjoy local delights such as *mezédhes*. The Apollo prepares Cypriot specialities with a contemporary twist. The menu also features Greek and Italian fare.

PROTARAS: Marcello's €
Italian   Map E3
Hotels Ave, 5310
Tel *23 831 501*
Savour pizzas baked in a wood-fired oven, fresh pasta, risotto and hot and cold *antipasti* while watching the busy street outside. Good selection of Italian wines.

PROTARAS: Knight's Pub €€
International   Map E3
Perneras 58, 5295
Tel *23 831 497*
From delectable steaks and tasty Thai curries to divine *moussaka*, Knight's Pub caters to all tastes. The impressive drinks menu offers fresh margaritas, wines and beers.

PROTARAS: Spartiatis Tavern €€
Seafood   Map E3
Konnou 79B, 5297
Tel *23 831 386*
Fresh fish and seafood are the specialities at this restaurant overlooking Konnos Bay. Apart from the "catch of the day", try fish *mezédhes* before finishing your meal with home-made desserts.

SOTERA: Mousikos Tavern €
Cypriot   Map E3
K. Matsi, Sotera, 5390
Tel *23 828 833*
Ten minutes' drive from Protaras, this tavern is set in a pretty yard during summer and shifts indoors to a restored traditional house in winter. Superb *mezédhes, souvlakia, kleftiko* and fresh *halloumi*.

Troodos Mountains

FINI: Neraida €
Cypriot   Map B3
Fini village, 4814
Tel *25 421 680*
Located over the Diarizos river, Neraida offers magical views. Try the traditional oven-roasted meat stew, grilled trout, *souvlakia* and *souvla* (chargrilled meat).

**KAKOPETRIA: Mylos
Restaurant** €€
Cypriot   Map B3
The Mill Hotel, Mylou 8, 2800
Tel *22 922 536*
Spacious restaurant with a wooden vaulted ceiling and fabulous mountain views. Enjoy *tahini* and *tzatziki* dips, and Cypriot ravioli and *moussakas*. Its signature dish is trout grilled and served with lemon sauce and garlic.

**KAKOPETRIA: Tziellari
Argentina** €€
Argentinian   Map B3
Paleas Kakopetrias 72, 2800
This cosy restaurant specializes in steaks, served with *chimichurri* (Argentinian green sauce used for grilled meat) and other delights such as *empanadas* (stuffed pastry) and sausage.

**KALOPANAGIOTIS: To
Palio Sinema** €
Cypriot   Map B3
M. Drakou 44A, 2862
Tel *99 130 275*
The name translates as "the old cinema" and photographs of famous film stars adorn the restaurant walls. *Mezédhes* and other seasonal dishes are on offer. Do try the *anari bourekia*.

**KAMINARIA: Kaminaria by
Leonidas Markou** €
Cypriot   Map B3
Kaminaria village, 4843
Tel *99 945 975*
This cosy *kafenia* is as home-made as it can get. Savour delicious traditional food such as fried greens with eggs, meatballs, *souvla* and roasted potatoes. Casual ambience.

LANEIA: Lania Tavern €
Cypriot   Map B4
Laneia village, 4744
Tel *25 432 398*
Traditional eatery in the centre of a pretty artists' village. Excellent Cypriot cuisine served daily for lunch and on Friday and Saturday evenings. Dine inside or on the terrace.

Quirky interior adorned with plates at Ta Piatakia, Limassol

**LOFOU: Lofou Traditional
Tavern** €
Cypriot **Map** B4
Tsindouri, Lofou village, 4716
Tel *25 470 202*
For a real Cypriot experience
this lovely tavern housed in an
old stone cottage serves home-
made local dishes and fine wines.
Listen to the jovial owner Costas
playing traditional folk music in
the background.

**MONIATIS: Paraskeuas
Restaurant** €
Cypriot **Map** B3
Moniatis village, 4747
Tel *25 433 626*
Serves a good variety of grilled
dishes such as pork ribs,
souvlakia, sheftalia and chicken
kebabs. Eat inside or alfresco on
its vine-covered terrace.

OMODOS: Stou Kir Yianni €
Greek/Cypriot **Map** B4
Linou 15, 4760
Tel *25 422 100*
Housed in a restored village
house, this eatery serves an
interesting array of Greek, Cypriot
and Middle Eastern dishes. Live
folk music on weekends.

DK Choice

**PANAGIA: Vouni
Panagias** €
Cypriot **Map** A3
*Archiepiskopou Markariou
III 60, 8640*
Tel *26 722 770*
Enjoy gorgeous panoramic
views while dining at the
restaurant and outdoor
terrace of this winery. Classic
Cypriot dishes with an
emphasis on fresh organic
produce are accompanied by
the winery's own labels. The
menu changes regularly to
feature seasonal vegetables.

PEDOULAS: Platanos €
Cypriot **Map** B3
V. Hadjioannou, 2850
Tel *99 438 820*
Visit this coffee shop to sample
traditional delicacies such as
mezédhes, souvlakia, home-made
sausages, *sheftalia, halloumi* and
"village salad". End your meal with
Cypriot coffee and spoon sweets.

PELENDRI: Symposio €
Cypriot **Map** B3
Prodromou 61, 4878
Tel *99 404 348*
A lovely tavern serving *mezédhes,
souvla* and *kleftiko* along with
home-made bread. The
ingredients are sourced from
the owner's garden.

PLATRES: Psilo Dendro €
Cypriot **Map** B3
13 Aidonion, 4820
Tel *25 813 131*
Busy restaurant with a great
location near the waterfalls.
Try the legendary freshly caught
trout cooked with herbs and
lemon, sourced from the owner's
own trout farm.

**STATOS-AGIOS FOTIOS: Kolios
Restaurant** €
Cypriot **Map** A3
Kolios Winery, 2651
Tel *26 724 090*
This large, modern restaurant
is part of the Kolios Winery
complex. After a tour of the
winery, sit back and enjoy local
delicacies such as *mezédhes*.
Reservation recommended.

**TROODOS: Fereos Park
Restaurant** €
Cypriot **Map** B3
Troodos village, 1504
Tel *25 420 114*
Fereos Park is an attractive little
eatery that serves local dishes. Try
the excellent *souvlakia* and
barbecued *sheftalia*.

VASA: Ariadne Restaurant €€
Cypriot **Map** B4
Vasa village, 4505
Tel *25 944 064*
Sample from an extensive
selection of *mezédhes* dishes,
including *tahini* and *skordalia*
dips, grilled *halloumi* and herb
sausages with fresh bread. Lovely
courtyard seating.

VOUNI: Orea Ellas €€
Greek **Map** B4
Ellados 3, 4772
Tel *25 944 328*
Housed in a beautiful building,
Orea Ellas dishes up sumptuous
dishes such as *saganaki* (a Greek
appetizer), oven-baked pies, cour-
gette balls and Greek sausage.

Central Cyprus

DK Choice

AGROS: Kelada €
Cypriot **Map** C3
Agros Ave, 4860
Tel *25 521 303*
Located on the central square
of Agros, Kelada offers a taste of
the authentic cuisine of Cyprus.
Souvla (pork, lamb or chicken),
*koupepia, makaronia tou
fournou* (pasta with béchamel
sauce and minced pork) are
some of its specialities. Dine at
the outdoor patio in summer.

**AGROS: Rodon Hotel
Restaurant** €
International **Map** C3
Rodon Hotel, Rodou 1, 4860
Tel *25 521 201*
Cypriot and international cuisine
are served in this bright and
spacious fine-dining restaurant
located in a renovated country
house. Imaginative home-
made desserts.

**AGROS: To Mpakaliko
toy Hapsi** €
Cypriot **Map** C3
114 Agros Ave, 4860
Tel *99 409 108*
Enjoy lovely views over Agros
while sipping coffee or tea at this
traditional *kafenia*. When hungry,
order the platter of charcuterie
and local cheese, accompanied
by Greek or Cypriot wines.

DALI: Daliou Mills €
Cypriot **Map** D3
Archbishop Makarios III 41, 2540
Tel *22 521 308*
One of Dali's few eateries, and
believed to be its oldest taverna,

Scenic views from the alfresco dining terrace at Vouni Panagias, Panagia

The charming, homely dining room at Archontiko Papadopoulou, Kornos

the Daliou Mills is best known for its *mezédhes* platters and scrumptious *kleftiko*. Call ahead.

FIKARDOU: O Yiannakos €
Cypriot **Map** C3
Fikardou village, 2623
Tel *22 633 311*
Popular restaurant housed in a renovated centuries-old stone house. Good Cypriot menu with *koupepia* and *sheftalia* highly recommended. Call ahead for opening times.

KORNOS: Archontiko Papadopoulou €€
Cypriot **Map** C3
Archbishop Makarios III 67, 7640
Tel *22 531 000*
Set in a beautifully restored village house, this restaurant dishes up local cuisine with a creative twist. Try their *mezédhes* named *Ta Pilina*, as the food is served in little clay pots (*pilos*). Good wine list.

LAKATAMIA: Mageirisses €
Cypriot **Map** C3
Archbishop Makarios III 110, 2323
Tel *22 381 822*
True to its name, which means two women cooks, this modern tavern is run by two sisters. Offers *souvlakia*, *sheftalia*, *ttavas* (a casserole dish) and other Cypriot dishes.

LAZANIA: Estiatorio Mageia €
Cypriot **Map** C3
Lazania village, 2618
Tel *22 781 083*
Estiatorio Mageia is one of a handful of small eateries in this traditional cobbled village. Known for its delicious *kleftiko*, which is cooked in its outside domed oven, and *souvlakia* that sizzles on the barbecue.

South Nicosia

Café La Mode €
International **Map** C3
Archbishop Makarios III 12A, 1065
Tel *22 510 788*
One of five branches in the city, this lovely café serves everything from salads and light lunches to steaks, along with delicious coffees and desserts.

Fanous Lebanese Restaurant €
Lebanese **Map** C3
Solonos 7C, 1011
Tel *22 666 663*
Choose from a menu of traditional and contemporary Lebanese and Palestinian dishes. There is belly dancing on Saturdays.

Il Forno €
Italian **Map** C3
Ledras 216–218, 1011
Located on the busiest pedestrian street of the capital. The menu is simple and consists of thin-crust pizzas baked in a wood-fired oven, savoury pastas and *antipasti*.

Zanettos €
Cypriot **Map** C3
Trikoupi 65, 1016
Tel *22 765 501*
One of the best places in South Nicosia to taste *mezédhes*. Choose from an extensive selection of dishes – "village salad", *koupepia*, *souvlakia*, dips, village pasta and lots more. First-rate wine list.

Aigaio €€
Cypriot/Greek **Map** C3
Ektoros 40, 1016
Tel *22 433 297*
Favoured by loyal diners for over 25 years, Aigaio dishes up the best of classic Cypriot and Greek cuisines. Superb selection of wines. Reservations are advised.

Akakiko €€
Asian **Map** C3
Achaion 1, 2413
Tel *77 778 022*
Relish flavourful Japanese, Thai and Korean dishes at this modern Asian restaurant located adjacent to Hilton Park Hotel. There is a wide range of sushi on offer. Advance booking is recommended.

DK Choice

Brasserie Au Bon Plaisir €€
French **Map** C3
97 Larnakos Ave, 1046
Tel *96 755 111*
The only French restaurant in Nicosia, this fine-dining establishment serves delectable dishes such as *foie gras* in a Madeira sauce, oysters, mussels, beef bourguignon, *Charolaise* steak and veal with a Béarnaise sauce. Guests can choose from a good list of French and Cypriot wines. Cosy, welcoming interior.

D.O.T €€
International **Map** C3
6A Athinas Ave, 1016
Tel *22 101 228*
Enjoy Mediterranean-inspired cuisine in a lovely industrial-chic setting. From tasty burgers to artfully prepared salads and pastas, the seasonally changing menu offers good choices to diners. Brunch is served throughout the week.

For more information on types of restaurants *see pp166–7*

The Gym €€
International Map C3
Onasagorou 85–89, 1011
Tel *22 002 001*
This bustling place lives up to
the definition of a gastro bar. The
creatively cooked dishes use
seasonal ingredients. Superb
selection of wines and cocktails.

No Reservations €€
International Map C3
16 Stasinou Ave, 1060
Tel *22 376 584*
Gourmet restaurant offering a
modern interpretation of classic
Mediterranean cuisine. The set
menu provides two options; one
with fewer dishes. The menu
changes often as it is based on
seasonal produce. Good wine list.

DK Choice
**Pantopoleion
Kali Orexi** €€
Greek Map C3
Vassileos Pavlou 7, 1096
Tel *22 675 151*
Dine on an authentic Greek
menu consisting of fava,
saganaki, feta cheese baked in
fyllo pastry and chicken
souvlaki with yogurt sauce at
this modern taverna. The
interior is beautifully decorated
in Athenian style. The wine list
is noteworthy.

**Vinocultura Wine Bar &
Tapas Bar** €€
International Map C3
K. Matsi 20, 1082
Tel *22 676 707*
Atmospheric wine bar with an
impressive list of options to
choose from. A good range of
tasty tapas from various cuisines
to accompany your drink. Try
the cocktails too.

Bastione €€€
International Map C3
6 Athinas Ave, 1016
Tel *22 730 025*
Located right next to Famagusta
Gate, this modern establishment
dishes up an interesting blend
of Mediterranean, Greek and
Asian flavours. Good wine and
cocktail lists.

**Domus Lounge Bar and
Restaurant** €€€
International Map C3
Adamantiou Korai 5, 1016
Tel *22 433 722*
Lavishly decorated fine-dining
spot serving international à la
carte cuisine. After dinner, the
restaurant transforms into a
swanky bar and lounge.

DK Choice
**Souxou Mouksou
Mantalakia** €€€
International Map C3
Onasagorou 45–47, 1010
Tel *22 666 600*
Gourmet cuisine served in a
charmingly decorated dining
room. The menu includes
appetizers, steaks, seafood,
imaginative salads and delicious
desserts. First-class selection
of wines.

North Cyprus

**BELLAPAIS: The Abbey
Bell Tower** €
International Map C2
Bellapais village
Tel *0392 815 75 07*
With a first-floor terrace
commanding panoramic views,
the Abbey Bell Tower offers
Turkish and Cypriot cuisine along
with lots of international dishes.

**BELLAPAIS: Altinkaya Fish
Restaurant** €
Seafood Map C2
Bellapais village
Tel *0392 081 55 001*
Popular eatery specializing in fish
dishes, each well-cooked and
beautifully presented. Excellent
service. Good value for money.

BELLAPAIS: Bella Moon €
Cypriot Map C2
Bellapais village
Tel *0392 815 43 11*
Located near the abbey ruins,
this alfresco eatery serves Cypriot
dishes on its airy terrace. Great
local desserts.

**BELLAPAIS: Bellapais Gardens
Hotel & Restaurant** €€
International Map C2
Crusader Rd
Tel *0392 815 60 66*
Good restaurant inside the
Bellapais Gardens hotel complex.

Gourmet-style dishes on the
menu include *carpaccio* of beef
and steak in brandy cream sauce.
Champagne menu available.

**DIPKARPAZ: Big Sand Beach
Restaurant** €€
International Map F1
Dipkarpaz village
Tel *0533 844 13 22*
One of the few good restaurants
on the Karpaz peninsula, the Big
Sand Beach, located at the
famous Golden Beach, serves
delectable international cuisine.
Terrace seating overlooks the sea.

FAMAGUSTA: DB Café €
International Map E3
Namik Kemal Meydanı 14
Tel *0392 366 66 10*
Lively eatery specializing in pizzas
with an array of toppings to
choose from. Also on offer are
burgers, sandwiches and kebabs.

**FAMAGUSTA: Petek
Patisserie** €
International Map E3
Liman Yolu Sok 1
Tel *0392 366 71 04*
Popular spot serving international
and Turkish dishes, including delicious pastries. Fun decor with
indoor fountains and ornaments
on display. The outside terrace
overlooks the Famagusta harbour.

**FAMAGUSTA: Bedis Bar and
Restaurant** €€
International Map E3
Near Salamis Ruins
Tel *0392 378 82 25*
Eat outside on the terrace or in
the cosy interior dining hall at
this popular spot servicing
visitors to the Salamis ruins.
Turkish and international cuisine.

KYRENIA: Al Shaheen €€
Indian Map C2
Uğur Mumen 2
Tel *0392 815 73 90*
The restaurant features Indian
cuisine on its menu. Outside
dining is on a wonderful terrace
surrounded by palm trees.

Lovely alfresco seating at Bellapais Gardens Hotel & Restaurant, Bellapais

Indian cuisine in an outdoor setting at Jashan's, Kyrenia

KYRENIA: Buffavento €€
Turkish/Cypriot Map C2
Mağusa Dağ Yolu, Beşparmak Zirvesi
Tel *0533 864 53 88*
Mountainside restaurant with
panoramic views of the Kyrenia
coastline and a lengthy menu
featuring Cypriot and Turkish
cuisine. Try their grills and
delicious *börek* cheese pastries.

KYRENIA: Canlı Balık €€
International Map C2
Kyrenia Harbour
Tel *0392 815 21 82*
Housed in a period building on the
harbour. Choose from grills and
vegetarian dishes, or try the daily
specials of locally caught fish.

KYRENIA: Carpenters €€
Turkish/Cypriot Map C2
Karaoğlanoğlu
Tel *0392 822 22 51* **Closed** *lunch*
Welcoming, family-run restaurant
close to the harbour. Sample local
Turkish dishes such as *börek*,
kebabs, steaks and honey-
drenched dessert pastries.

KYRENIA: Chinese House €€
Chinese Map C2
Karaoğlanoğlu
Tel *0392 815 21 30*
Dine inside or on a pretty terrace
surrounded by flowers. Authentic
Chinese delicacies are on offer
along with a good choice of wines.

**KYRENIA: Güler's Fish
Restaurant** €€
Seafood Map C2
Coast Rd
Tel *0392 822 27 18*
Visit Güler's for some of Kyrenia's
best seafood, with a Cypriot twist.
Memorable dining experience in
a beautiful beachside setting.

**KYRENIA: Hürdeniz Fish
Restaurant** €€
Seafood Map C2
Naci Talat Cad 40C
Tel *0392 816 12 33*
One of the best places in Kyrenia
to enjoy fresh fish dishes,

especially fish *meze*. Popular spot
among locals. Advance booking
is recommended.

KYRENIA: I Belli €€
Italian Map C2
Namik Kemal 52
Tel *0392 815 46 70*
Among the best Italian dining
venues in North Cyprus, I Belli
prepares savoury pizzas, risotto,
pastas, seafood dishes and delicious desserts. Do not miss their
home-made Limoncello liquor.

KYRENIA: Jashan's €€
Indian Map C2
Karaoğlanoğlu
Tel *0392 822 20 27*
Long-established eatery popular
with locals for its superb Indian
cuisine. Try the speciality curry
and *tandoori* dishes. Also serves
some international dishes and
has an excellent wine list.

**KYRENIA: Missina Fish and
A La Carte Restaurant** €€
International Map C2
Omer Faydeh 12, Karaoğlanoğlu
Tel *0392 822 38 44*
An à la carte and fish restaurant
in the heart of Kyrenia, Missina
has a lengthy menu and excellent
wine selection. Eat outdoors on
its large terrace or inside in the
elegantly decorated dining hall.

KYRENIA: Niazi Restaurant €€
Turkish/Cypriot Map C2
Kordonboyu
Tel *0392 815 21 60*
Well-established restaurant near
the town centre. Order their
speciality *meze* and enjoy the
excellent *meze* or small dishes of
Turkish Cypriot classics brought
to the table.

KYRENIA: No. 14 €€
International Map C2
14 Yazicade Sokak
Tel *0542 859 20 72*
An elegant bistro-style eatery in
the heart of the town's old quarter.
Serves international cuisine,

including Turkish dishes such as
bamya basti (vegetarian stew).
Lovely seating around a pool.

**KYRENIA: Patina A La Carte
Restaurant** €€
Cypriot Map C2
13 Sinir Sok, Ozanköy
Tel *0533 837 97 42*
Artfully presented gourmet-
style dishes are served at this
atmospheric restaurant featuring lovely red decor and
white linens. Try the steak meals
or the speciality *oska buka olla
marina* (beef medallions in a
watercress cream sauce).
Reservations recommended.

KYRENIA: The Dragon €€€
Chinese Map C2
Kordonboyu Cad
Tel *0533 830 06 55*
Savour Chinese delicacies and
freshly prepared sushi at this
delightful restaurant housed in
the Rocks Hotel. Traditional
Chinese ambience.

LAPITHOS: The Wild Duck €
International Map C2
Lapithos village
Tel *0533 863 03 02*
A casual, family-friendly café set
inside a pretty garden. Offers
burgers, salads, sandwiches and
some Turkish delicacies.

**NORTH NICOSIA (LEFKOŞA):
Biyer Restaurant** €€
International Map C3
Mehmet Akif Cad 61
Tel *0392 229 17 50*
Serves a mix of international and
Turkish cuisine. The restaurant
offers a selection of kebabs and
meze, while the café next door
dishes up international fare.

**NORTH NICOSIA (LEFKOŞA):
Boghjalian Konak** €€
Cypriot Map C3
Şehit Salahi Şevket Sok, Arabahmet
Tel *0392 228 07 00*
Housed in a grand building with
an Ottoman-style banqueting
hall and a courtyard. Go for the
speciality *meze*.

**NORTH NICOSIA (LEFKOŞA):
Californian Bar and Grill** €€
International Map C3
Mehmet Akif Cad 74
Tel *0392 227 07 00*
While the decor downstairs is
reminiscent of an American diner,
there is also an elegant dining
area upstairs. Choose from
sizzling steaks, grilled chicken,
burgers and kebabs.

For more information on types of restaurants *see pp166–7*

SHOPPING IN CYPRUS

Cyprus is famous for its handicrafts, especially the intricate laces and beautifully embroidered fabrics created by Cypriot women. Artisan food and drink, such as honey and jam, as well as spoon sweets and local wines such as Commandaria and *zivania*, are widely available. A variety of rose products, including oils, soap and perfume, are also quite unique. Other popular gifts are silver and copper jewellery based on traditional designs, and inexpensive leather goods. One of the pleasures of a trip to Cyprus is sampling the local food, whether in a market (where fresh fruit and spices abound) or bakery. *Halloumi* cheese, eaten on its own or grilled in a sandwich with tomatoes and *lountza* (cured pork), tastes delicious.

Where to Shop

Souvenirs can be bought anywhere on the island. Shops, boutiques and street stalls are found in abundance in the larger towns and along the promenades of the famous resorts. In the mountain villages, small family-run shops sell basic commodities, while home-made foodstuffs, such as orange marmalade, jam and excellent honeys, can be bought directly from their producers at the workshops or from stalls at various locations throughout Cyprus.

Near every major historic site you will find a stall that sells typical local souvenirs, postcards and handicrafts. The most common items for sale are clay amphorae and jugs, baskets and traditional lace and embroidery.

Supermarkets and small local shops, which are usually open late, have the best prices for foodstuffs, but you can also buy cold drinks and snacks at the beach or from one of the many kiosks found everywhere. The larger hotels have their own shops.

Opening Hours

The peak holiday season is June to mid-September, when shops

A shop selling handicrafts in the centre of Larnaka

have the longest hours. They open between 7am and 9am until 8pm (7:30pm in winter), some with a 3-hour lunch break (1–4pm). On Wednesdays and Saturdays most shops close between 1pm and 3pm.

Many larger shops now open on Sundays in the summer months, usually from around 7am or 8am until 4pm. Supermarkets generally have longer opening hours.

Markets are best seen early in the morning, when the choice of produce is largest.

How to Pay

In beach shops, open markets and small shops in villages, it is customary to pay by cash. Credit cards are widely accepted in larger establishments, including supermarkets, and souvenir and jewellery shops.

A stall with a variety of home-preserved fruits and jams

Markets

An inherent feature of the Mediterranean scenery, markets are found in all larger towns of Cyprus. The most picturesque are the fruit and vegetable markets in Nicosia, Limassol, Pafos and Larnaka. Their local colour and character make them a great tourist attraction. Haggling is a common practice. Most markets sell fresh fruit, vegetables and spices. Those in seaside resorts may also have interesting costume jewellery, flip-flops and beach bags.

Markets that specialize in fresh local produce are best visited early in the morning. At that time of day, the air is cool and you can take a leisurely stroll between the rows of stalls, savouring the flavours and scents. Here you will find readily available fresh produce, including exotic fruit and vegetable varieties little known

A typical Cypriot market, brimming with fresh produce

in mainland Europe. You can also buy traditional cheeses, sausages, many types of fish, and a variety of nuts and sweets. Sacks full of fragrant, colourful spices stand next to the stalls.

Every now and then you can also find antiques offered at reasonable prices.

Food

One of the island's specialist foods is *halloumi* – the traditional goat's cheese, which is excellent in salads and delicious when fried or grilled. Another tasty delicacy is *soujoukkos* – a sweet almond filling covered with thickened grape juice.

The best souvenir from Cyprus is the sweet "Cyprus sun" – the local full-bodied Commandaria wine with its rich, warm and truly sunny bouquet. Another noteworthy beverage is *zivania* (alcohol produced from grape seeds), classified as *eau-de-vie*. Look for the popular brands as well as the ones sold at local wineries. Other good food purchases include delicious dried fruit, and rose petal jam. The sweet fruit jellies – *loukoumi* – are the Cypriot version of Turkish delight. They are mainly produced in Lefkara and Geroskipou villages. The Fini village prepares a different version of *loukoumi*. The highlanders produce exquisite herb-scented honey. The popular spices on the island are oregano, thyme and most of the Mediterranean herbs and spices.

A well-stocked wine shop in Omodos, in the Troodos mountains

Souvenirs

A wide range of souvenirs is available for sale to tourists in Cyprus, but by far the most popular take-home items are

The owner of a jewellery studio at work on a new piece

ceramics and wickerwork. The Cyprus Handicraft Service has shops and workshops that sell such handicrafts in many towns and cities around the islands.

Traditional Cypriot lace is produced in the villages of Lefkara and Omodos, and makes a beautiful souvenir or gift. In North Cyprus you can buy embroidery based on traditional Turkish designs.

Exquisite icons are sold in the mountain monasteries, sometimes hand-crafted and painted by the monks themselves.

Traditional copper pots and bowls, and attractive and inexpensive leather goods, are available throughout Cyprus and make good gifts.

DIRECTORY

Markets

Larnaka
Municipal market, Old Market Square. **Open** 4am–2pm Sat. Flea market, Kellia. **Open** 9am–5pm Mon–Sat.

Limassol
Central market. **Open** 6am–2pm Mon–Sat. Town market near the old hospital. **Open** 6am–1pm Sat. Linopetra. **Open** 7am–5pm Sat.

Nicosia
Market Square. **Open** 6am–5pm daily. Strovolos, Dimitri Vikellou Str. **Open** 6am–6pm Fri. Ochi Square. **Open** 6am–6pm Wed & Sat.

Pafos
Agora Str. **Open** 8am–5pm Mon–Sat (to 2:30pm Wed & Sat). Timi. **Open** 8am–2pm.

Cyprus Handicraft Service

Larnaka
Cosma Lysioti 6. **Tel** 24 304 327.

Limassol
Themidos 25. **Tel** 25 305 118.

Nicosia
Leoforos Athalassas 186. **Tel** 22 305 024.

Pafos
Leoforos Apostolou Pavlou 64. **Tel** 26 306 243.

Beautifully embroidered, colourful shawls from Lefkara

What to Buy in Cyprus

Thanks to the centuries-long influence of a variety of cultures, Cyprus offers its visitors a wealth of souvenirs of every description, from beautiful icons in the south, to typical Turkish water pipes in the north. Some towns are famous for their unique lace designs, ceramics and exquisite jewellery. Leather goods are particularly attractive in the northern part of the island. The choice of souvenirs is truly astounding, and searching for that original item to take home with you is half the fun.

Icons
Icons, painted by Greek Orthodox monks, are very popular with tourists. They vary from simple to elaborate designs, some with robes depicted in silver or with golden floral motifs.

Madonna and Child icon

South Cyprus

A beautifully embroidered tablecloth – a handsome gift

Textiles
Colourful stripes form the traditional pattern seen on tablecloths and rugs. The hand-woven fabric used in these articles is called *lefkonika*. Its name comes from the town of Lefkonikon (now in North Cyprus) where the fabric was first produced.

Lace
The most famous Cypriot lace – *lefkaritika* – comes from Lefkara. The best-known motif is the Da Vinci pattern, which, according to legend, was passed on to local lace-makers by the famous Italian artist.

Exquisite lace

Woven rug with the distinctive striped pattern

Tin and Copperware
Tin-plated kettles decorated with fine patterns are a practical, as well as a decorative present. Copper ornaments are also popular. The most beautiful of these include bracelets with traditional Greek designs.

An original tin kettle

A beautifully decorated silver trinket

Tray decorated with a map of Cyprus

Tourist Souvenirs
The most common souvenirs from Cyprus are plates, ashtrays, mugs and T-shirts decorated with the image of Aphrodite or a map of the island. But the inventiveness of the souvenir producers knows no bounds, and stalls are loaded with fancy knick-knacks.

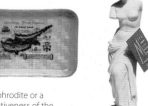

Silver
In addition to lace, Lefkara prides itself on its silver creations. Here, you can find the finest jewellery made to unusual designs, and intricately decorated trinkets.

Statuette of Aphrodite – the patron goddess of Cyprus

Alcoholic Beverages

One of the best souvenirs from the island is "Cyprus sun" – sweet local Commandaria wine, full-bodied, with a rich bouquet of aromas and flavours. Other noteworthy beverages include wines made from indigenous grape varieties and *zivania*, which belongs to the *eau-de-vie* category.

"Cyprus sun" – the sweet Commandaria

Bottle of Cypriot rosé wine

Wicker basket

Wickerwork

Inexpensive wicker baskets can be bought in the markets of Nicosia, Limassol and Larnaka, or directly from their makers in the villages of Liopetri or Sotira, near Agia Napa.

Cypriot Music

Traditional Cypriot music is based on Mediterranean motifs. The famous "Zorba's Dance" is a favourite with tourists.

CD of traditional Cypriot music

Local Delicacies

The outstanding local delicacy is *halloumi* – a goat's cheese. People with a sweet tooth should try *soujoukkos* – made of almonds and grape juice, or *loukoumi* (Cyprus delight).

Cypriot sweets

Pottery

Cypriot markets are full of clay jugs, bowls and other vessels, of all shapes and sizes, often richly ornamented.

Clay water jug

North Cyprus

Ceramics

A wide variety of ceramic products is on offer. Available in all shapes and sizes, they are decorated in traditional patterns. The loveliest and most popular with tourists are the traditional bowls and jugs.

A jug – a popular form of earthenware

Hookah (or narghile)

The hookah is a typical souvenir from the north. Tourists buy these water pipes, tempted by the fruity aroma of tobacco. The full set also includes charcoal and tobacco.

A hookah – a typical souvenir from North Cyprus

Tourist Souvenirs

The most popular souvenirs are hand-woven rugs and tablecloths, and plates decorated with pictures of popular historical sites, with commemorative inscriptions. The selection of souvenirs is not great, but prices are reasonable. Stalls selling souvenirs can be found at the main tourist sites.

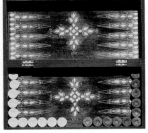

An encrusted wooden box for the popular game backgammon

A colourful souvenir plate

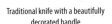

Traditional knife with a beautifully decorated handle

ENTERTAINMENT IN CYPRUS

Every visitor to Cyprus, whether young or old, will find plenty of entertainment to enjoy. Hotels stage folk evenings, accompanied by traditional music and dancing. Guests can dance to Greek and Cypriot tunes, watch an unusual display in which a dancer wearing the typical Cypriot attire places a tower of glasses on his head, or join in games of skill based on traditional Greek entertainment.

In addition to this, every major resort has modern bars, pubs and clubs playing live music, which mostly includes contemporary international tracks. Festivals, casinos and amusement parks on the island provide even more diversions.

CTO office in Pafos

Information

Information on current cultural events can be obtained from tourist offices and hotel reception desks. Even before leaving for your trip, it's worth checking out Cyprus on the Internet, so that you can time your arrival to coincide with local festivals, such as the wonderful wine festivals, which are accompanied by free tastings, and the music festivals taking place mostly during summer at various locations all over the island (see also pp26-9). Leaflets handed out on the streets may contain interesting information on local events, as do posters displayed in public places and English language newspapers (see p197).

Nightlife and Culture

The island has a thriving nightlife. In addition to the bars in major resorts, there is a good selection of clubs, wine bars and pubs in the cities. People looking for all-night parties and dancing should stay in Limassol – the centre of entertainment on the island. Agia Napa, is considered Cyprus' party town, dotted with clubs hosting internationally renowned DJs every summer.

Tickets to the largest clubs can be booked in advance over the telephone or via the Internet.

Cultural life in Cyprus is not limited to bars, cafés, nightclubs and folk shows staged on hotel terraces. Larger towns also have theatres performing a classical repertory as well as modern plays in historic settings. It is worth dropping into one of the stylish cafés in the old part of Nicosia, to taste Cypriot coffee and indulge in people-watching. Served in small glasses, this strong and sweet coffee will revive you in no time at all.

Hotel Entertainment

Many hotel concierges and travel agents will arrange activities for visitors, including equipment hire for anything from tennis rackets or bicycles to a luxury yacht. They can also organize lessons for you. Their offers are displayed in hotels, where you can also book a boat cruise, an excursion or a diving course. Most hotels also sell tickets to concerts, dance

Children at the Wild Flower Festival in Larnaka

shows and other performances by local artists. In some venues, Cypriot orchestras entertain dinner guests nightly. Other traditional Cypriot evenings are popular and easy to book.

Feasts and Festivals

Traditional religious festivals in Cyprus coincide with those celebrated in Europe. On New Year's Day, Cypriots exchange presents and eat the traditional New Year cake – vassilopitta. Epiphany is celebrated in the seaside towns with a swimming competition: the winner is the person who recovers the

Nissi Beach in Agia Napa, popularly known as "Cypriot Ibiza"

crucifix hurled out over the water. During Holy Week, an effigy of Judas is burned, and icons are covered with a black pall. Anthestiria – the flower festival held in May – heralds the arrival of spring. In September, the annual arts festival Ta Kypria is held in Nicosia and other cities as well as the Limassol wine festival.

The North celebrates mainly Muslim festivals, the most important and widely celebrated is Şeker Bayramı.

Casinos

Gambling is not particularly popular in Cyprus, but Roulette and blackjack attract mainly tourists from Turkey. Casinos are only found in North Cyprus. The best are found in the more upmarket hotels of Kyrenia and Famagusta.

A casino in the Colony Hotel *(see p165)*, located in Kyrenia

Excursions

Information about organized excursions and sightseeing bus tours can be obtained from hotel reception desks or tourist information centres. The most popular excursions are day trips to major tourist attractions and historic sites, visits to traditional villages, and Cypriot evenings with traditional food, drink and dancing. Boat cruises along the coast are also available.

Amusement Parks

Unlike most rival Mediterranean resorts, Cyprus has lots of purpose-built attractions for

The colourful Waterworld Waterpark in Agia Napa

younger visitors. A visit to a waterpark or a mini-zoo is a must when on holiday with children. The vast waterparks, usually occupying several hectares, offer numerous amusements for all age groups. In addition to swimming pool complexes, they have scenic routes that can be travelled by small boat, while admiring Greek ruins scattered along the shores. Large swimming pools have secret coves, artificial waves, thickets and diving sites. They vie with oneanother to provide the most unusual attractions, such as the Zeus Zenith slide with its 370 bends at the Agia Napa waterpark. This waterpark styled after ancient Greek designs, combines entertainment with a lesson in history. Waterparks, being outdoor attractions, are open only during high season.

Educational parks and their collections of island fauna and flora are also sources of unforgettable delight, knowledge building and exploration for youngsters.

In the summer the most popular parks are very crowded. Every amusement park is virtually a small town in itself, with shops, restaurants and numerous attractions where you can easily spend an enitre day.

Those who fail to get their fill of fun during the daytime can take a stroll along the seaside promenades during the evening, and drop into a funfair for a ride on a carousel. Limassol *(see pp72–7)* and other large resorts have such funfairs.

DIRECTORY

Excursions

CitySightseeing Pafos
Harbour Coach Park, Pafos.
Tel 99 393 766.
Open 10am–4pm daily.
cypruscitysightseeing.com

Salamis Tours Excursions
Salamis House,
28 Oktovriou, Limassol.
Tel 25 860 000.
salamisinternational.com

Waterparks

Aphrodite Waterpark
Poseidonos Ave, Geroskipou-Pafos.
Tel 26 913 638.
Open May & Jun: 10:30am–5:30pm daily; Jul & Aug: 10am–6pm daily; Sep & Oct: 10am–5pm daily.
aphroditewaterpark.com

Fasouri Water Mania Waterpark
Near Trahoni village, Limassol.
Tel 25 714 235.
Open May, Sep & Oct: 10am–5pm daily; Jun–Aug: 10am–6pm daily.
fasouri-watermania.com

Waterworld Waterpark
Agia Napa.
Tel 23 724 444.
Open May–Sep: 10am–6pm daily Apr & Oct: 10am–5pm daily; May–Sep: 10am–6pm daily.
waterworldwaterpark.com

OUTDOOR ACTIVITIES

Contrary to popular belief, Cyprus offers much more in the way of recreation than splashing in the sea and sunbathing on the beaches. Certainly many visitors are drawn by the prospect of sunshine, peace and tranquillity. But the island's mild, warm climate, combined with its unique topography, attracts all types of outdoor enthusiasts. Visitors seeking an active holiday will find numerous facilities for sport, as well as knowledgeable and professional coaching and instruction. You can enjoy a wide array of watersports, including snorkelling, diving and windsurfing. On land there is excellent hiking, horse-riding and cycling. In winter, you can even learn to ski or snowboard on the slopes of Mount Olympus.

Hiking in the Troodos mountains

Hiking

The island's best hiking areas are in the mountain regions. Clearly signposted walking trails and scenic nature trails, found mainly in the Troodos mountains and on the Akamas peninsula, help hikers to discover the most fascinating corners of Cyprus. The most enjoyable island hikes lead through nature reserves.

When hiking, you should always carry a detailed map of the region. And before setting off, it is important to pack appropriate warm clothing; even when it is hot on the coast, it can be quite chilly high up in the mountains. Also be sure to bring plenty of drinking water and sunblock.

There are registered nature trails that offer a good opportunity to explore the island. Information on these trails is available through the tourist information centres and the CTO website.

Cycling Trips

Virtually all tourist resorts on Cyprus have bicycles available for hire. The island's cycling routes are magnificent, particularly in the mountains, and this is a great way to enjoy the scenery. Maps showing the routes are available from tourist information centres in every resort and larger town.

It is a good idea to carry a pump with the correct tip, and self-adhesive patches for inner-tubes in case of punctures. For more complicated repairs, you can ask for help from a specialist bicycle shop.

Horse-riding

Cyprus' hills provide the ideal terrain for horse-riding. Horse-lovers will appreciate a beautiful

A leisurely family cycling trip

ride along the paths that wind their way gently through the pine-clad hills. An unhurried walk through a cypress grove, or a wild gallop over wooded hills, will be a memorable part of your holiday in Cyprus.

Donkey rides are also available in Cyprus. Resorts and hotels can provide information about horse and donkey farms.

Snowboarder on the slopes of Mount Olympus

Skiing and Snowboarding

Depending on the weather, it is possible to ski and snowboard on the northeast slopes of Mount Olympus between December and mid-March. The island's highest mountain provides good snow conditions, with four ski lifts and an equipment hire centre for visitors. Individual and group tuition is available for both skiers and snow boarders to help novices negotiate the complexities of a downhill run. If you are planning to engage in snow sports during your holiday in Cyprus, keep an eye on the weather forecast and snow conditions by checking on the Internet, with the Cyprus Ski Federation, or asking your tour operator.

Tennis

Most top hotels on the island have their own hard courts and tennis schools, and floodlit, all-weather public tennis courts can be found in most major towns. Aficionados will enjoy a game played at high altitude (above 1,500 m/ 4,900 ft), amid the pine and cedar woods. This is made possible by the location of one of the most scenic courts which can be found in the Troodos National Forest Park.

Golf

Cyprus has perfect golfing weather for much of the year, though some may find July and August uncomfortably hot. There are several 18-hole courses, all offering golf clubs for hire. Particularly noteworthy is the Minthis Hill Golf Club, situated near Pafos on the picturesque grounds of a 12th-century monastery. There are many other high-quality, scenically located golf courses of varying degrees of difficulty for golfers of every ability.

The north of the country has no public golf courses, but

Tourists relaxing and bathing at Fig Tree beach, Protaras

visitors may use the golf course in Pentayia, which is located to the southwest of the town of Morfou (Güzelyurt).

Other Activities

Increasingly popular trips in four-wheel-drive vehicles give visitors the chance to discover the lesser-known parts of the island and to admire its beauty away from the tourist centres.

Rock-climbers may head for the crags of Troodos, Drouseia or Cape Gkreko. Novice climbers should always be assisted by an experienced instructor.

Cyprus is full of ancient relics, and among its main attractions are the archaeological sites. The ruins at Amathous, near Limassol, are partially flooded, so they can be viewed while swimming in the sea. Other important sights are Kato Pafos and Salamis, in the north.

Car Rallies

Drivers travelling around Cyprus will get enough excitement from driving the narrow streets of Nicosia or steep roads of the Troodos mountains. But if you want even more driving thrills, you can attend one of Cyprus' several car rallies, sprints or hill climbs. These are held at various locations including Limassol, Larnaka, Nicosia and Pafos. Further details, including the routes and the results of recent years, can be obtained from the website of the **Cyprus Motor Sports Federation** or from any of the individual towns' automobile clubs.

Churning up clouds of dust at the popular International Cyprus Rally

Watersports

The beaches of Cyprus are fun places for the whole family. Sunbathing, volleyball and all kinds of watersports are available to keep you entertained. The numerous attractions include snorkelling, diving, windsurfing, waterskiing, sailing and a lot more. Sea breezes moderate the high temperatures, and the clear water is ideal for swimming. There is no shortage of places to hire equipment, allowing you to practise even the most ambitious watersports or take a scuba-diving course.

Snorkelling in the clear blue waters near rock formations

Diving

The clear, clean coastal waters of Cyprus invite underwater exploration. Diving is extremely popular in Cyprus, and there are diving schools and centres in virtually every seaside resort on the island.

The greatest thrills can be experienced from underwater explorations in the regions of Larnaka, the Akamas peninsula and Agia Napa, famous for the island's loveliest beaches. Experienced divers may look for the local wrecks of cargo boats and naval vessels. This is quite a unique attraction since, unlike many countries, the Cyprus Tourism Organization allows the exploration of vessels that have sunk off its coast. One of the most famous wrecks is the Wreck of the Zenobia, close to Larnaka.

Visitors will be flooded with offers from diving clubs and schools. These organizations provide not only diving lessons for novices and children, but also sea cruises along with diving. The initial lessons can often be taken in the hotel, since many of them run their own diving schools.

Snorkelling

There is plenty to see underwater, even within a few metres of the shore if you are a beginner at this sport. The shallows teem with tiny fish, sea anenomes and urchins clinging to the rocks. If you're lucky, you may even see an octopus slither past.

It's worth heading out to the more rocky shores where there is more to see than on the sandy bottom. One of the best places for snorkelling is the north coast of the Akamas peninsula, where rocky coves and tiny offshore islands abound in sealife.

Many hotels hire out snorkelling equipment. You can also buy masks with snorkels and flippers at local sports shops; these do not cost much.

It is prohibited to collect sponges or any archaeological items found on the seabed.

Windsurfing and Kiteboarding

Almost all beaches run courses for windsurfing, though the gentle afternoon breezes may not meet the expectations of the more competitive windsurfers. The best winds blow around the capes, between Agia Napa and Protaras, and in the region of Larnaka and Pafos. Kiteboarding, which involves being towed at high speeds by a giant parachute-like kite, can be practised in almost all coastal regions of Cyprus, where there are training schools in each area.

Yachts moored in Larnaka marina

Sailing

Sailing is very popular in Cyprus, and the island's marinas play host to vessels from practically every European country. Skippered yachts can be chartered from island marinas (Larnaka and Limassol are the main centres) by the day or for longer cruises, and smaller dinghies and catamarans are available by the day or half-day from beaches around Agia Napa, Protaras, Limassol and Latsi. The many boat charter companies have their offices in coastal resorts, where you will also find sailing schools.

The waters around Cyprus offer magnificent sailing conditions, and the island is often referred to as a "sailor's paradise". Southwesterly winds prevail in the summer. The delicate westerly breeze blowing in the morning

A diver exploring the sights under water

Holidaymakers enjoying a "banana ride" at a Cyprus resort

changes gently around noon to a westerly wind of 15–20 knots. In the winter, the temperatures are milder and the sun less scorching. In December and January the winds are mainly 10–20 knots from the southeast. There can be occasional rain at this time, but the prevailing clear weather makes sailing conditions close to ideal.

From Cyprus you can sail to nearby Israel, Lebanon, Egypt, the Greek islands and Turkey.

Beach Sports

For the most part, beaches are found close to hotels, and are watched over by lifeguards in the summer, making them peaceful and comfortable recreation grounds. The beautiful sandy beaches in small sheltered coves provide beautifully idyllic spots for a refreshing dip and are particularly welcoming to those who are lured by the charm and appeal of Aphrodite's island.

Colourful inflatable rings for children

The best known of these scenic beaches is the rocky coast by Petra tou Romiou – the Rock of Aphrodite.

Private hotel beaches as well as public beaches become very crowded during peak season. One of the most famous beaches in Cyprus – Agia Napa's Nissi Beach – buzzes with activity from morning until night. Tourists remain in beach bars and nearby clubs until the small hours and, after a night of partying, head

straight for the beach to enjoy a refreshing swim. Named after the nearby island (the word *nissi* means "island"), Nissi Beach has consequently been nicknamed the "Cypriot Ibiza". The beach lures visitors with its clear water and sand, not seen in other parts of south Cyprus. According to legend, the sand was brought here from the Sahara.

Less famous but equally beautiful beaches can be found in the northern part of the island, in the region of Famagusta (Gazimağusa). Deckchairs, umbrellas and towels are available for hire, but be aware that in some places the owners charge exorbitant prices. Many beaches are set up with volleyball courts; you can also have a game of beach ball or frisbee. Numerous sport centres hire out diving or snorkelling equipment, as well as boats and canoes.

Since there is no shortage of daredevils, Cyprus' beaches also offer more extreme and thrilling activities such as bungee jumping, waterskiing, water scooters, paragliding, jet skiis and "banana" rides behind a motorboat.

The very popular jet ski

DIRECTORY

Diving

Aquanaut
Green Bay, Protaras.
Tel 99 091 170/99 658 271.
w aquanaut.com.cy

Blue Dolphin Scuba Diving
Jasmine Court Hotel, Kyrenia (Girne).
Tel 0542 851 5113.
w bluedolphin.4mg.com

Cydive Diving Centre
1 Poseidonos Ave, Marina Court 44–46, Pafos.
Tel 26 934 271.
w cydive.com

Cyprus Federation of Underwater Activities
1510 Nicosia.
Tel 22 754 647.
w cfua.org

Boat and Yacht Charter

Blue Point Yatching
Larnaka Marina, Larnaka.
Tel 24 539 600.

Interyachting Ltd
3722 Limassol.
Tel 25 811 900.
w interyachting.com.cy

Latchi Yatching
Vladimirou Iracleous 7, Pafos.
Tel 26 949 424.
w latchi-yachting.com

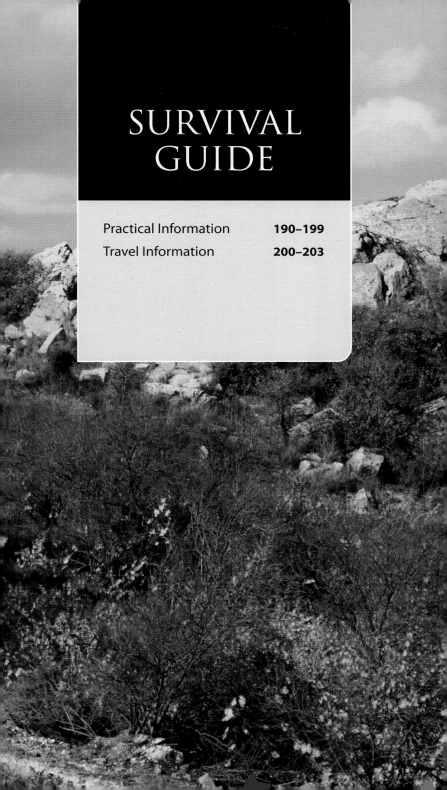

SURVIVAL GUIDE

Practical Information   190–199

Travel Information   200–203

PRACTICAL INFORMATION

Cyprus is a popular year-round destination, due to its Mediterranean climate. It is easily accessible from mainland Europe and the Middle East, yet being an island it feels like a true getaway. The Cypriots are extremely friendly and well inclined towards tourists.

The Greek South and Turkish North have very different characters. Entry requirements are straightforward for visitors who travel solely to either the South or the North. But due to the island's partition, visitors wanting to see both parts of the island should follow the latest advice. The Cyprus Tourism Organization (CTO), representing Southern Cyprus, has offices overseas and throughout the South. The Turkish Republic of Northern Cyprus Ministry of Economy and Tourism represents the North.

When to Go

Cyprus is a year-round destination, so any time of year is suitable for a visit. The main tourist season runs from April until October, and peaks during July and August, when the air and water temperatures are at their highest. At this time the late-night bars, tavernas and restaurants fill up to capacity, and the beaches are packed with sun-worshippers. The hotel swimming pools, bars and restaurants are equally crowded. During peak season you can hear an international mix of languages in the streets, dominated by English, German and Russian.

Those who enjoy the mild, warm climate but prefer to avoid the crowds should visit Cyprus outside the peak season. In April, May and October it is warm enough to swim in the sea, but the beaches are not crowded. In winter (December–February), it is cool for swimming, but good for beach walks, while in the Troodos mountains you can even ski. In spring, Cyprus is an ideal place for hiking, cycling and horse-riding.

The pretty harbour of Kyrenia, North Cyprus

Passports & Visas (The South)

Most visitors, including citizens of the EU, the USA, Canada, Australia and New Zealand, do not require a visa to visit the Republic of Cyprus, and can stay there for up to three months. However, entry to the South may be refused if visitors' passports show they have previously entered North Cyprus.

Tourists may be asked to show that they have adequate means to support themselves for the duration of their stay. No vaccinations or health certificates are required.

Passports & Visas (The North)

To visit North Cyprus, most visitors (including citizens of the EU, USA, Canada, Australia and New Zealand) require only a valid passport. But to avoid being refused entry on later visits to the South, passports should be stamped on a separate loose sheet of paper.

There are no currency restrictions in the North, which has no currency of its own and uses the Turkish lira.

Crossing the Border

Until 2003, the only entry route to North Cyprus was via plane or ferry from Turkey. Nowadays, visitors can fly directly to the Republic of Cyprus and from there travel to the buffer zone. Most visitors do not require a visa to visit North Cyprus, but you will be issued a document free of charge when crossing the border between the two parts of the island. There are seven border crossings (two for pedestrians and one for cars in Nicosia; a further four for cars outside the capital).

Cycling, a popular pastime in Cyprus

 Mountain biking along the rural roads of Cyprus

Apart from the largest cities, such as North Nicosia, Kyrenia and Famagusta, North Cyprus is less crowded than the South of the island. The climate is the same, so in spring it is pleasant to stroll among the orange groves, and in the summer to enjoy the beaches and the sea.

Customs

Customs regulations allow visitors to bring in, duty free, 200 cigarettes, 1 litre of spirits and 2 litres of wine. The import of perishable food items is strictly prohibited. Visitors may import any amount of banknotes, which should be declared to customs on arrival.

Embassies & Consulates

Many countries have embassies or consulates in southern Nicosia, the capital of the Republic of Cyprus. There are no embassies or consulates north of the Green Line because North Cyprus is not recognized as an independent country.

What to Take

For the most part, Cyprus is a relaxed, casual holiday destination. Visitors should pack beachwear, sunglasses, hats and smart casual wear for the resorts. If you're staying in an upmarket hotel, or dining in a fancy restaurant, you will fit in better if you dress up more, as the Cypriots themselves do.

In summer you will seldom need a sweater, but in late autumn, winter and early spring, temperatures are cooler and you will need to bring some warm clothing for the evenings.

If you plan to visit the mountains, at any time of year, it is advisable to bring warm clothes and rain gear. Visitors taking medication should travel with an adequate supply. It's also a good idea to bring high-factor sun lotion and insect repellent.

Some hotels don't supply bath or sink plugs, so you may consider bringing your own.

Etiquette

When visiting religious buildings, modest attire is expected. For churches, monasteries and mosques this means long trousers or skirts, and a shirt that covers your back and shoulders. Shoes must be removed before entering a mosque.

Tourist Organizations

Tourist information bureaux can be found easily in all major tourist centres, such as Nicosia, Larnaka, Limassol, Pafos and Agia Napa. They distribute free information packs and maps, as well as providing useful advice on sightseeing. The **Cyprus Tourism Organization (CTO)**, with offices in many European cities, has a website with lots of information on the Republic of Cyprus. Visit their website at: www.visitcyprus.com.

The **Turkish Republic of Northern Cyprus Ministry of Economy & Tourism** has overseas offices, too. You can learn more about the North at **www.welcometonorthcyprus.co.uk**. Travel agents, hotels, car hire companies, and organizations that offer special activities have their

Automatic tourist information kiosk

own websites detailing the services they offer. It's a good idea to browse through these sites for any potential offers before travelling; many arrangements can be made before you leave home, allowing you to start enjoying your visit from the moment you arrive in Cyprus. Just be sure to check when the website was last updated, as some of the information, particularly for the North, may be out of date and quote the last season's prices.

A range of brochures and illustrated booklets covering individual tourist sights are usually available for sale at the sights themselves.

Languages

Two languages – Greek and Turkish – have coexisted in Cyprus in the centuries between the Turkish conquest of 1571 and the partition of the island in 1974. Due to the current political situation, however, you will find that Southern Cyprus uses only Greek and Northern Cyprus uses only Turkish. In the main holiday resorts in the Southern part of the island, English (as well as German and Russian) is commonly understood and spoken widely. Restaurant menus and shop signs are written in several languages.

In the North it can be more difficult to communicate in English and other European languages, although there is usually no problem when staying in hotels. Road signs throughout the island carry the names of towns written in the Latin alphabet. In the North, however, only the Turkish names are given, so check your map or satellite navigation to ensure that you are travelling in the correct direction for your destination.

A tourist information centre

Religion

The Cypriot Orthodox Church, which is dominant in the south of the island, is independent of the Greek Orthodox Church. It is also the oldest national church in Christendom, its history tracing back to the time of St Paul.

In the towns, you often encounter Orthodox priests dressed in long black robes. The main Orthodox services, lasting 2 to 3 hours, are held on Saturday evenings and Sunday mornings.

Monasteries have served as Cypriot pilgrimage sites for centuries. Today, they are visited by tourists in such vast numbers that access to some of them has been restricted.

In the North, the dominant religion is Islam, though, like Turkey, the North is a secular state. All larger towns and cities have mosques, from which the muezzin's voice calls the faithful to prayer five times a day. Services are held on Friday afternoons.

Façade of a Cypriot mosque with an imposing minaret

Travelling with Children

Major brands of baby food, medicines and toiletries, including nappies (diapers), are sold in all supermarkets and pharmacies. Both parts of the island are family-friendly, with children welcomed everywhere and plenty of kids' facilities. However, risks for smaller children include sunburn, occasional rough waters and pests such as jellyfish, sea urchins and stinging insects.

Worshipper inside an Orthodox church in southern Cyprus

Young Visitors

Cyprus is an ideal holiday destination for young people. Its sunny beaches, clean waters, watersports facilities, and rich and varied nightlife attract young people in thousands. Hundreds of nightclubs, discos, pubs and bars await the revellers.

Holders of ISIC or Euro<26 cards qualify for discounts on public transport and reduced admission to museums and some other tourist sights.

Women Travellers

Women travelling alone or together should exercise normal caution. However, Cyprus is generally safe for women.

Disabled Visitors

Facilities for the disabled have improved considerably in the last few years. However, many museums are housed in older buildings without the provision of lifts. Access to archaeological sites is also difficult. Pavements in towns and villages are often uneven. A leaflet with information on facilities for wheelchair users is available from the CTO.

An increasing number of museums and archaeological sites in the South (and none in the North) offer Braille or audio guides for visually impaired people or induction loop devices for those with hearing difficulties. The British charity RADAR (for people with hearing and visual impairment) can supply information on facilities in Cyprus (www.radar.org.uk).

Gay and Lesbian Visitors

Homosexuality is no longer illegal in Southern Cyprus, and gay visitors are generally welcomed; there are gay clubs and bars in Agia Napa, Larnaka, Limassol and Pafos. Furthermore, the majority of bars, clubs, cafés and restaurants are gay-friendly.

In North Cyprus, homosexuality is still illegal.

Single Travellers

Most visitors to Cyprus come as couples, families or groups of singles, and most hotels offer only double or twin rooms and charge a "single supplement" for those travelling alone. Individuals travelling independently may be able to negotiate a better deal out of season. Several companies specialize in tours for singles: lists are available from the CTO or the Association of Independent Tour Operators in the UK.

Senior Citizens

Both Cypriot communities are notably respectful to older people, but hazards include urban traffic (Cypriot drivers sometimes ignore pedestrian

Sign in Greek prohibiting photography

crossings) and noise – Agia Napa, especially, is geared to younger visitors.

Photography

Be aware that taking photographs of military bases or facilities, and the border between Southern Cyprus and the North is strictly prohibited. United Nations soldiers guarding the Green Line are used to groups of tourists, but taking photographs at any point is strictly forbidden.

Archaeological sites can be photographed and filmed free of charge; however, the state museums generally charge a fee for taking photographs.

In places of worship, ask in advance whether photography is permitted. Most churches will not allow you to use flash photography.

Electrical Equipment

The mains supply on the island is 220/240V, with standard British triple rectangular-pin plugs. Anyone travelling from outside of the EU should ensure they have a suitable adaptor but if needed most hotel reception desks will provide you with the correct type for your devices. Some hotel rooms are equipped with hair dryers, and irons are usually available to borrow.

Time

Cyprus lies within the Eastern-European time zone, and local time is 2 hours ahead of GMT. Like the UK, Cyprus puts its clocks forward by 1 hour from late March to late October. "Morning" in South Cyprus is *proí*; "afternoon" – *mesiméri*; "evening" – *vrádhi*; and "night" – *níchta*.

Weddings

Cyprus is one of the world's most popular wedding destinations and some hotels have their own wedding chapel as well as wedding planners to assist with the preparation for the big day. The bride and groom are required to have all the correct documentation.

Discussing Politics

The events of 1974, when the island was divided between the Turkish and the Greek Cypriots, are still remembered with bitterness. In both the South and the North, local people vehemently argue the justice of their cause. Politics and recent history are therefore subjects that are best avoided for open discussion.

Military Zones

Britain's sovereign bases in the south, at Akrotiri (Episkopi) and Dhekelia, are also used by US forces and are likely to be on heightened alert in these security-conscious times. Do not intrude on military installations. The same applies to Turkish Army personnel, equipment and installations in the occupied North.

DIRECTORY

Embassies & Consulates

Australia
Pindarou 27, Nicosia.
Tel 22 753 001.
w cyprus.
highcommission.gov.au

Germany
Nikitaras 10, Nicosia.
Tel 22 451 145.
w nikosia.diplo.de

Ireland
Aiantos 7, 1082 Nicosia.
Tel 22 818 183.
w embassyofireland.
com.cy

Representation of the European Commission
Byron 30, 1096 Nicosia.
Tel 22 817 770.
w ec.europa.eu/cyprus

Russia
Arch. Makarios III, 2406 Engomi, Nicosia.
Tel 222 774 622.
w cyprus.mid.ru

UK
Alexandrou Palli 1,
1106 Nicosia.
Tel 22 861 100.
w ukincyprus.fco.
gov.uk/en

USA
Ploutarchou, Nicosia.
Tel 22 393 939.
w american embassy.
org.cy

Tourist Organizations

Association of Independent Tour Operators
w aito.co.uk

Cyprus Hotel Association
Andreas Araouzos 12,
1303 Nicosia.
Tel 22 452 820.
w cyprushotel
association.org

Cyprus Tourism Organization (CTO)
Leoforos Lemesou 19,
Nicosia.
Tel 22 691 100.
w visitcyprus.com

Cyprus Tourist Guides Association
Spyrou Kyprianou 14, 1640
Nicosia. **Tel** 22 765 755.
w cytouristguides. com

North Cyprus Tourism Centre
w welcometonorthcyprus.
co.uk

Turkish Republic of Northern Cyprus Ministry of Economy & Tourism
Tel 0392 228 96 29.

Weddings

Union of Cyprus Municipalities
Rigenis 78, Nicosia.
Tel 22 445 170.
w ucm.org.cy

Useful Websites in the Republic of Cyprus

w cyprus-mail.com
w visitcyprus.com
w kypros.org
w pio.gov.cy
w windowon
cyprus.com
w in-cyprus.com

Useful Websites in North Cyprus

w cypnet.com
w northcyprus.net

Personal Security and Health

Cyprus has a low crime rate, but even here crimes do occur; chances can be minimized by taking simple precautions. The risk of theft is greatest in crowded places. Take extra care on crowded promenades or streets and in markets to protect your belongings. Keep documents, money and credit cards hidden from view, and leave what you don't need in the hotel safe. Never leave anything visible in your car when you park it. When in need, you can always ask a policeman for help. Basic medical advice is available at pharmacies. All medical treatment must be paid for; insurance is strongly advised.

Entrance to a police station in the North

Personal Belongings

Before travelling abroad, it is wise to ensure that you have adequate insurance to protect yourself financially from the loss or theft of your property. Even so, it is advisable to take precautions against loss or theft in the first place. Be vigilant when you are out and about but especially in crowded places, where the risk of theft is greatest.

Make photocopies of your important documents and keep these with you, leaving the originals behind in the hotel safe (where you can also deposit money and jewellery).

Make a note of your credit card numbers and the phone number of the issuing bank, in the event of loss or theft.

Cameras and camcorders should be carried on a strap or inside the case. Your car should always be locked, with any valuables kept well out of sight.

Any case of theft should be reported immediately to the police. Passport theft should also be reported to your embassy in Nicosia.

Cyprus Police

The police in Cyprus are friendly towards tourists and ready to offer advice. The majority of them also speak English. But in the event that you are caught breaking the law, they can be stern and unwilling to accept excuses.

Heavy fines are levied for failing to wear a seat belt and for using a mobile telephone when driving a vehicle.

Personal Security in the North

In terms of personal safety, North Cyprus is no different from the south. Special care should be taken when visiting the buffer zone and when passing by military facilities, of which there is no shortage. In particular, resist the temptation to photograph any military installations, vehicles or soldiers. The latter are visible in great numbers, but if you follow the rules of normal behaviour, they will not interfere with your visit.

Roads in North Cyprus are comfortable, wide and of very high quality, including the mountain roads.

Manned lifeguard post at one of the beaches

Beaches

During the holiday season, most beaches employ lifeguards. The areas allocated for swimming are marked with coloured buoys. While swimming outside the marked areas is not prohibited, it is inadvisable, particularly for weaker swimmers. Some beaches have first-aid stations, with lifeguards trained to help casualties.

Beach facilities, such as showers, are standard almost everywhere. Hotels with direct access to the sea have stretches of beach allocated to them.

Smaller beaches have no lifeguards; they are generally found in coves sheltered from the open sea, so their waters are calm and safe. The most beautiful beaches are found in the regions of Agia Napa in the South, and Famagusta in North Cyprus. The south coast beaches are generally rocky and pebbly.

In summer, Cyprus has some of the highest temperatures in Europe, and it's easy to get sunburned anytime from early April to late October. Young children are especially vulnerable to the hot sun. Avoid being directly in the sun during the middle of the day, when the rays are strongest. Sunhats, sunglasses, a high factor

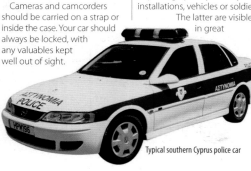

Typical southern Cyprus police car

sunscreen and sunblock are vital to protect your skin. During the day, carry bottled water with you, and drink lots of it, to avoid dehydration.

Medical Care

Cyprus is free from most dangerous infectious diseases (although AIDS is present), and no immunizations are required. Drinking tap water is safe. However, all medical treatment must be paid for, and comprehensive insurance to cover hospital and medical charges, as well as emergency repatriation, is advisable. Before travelling to the North, double check that your insurance policy will cover you there.

Some medical procedures (such as dental treatment) are not covered by insurance.

Emergency medical care in the Republic of Cyprus is free for all European Union citizens. The European Health Insurance Card (EHIC), available from the UK Department of Health or from a main post office, provides access to healthcare at a reduced cost or sometimes for free. The card comes with a booklet that contains general health advice and information about how to claim medical treatment when travelling abroad. You may find that you have to pay and reclaim the money later.

Hotels can usually recommend a local doctor or dentist, many of whom speak English. All bills must be settled at the time of treatment, but these practitioners will provide a receipt for you to

Pharmacy sign with the easily recognizable green cross

claim a refund from your insurance company.

Visitors on package holidays to Cyprus should check with their tour operator if medical insurance is included.

Pharmacies

Most pharmacies keep normal shop opening hours *(see p178)*. They display the green cross sign and the word *farmakeio* or *eczane*. A list of pharmacies that open at night and on holidays can be found in the English-language *Cyprus Mail* and *Cyprus Weekly*. In an emergency, an all-night pharmacy can offer medical help and advice.

In tourist resorts and large cities pharmacists speak English. They can usually advise on remedies for minor ailments and injuries, but if you need specialist prescription drugs it is best to bring an adequate supply.

A uniformed fireman

Fire Service

Winters are dry and mild, and summers are hot, creating prime conditions for fires, which can spread with alarming speed and present a particular danger to forests. Mountain fires, especially, are difficult to put out.

Cyprus has two types of fire brigade; one that responds to general emergency calls, the other specifically dedicated to forest fires.

During excursions to the island's drier inland areas, or when camping, you must take particular care not to start a fire, or keep one under control. Be especially careful to extinguish cigarettes thoroughly and dispose of them safely. When leaving a picnic area or campsite, ensure that any bonfires are completely extinguished when you are leaving, and take all glass bottles with you to prevent accidental fires.

DIRECTORY

Emergency Services

Police
Tel 112 (South), 155 (North).

Fire Brigade
Tel 112 (South), 199 (North).

Forest Fire Teams
Tel 1407 (South), 177 (North).

Ambulance
Tel 112.

Hospitals

General Hospitals
Agia Napa/Paralimni.
Tel 23 200 000.
Famagusta.
Tel 0392 366 28 76.
Kyrenia.
Tel 815 2266.
Larnaka.
Tel 24 800 500.
Limassol.
Tel 25 801 100.
Nicosia.
Tel 22 603 000.
North Nicosia.
Tel 228 5441.
Pafos.
Tel 26 803 100.

Pharmacies

Information in English
Famagusta.
Tel 90 901 413.
Larnaka.
Tel 90 901 414.
Limassol.
Tel 90 901 415.
Nicosia.
Tel 90 901 412.
Pafos.
Tel 90 901 416.

Standard fire engine of the Cyprus Fire Brigade

Communications

The quality of telecommunications services in Cyprus is very good, especially in the south. Public telephone booths are widespread. In larger towns and cities, you will have no trouble finding an Internet café, if your hotel doesn't have access. Postal services are efficient. A good selection of newspapers and magazines is available, and there's no shortage of TV or radio stations.

Telephone and discount card

Using the Telephone

Cyprus has a well-developed telephone network. Public phones accept coins, as well as phonecards, which can be purchased from newsagent kiosks, post offices and banks in various denominations. Instructions for using the phone are provided in both Greek and English. Calls to the police, fire brigade or ambulance service are free.

Hotel rooms are equipped with telephones, but calls made from them are usually very expensive; make sure you check the rates before using them. The country code for Cyprus is 357 except for North Cyprus, where it is 90 (for Turkey) followed by (0)392. Local area codes in Cyprus include: Nicosia 22; Limassol 25; Larnaka 24; Pafos and Polis 26; Agia Napa and Protaras 23.

When making an international call from Cyprus, first dial 00,

followed by the country code, and then the area code (omitting the zero that precedes some area codes). Useful country codes are: UK (44), USA and Canada (1), Ireland (353), Australia (61), New Zealand (64) and South Africa (27). All public telephones in the South can be used to make international calls. Calls are cheaper at night (after 6pm) and at weekends.

Every hotel and many public buildings have Yellow Pages directories where, in addition to local phone numbers, you can find information on hotels, restaurants, and many outfits offering activities and entertainment.

Telephones in North Cyprus

There are fewer public telephones in the North than in the South and the quality of connections can be poor. In the North, phones don't accept coins; instead you insert a pre-paid phone card (*telekart*). These are available from *Telekomünikasyon* offices, post offices and newsagents. There are also metred counter phones (*kontürlü telefon*) where you speak first and pay after completing the call. These calls are more expensive than card-operated phones. Metered phones can be found in *Telekomunikasyon* branches.

Hotel room telephones are the most expensive. To avoid unpleasant surprises, check the rates first.

The area codes for Northern Cyprus are as follows:
228 for Nicosia (Lefkoşa);
822 for Kyrenia (Girne);
366 for Famagusta (Gazimağuza);
723 for Morfou (Güzelyurt);

and 660 for Lefke. The remaining area codes are the same as for Southern Cyprus.

Mobile Phones

The Cyprus mobile telephone (cellphone) network covers most of the island, although reception may be patchy, especially in the mountainous regions. Mobile phone usage is widespread in Cyprus, and international visitors who bring their own mobile phone are likely to experience few problems, although individual calls will invariably cost more than at home.

Making and receiving calls requires an active roaming facility on the phone. While abroad, mobile telephone users are charged for both outgoing and incoming calls, as well as text messages. Information on the cost of calls, travel bundles and packages and how to activate international roaming can be obtained from individual network providers.

A cheaper alternative may be to buy a prepaid SIM card upon arrival in Cyprus to use with your mobile. Handsets must be GSM-compatible, and users will need to check with their local service provider that the handset is unlocked to allow for a new SIM card.

Prepaid SIM cards and top-up vouchers are available from newspaper stands, petrol stations and convenience stores. The SIM card gives the user a local mobile number, allowing for standard local rates, very reasonable international rates and free incoming calls. Prepaid data packages are also available for smartphones.

Useful Numbers

- Directory enquiries 11892 (South), 192 (North)
- International directory enquiries 11894 (South), 192 (North)
- International calls via the operator 80000198
- Speaking clock 1895
- Infoline 132
- International access code 00

Public phone booths

Internet

The Internet is a great way to research your trip before heading off. Hotels will have their own websites where you can view the facilities available, make reservations and plan your trip. The same is true of car hire companies and various organized activities. A particularly informative site is the CTO's own website www.visitcyprus.com.

Once you're in Cyprus, the Internet is a valuable resource to stay in touch with people back home, and to learn more about Cyprus. Internet cafés can be found in all the island's major towns, and most hotels provide Internet access. Visitors can enjoy access to free Wi-Fi in almost all cafés, bars and restaurants in towns and cities.

Postal Services

Most post offices in the South are open from 7:30am to 5:30pm in towns and from 8am to 3pm in rural areas (except in July and August, when they close daily at noon). They are closed from noon on Wednesdays. Letters and postcards sent to European countries arrive quite quickly, taking about four days to reach their destination.

In the North, post offices are open from 8am until 5pm on weekdays, with a lunch break from 1 to 2pm; and on Saturdays from 9am until noon.

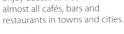

Postage stamp vending machine

Post offices accept letters and parcels and postage stamps can be bought at post offices and almost any shop that sells postcards. You can also post your letter at the reception desk in most hotels.

Beware posting mail in the North – it will invariably take longer to reach its destination. This is due to the international non-recognition of North Cyprus, all mail sent from here has to travel via Turkey to reach its destination.

Radio and Television

Cyprus has an extraordinary number of TV channels for a country of its size.

In the South there are five free-to-air island-wide channels plus several local stations in each town. Many Cypriots also subscribe to one or more Pay-TV channels. Greek national TV is relayed to the South and Turkish TV to the North. Most large hotels have satellite TV tuned to CNN, BBC World and other foreign-language channels.

The most popular of the English-language radio stations in Cyprus is BFBS (www.bfbs. com), which is primarily aimed at the British Forces stationed on Cyprus, but is listened to by English-speakers throughout the island. Its two channels resemble BBC Radio 1 and BBC Radio 2, though the latter also transmits programmes from BBC Radio 4 and Radio 5 Live.

Cyprus has its own national broadcaster, CyBC (www.cybc. com.cy), which provides a limited English-language TV service on Channel 2, and there are also several independent English-language stations to tune in to, including Radio Napa (106.3 FM broadcast in Agia Napa) and Coast FM (91.4 FM broadcast in Limassol).

Range of English-language newspapers available at Larnaka airport

Press

English-language newspapers published in southern Cyprus include the daily *Cyprus Mail* and the weekly *Cyprus Weekly*, as well as the *Cyprus Lion* – the British Forces newspaper. In the North, you can find the English-language *Cyprus Times*. Many popular British newspapers (*Daily Mail*, *Daily Express* and *Mirror*) are on sale on the day of publication.

These newspapers are sold at newsagent kiosks, airports and hotels. There are also a dozen or so local papers published in Cyprus. The cultural bulletins, published in several languages, contain information on current events and activities, and may be useful to visitors interested in what's happening on the island.

Post office in Pafos, with the bright-yellow letter box outside

Banking and Local Currency

Banks in Cyprus operate efficiently. There is a wide bank network on the island, and many foreign banks also have branches here. Cash machines can be found along the main streets and in hotel lobbies, making debit and credit cards a convenient way to withdraw cash. Most larger shops and boutiques, as well as hotels and restaurants, accept credit and debit cards.

Tourists drawing money from a cash machine

Banks and Cash Machines

Bank opening hours are from 8:15am to1:30pm (Monday to Friday) in summer (8:30am–1:30pm, 3:15–4:45pm in winter); closed Saturday and Sunday. Some banks in the tourist resorts are open every afternoon, from 3 to 5pm. The bank desks in Larnaka and Pafos airports remain open until the last plane of the day lands.

Cash machines operate around the clock. They are typically installed outside banks and in some hotels, as well as in larger towns and holiday resorts. You can withdraw cash using all major credit cards. VISA, MasterCard and American Express are widely accepted.

Money Exchange

Bureaux de change are found in the centres of larger towns and at the airports. They are open 24 hours a day; currency exchange counters in the banks are open during normal banking hours. Money exchange transactions are always subject to a commission fee; look around to get the best deal – the rates are clearly posted for you to see.

Hotels also offer exchange facilities, but their rates of exchange tend to be less favourable than either banks or bureaux de change, and they usually charge a higher commission, too.

Both foreign currency and travellers' cheques are accepted, in exchange for euro or Turkish lira. Travellers' cheques are also honoured by many hotels, shops and restaurants.

Many shops in both the Republic of Cyprus and in North Cyprus accept common foreign currencies, including US dollars and British pound sterling.

Cash machine in one of Nicosia's streets

Banks and Currency Exchange in North Cyprus

In North Cyprus, the bank networks are less extensive than in the south. Banks are open from 8am until noon. Travellers' cheques are widely accepted in shops, hotels and restaurants. They can also be exchanged for Turkish lira in banks and bureaux de change. When exchanging money, use only reputable dealers. In light of the high rate of inflation, it is worth changing smaller amounts of money more frequently, rather than a large amount.

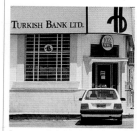

Entrance to a Turkish bank in North Cyprus

Traveller's Cheques and Credit Cards

Banks, bureaux de change and other exchange facilities will cash your traveller's cheques into either euros or Turkish lira.

Credit cards are accepted by most larger shops, restaurants and hotels, although in markets and small shops only cash is accepted. Many debit cards are accepted, but check with your bank that your card is valid internationally. It may be difficult to find a cash machine in provincial towns and villages, so it is advisable to bring enough cash with you. Banks and credit card providers will charge foreign transaction fees on charges made while you are abroad so check the rates before you travel to avoid an unecessarily large bill.

Currency

The Republic of Cyprus joined the Eurozone on 1 January 2008. Following a changeover period of one month, during which time both the Cyprus pound and the euro were in circulation, the Cyprus pound ceased to be legal tender.

The currency used in North Cyprus is the Turkish lira (TL or, more officially, TRY). This currency is not readily available abroad, so you need to change money on arrival in the island. North Cyprus also accepts payments in euros.

Republic of Cyprus

Banknotes

Euro banknotes have seven denominations. The 5 note (grey in colour) is the smallest, followed by the 10 note (pink), 20 note (blue), 50 note (orange), 100 note (green), 200 note (yellow) and 500 note (purple). All notes show the 12 stars of the European Union.

Coins

The euro has eight coin denominations: 2 and 1; 50 cents, 20 cents, 10 cents, 5 cents, 2 cents and 1 cent. The 1 and 2 coins are both silver and gold in colour. The 50-, 20- and 10-cent coins are gold. The 5-, 2- and 1-cent coins are bronze.

5 euros

10 euros

20 euros

50 euros

100 euros

200 euros

500 euros

North Cyprus

Banknotes

North Cyprus does not have its own currency; it uses the Turkish lira (abbreviated to TL). The banknotes, in six denominations from 5 to 200 TL, come in a range of colours, and bear Turkish national symbols and major historical figures. The euro is also accepted in the North.

Coins

There are six coins in circulation, ranging in value from 1 kuruş, 5 kuruş, 10 kuruş, 25 kuruş and 50 kuruş to 1 TL – equal to (100 kuru).

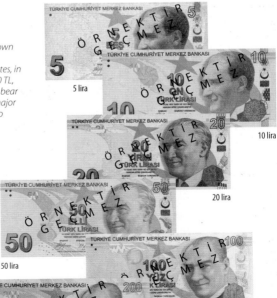
5 lira

10 lira

20 lira

50 lira

100 lira

200 lira

TRAVEL INFORMATION

Most visitors travel to Cyprus on a package holiday combining flights, accommodation, transport to and from the airport, and often car hire. International airports are located in Larnaka and Pafos and handle both scheduled flights and charters. Fares and schedules can be obtained from travel agents, airline offices and via the Internet. It is difficult to reach Cyprus by boat as passenger services no longer operate from Greece. The only ferry routes now available link Turkey to Kyrenia and Famagusta in North Cyprus. Cruises between Greece and Cyprus are also an option.

Road networks are good, with clearly marked signs. Cars drive on the left side of the road. A decent bus service operates between main towns and big resorts.

Air Travel

The international airports in Pafos and Larnaka, both in the Republic of Cyprus, handle flights by the majority of European airlines, serving many European capital cities and regional hubs. Budget airlines, such as easyJet and Ryanair, also fly to Cyprus. During summer, the airports become crowded due to the large number of charter flights. Scheduled flight tickets are generally more expensive than charters, but offer more flexibility and greater comfort.

Charter flights are at their busiest from April through October, with weekly departures. Most seats on charter flights are bought in blocks by tour operators, as part of their holiday packages, but "flight-only" charters are also available. These can be an affordable and convenient option for holiday-makers who prefer independent arrangements. Information on ticket availability can be obtained from travel agents

Pafos international airport

and from airline representatives. The airports have duty-free shops, cafés and restaurants, but the food and beverages on offer are over-priced.

Bus services from the airports to the main towns are frequent but it is worth checking the schedule to your destination in advance. The tourist information centres should be able to help you with this.

The best way of getting to town is by taxi or hired car. Taxi ranks are situated immediately next to the exit from the arrivals hall. For short distances, taxis are a comfortable and affordable mode of transport. Many of the larger car hire companies have offices at the airports, as well as in major towns on the island.

Visitors travelling to Larnaka airport with a tour operator should turn left, towards the coach parking, after leaving the terminal building. Visitors hiring a car should take care to follow the signs after leaving the terminal building.

At Larnaka, as well as at Pafos airport, services, amenities and transport links are clearly signposted at the terminal.

Ferries

Travel by ferry is often cheaper than flying, but currently there are few options to travel to Cyprus by sea. There are no passenger ferries to South Cyprus at the present time. The only regular ferry services available for tourist travellers sail from Turkey to North Cyprus.

Determined budget travellers can sail into Limassol from ports such as Piraeus (the port of Athens) and from some of the Greek islands, such as Patmos or Rhodes, but often this will be aboard a cargo ship. Journey times can be long: a direct sailing from Piraeus to Cyprus can take around 40 hours.

Cruise ships provide regular links between Cyprus and Haifa (Israel), Beirut (Lebanon) and

Interior of Larnaka international airport

Port Said (Egypt). These services begin in spring, at the start of the tourist season. Between May and October, the ferries sailing to the Middle East are used mainly by people on holiday in Cyprus. From the South there are a number of popular trips, including the journeys to Israel, Egypt, Lebanon and the Greek islands.

Some travel operators offer organized three-day trips to Egypt and the Holy Land, which include visits to Jerusalem and Bethlehem. These excursion vessels depart from Limassol Port.

There are a number of luxury cruiseliners that travel the Mediterranean and Middle East, with Cyprus being a popular stopping-off point.

North Cyprus

The quickest way to reach North Cyprus is by plane. All flights to Ercan airport originate in Turkey – from Alanya, Dalaman, Istanbul and Izmir. It is not possible to fly direct to North Cyprus from any other country. Flights are operated by Turkish Airlines. In order to reach Ercan airport you have to travel to Turkey from one of the European airports and then change for the flight to North Cyprus.

Convenient package holidays offer the same combination of flights, accommodation, airport transfers and, generally, car hire as those to the South, making this the easiest way to visit. You can also reach the North by ferry, which is a cheaper

Ferry harbour in Kyrenia, North Cyprus

option, recommended for those who wish to bring their own car to the island. Ferry journeys which set sail from southern Turkey take much longer than flying. The journey from Taşucu to Kyrenia lasts 6 hours while from Mersin to Famagusta, it can take up to 10 hours.

Travelling to North Cyprus can test your patience, as it usually involves long hours of waiting at Turkish airports for connecting flights – an important consideration when travelling with children or the elderly. These delays are due to the timetables not being very well coordinated.

Since the Republic of Cyprus joined the European Union in 2004, all citizens from the South are allowed to cross the border into North Cyprus without any hindrance, at least in theory, and stay as long as they wish. Visitors to the South who want to see North Cyprus can also cross the border to the North at the official checkpoints. Crossing anywhere other than an official checkpoint may result in arrest.

DIRECTORY

Cyprus Tourism Organization (CTO)

[w] visitcyprus.com
Larnaka.
Tel 24 654 322.
Limassol.
Tel 25 362 756.
Nicosia.
Tel 22 674 264.
Pafos.
Tel 26 932 841.
Troodos.
Tel 25 421 316.

International Airports

Ercan.
Tel 0392 600 5000.
[w] ercanhavalimani.com
Larnaka.
Tel 77 778 833.
[w] hermesairports.com
Pafos.
Tel 77 778 833.
[w] hermesairports.com

Ports

Cyprus Ports Authority (covers ports in Famagusta, Larnaka, Limassol and Pafos).
Tel 22 817 200.
[w] cpa.gov.cy

Airport Transfer

Kapnos Airport Shuttle
Nicosia to Pafos and Larnaka.
Tel 77 771 477.
[w] kapnosairportshuttle.com

Limassol Airport Express
Limassol to Pafos and Larnaka.
Tel 77 777 075.
[w] limassolairportexpress.eu

Airport terminal building at Ercan, North Cyprus

Getting Around Cyprus

Most visitors to Cyprus explore the island by bus or hire car. Buses provide good links between the towns, while for shorter distances taxis are a good option – both comfortable and affordable. In Cyprus, vehicles are right-hand drive. The roads throughout the island are in good condition, and signposting is clear.

North Cyprus sign indicating cars should drive in the left lane

Car Hire

It is expensive to hire a car on the island, especially in the main tourist season from April through October. You may find more attractive prices during low season. The price usually includes full insurance, a certain mileage allowance and VAT (value-added tax). Drivers under the age of 25 require additional insurance. Cypriot authorities honour international diving licences, as well as foreign licences. Both manual and automatic cars are available for hire, as are motorcycles and scooters.

You only need a four-wheel-drive vehicle if you are planning to tour the mountain regions in winter using some of the rough tracks, or go off-road in the Akamas peninsula. Major international car hire companies – Hertz, Avis and Europcar – have offices at the airports and in large cities, including Nicosia, Larnaka, Limassol and Pafos. Driving a hire car across the border to North Cyprus is not prohibited, but you will have to take out extra insurance on the Turkish side.

Rules of the Road

Driving is the easiest way to get around Cyprus. Roads are good, with motorways connecting Nicosia with Larnaka, Limassol, Pafos and Agia Napa. Distances are short – it is less than 160 km (100 miles) from Pafos to Nicosia.

Cypriots drive on the left side of the road, and drivers should give way to vehicles approaching from the right. Road signs are provided in both Greek and English in the South.

Distances and speed limits are in kilometres – 100 km/h (60 mph) on motorways, 80 km/h (50 mph) on most other roads, and 50 km/h (30 mph) in built-up areas. There are on-the-spot fines for speeding and for failing to wear a seat belt. Driving under the influence of alcohol is a criminal offence with serious consequences, as is using a mobile phone while driving.

Road sign in the South: sharp bend

Roads

The condition of the roads in Cyprus is very good. Since the 1980s, many stretches of road have been built, and others modernized. Roundabouts (traffic islands) have also appeared at intersections; the right of way goes to drivers approaching from the right.

Finding your way to the major historic sites is not difficult, as road signs show the way. Difficulties may arise, however, in the narrow streets of small towns, where signs are usually absent.

Pedestrians, especially those who may not be used to left-hand traffic, should exercise caution when crossing the road, and warn children to be particularly careful when stepping into the road.

Maps

When hiring a car, you will usually be given a very basic road map of the island. It is certainly worth purchasing a more detailed map of Cyprus or the part of the island you'll be exploring; these are available in many book stores and petrol stations. It may be easier to purchase a map from home and bring it with you, so that you'll be prepared from the outset. Bear in mind that many mountain roads are accessible only by four-wheel drive vehicle or motorcycle (or scooter).

Remember, too, that place names in the North may be different from those on a map purchased in the South, so you may have to cross-reference maps.

Driving in Nicosia

The capital of Cyprus is the biggest and most congested city on the island. Traffic jams occur during rush hour and tourists may have difficulty negotiating the traffic at these times, especially in the narrow streets of parts of the city. The worst congestion

A well-maintained road in the Troodos mountains

can be expected on the trunk roads leading into and out of the city and – particularly in high season – on roads to the main historical sites. Outside of rush hour, driving in Nicosia is relatively easy and comfortable.

Street names throughout the city are clearly visible, and major tourist attractions are well signposted.

Buses

Bus services between the large towns are efficient and comfortable, and tickets are inexpensive. There are at least six services daily between the four main southern towns. Transport links to major seaside resorts are also good.

Local buses also connect outlying communities with the nearest main town, but they are geared to the needs of school children and villagers, so departures are only early morning and mid-afternoon. Travellers will find it hard to get to and from the smaller towns and villages by bus.

Before travelling, check the timetable to see when the last return bus departs, to ensure that you will be able to get back. At weekends, there are reduced services.

Taxis

Metered taxis operate in all the main towns in Cyprus. Unmetered rural taxis serve most larger villages, charging 31–49 cents per kilometre.

Traffic moving along one of Kyrenia's busy streets

There are also shared "service taxis" or minibuses, which take passengers door to door so you can choose the most convenient point for getting on or off. Service taxis operate between all the major towns half-hourly between 6am and 6pm (to 7pm in summer) Monday to Friday, and 7am to 5pm at weekends.

A taxi sign in North Cyprus

Taxi fares are reasonable – particularly when you take a larger car and share the cost between several people – and provide a very convenient way of getting around.

Hitchhiking

Hitchhiking is not illegal in Cyprus but it is better avoided altogether in the larger towns, where a decent public transport system and affordable taxis provide safer alternatives. In more remote areas, the locals readily give lifts to people standing by the road.

It can be difficult to hitch a lift during the peak holiday season, and temperatures soar, making the wait uncomfortable. Be sure to carry a bottle of water with you and wear a sunhat. Women who hitchhike should take special care.

DIRECTORY

Buses

Intercity
Intercity Buses. **Tel** 80 00 77 89.
w intercity-buses.com

Larnaka
Zinonas Buses. **Tel** 80 00 77 44.
w zinonasbuses.com

Nicosia
OSEL. **Tel** 77 77 77 55.
w osel.com.cy

Pafos
Osypa Limited. **Tel** 80 00 55 88.
w pafosbuses.com

Taxis

Acropolis Vassos Taxi
Akamia Centre, Larnaka.
Tel 24 622 000.

Cyprus Taxi
w cyprustaxi.com

Euro Taxi
Ifigenias 24, Nicosia.
Tel 22 513 000.

Golden Taxi
Lysis Fasis 33, Limassol.
Tel 70 000 882.

Mayfair Taxi
Agapinoros 46, Pafos.
Tel 26 954 200.

Car Hire

Avis
Tel 22 713 333.
w avis.com.cy

Europcar
Tel 25 880 222.
w europcar.com.cy

Hertz
Tel 22 208 888.
w hertz.com.cy

A local Cypriot bus

General Index

Page numbers in **bold** refer to main entries.

A

Abbeys
  Bellapais 9, 12, 18, 22, **149**
  see also Monasteries
Abd al-Malik, Caliph 36
Achilles' House (Kourion) 70
Acropolis (Larnaka) **82**
Adonis 59, 112
Adonis Baths 51
Afamia Grape and Wine Festival (Koilani) 28
Afxentiou, Grigorios 114
A.G. Leventis Gallery (South Nicosia) **127**
Agaperon 48
Agia Eirini 105
Agia Faneromeni (Larnaka) **84**
Agia Kyriaki (Pafos) 10, **54**
Agia Napa 19, 64, **86**
  beaches 27, 65
  festivals 28, 29
  hotels 162
  restaurants 171
Agia Napa Cathedral (Limassol) **72–3**
Agia Napa International Festival 28
Agia Solomoni catacombs (Pafos) 10, **54–5**
Agia Thekla 86
Agia Trias *see* Sipahi
Agia Zoni (Famagusta) **140**
Agios Andronikos (Limassol) **72**
Agios Georgios 47, **58**
Agios Georgios Alamanos **78**
Agios Ioannis (Famagusta) **142**
Agios Ioannis Lampadistis 11, **92–3**
Agios Ioannis Lampadistis festival (Kalopanagiotis) 28
Agios Irakleidios Monastery 107, **111**
Agios Kendas (Pafos) **52**
Agios Konon 59
Agios Lazaros (Larnaka) **84**
Agios Loukas 28
Agios Minas **79**
Agios Neofytos 8, 13, **51**
  festivals 29
Agios Nikolaos (Famagusta) **140**
Agios Nikolaos tis Stegis (Troodos Mountains) 11, 42, **102–3**
Agios Nikolaos ton Gaton (St Nicholas of the Cats) 65, **69**
Agios Sozomenos 112
Agios Theodoros (Pafos) **52**
Agios Thyrsos 12, **145**
Agora (Pafos) 10, **52**
Agros 11, 107, **115**
  hotels 164
  restaurants 174
Agrotourism 160–61
Air travel **200–201**
Akamas peninsula 8, 13, 17, 45, **59**
  landscape and wildlife 20, 21
  walking in **60–61**
Akdeniz (Agia Irini) 155
Akdoğan *see* Lysi
Akhyronas barn 87
Akıncı, Mustafa 39
Akrotiri peninsula 18, 65, **69**
Alashia, Kingdom of **97**
Alasia **136**
Alcohol 167
  what to buy 181

Alexander the Great 34
  "Kyrenia Ship" 86
  Tamassos 111
Algadi beach 12
Amathous 33, 34, 65, **78**
  festivals 29
Amathus 78
Ambulances 195
Ammochostos *see* Famagusta
Amphitheatre (Salamis) 139
Amusement parks 183
Analiontas, festivals 28
Anastasiades, Nico 39
Ancient architecture 22
Ancient Greek Drama Festival (Pafos) 27
Andrew, St 145
Anthistiria Flower Festival (Pafos) 26
Antifonitis Monastery 12, **148**
Antony, Mark 98
Aphendrika 145
Aphrodite 17, 33, 45, **48**
  Baths of Aphrodite 13, **59**
  Idalion 112
  Rock of Aphrodite 13, **48**
  Temple of Aphrodite (Palaipafos) 13, **48–9**
Aphrodite Opera Festival (Pafos) 28
Aphrodite Waterpark 183
Apollo, Sanctuary of Apollo Ylatis 2–3, **68**
Apostolic Nunciature (South Nicosia) 127
Apostolos Andreas monastery 12, 28, **145**
Aquariums, Ocean Aquarium (Protaras) 87
Aqueducts
  Larnaka **85**
  Salamis 139
Arab Ahmet Pasha 135
Arab invasions 36
Arabahmet District (North Nicosia) 10, **135**
Arabahmet Mosque (Arabahmet Camii) (North Nicosia) 10, **135**
Aradippou, festivals 28
Araplar Mosque (South Nicosia) 10, **126**
Archaeological Museum (Larnaka) **82**
Archaeological Museum (Pafos) 10, **55**
Archaeological Museum (St Barnabas Monastery) 137
Archaeology and Natural History Museum (Morfou) 156
Archaic era 33
Archangelos Church (Kyrenia) **151**
Archangelos Michael 109, **110**
Archangelos monastery (Monagri) 99
Archbishop Makarios Cultural Centre (South Nicosia) 120, **122**
Archbishop's Palace (South Nicosia) 120
Architecture **22–3**
Arnaoutis, Cape 59
Arodes 58
Art, Cypriot church frescoes **113**
Askas, hotels 164
Aspro, Cape **68**
Asprokremmos reservoir 63
Assumption of the Virgin Mary 27
Atatürk (Mustafa Kemal Atatürk), statue 156
Atatürk Square (Saray Square, North Nicosia) **135**

Athalassa forest 110
Atmese, King of Tamassos 111
ATMs 198
Augustinian order 149
Augustus, Emperor 139
Authentou, Leon 104
Autumn in Cyprus 28
Auxibius, Bishop of Soloi 156
Avakas Gorge 8, 13, **58**
Avdimou beach 75
Axenti, Simeon 103
Aya Sofya Cathedral (North Nicosia) **132–3**

B

Bank of Cyprus Cultural Foundation (South Nicosia) **126**
Banking 198
Baptistry (Kourion) 70
Barbaro bastion (North Nicosia) 134
Barnabas, St **24**, 35, **137**
  Agios Irakleidios Monastery 111
  relics 123
  tomb 36, 137
Basilica (Kourion) 70
Basketware 181
Baths
  Baths of Aphrodite 13, **59**
  Büyük Hamam (North Nicosia) **134**
  Fountain and Jafar Pasha Baths (Famagusta) **140**
  Kourion 71
  Salamis 138
Bayraktar Mosque (South Nicosia) 125
Bazaars
  Belediye Ekpazarıı (North Nicosia) 129, **132**
  see also Markets
Beaches
  Agia Napa 64, 86
  Akamas Peninsula 59
  beach sports 187
  Coral Bay **51**, 55
  Kyrenia 12
  Lady's Mile (Akrotiri Peninsula) 69, 75
  Lara 58
  Larnaka 85
  Limassol 75
  Nangomi (Golden) Beach 12, 145
  Pafos 10, **55**
  Polis 62
  Protaras 16, 87
  safety 194–5
Bedesten (North Nicosia) **132**
Beer 167
Belediye Ekpazarıı (North Nicosia) 129, **132**
Bellapais 12, 22, 129, **149**
  festivals 26, 28
  hotels 165
  restaurants 176
Bellapais Abbey 9, 12, 18, 22, **149**
Berengaria of Navarre 65, 75, 76
Biddulph, Sir Robert 143
Biddulph Gate (Famagusta) **143**
Birds 17–18
  Klidhes islets 145
  Salt Lake 81
  see also Wildlife
Bishop's Palace (Kourion) 70
Bishop's Palace (Pafos) **53**
Boats
  ferries **200–201**
  sailing 186–7

Bogazi (Boğaz) **144**, 145
Boltaşlı (Lythrangkomi) 145
Border crossings 190–91, 201
Bragadino 37
Breakfast 166
British rule **38–9**
Bronze Age 32–3
    see also Prehistoric sites
Buffavento Castle 12, 43, 129, **148**
Bureaux de change 198
Buses 203
Büyük Cami (Larnaka) **84–5**
Büyük Hamam (North Nicosia) **134**
Büyük Han (North Nicosia) 10, 23, **132**
Byzantine Empire 36
Byzantine Museum (Larnaka) **84**
Byzantine Museum (Pafos) 10, **53**
Byzantine Museum (South Nicosia) 122
Byzantine Tower (Kyrenia) **150**

C
Cafés 182
Caledonia waterfall 97
Cami Kebir (Grand Mosque) (Pafos) **52**
Campsites 161
Canbulat 142
Canbulat Bastion (Famagusta) **142**
Cape Arnaoutis 59
Cape Aspro **68**
Cape Drepano 47, 58, 59
Cape Gkreko 19, 67, **86–7**
Cape Kormakitis (Korucam Burnu) **155**
Car hire 202, 203
Car rallies 185
Carnival (Limassol) 29
Carob Museum (Limassol) **73**
Carols Evening (Agia Napa) 29
Cars **202–3**
Cash machines 198
Casinos 183
Castles and fortifications
    Buffavento Castle 12, 43, 129, **148**
    Byzantine Tower (Kyrenia) **150**
    Canbulat Bastion (Famagusta) **142**
    Citadel (Othello's Tower) (Famagusta) 12, **142**
    Costanza bastion (South Nicosia) **125**
    Famagusta Gate (South Nicosia) 10, **124**
    Kantara Castle 12, 128, 129, **144**
    Kato Pafos 56
    Kolossi 65, **69**
    Kyrenia Castle 9, **152–3**
    Kyrenia Gate (North Nicosia) **134**
    Larnaka Fort **85**
    Limassol Castle **76–7**
    St Hilarion Castle 9, 12, 36, 129, 131, **149**
    Saranda Kolones (Kato Pafos) 57
    Venetian Walls (Famagusta) **142**
    Venetian Walls (North Nicosia) **134**
    Venetian Walls (South Nicosia) **124**
Catacombs of Agia Solomoni (Pafos) 10, **54–5**
Cathedrals
    Agia Napa Cathedral (Limassol) **72–3**
    Agios Theodoros (Pafos) **52**
    Aya Sofya Cathedral (North Nicosia) **132–3**
    St John the Theologian (South Nicosia) 121, **123**
    see also Abbeys; Churches; Monasteries

Catherine, St 136
Cedar Valley 8, 13, 45, **92**
Cenotaph of Nikokreon 136
Central Cyprus **106–15**
    hotels 164
    map 108–9
    restaurants 174–5
    travel 108
Central Market (Limassol) **72**
Centre of Visual Arts and Research (South Nicosia) **124**
Ceramics 181
Chalcanor, King 112
Chalcolithic era 31, 32
Chamber Music Festival (Nicosia) 26
Chantara waterfall 96
Chapels
    Agia Faneromeni (Larnaka) **84**
    Agia Mavra (Koilani) 98
    Latin Chapel (Agios Ioannis Lampadistis) 93
    Metamorfosis tou Sotiros (Palaichori) 114
    Prophitis Elias (Protaras) 87
    St Catherine (Pyrga) 80
    St Mamas (Louvaras) 11, **115**
    Terra Santa (Kyrenia) 151
Charlotte de Bourbon 80
Children 192
Chionistra see Mount Olympus
Choirokoitia 31, 32, 65, **79**
Christ, relics of 97
Christianity **24–5**
    introduction of 35–6
Christmas 29
Christodoulou, Lefkos 115
Chrysanthos, Bishop of Pafos 52
Chrysochou Bay 8, 13, 45, 59, 62
Chrysorrogiatissa monastery see Panagia Chrysorrogiatissa
Chrysostomos, Bishop of Pafos 53
Churches
    dress code 191
    Agia Faneromeni (South Nicosia) 10, **126**
    Agia Kyriaki (Pafos) 10, **54**
    Agia Moni (near Panagia Chrysorrogiatissa) 63
    Agia Paraskevi (Geroskipou) 13, **50**
    Agia Paraskevi (Panagia tis Podithou) 103
    Agia Zoni (Famagusta) **140**
    Agii Anargyri (Cape Gkreko) 87
    Agios Andronikos (Limassol) **72**
    Agios Andronikos (Polis) 13, **62**
    Agios Antonios (Diarizos Valley) 63
    Agios Georgios (Kakopetria) 103
    Agios Georgios (Vasa) 97
    Agios Gregorios (Kormakitis) 155
    Agios Ioannis (Famagusta) **142**
    Agios Ioannis Lampadistis **92–3**
    Agios Kendas (Pafos) **52**
    Agios Lazaros (Larnaka) **84**
    Agios Mamas (Agios Sozomenos) 112
    Agios Mamas (Morfou) 156
    Agios Nikolaos (Famagusta) **140**
    Agios Nikolaos (Orounta) 110
    Agios Nikolaos tis Stegis (Troodos Mountains) 11, 42, **102–3**
    Agios Philon (Karpatia) 12, **145**
    Agios Rafael (Polis) 62
    Agios Sozomenos (Panagia tis Podithou) 103
    Annunciation (Lofou) 99

Churches (cont.)
    Antifonitis Monastery **148**
    Archangel Michael (Pedoulas) 11, **93**
    Archangel Michael (Vyzakia) 11, **104**
    Archangelos (Kakopetria) 103
    Archangelos (Kyrenia) **151**
    Archangelos Michael 109, **110**
    Armenian Church (Famagusta) 143
    Byzantine-style church (near St Barnabas Monastery) 137
    Chrysospiliotissa church (Kyrenia) 150
    frescoes **11**, **113**
    Holy Apostles (Pera Chorio) 112
    Holy Cross (North Nicosia) 135
    Holy Cross (South Nicosia) 127
    Knights Hospitaller (Famagusta) 12, **141**
    Knights Templar (Famagusta) 12, **141**
    Koimisis tis Panagias (Kourdali) 105
    Nestorian Church (Famagusta) **141**
    Painted Churches of the Troodos **11**, **133**
    Panagia Angelokisti (Kiti) 22, **80–81**
    Panagia Chrysaliniotissa (South Nicosia) 10, **124**
    Panagia Chryseleoussa (Empa) 13, **51**
    Panagia Chrysopolitissa (Larnaka) 66
    Panagia Chrysopolitissa (Palaipafos) 49
    Panagia Chrysospiliotissa 27, 107, **110–11**
    Panagia Forviotissa (Panagia tis Asinou) 6–7, 11, **104**
    Panagia Katholiki (Pelendri) 102
    Panagia Pergaminiotissa (near Kantara Castle) 144
    Panagia Thetokos (Trikomo) 9, 12, **144**
    Panagia tis Amasgou (Kouris Valley) 99
    Panagia tis Podithou (Troodos Mountains) 11, **103**
    Panagia tou Araka (Troodos Mountains) 11, 36, **104–5**
    Panagia tou Moutoulla (Our Lady of Moutoulla) 11, **93**
    St Andrew (Kyrenia) 151
    St Anna (Famagusta) 143
    St Anthony (Kellia) 81
    St Barnabas and St Hilarion (Peristerona) 110
    St Catherine's Catholic Church (Limassol) **74**
    St George (Agios Georgios) 58
    St George (Chlorakas) 51
    St George of the Greeks (Famagusta) **143**
    St Irakleidios (Agios Ioannis Lampadistis) 92
    St James (Trikomo) 144
    St John (Latin) (Famagusta) **141**
    St Mary of Carmel (Famagusta) 130, **143**
    Stavros tou Agiasmati 11, **105**
    Theotokos Archangelos 90
    Timios Stavros (Troodos Mountains) 11, **102**
    Timiou Stavrou (Agia Eirini) 105
    Tripiotis Church (South Nicosia) 10, **126**
    see also Abbeys; Cathedrals; Chapels; Monasteries

Cigarettes, duty-free allowances 191
Citadel (Othello's Tower) (Famagusta) **142**
Classical Period 34
Cleopatra 98
Climate 17, 27–9, 190
Clothes, what to take 191
Clubs 182
Coast, landscape and wildlife 20
Coffee 169
Colonial architecture 23
Commandaria Festival (Kalo Chorio) 27
Communications **196–7**
Constantia 36
Constantine, Emperor 35
Consulates 191, 193
Copper Age 32
Coral Bay **51**, 55
    hotels 162
Cornaro, Queen Caterina 37
Coro, Dimitrios 103
Coro family 103
Costanza bastion (South Nicosia) **125**
Credit cards 198
    in shops 178
Crime 194
Crossing the border 190–91, 201
Crusades 36–7
Cultural Winter (Agia Napa) 28
Curium see Kourion
Currency **198–9**
Customs regulations 191
Cycling 184, 185
Cypriot National Guard 39
Cyprus College of Art (Lempa) 50, 51
Cyprus Handicraft Centre (Limassol) **72**
Cyprus Handicraft Centre (South Nicosia) 127
Cyprus International Rally 26
Cyprus Museum (South Nicosia) 10, 117, **126–7**
Cyprus Parliament (South Nicosia) 127
Cyprus Tourism Organization (CTO) 160, 161, 191, 193, 201
Cyprus Wine Museum (Limassol) **74–5**

D

Dali 108, 112
    restaurants 174–5
De Montfort, John 123
Dede, Selim 134
Dentists 195
Dervish Pasha 135
Dervish Pasha Mansion (North Nicosia) **135**
Deryneia 87
    festivals 29
Dialling codes 196
Diamantis, Adamantios 75, 127
Diarizos Valley **63**
Digenis Akritas 48
Dionysia (Stroumbi) 27
Dipkarpaz (Rizokarpaso) 12, **145**
    restaurants 176
Disabled visitors 192
    in hotels 161
District Archaeological Museum (Limassol) **74**
Divine liturgy 25
Diving 186, 187
Djafer Pasha 150
Djafer Pasha Mosque (Cafer Paşa Camii) (Kyrenia) **150**
Doctors 195

Dominicans 79
Donkeys 21
    Vouni Donkey Sanctuary 98
Drepano, Cape 47, 58, 59
Driving 202–3
Drouseia 13, 58, 61
Durrell, Lawrence 149
Duty-free allowances 191

E

Easter 26
Economy 19
Egyptians 34–5
Electrical equipment 193
Elevation of the Holy Cross 28
Elhey Bekir Pasha 85
Elizabeth II, Queen 135
Elymas 54
Embassies 191, 193
Embroidery 179
Emergency services 195
Empa 13, **51**
Engomi-Alasia 129, **136**
Enosis (unification with Greece) 38, 39
Entertainment **182–3**
    amusement parks 183
    casinos 183
    clubs and cafés 182
    excursions 183
    feasts and festivals 26–9, 182–3
    hotel entertainment 182
    information 182
EOKA (National Organization of Cypriot Fighters) 39
    Akhyronas barn 87
    Bitter Lemons (Durrell) 149
    Church of St George 51
    Liberty Monument (South Nicosia) 124
    Machairas Monastery 114
    monuments 105, 148
    National Struggle Museum (South Nicosia) 122
Epifanos, St 143
Ethnological Museum (North Nicosia) 135
Ethnographic Museum (Pafos) 10, **53**
Ethnological Museum (South Nicosia) 119, 120, 123
Etiquette 191
    photography 193
European Union 39
Evagoras, King of Salamis 34
Evangelismós 26
Excursions 183

F

Fabrica Hill (Pafos) **54–5**
Famagusta (Ammochostos/ Gazimağusa) 9, 12, 43, 129, **140–43**
    festivals 27
    history 36, 37
    hotels 165
    map 141
    restaurants 176
    view from Deryneia 87
Famagusta Bay 20, 129
Famagusta Gate (South Nicosia) 10, **124**
Faneromeni High School (South Nicosia) 23, 126
Fasouri Watermania Waterpark (Limassol) **75**, 183
Feast of Archangels Gabriel and Michael (Analiontas) 28
Feasts 182–3
Fenargos Music Festival (Kato Drys) 27

Ferries **200–201**
    see also inside back cover
Festivals **26–9**, 182–3
Fikardou 19, 107, **114–15**
    restaurants 175
Filaretos 99, 123
Fine Arts Museum (Kyrenia) **151**
Fini (Foini) 96
    restaurants 173
Fire service 195
Flatro bastion (North Nicosia) 134
Flavours of Cyprus **168–9**
Foini see Fini
Folk Art Museum (Geroskipou) 50
Folk Art Museum (Kyrenia) **150**
Folk Art Museum (Limassol) **74**
Folk Art Museum (South Nicosia) 121, **122**
Fontana Amorosa 59
Food and drink
    Flavours of Cyprus **168–9**
    shops 179
    what to drink 169
    what to eat 166–7
    wines **98**
    see also Restaurants
Forest fires 195
Foscari, Nicolo 142
Fóta (Epiphany) 29
Fountain and Jafar Pasha Baths (Famagusta) **140**
Frangoudis 75
Frederick II, Emperor 149
Frescoes, church 11, **113**
Fytl 8, 13

G

Galleries see Museums and galleries
Gardens see Parks and gardens
Gay and lesbian visitors 192
Gazimağusa see Famagusta
Gemikonağı (Karavostasi) 156
Genoese 37
Geological Exhibition (Pafos) **53**
George, St 58
Germanos, Archbishop 126
Geroskipou 13, **50**
Gialia 13
Girne see Kyrenia
Gkreko, Cape 19, 67, **86–7**
Goats 61
Golden Beach see Nangomi Beach
Golf 185
Goul, Philip 105
Gourri 107, 114
Grand Mosque (Limassol) **73**
Grand Mosque (Pafos) **52**
Greek Orthodox Church **24–5**
Greek phrase book 213–14
Greek War of Independence 38
Greeks 18–19, 32–3, 34
"Green Line" 39, 107
    at Deryneia 87
    at Potamia 112
    crossing the border 190–91, 201
    Ledra Street checkpoint (South Nicosia) 10, **125**
    North Nicosia 134, 135
    photography 193
Grivas, General George 39, 51
Gunzburg, Benjamin 72, 75
Güzelyurt see Morfou

H

Hadid, Zaha 125
Hadjigeorgakis Kornesios House (South Nicosia) 10, 120, **123**
Hadrian, Emperor 35
Hala Sultan Tekke 23, 65, **81**
Handicrafts 179, 180–81

Harbour (Kyrenia) 146–7, **150–51**
Harbours (Larnaka) **85**
Haydarpaşa Mosque (North Nicosia) **133**
Health **195**
Helen, Queen 124
Helena, St 35, 65, 105
  Agios Nikolaos ton Gaton (St Nicholas of the Cats) 69
  Stavrovouni monastery 66, 80
  Timiou Stavrou monastery (Omodos) 97
Hellenism 34–5
Henry II Lusignan, King 37
Heracleidius, Bishop of Tamassos 111
Herod the Great 111
Hiking 184
Hilarion, St 149
History **31–9**
Hitchhiking 203
Holidays, public 27, 29
Homer 111
Horse-riding 184, 185
Hospitals 195
Hostels 161
Hotels **160–65**
  Central Cyprus 164
  disabled travellers 161
  entertainment 182
  North Cyprus 165
  package deals 160
  rates 160
  reservations 161
  single travellers 192
  South Nicosia 164–5
  Southern Cyprus 162–3
  Troodos Mountains 164
  West Cyprus 162
House of Aion (Kato Pafos) 56
House of Dionysos (Kato Pafos) 56
House of Eustolios (Kourion) 71
House of the Gladiators (Kourion) 71
House of Leda (Palaipafos) 49
House of Theseus (Kato Pafos) 56
Hugo III, King 149
Hugo IV, King 149
Hugo V, King 102

I
Iaskos, Bishop of Pafos 53
Ibelin, Jean d' 149
Icons 24, 25
  Byzantine Museum (South Nicosia) 122
  Icon of the Most Merciful Virgin 94
  Icon Museum (Kyrenia) **151**
  Icon Museum (Morfou) 156
  Icon Museum (St Barnabas Monastery) 137
  Icon Museum (Trikomo) 144
Idalion 34, 107, **112**
Independence 39
Ineia 13, 58
Insurance
  medical 195
  travel 194
International Dog Show (Pafos) 28
International Music Festival (Famagusta) 27
International North Cyprus Music Festival (Bellapais) 28
International Skiing Competition 26
International Spring Concerts 26
Internet 197
Iron Age 33
Isaac Komnenos, Prince 37, 75
İskele see Trikomo
Islam
  architecture 23
  Hala Sultan Tekke **81**

Islam (cont.)
  Medresa (Famagusta) **143**
  see also Mosques
Itineraries **8–13**
  Painted Churches of the Troodos 8, **11**
  Two Days in Nicosia 8, **10**
  Two Days in Pafos 8, **10**
  A Week in Northern Cyprus 9, **12**
  A Week in Western Cyprus 8, **13**

J
Jafar Pasha 140
Jafar Pasha Baths (Famagusta) **140**
Janus, King 80
Jazz festivals 27
John II, King 124
John Lampadistis, St, tomb 92
Joseph of Arimathea 51
Justinian II, Emperor 36

K
Kakopetria 11, **103**
  hotels 164
  restaurants 173
Kalavasos 65, **78**
  festivals 26
Kallinikos, Father 24, 80
Kalopanagiotis 11, 92, **93**
  festivals 28
  restaurants 173
Kamares Aqueduct (Larnaka) 43
Kaminaria, restaurants 173
Kantara Castle 12, 128, 129, **144**
Kanthos 75
Karavostasi see Gemikonağı
Kargotis river 103
Karman (Karmi) 154
Karpasia peninsula 9, 12, 20, 21, 129, **144–5**
Kashialos, Michael 75, 83
Kastros 12, 145
Kathikas 13, 58
  restaurants 170
Kato Drys, festivals 27
Kato Lefkara 65
Kato Pafos 10, 35, 52, **56–7**
  festivals 27
Kellia 81
Kemal Pasha 135
Kimon 34
Kingdom of Alashia **97**
Kinyras 49
Kite-flying Competition (Deryneia) 29
Kiteboarding 186
Kiti **80–81**
Kition (Kitium) 33, 34, 65, **82**
Kittim 82
Klidhes islets 145
Klirou, festivals 26
Knights Hospitaller of St John 97
  Church of the Knights Hospitaller (Famagusta) 12, **141**
Knights of St John of Jerusalem, Kolossi 69
Knights Templar 37
  Church of the Knights Templar (Famagusta) 12, **141**
  Kolossi 69
Koilani **98**
  festivals 28
Koimisis tis Panagias (Kourdali) 105
Kokkinohoria 87
Kolossi 65, **69**
Komi 145
Komnenos artistic style 102, 104, 105, 112
Komnenos, Isaac 144, 145
Korakou, festivals 28
Kormakitis (Koruçam) **154–5**

Kormakitis, Cape (Koruçam Burnu) **155**
Kornesios, Hadjigeorgakis 123
Kornos 80
  restaurants 175
Kornos beach (Protaras) 16
Koruçam see Kormakitis
Koruçam Burnu see Cape Kormakitis
Kourdali 105
Kourion 34, 35, 65, **70–71**
  architecture 22
  beach 75
  festivals 27
Kouris dam 99
Kozan see Larnaka tis Lapithou Ktima
Kykkos 25, 27, 88, **94–5**
Kyprianos, Archbishop 38, 123
Kyrenia (Girne) 12, 129, 131, 146–7, **150–53**
  history 34, 37
  hotels 165
  map 151
  restaurants 176–7
Kyrenia Mountains 20, 21
Kyrenia Castle and Shipwreck Museum 9, **152–3**
Kyrenia Gate (North Nicosia) **134**

L
Lace and Silverware Museum (Lefkara) 79
lacework 8, 13, 19, 79, 179
Lady's Mile (Akrotiri peninsula) 69, 75
Laiki Geitonia (South Nicosia) 116, 117, **125**
Lakatamia, restaurants 175
Lakhas, Francis 141
Lala Mustafa Pasha 37, 123
Lala Mustafa Pasha Mosque (Famagusta) 9, 12, **140**
Lambousa (Lambusa) **154**
Landscape **20–21**
Laneia (Lania) 99
  restaurants 173
Languages 191
  Greek phrase book 213–14
  Turkish phrase book 215–16
Lania see Laneia
Laona region 58
Lapidary Museum (North Nicosia) **133**
Lapithos (Lapta) **154**
  hotels 165
  restaurants 177
Lara 8, 13, **58**
Larnaka 18, 19, 43, 65, **82–5**
  airport 200, 201
  architecture 23
  festivals 26, 27
  hotels 162–3
  map 83
  restaurants 171–2
  shopping 179
Larnaka Fort **85**
Larnaka tis Lapithou (Kozan) **154**
Latsi (Latchi) 59
  hotels 162
Lazanias 107, 114
  restaurants 175
Lazarus, St **84**
  Agios Lazaros Church (Larnaka) 84
  Salt Lake 81
Leda, Queen 49
Ledra Palace Hotel (South Nicosia) 127
Ledra Street (South Nicosia) 10, 125
Léfka (Lefke) **156**
  hotels 165
Lefkara 22, **79**
  hotels 163

Lefke *see* Léfka
Lefke European University (Léfka) 156
Lefkoşa *see* North Nicosia
Lemesos *see* Limassol
Lempa 46, **50–51**
Lempa Experimental Village 50–51
Leo VI, Emperor 84
Leonardo da Vinci 79.65
Leventis, Anastasios George 127
Leventis Museum (South Nicosia) 10, **125**
Liberty Monument (South Nicosia) 121, 124
Library, Sultan Mahmut II (North Nicosia) **133**
Lighthouse (Kato Pafos) 57
Limassol (Lemesos) 19, 65, **72–7**
  architecture 23
  ferries 200, 201
  festivals 26, 27, 28, 29
  hotels 163
  map 73
  restaurants 172–3
  shopping 179
Limassol Castle **76–7**
Liopetri 87
Lipertis, Dimitris 97
Lizards 20, 61
Lofou **98–9**
  festivals 27
  restaurants 174
Loredano bastion (North Nicosia) 134
Louvaras 11, **115**
Luke, St 17, 62
  Icon of the Most Merciful Virgin 94
  Trooditissa 96
Lusignan, Guy de 37, 148
Lusignan, Jean de 102
Lusignan Court (Palaipafos) 49
Lusignan Dynasty **37**
  Buffavento Castle 148
  Chapel of St Catherine (Pyrga) 80
  Chrysospiliotissa church (Kyrenia) 150
  Citadel (Othello's Tower) (Famagusta) 142
  Gothic Selimiye Camii (Aya Sofya Cathedral) (North Nicosia) 132–3
  Harbour (Kyrenia) 151
  Haydarpaşa Mosque (North Nicosia) 133
  Kato Pafos 56, 57
  Kyrenia Castle 152
  Limassol Castle 76–7
  Potamia 112
  St Hilarion Castle 149
  Venetian Palace (Famagusta) 140
Lysi (Akdoğan) **136**
Lysos 13
Lythrangkomi *see* Boltaşlı
Lythrodontas 114
  hotels 164

M

Maa Paleokastro 51
Machairas Monastery 106, 107, **114**
Magnac, Louis de 69
Maistros, Nikiforos 104
Makarios III, Archbishop 39
  Archbishop Makarios Cultural Centre (South Nicosia) 120, 122
  birthplace and family home (Panagia) 63
  heart 122
  New Archbishop's Palace (South Nicosia) 122
  Presidential Palace (South Nicosia) 127
  tomb 63
Makronissos Beach 86
Mamas, St 115, 156

Manuel Komnenos, Emperor 114
Maps
  Akamas Peninsula 60–61
  Central Cyprus 108–9
  Cyprus at a Glance 42–3
  Famagusta 141
  Kato Pafos 56–7
  Kourion 71
  Kyrenia 151
  Larnaka 83
  Limassol 73
  Nicosia: North Nicosia 133
  Nicosia: South Nicosia 118–19
  Nicosia: South Nicosia street-by-street 120–21
  North Cyprus 130–31
  Pafos 53
  Putting Cyprus on the Map 14–15
  Road Map of Cyprus *see* inside back cover
  road maps 202
  Salamis 139
  South Nicosia 118–19
  South Nicosia street-by-street 120–21
  Southern Cyprus 66–7
  Troodos Mountains 90–91
  West Cyprus 46–7
Marathassa valley 93
Marion 34, **62**
Marion-Arsinoe Archaeological Museum (Marion) 8, 13, **62**
Mark, St 137, 156
Markets 178–9
  Bedesten (North Nicosia) **132**
  Belediye Ekpazarı (North Nicosia) **132**
  Central Market (Limassol) **72**
  Kyrenia **150**
Maron, St 155
Maroni, river 79
Maronites 154–5
Medical care 195
Medieval architecture 22
Medieval Museum (Larnaka) **85**
Medresa (Famagusta) **143**
Mehmet Bey Ebubekir Hamam (Turkish Baths) (Pafos) 10, **52**
Meleti Forest 59
Mesaoria plain 21, 107, 110, 117
Mevlana (Celaleddin Rumi) 134
Mevlevi Tekke (North Nicosia) 10, **134**
Military zones 193
Mini-Zoo (Limassol) **74**
Mobile phones 196
Modern architecture 23
Mohammed, Prophet 135
Monagri **99**
Monasteries **25**
  dress code 191
  Agia Napa 86
  Agios Georgios Alamanos **78**
  Agios Ioannis Lampadistis 11, **92–3**
  Agios Irakleidios 107, **111**
  Agios Mamas (Morfou) 156
  Agios Minas **79**
  Agios Neofytos 8, 13, **51**
  Agios Nikolaos ton Gaton (St Nicholas of the Cats) 65, **69**
  Agios Savvas tis Karonos 63
  Antifonitis 12, **148**
  Apostolos Andreas 12, 28, **145**
  Archangelos (Monagri) 99
  Kykkos 25, 27, 88, **94–5**
  Machairas 106, 107, **114**
  Panagia Apsinthiotissa 148
  Panagia Chryseleoussa (Empa) 13, **51**
  Panagia Chrysorrogiatissa 8, 13, 27, 29, **62–3**

Monasteries (cont.)
  Panagia tou Sinti (Xeros Valley) 63
  Profitis Ilias (Kormakitis) 155
  Prophitis Elias (Machairas Forest) 114
  St Barbara 80
  St Barnabas 12, 129, 130, **137**
  Stavros tis Psokas (Pafos Forest) 13, **92**
  Stavrovouni 35, 65, 66, **80**
  Timiou Stavrou (Omodos) 97
  Trooditissa **96**
  see also Abbeys; Cathedrals; Churches
Money **198–9**
Moni-Fylagra (Pelendri) 102
Moniatis, restaurants 174
Morfou (Güzelyurt) 129, **156**
  festivals 26
Mosques
  dress code 191
  Arabahmet Mosque (Arabahmet Camii) (North Nicosia) 10, **135**
  Araplar Mosque (South Nicosia) 10, **126**
  Bayraktar Mosque (South Nicosia) 124
  Büyük Cami (Larnaka) **84–5**
  Djafer Pasha Mosque (Cafer Paşa Camii) (Kyrenia) **150**
  Grand Mosque (Limassol) **73**
  Grand Mosque (Pafos) **52**
  Haydarpaşa Mosque (North Nicosia) **133**
  Lala Mustafa Pasha Mosque (Famagusta) 9, 12, **140**
  Omar Mosque (Ömeriye Cami) (South Nicosia) 10, 120, **123**
  Peristerona Mosque 109, 110
  Piri Osman Pasha (Léfka) 156
  Selimiye Camii (Aya Sofya Cathedral) (North Nicosia) 10, 38, **132–3**
  Sinan Pasha Mosque (Famagusta) **140**
  Tanner's Mosque (Famagusta) **143**
Moufflons 21, 92
Mount Adhelfi 105
Mount Kyparissovouno 21
Mount Olympus (Chionistra) 21, 89, **96**
Mount Tripylos 92
Mount Zaharou 92
Mountains, landscape and wildlife 21
Moutoulla 93
Moutoullas, Ioannis 93
Mula bastion (North Nicosia) 134
Municipal Art Gallery (Limassol) **75**
Municipal Arts Centre (South Nicosia) 122
Municipal Cultural Centre (South Nicosia) 10, 124
Municipal Garden (South Nicosia) 127
Municipal Gardens (Limassol) **74**
Museums and galleries
  A.G. Leventis Gallery (South Nicosia) **127**
  Archaeological Museum (Larnaka) **82**
  Archaeological Museum (Pafos) 10, **55**
  Archaeological Museum (St Barnabas Monastery) 137
  Archaeology and Natural History Museum (Morfou) 156
  Archbishop Makarios Cultural Centre (South Nicosia) 120, **122**
  Bank of Cyprus Cultural Foundation (South Nicosia) **126**

Museums and galleries (cont.)
Byzantine Museum (Larnaka) **84**
Byzantine Museum (Pafos) 10, **53**
Byzantine Museum (South Nicosia)
122
Carob Museum (Limassol) **73**
Centre of Visual Arts and Research
(South Nicosia) **124**
Cyprus Museum (South Nicosia) 10,
117, 126, **126–7**
Dervish Pasha Mansion (North
Nicosia) **135**
District Archaeological Museum
(Limassol) **74**
Ethnographic Museum (North
Nicosia) 135
Ethnographic Museum (Pafos) 10,
53
Ethnological Museum (South
Nicosia) 119, 120, 123
Fine Arts Museum (Kyrenia) **151**
Folk Art Museum (Geroskipou) 50
Folk Art Museum (Kyrenia) **150**
Folk Art Museum (Limassol) **74**
Folk Art Museum (South Nicosia)
121, **122**
Geological Exhibition (Pafos) **53**
Icon Museum (Kyrenia) **151**
Icon Museum (Morfou) 156
Icon Museum (St Barnabas
Monastery) 137
Icon Museum (Trikomo) 144
Koilani 98
Kykkos 94
Lace and Silverware Museum
(Lefkara) 79
Lapidary Museum (North Nicosia)
133
Leventis Museum (South Nicosia)
10, **125**
Makarios Family Home (Panagia) 63
Marion-Arsinoe Archaeological
Museum (Marion) 8, 13, **62**
Medieval Museum (Larnaka) **85**
Mevlevi Tekke (North Nicosia) 10,
134
Municipal Art Gallery (Limassol) **75**
Museum of the Mycenaean
Colonization of Cyprus (Maa
Paleokastro) 51
Museum of Natural History
(Larnaka) **83**
National Struggle Museum (South
Nicosia) 121, **122**
Pierides Museum (Larnaka) 23,
82–3
Pilavakion Museum (Fini) 96
Rural Museum (Fikardou) 19, 115
Shipwreck Museum (Kyrenia)
152–3
State Gallery of Contemporary Art
(South Nicosia) **127**
Thalassa Museum of the Sea (Agia
Napa) 86
Tomb-Finds Gallery (Kyrenia) 152
Visitor Centre of the Troodos
National Forest Park 96
Vouni 98
Music festivals 26, 27, 28
Muslims *see* Islam; Mosques
Mycenaean culture 32–3
Alasia 136
Museum of the Mycenaean
Colonization of Cyprus (Maa
Paleokastro) 51
Mycenaean Site (Larnaka) **82**

N

Namik Kemal 140, 143
Nangomi (Golden) Beach 9, 12, 145

Naqshbandi order 156
National Struggle Museum (South
Nicosia) 121, **122**
Natural History Museum (Larnaka)
83
Nature reserves
Cape Gkreko 86
Cedar Valley 92
Karpasia Peninsula 145
Troodos Mountains 89
Nazim, Kibrisli Syke 156
Neo Chorio 61
Neofytos, St 51
Nestorian Church (Famagusta)
141
New Port (Limassol) **75**
New Year 29
Newspapers 197
Nicephorus II Phocas, Emperor 36
Nicocreon, King of Salamis 34–5
cenotaph of (Engomi) 136
Nicosia 107
history 36
see also North Nicosia; South
Nicosia
Nikiforos, Archbishop 121
tomb 110
Nikokleia 63
Nikokles, King of Palaipafos 49, 63
Nissi Beach 64, 86
Nomikos, George 122
North Cyprus **128–57**
air travel 201
banking and currency 198–9
ferries 201
food and drink 169
hotels 165
map 130–31
passports and visas 190
personal security 194
public holidays 29
restaurants 176–7
telephones 196
travel 131
websites 193
A Week in Northern Cyprus 9, **12**
North Nicosia (Lefkoşa) 117, 129,
132–5
driving in 202–3
hotels 165
map 133
restaurants 177
Two Days in Nicosia 8, **10**
Nymphaeum (Kourion) 70

O

Ocean Aquarium (Protaras) 87
Odeon (Kato Pafos) 57
Olympus, Mount (Chionistra) 21, 89,
96
Omar, Caliph 123
Omar Mosque (Ömeriye Cami)
(South Nicosia) 10, 120, **123**
Omodos **97**
restaurants 174
Onasagorou Street (South Nicosia)
125
Onesilos 34
Opening hours
banks 198
restaurants 166
shops 178
Orange Festival (Güzelyurt) 26
Orounta 110
Orthodox Church 18, 192
Osman Pasha, tomb 156
Othello's Tower (Famagusta)
142
Ottoman Empire 37, **38**
Outdoor activities **184–7**

P

Package deals 160
Pafos 17, 19, 42, 45, **52–7**
airport 200, 201
architecture 22
festivals 26, 27, 28
history 34, 35
hotels 162
Kato Pafos **56–7**
map 53
restaurants 170–71
shopping 179
Two Days in Pafos 8, **10**
A Week in Western Cyprus 13
Palaces
Archbishop's Palace (South Nicosia)
120
Bishop's Palace (Kourion) 70
Bishop's Palace (Pafos) **53**
New Archbishop's Palace (South
Nicosia) 122
Presidential Palace (South Nicosia)
127
Venetian Palace (Famagusta) **140**
Vouni (Vuni Sarayı) 129, **157**
Palaiochori **114–15**
Palaipafos 13, 34, 36, **48–9**
Paleologos artistic style 102
Palma di Cesnola, Luigi 83
Amathous 78
Idalion 112
Tomb of the Kings (Pafos) 54
Panagia 13, **63**
restaurants 174
Panagia Angeloktisti (Kiti) 22, **80–81**
Panagia Apsinthiotissa monastery 148
Panagia Chrysaliniotissa (South
Nicosia) 10, **124**
Panagia Chryseleoussa (Empa) 13, **51**
Panagia Chrysorrogiatissa 8, 13, **62–3**
festivals 27, 29
Panagia Chrysospiliotissa 27, 107,
110–11
Panagia Forviotissa (Panagia tis
Asinou) 6–7, 11, **104**
Panagia Limeniotissa (Kato Pafos) 56
Panagia tis Podithou (Troodos
Mountains) 11, **103**
Panagia tou Araka (Troodos
Mountains) 11, 36, **104–5**
Panagia tou Moutoulla (Our Lady of
Moutoulla) 11, **93**
Pancyprian Choirs Festival (Kato
Pafos) 27
Paphos *see* Pafos
Paralimni 87
Parks and gardens
Municipal Garden (South Nicosia)
127
Municipal Gardens (Limassol) **74**
Roccas bastion (North Nicosia) 134,
135
Passports 190
Pattichion Municipal Theatre
(Larnaka) **84**
Pattichion Theatre (Limassol) **75**
Paul, St **24**, 35, 137
Agios Irakleidios Monastery 111
"St Paul's Pillar" (Pafos) 54
Paulus, Sergius 24, 35, 54
Pediaios river 110
Pedoulas **93**
hotels 164
restaurants 174
Pegeia **58**
Pelendri **102**
restaurants 174
Pelicans 21
Pentadaktylos mountains 17, 21, 107,
129, 148, 149

Pentecost-Kataklysmos Fair 27
People 18–19
Pera Chorio **112**
Peravasa 63
Peristerona 107, 109, **110**
Peristerona river 114
Persian Wars 34
Pervolia, festivals 27
Petra tou Limniti 157
Petra tou Romiou (Rock of Aphrodite)
13, 20, 44, 45, **48**
Petratis Gorge 61
Pharmacies 195
Philip, St, relics of 97
Philocyprus, King of Aepea 156
Philotheos, Archbishop 137
Phoenicians 33, 34
Phokas II, Emperor 37
Photography 193
Phrase books
Greek 213–14
Turkish 215–16
Pierides, Demetrios 82–3
Pierides family 82
Pierides Museum (Larnaka) 23,
82–3
Pigadhes sanctuary 155
Pilavakion Museum (Fini) 96
Pilavakis, Theofanis 96
Piracy 36
Piri Osman Pasha mosque (Léfka)
156
Pissouri 48, 65, 68
beach 75
hotels 163
restaurants 173
Pitsillia 107, 114
Plateia Eleftheria (South Nicosia) 125
Platres 63, **97**
hotels 164
restaurants 174
Police 194, 195
Polis 13, **62**
hotels 162
restaurants 171
Politics, discussing 193
Pomos 13
restaurants 171
Pomos Jazz Festival 27
Ports 201
Postal services 197
Potamia **112**
Potamiou **98**
Potamos Liopetriou 87
Prehistoric sites **31–3**
Akdeniz (Agia Irini) 155
Choirokoitia **79**
Diarizos Valley **63**
Engomi-Alasia **136**
Idalion **112**
Kition (Kitium) 82
Lempa Experimental Village 50, 51
Maa Paleokastro 51
Morfou (Güzelyurt) 156
Palaipafos 48–9
Petra tou Limniti 157
Pigadhes sanctuary 155
Royal Tombs **136**
Tamassos **111**
Tenta 78
Zafer Burnu 145
Presentation of Jesus to the Temple
(Chrysorrogiatissa monastery) 29
Presidential Palace (South Nicosia)
127
Prioli, Nicolo 142
Private accommodation 160
Prodromos 93
restaurants 174
Profitis Ilias (Kormakitis) 155

Protagoras, King of Salamis 111
Protaras 16, 65, **87**
hotels 163
restaurants 173
Ptolemy I Soter, King of Egypt 34, 62,
136
Ptolemy II Soter, King of Egypt
62
Public holidays 27, 29
Pygmalion 49
Pyrga **80**

Q
Quirini bastion (North Nicosia)
134

R
Radio 197
Rainfall 28
Religion 192
Christianity and the Greek
Orthodox Church **24–5**
see also Islam
Renier, Giovanni 140
Republic of Cyprus 39, **44–127**
food and drink 168–9
public holidays 27
visas and passports 190
see also Central Cyprus; Southern
Cyprus; Troodos Mountains; West
Cyprus
Restaurants **166–77**
alcohol 167
Central Cyprus 174–5
choosing 166
Flavour of Cyprus **168–9**
North Cyprus 176–7
prices 167
South Nicosia 175–6
Southern Cyprus 171–3
Troodos Mountains 173–4
vegetarian food 167
West Cyprus 170–71
what to eat 166–7
when to eat 166
see also Food and drink
Rialto Theatre (Limassol) **73**
Richard the Lionheart 30, 65, **75**
Apostolos Andreas 145
Crusades 37
Kantara Castle 144
wedding 76
Rimbaud, Arthur 96
Rivettina (Ravelin) Bastion
(Famagusta) 142
Rizokarpaso see Dipkarpaz
Road travel **202–3**
Roccas bastion (North Nicosia) 134,
135
Rock of Aphrodite 20, **48**, 55
Rock climbing 185
Rock formations 20
Roman Empire 35
Agios Konon 59
Kato Pafos **56–7**
Kourion 70–71
Salamis **138–9**
Sanctuary of Apollo Ylatis **68**
Soloi 156–7
Roman Theatre (Kourion) 71
Roman Theatre (Salamis) 139
Roman Theatre (Soloi) 157
Roudia, Bridge of 13, 63
Royal Tombs 12,
136
Al Ruchi 133
Rules of the road 202
Rumi, Celaleddin 134
Rural Museum (Fikardou)
115

S
Sailing 186–7
St Andrew's Day 28
St Barnabas Monastery 12, 129, 130,
137
St Catherine's Catholic Church
(Limassol) **74**
St George of the Greeks Church
(Famagusta) **143**
St Hilarion Castle 9, 12, 36, 129, 131,
149
St John (Latin) Church (Famagusta)
141
St John the Theologian Cathedral
(South Nicosia) 121, **123**
St Leontios' Day (Pervolia) 27
St Mamas Chapel (Louvaras) **115**
St Mary of Carmel (Famagusta) 130,
143
St Neofytos' Day 29
St Nicholas of the Cats 65, **69**
St Theodore's Cathedral (Pafos) **52**
Saladin 36, 149
Salamis 9, 12, 43, 129, **138–9**
architecture 22
history 34, 35, 36
map 139
Salt lakes 20, 81
Sanctuary of Apollo Ylatis 2–3, **68**
Saranda Kolones (Kato Pafos) 57
Savorgnano, Giulio 124
"Sea peoples" 33
Seaside Promenade (Limassol) **72**
Security **194–5**
Şeker Bayramı (Sugar Festival) 29
Selim II, Sultan 18, 37
Selimiye Camii (North Nicosia) 10, 38,
132–3
Seljuk Turks 36
Senior citizens 192–3
Septimius Severus, Emperor 127
Setrachos Valley 93
Shakespeare, William 142
Shipwrecks
Cape Gkreko 87
Shipwreck Museum (Kyrenia)
152–3
Shopping **178–81**
food 179
how to pay 178
markets 178–9
opening hours 178
souvenirs 179
What to Buy in Cyprus 180–81
Sightseeing tours 183
Silikou 99
Sinan Pasha Mosque (Famagusta)
140
Single travellers 192
Sipahi (Agia Trias) 9, 12, **145**
Skiing 184–5
Mount Olympus 96
Skinner, Mary and Patrick 98
Skouriotissa 20
Snorkelling 186
Snowboarding 184–5
Society 18–19
Soloi (Soli Harabeleri) 12, 34, 129,
156–7
Solomoni 54
Solon 156
Sotera, restaurants 173
South Nicosia 19, 42, **116–27**
architecture 23
driving in 202–3
festivals 26, 27
hotels 164–5
map 118–19
restaurants 175–6
shopping 179

South Nicosia (cont.)
  street-by-street map 120–21
  travel 119
  Two Days in Nicosia 8, **10**
Southern Cyprus **64–87**
  hotels 162–3
  map 66–7
  restaurants 171–3
  travel 67
Souvenirs 180–81
  shops 179
Spilia 105
Sports **184–7**
Spring in Cyprus 26
Standard of living 19
State Gallery of Contemporary Art
  (South Nicosia) **127**
Statos-Agios Fotios, restaurants
  174
Stavros tis Psokas (Pafos Forest) 13,
  92
Stavros tou Agiasmati 11, **105**
Stavrovouni monastery 35, 65, 66,
  80
Stoicism 81
Stone Age 31
Storrs, Sir Ronald 127
Strabo 68
Stroumbi, festivals 27
Sultan Mahmut II Library (North
  Nicosia) **133**
Summer in Cyprus 27
Sun protection 194–5
Sunshine 27
Swimming 194

T

Ta Kypria International Festival 28
Tamassos 107, **111**
Tanner's Mosque (Famagusta) **143**
Taxis 203.
Telephones **196–7**
Television 197
Temperatures 29
Temple of Aphrodite (Palaipafos) 13,
  48–9
Tennis 185
Tenta 32, 78
Textiles 180
Thalassa Museum of the Sea (Agia
  Napa) 86
Theft 194
Theodosius the Great, Emperor 49,
  68
Tilliria 13, **92**
Time zone 193
Timios Stavros (Troodos Mountains)
  11, **102**
Timiou Stavrou Monastery (Omodos)
  97
Tochni 78
Tomaritis, George 86
Tombs
  Royal Tombs **136**
  Tomb-Finds Gallery (Kyrenia)
    152
  Tombs of the Kings (Pafos) 10, **54**
Tourism 19
Tourist organizations 191, 193
Town Hall (Kyrenia) **150**
Town Hall (Limassol) **72**
Town Hall (Pafos) **52**
Town Hall (South Nicosia) **125**
Trachonas Hill 68
Trakofryges of Asia Minor 111
Travel **200–203**
  air 200–201
  bus 203
  Central Cyprus 108
  ferry 200–201

Travel (cont.)
  hitchhiking 203
  North Cyprus 131
  road 202–3
  South Nicosia 119
  Southern Cyprus 67
  taxis 203
  Troodos Mountains 91
  West Cyprus 46
Traveller's cheques 198
Trikomo (Iskele) 8, **144**
Trimiklini 99
Tripiotis Church (South Nicosia) 10,
  126
TRNC Foundation Day 28
Trooditissa **96**
Troodos **96**
  hotels 164
  restaurants 174
Troodos Mountains 17, 20, 21,
  88–105, 107
  festivals 26
  hotels 164
  map 90–91
  Painted Churches of the Troodos 8,
    11
  restaurants 173–4
  travel 91
Tsolakis, Chris 115
Turkish Baths (Pafos) 52
Turkish Cypriots 18, 19, 39
Turkish delight 179, 181
Turkish National Day 28
Turkish phrase book 215–16
Turkish Republic of Northern Cyprus
  (TRNC) 39, **128–57**
  see also North Cyprus
Turkish Resistance Organization
  (TNT) 39
Turtles
  endangered **155**
  Karpasia Peninsula 145
  Lara Bay 8, 58
  Nangomi (Golden) Beach 12
Tychon, St, Bishop of Amathous 78

U

Umm Haram, tomb 23, 81
UNESCO World Heritage Sites 17
  Agios Ioannis Lampadistis 92–3
  Agios Nikolaos tis Stegis 42
  Byzantine churches 113
  Choirokoitia 79
  Church of the Archangel Michael
    (Pedoulas) 93
  Kato Pafos **56–7**
  Panagia Forviotissa (Panagia tis
    Asinou) **104**
  Troodos Mountains frescoes 24
United Nations (UN) 39, 127
  Peacekeeping Forces 127

V

Varosha (Famagusta) 87, 140, 142
Vasa 97
  restaurants 174
Vavla 79
Vegetarians 167
Venetian Palace (Famagusta) **140**
Venetian rule 37
Venetian Walls
  Famagusta **142**
  North Nicosia **134**
  South Nicosia.124
Visas 190
Visitor Centre of the Troodos National
  Forest Park 96
Volleyball 187
Vouni (Troodos Mountains) **98**
  restaurants 174

Vouni (Vuni Sarayi) 12, 129, **157**
Vyzakia 11, **104**

W

Walking
  Akamas Peninsula 60–61
  Baths of Aphrodite 59
  hiking 184
Walls, city see Castles and
  fortifications
Water, drinking 195
Waterfalls
  Adonis Baths 51
  Caledonia waterfall 97
  Chantara waterfall 96
Waterparks
  Aphrodite Waterpark 183
  Fasouri Watermania Waterpark
    (Limassol) **75**, 183
  Waterworld Waterpark (Agia Napa)
    183
Watersports **186–7**
Waterworld Waterpark (Agia Napa)
  183
Weather 17, 27–9, 190
Websites 193
Weddings 193
Welcoming the New Year 29
West Cyprus **44–63**
  hotels 162
  map 46–7
  restaurants 170–71
  travel 46
  A Week in Western Cyprus 8, **13**
Wheelchair access see Disabled
  travellers
Whirling Dervishes 134
Wild Flower Festival 26, 27
Wildlife **20–21**
  Akamas peninsula 61
  Cedar Valley 92
  sea turtles 58, **155**
  Xeros Valley 63
  see also Aquariums; Birds; Nature
    reserves; Zoos
Windsurfing 186
Wine **98**, 169
  Cyprus Wine Museum (Limassol)
    74–5
  duty-free allowances 191
  festivals 28
  in restaurants 167
  shopping 181
Wine Festival (Limassol) 28
Winter in Cyprus 29
Winter Solstice 29
Women travellers 192
World Council of Churches
  Ecumenical Conference Centre
    (Agia Napa) 86
World War I 38
World War II 38

X

Xarkis Festival (Lofou) 27
Xeros Valley **63**

Y

Yialousa (Yenierenköy) 145
Young visitors 192

Z

Zafer Burnu 145
Zamboulakis, Andreas 50
Zeno, Emperor 36, 123, 137
Zeno of Kition 65, **81**
Zoos
  Mini-Zoo (Limassol) **74**
  Vouni Donkey Sanctuary 98
  see also Wildlife

Acknowledgments

Dorling Kindersley and Wiedza i Życie would like to thank the following people and institutions, whose contributions and assistance have made the preparation of this guide possible.

Publishing Manager
Kate Poole

Managing Editors
Vivien Antwi, Vicki Ingle

Publisher
Douglas Amrine

Senior Cartographic Editor
Casper Morris

Senior DTP Designer
Jason Little

Additional Picture Research
Rachel Barber, Rhiannon Furbear, Ellen Root

Revisions Editor
Anna Freiberger

Revisions Designer
Maite Lantaron

Revisions Team
Beverley Ager, Emma Anacoootee, Uma Bhattacharya, Emma Brady, Emer FitzGerald, Carole French, Swati Handoo, Vinod Harish, Mohammad Hassan, Shobhna Iyer, Jasneet Kaur, Juliet Kenny, Sumita Khatwani, Vincent Kurien, Laura Jones, Jude Ledger, Maria Massoura, Deepak Mittal, Alison McGill, Sonal Modha, Catherine Palmi, Helen Peters, Andrea Pinnington, Rada Radojicic, Erin Richards, Lokamata Sahoo, Sands Publishing Solutions, Avijit Sengupta, Ankita Sharma, Azeem Siddiqui, Rituraj Singh, Christine Stroyan, Roseen Teare, Priyansha Tuli, Dora Whitaker, Sophie Wright

Production Co-ordinator
Wendy Penn

Jacket Design
Tessa Bindloss

Consultant
Robin Gauldie

Factchecker
John Vickers

Proofreader
Stewart Wild

Index
Hilary Bird

Additional Photography
Wojciech Franus, Carole French, Robin Gauldie, Konrad Kalbarczyk, Grzegorz Micuła, Bernard Musyck, Ian O'Leary, Ronald Sayegh, Jon Spaull, Andrzej Zygmuntowicz

Special Assistance
Dr. Fotos Fotiou, Aleksander Nikolaou, Irfan Kiliç, Suleyman Yalin, Latif Ince, Artur Mościcki, Joanna Egert-Romanowska, Maria Betlejewska, Małgorzata Merkel-Massé.Latif Ince, Artur Mościcki, Joanna Egert-Romanowska, Maria Betlejewska, Małgorzata Merkel-Massé.

The publishers would also like to thank all the people and institutions who allowed us to use photographs from their archives:

Bernard Musyck, Ronald Sayegh (www.CyprusDestinations.com, skiing and agrotourism site)

Picture Credits
a = above; b = below/bottom; c = centre; f = far; l = left; r = right; t = top.

7 St. Georges Tavern: 170br; A. G. Leventis Gallery, Nicosia, Cyprus: 127bl; Almyra Hotel: 160cla; Alamy Images: Ros Drinkwater 158-9; Greg Balfour Evans 45b, 116; Peter Horree 169tl; Hemis 11tc; Doug Houghton40 203bl; Iconotec 17b; imagebroker/ Maria Breuer 190cra; imagebroker/Siepmann 169c; iWebbtravel 106; LOOK Die Bildagentur der Fotografen GmbH 13tr; Victor Lucas 186–7; nagelstock.com 2–3; David Newham 10tr; Piamen Peev 55bl; Stuwdamdorp 197cr; Peter Titmuss 200c; Rawdon Wyatt 203tc; StockFood GmbH 5cr; Zoonar GmbH 1c. Archontiko Papadopoulou: 175t; Bellapais Gardens Hotel & Restaurant: 176br; The Trustees of the British Museum 97bc; Cleopatra Lebanese Restaurant: 172t; Corbis Bettmann 30, 38clb, 75br; Jonathan Blair 28c, 29cra, 38tr; Tom Brakefield 155cr; James Davis/ Eye Ubiquitous 20clb, 95crb, 152cla; John Heseltine 168cl; Jo Lillini 26bc, 185bl; Chris Lisle 28bl; Hans Georg Roth 6–7; Cyprus Police 194bl; Cyprus Tourism Organisation: 13bc, 56tr; Y.Vroullou 10bl; 123tc, Y. Vroullou 112clb; Domus Lounge Bar & Restaurant: 167tr; Dreamstime.com: Rostislav Ageev 12tr; Senai Aksoy 12br; Ruzanna Arutyunyan 128, 182cra; Debu55y 9tr, 9cr; Evgeniy Fesenko 85br; Gillian Hardy 8br; Bensliman Hassan 100–1; Kirill Makarov 18t, 19br, 40-1; Noamfein 200bl; Nushahru 8cl; Otk1986 182br; Michalakis Ppalis 11b, 185tr; Tupungato 64; Tetiana Zbrodko 16; Episkopiana Hotel: 160br; Carole French 196bl; Getty Images: Esen Tunar Photography 44; Nejdetduzan 146-7; Hill View: 163tr; Hilton Cyprus: 161bc, 165br; Jashan's: 177tl; Karatello Tavern, member of Carob Mill Restaurants Ltd.: 172bc; KEO Beer: 181tc; The Leventis Municipal Museum of Nicosia: 125br; Maria Massoura: 22tr; George Mitletton: 52bl; Grzegorz Micuła 21ca/bl, 23br, 56cb, 53c, 71cr, 96tr, 186br, 187tl, 196cla; George Mitletton: 52bl; Bernard Musyck: 29bl; New Helvetia Hotel: 164tc; Oliveto Stonegrill Dining: 167tr; Onar Holiday Village: 161tl; Ta Piatakia: 173br; Superstock: imagebroker.net 88; TAGO Konrad Kalbarczyk 17b, 182t; Thanos Hotels - Anassa: 162bl; Vouni Panayia Winery: 174bl; Zambartas Wineries: 181tl.

Front Endpaper

Alamy Images: Greg Balfour Evans Rcra; iWebbtravel Lbl; Dreamstime.com: Ruzanna Arutyunyan Rbr; Tupungato Rbc; Getty Images: Esen Tunar Photography Ltl; Superstock: imagebroker.net Ltr.

Jacket
Front and Spine – 4Corners: Johanna Huber / SIME.

All other images © Dorling Kindersley

For further information see www.dkimages.com

English–Greek Phrase Book

There are no clear-cut rules for transliterating modern Greek into the Latin alphabet.
The system employed in this guide follows the rules generally applied in Greece, adjusted to fit in with English pronunciation. On the following pages, the English is given in the left-hand column, the right-hand column provides a literal system of pronunciation and indicates the stressed syllable in bold.
It is also worth remembering that both the Cypriot Greek and Cypriot Turkish alphabets differ slightly from those used on the mainland, and their accents are distinctive, too.

In Emergency

Help!	**Voítheia**	vo-ee-theea
Stop!	**Stamatíste**	sta-ma-tee-steh
Call a doctor!	**Fonáxte éna yatro**	fo-nak-steh e-na ya-tro
Call an ambulance!	**Kaléste to asthenofóro**	ka-le-steh to as-the-no-fo-ro
Call the police!	**Kaléste tin astynomía**	ka-le-steh teen a-sti-no mia
Call the fire brigade!	**Kaléste tin pyrosvestikí**	ka-le-steh teen pee-ro-zve-stee-kee
Where is the nearest telephone?	**Poú eínai to plisiéstero tiléfono?**	poo ee-ne to plee-see-e-ste-ro tee-le-pho-no?
Where is the nearest hospital?	**Poú eínai to plisiéstero nosokomeío?**	poo ee-ne to plee-see-e-ste-ro no-so-ko-mee-o?
Where is the nearest pharmacy?	**Poú eínai to plisiéstero farmakeío?**	poo ee-ne to plee-see-e-ste-ro far-ma-kee-o?

Communication Essentials

Yes	**Nai**	neh
No	**Ochi**	o-chee
Please	**Parakaló**	pa-ra-ka-lo
Thank you	**Efcharistó**	ef-cha-ree-sto
Excuse me	**Me synchoreíte**	me seen cho-ree-teh
Goodbye	**Antío**	an-dee-o
Good morning	**Kaliméra**	ka-lee-me-ra
Good evening	**Kalinychta**	ka-lee-neech-ta
Morning	**Proí**	pro-ee
Afternoon	**Apógevma**	a-po-yev-ma
Evening	**Vrádi**	vrath-i
Yesterday	**Chthés**	chthes
Today	**Símera**	see-me-ra
Tomorrow	**Avrio**	av-ree-o
Here	**Edó**	ed-o
There	**Ekeí**	e-kee
What?	**Tí?**	tee?
Why?	**Giatí?**	ya-tee?
Where?	**Poú?**	poo?
How?	**Pós?**	pos?

Useful Phrases

How are you?	**Tí káneis?**	tee ka-nees
Very well, thank you	**Poly kalá, efcharistó**	po-lee ka-la, ef-cha-ree-sto
Pleased to meet you	**Chaíro polę**	che-ro po-lee
What is your name?	**Pós légeste?**	pos le-ye-ste?
Where is/where are…?	**Poú eínai?**	poo ee-ne?
How far is it to…?	**Póso apéchei…?**	po-so a-pe-chee?
I understand	**Katalavaíno**	ka-ta-la-ve-no
I don't understand	**Den katalavaíno**	then ka-ta-la-ve-no
Can you speak more slowly?	**Miláte lígo pio argá parakaló?**	mee-la-te lee-go pyo ar-ga pa-ra-ka-lo?
I'm sorry	**Me synchoreíte**	me-seen-cho-ree teh

Useful Words

big	**Megálo**	me-ga-lo
small	**Mikró**	mi-kro
hot	**Zestó**	zes-to
cold	**Kreyo**	kree-o
good	**Kaló**	ka-lo
bad	**Kakó**	ka-ko
open	**Anoichtá**	a-neech-ta
closed	**Kleistá**	klee-sta
left	**Aristerá**	a-ree-ste-ra

right	**Dexiá**	dek-see-a
straight	**Eftheía**	ef-thee-a
between	**Anámesa/ Metaxey**	a-na-me-sa/ Metaxy
on the corner….	**Sti gonía tou…**	stee go-nee-a too
near	**Kontá**	kon-da
far	**Makriá**	ma-kree-a
up	**Epáno**	e-pa-no
down	**Káto**	ka-to
early	**Norís**	no-rees
late	**Argá**	ar-ga
entrance	**I eísodos**	ee ee-so-thos
exit	**I éxodos**	eee-kso-dos
toilets	**Oi toualétes**	eee-kso-dos

Shopping

How much is it?	**Póso kánei?**	po-so ka-nee?
Do you have…?	**Échete…?**	e-che-teh
Do you accept credit cards?	**Décheste pistotikés kártes**	the-ches-teh pee-sto-tee-kes kar-tes
Do you accept travellers' cheques?	**Décheste pistotikés travellers' cheques?**	the-ches-teh pee-sto-tee-kes … travellers' cheques
What time do you open?	**Póte anoígete?**	po-teh a-nee-ye-teh?
What time do you close?	**Póte kleínete?**	po-teh klee-ne-teh?
this one	**Aftó edó**	af-to e-do
that	**Ekeíno**	e-kee-no
expensive	**Akrivó**	e-kree-vo
cheap	**Fthinó**	fthee-no
size	**To mégethos**	to me-ge-thos
white	**Lefkó**	lef-ko
black	**Mávro**	mav-ro
red	**Kókkino**	ko-kee-no
yellow	**Kítrino**	kee-tree-no
green	**Prásino**	pra-see-no
blue	**Mple**	bleh
antique shop	**Magazí me antíkes**	ma-ga-zee me an-dee-kes
bakery	**O foúrnos**	o foor-nos
bank	**I trápeza**	. I trápeza
bazaar	**To pazári**	to pa-za-ree
bookshop	**To vivliopoleío**	o vee-vlee-o-po-lee-o
pharmacy	**To farmakeío**	to far-ma-kee-o
post office	**To tachy- dromeío**	to ta-chee -thro-mee-o
supermarket	**Supermarket**	"Supermarket"

Sightseeing

tourist information	**CTO**	CTO
beach	**I paralía**	ee pa-ra-lee-a
Byzantine	**vyzantinós**	vee-zan-dee-nos
castle	**To kástro**	to ka-stro
church	**I ekklisía**	ee e-klee-see-a
monastery	**moní**	mo-ni
museum	**To mouseío**	to moo-see-o
national	**ethnikós**	eth-nee-kos
river	**To potámi**	to po-ta-mee
road	**O drómos**	o thro-mos
saint	**ágios**	a-yee-os
theatre	**To théatro**	to the-a-tro

Travelling

When does the … leave?	**Póte févgei to…?**	po-teh fev-yee to..
Where is the bus stop?	**Poú eínai i stási tou leoforeíou?**	poo ee-neh ee sta-see too le-o-fo-ree-oo?
Is this bus going to…?	**Ypárche I leoforeío gia…?**	ee-par-chee le-o-fo-ree-o yia…?
bus ticket	**Eisitírio leoforeíou**	ee-see-tee-ree-o le-o-fo-ree-oo?
harbour	**To limáni**	to lee-ma-nee
bicycle	**To podílato**	to po-thee-la-to
taxi	**To taxi**	to tak-see
airport	**To aero- drómio**	to a-e-ro-thro- mee-o
ferry	**To "ferry-boat"**	to fe-ree-bot

alternatives for a female speaker are shown in brackets

In a Hotel

Do you have a vacant room?	**Echete domátia?**	e-che-teh tho-ma-tee-a?
double room	**Díklino me dipló kreváti**	thee-klee-no meh thee-plo kre-va-tee
single room	**Monóklino**	mo-no-klee-no
room with bathroom	**Domátio me mpánio**	tho-ma-tee-o meh ban-yo
shower	**To douz**	To dooz
key	**To kleidí**	to klee-dee
I have a reservation	**Echo kánei krátisi**	e-cho ka-nee kra-tee-see
room with sea view	**Domátio me théasti thálassa**	tho-ma-tee-o meh the-a stee tha-la-sa
room with a balcony	**Domátio me théasti mpalkóni**	tho-ma-tee-o meh the-a stee bal-ko-nee
Does the price include breakfast	**To proïnó symperi-lamvánetai stin timí?**	to pro-ee-no seem-be-ree-lam-va-ne-tehsteen tee-mee?

Eating out

Have you got a free table?	**Echete trapézi?**	e-che-te tra-pe-zee?
I'd like to reserve a table	**Thélo na kratíso éna trapézi**	the-lo na kra-tee-so e-na tra-pe-zee
The bill, please	**Ton logariazmó parakaló**	tonlo-gar-yas-mo pa-ra-ka-lo
I'm a vegetarian	**Eímai chortofágos**	ee-meh chor-to-fa-gos
menu	**O katálogos**	o ka-ta-lo-gos
wine list	**O katálogos me ta oin-opnevmatódi**	o ka-ta-lo-gos meh ta ee-no-pnev-ma-to-thee
glass	**To potíri**	to po-tee-ree
bottle	**To mpoukáli**	to bou-ka-lee
knife	**To machaíri**	to ma-che-ree
fork	**To piroúni**	to pee-roo-nee
spoon	**To koutáli**	to koo-ta-lee
breakfast	**To proïnó**	to pro-ee-no
lunch	**To mesimerianó**	to me-see-mer-ya-no
dinner	**To deípno**	to theep-no
main course	**To kyrios gévma**	to kee-ree-os yev-ma
starter	**Ta orektiká**	ta o-rek-tee-ka
dessert	**To glykó**	to ylee-ko
dish of the day	**To piáto tis iméras**	to pya-to tees ee-me-ras
bar	**To "bar"**	To bar
tavern	**I tavérna**	ee ta-ver-na
café	**To kafeneío**	to ka-fe-nee-o
wine shop	**To oinopoleío**	to ee-no-po-lee-o
restaurant	**To estiatório**	to e-stee-a-to-ree-o
ouzeria	**To ouzerí**	To ouzerí
kebab take-away	**To souvlatzídiko**	To soo-vlat-zee dee-ko

Menu Decoder

coffee	**O Kafés**	o ka-fes
with milk	**me gála**	me ga-la
black coffee	**skétos**	ske-tos
without sugar	**chorís záchari**	cho-rees za-cha-ree
tea	**tsái**	tsa-ee
wine	**krasí**	kra-see
red	**kókkino**	ko-kee-no
white	**lefkó**	lef-ko
rosé	**rozé**	ro-ze
raki	**To rakí**	to ra-kee
ouzo	**To oúzo**	to oo-zo
retsina	**I retsína**	ee ret-see-na
water	**To neró**	to ne-ro
fish	**To psári**	to psa-ree

cheese	**To tyrí**	to tee-ree
halloumi cheese	**To chaloúmi**	to chal-oo-mee
feta	**I féta**	ee fe-ta
bread	**To psomí**	to pso-mee
hummus	**To houmous**	to choo-moos
halva	**O chalvás**	o chal-vas
Turkish Delight	**To loukoúmi**	to loo-koo-mee loo-koo-mee
baklava	**O mpaklavás**	o bak-la-vas
kléftiko (lamb dish)	**To kléftiko**	to klef-tee-ko

Numbers

1	**éna**	e-na
2	**dyo**	thee-o
3	**tría**	tree-a
4	**téssera**	te-se-ra
5	**pénte**	pen-deh
6	**éxi**	ek-si
7	**eptá**	ep-ta
8	**ochtó**	och-to
9	**ennéa**	e-ne-a
10	**déka**	the-ka
100	**ekató**	e-ka-to
200	**diakósia**	thya-kos-ya
1,000	**chília**	cheel-ya
2,000	**dychiliádes**	thee-o cheel-ya-thes
1,000,000	**éna ekat--ommyrio**	e-na e-ka-to-mee-ree-o

Days of the Week, Months, Time

one minute	**éna leptó**	e-na lep-to
one hour	**mía óra**	mee-a o-ra
half an hour	**misí óra**	mee-see o-ra
a day	**mía méra**	mee-a me-ra
week	**mía evdomáda**	mee-a ev-tho-ma-tha
month	**énas mínas**	e-nas mee-nas
year	**énas chrónos**	e-nas chro-nos
Monday	**Deftéra**	thef-te-ra
Tuesday	**Tríti**	tree-tee
Wednesday	**Tetárti**	te-tar-tee
Thursday	**Pémpti**	pemp-tee
Friday	**Paraskeví**	pa-ras-ke-vee
Saturday	**Sávvato**	sa-va-to
Sunday	**Kyriakí**	keer-ee-a-kee
January	**Ianouários**	ee-a-noo-a-ree-os
February	**Fevrouários**	fev-roo-a-ree-os
March	**Mártios**	mar-tee-os
April	**Aprílios**	a-pree-lee-os
May	**Máios**	ma-ee-os
June	**Ioúnios**	ee-oo-nee-os
July	**Ioúlios**	ee-oo-lee-os
August	**Avgoustos**	av-goo-stos
September	**Septémvrios**	sep-tem-vree-os
October	**Októvrios**	ok-to-vree-os
November	**Noémvrios**	no-em-vree-os
December	**Dekémvrios**	the-kem-vree-os

alternatives for a female speaker are shown in brackets

English-Turkish Phrase Book

Pronunciation

Turkish uses a Roman alphabet. It has 29 letters: 8 vowels and 21 consonants. Letters that differ from the English alphabet are: **c**, pronounced "j" as in "jolly; **ç**, pronounced "ch" as in "church"; **ğ**, which lengthens the preceding vowel and is not pronounced; **ı**, pronounced "uh" as in "further"; **ö**, pronounced "ur" (like the sound in "further"); **ş**, pronounced "sh" as in "ship"; **ü**, pronounced "ew" as in "few".

In an Emergency

Help!	**İmdat!**	eem-**dat**
Stop!	**Dur!**	door
Call a doctor!	**Bir doktor çağrın!**	beer dok-**tor chah-**ruhn
Call an ambulance!	**Bir ambulans çağrın!**	beer am-boo-**lans chah-**ruhn
Call the police!	**Polis çağrın!**	po-**lees chah-**ruhn
Fire!	**Yangın!**	yan-**guhn**
Where is the nearest telephone?	**En yakın telefon nerede?**	en ya-**kuhn** teh-leh-**fon neh-**reh-deh
Where is the nearest hospital?	**En yakın hastane nerede?**	en ya-**kuhn** has-ta-**neh neh-**reh-deh

Communication Essentials

Yes	**Evet**	eh-**vet**
No	**Hayır**	h-**eye-**uhr
Thank you	**Teşekkür ederim**	teh-shek-**kewr eh-**deh-reem
Please	**Lütfen**	lewt-fen
Excuse me	**Affedersiniz**	af-feh-der-see-neez
Hello	**Merhaba**	mer-ha-ba
Goodbye	**Hoşça kalın**	hosh-**cha ka-**luhn
Good morning	**Günaydın**	gewn-**eye-**duhn
Good evening	**İyi akşamlar**	ee-**yee** ak-sham-**lar**
Morning	**Sabah**	sa-**bah**
Afternoon	**Öğleden sonra**	ur-leh-**den son-**ra
Evening	**Akşam**	ak-**sham**
Yesterday	**Dün**	dewn
Today	**Bugün**	**boo-**gewn
Tomorrow	**Yarın**	**ya-**ruhn
Here	**Burada**	**boo-**ra-da
There	**Şurada**	**shoo-**ra-da
Over there	**Orada**	o-ra-da
What?	**Ne?**	neh
When?	**Ne zaman?**	neh **za-**man
Why?	**Neden**	neh-**den**
Where?	**Nerede**	**neh-**reh-deh

Useful Phrases

How are you?	**Nasılsınız?**	na-suhl-suh-nuhz
I'm fine	**İyiyim**	ee-**yee-**yeem
Pleased to meet you	**Memnun oldum**	mem-**noon ol-**doom
That's fine	**Tamam**	ta-**mam**
Where is/are ...?	**... nerede?**	...**neh-**reh-deh
How far is it to ...?	**... ne kadar uzakta?**	...**neh ka-**dar oo-zak-ta
I want to go to ...	**... a/e gitmek istiyorum**	... a/eh geet-**mek** ees-**tee-**yo-room
Do you speak English?	**İngilizce biliyor musunuz?**	een-geel-**eez**-jeh bee-**lee-**yor moo-soo-nooz?
I don't understand	**Anlamıyorum**	an-**la-**muh-yo-room
Can you help me?	**Bana yardım edebilir misiniz?**	ba-na yar-**duhm** eh-deh-bee-**leer** mee-see-neez?

Useful Words

big	**büyük**	bew-**yewk**
small	**küçük**	kew-**chewk**
hot	**sıcak**	suh-**jak**
cold	**soğuk**	soh-**ook**
good/well	**iyi**	ee-**yee**
bad	**kötü**	kur-**tew**
open	**açık**	a-**chuhk**
closed	**kapalı**	ka-pa-**luh**
left	**sol**	sol
right	**sağ**	saa
straight on	**doğru**	doh-**roo**
near	**yakın**	ya-**kuhn**
far	**uzak**	oo-**zak**
early	**erken**	er-**ken**
late	**geç**	gech
entrance	**giriş**	gee-**reesh**

exit	**çıkış**	chuh-**kuhsh**
toilets	**tuvaletler**	too-va-let-**ler**

Shopping

How much is this?	**Bu kaç lira?**	boo **kach** lee-ra
I would like ...	**... istiyorum**	... ees-**tee-**yo-room
Do you have ...?	**... var mı?**	...**var** muh?
Do you take credit cards?	**Kredi kartı kabul ediyor musunuz?**	**kreh-**dee **kar-**tuh ka-**bool** eh-**dee-**yor moo-soo-nooz?
What time do you open/close?	**Saat kaçta açılıyor/ kapanıyor?**	Sa-**at** kach-ta a-chuh-**luh**-yor/ ka-pa-**nuh-**yor
this one	**bunu**	boo-**noo**
that one	**şunu**	shoo-**noo**
expensive	**pahalı**	pa-ha-**luh**
cheap	**ucuz**	oo-**jooz**
size (clothes)	**beden**	beh-**den**
size (shoes)	**numara**	noo-ma-**ra**
white	**beyaz**	bay-**yaz**
black	**siyah**	see-**yah**
red	**kırmızı**	kuhr-muh-**zuh**
yellow	**sarı**	sa-**ruh**
green	**yeşil**	yeh-**sheel**
blue	**mavi**	ma-**vee**
bakery	**fırın**	fuh-**ruhn**
bank	**banka**	**ban-**ka
cake shop	**pastane**	pas-ta-**neh**
chemist's/pharmacy	**eczane**	ej-za-**neh**
hairdresser	**kuaför**	kwa-**fur**
barber	**berber**	ber-**ber**
market/bazaar	**çarşı/pazar**	char-**shuh/pa-zar**
post office	**postane**	pos-ta-**neh**
travel agency	**seyahat acentesi**	say-ya-**hat** a-jen-teh-**see**

Sightseeing

castle	**hisar**	hee-**sar**
church	**kilise**	kee-**lee-**seh
mosque	**cami**	**ja-**mee
museum	**müze**	**mew-**zeh
square	**meydan**	may-**dan**
theological college	**medrese**	med-**reh-**seh
tomb	**türbe**	tewr-**beh**
tourist information office	**turizm danışma bürosu**	too-**reezm** da-nuhsh-**mah bew-**ro-soo
town hall	**belediye sarayı**	beh-leh-dee-**yeh** sar-**eye-**uh
Turkish bath	**hamam**	ha-**mam**

Travelling

airport	**havalimanı**	ha-**va-**lee-ma-nuh
bus/coach	**otobüs**	o-to-**bewss**
bus stop	**otobüs durağı**	o-to-**bewss** doo-**ra-**uh
ferry	**vapur**	va-**poor**
taxi	**taksi**	**tak-**see
ticket	**bilet**	bee-**let**
ticket office	**bilet gişesi**	bee-**let** gee-sheh-**see**
timetable	**tarife**	ta-ree-**feh**

Staying in a Hotel

Do you have a vacant room?	**Boş odanız var mı?**	bosh o-da-**nuhz var** muh?
double room	**iki kişilik bir oda**	ee-**kee** kee-shee-**leek** beer o-**da**
twin room	**çift yataklı bir oda**	**cheeft** ya-**tak-**luh beer o-**da**
single room	**tek kişilik**	**tek** kee-shee-**leek** with
room room a bathroom	**banyolu bir oda**	**ban-**yo-loo beer o-**da**
key	**anahtar**	a-nah-**tar**
room service	**oda servisi**	o-**da** ser-vee-**see**
I have a reservation	**Rezervasyonum var**	reh-zer-vas-yo-**noom** var
Does the price include breakfast?	**Fiyata kahvaltı dahil mi?**	fee-ya-**ta** kah-val-tuh da-**heel** mee?

Eating Out

Do you have a table	**... kişilik bir masa**	... kee-shee-**leek** for ...people
The bill please	**Hesap lütfen**	heh-**sap** lewt-fen
I am a vegetarian	**Et yemiyorum**	et **yeh-**mee-yo-room
restaurant	**lokanta**	lo-**kan-**ta
waiter	**garson**	gar-**son**

menu	**yemek listesi**	ye-**mek lees**-teh-see
wine list	**şarap listesi**	sha-**rap lees**-teh-see
breakfast	**kahvaltı**	kah-val-**tuh**
lunch	**öğle yemeği**	ur-**leh** yeh-meh-**ee**
dinner	**akşam yemeği**	ak-**sham** yeh-meh-**ee**
starter	**meze**	**meh**-zeh
main course	**ana yemek**	a-**na** yeh-**mek**
dish of the day	**günün yemeği**	gewn-**ewn** yeh-meh-**ee**
dessert	**tatlı**	tat-**luh**
glass	**bardak**	bar-**dak**
bottle	**şişe**	shee-**sheh**
knife	**bıçak**	buh-**chak**
fork	**çatal**	cha-**tal**
spoon	**kaşık**	ka-**shuhk**

Menu Decoder

bal	bal	honey
balık	ba-**luhk**	fish
bira	**bee**-ra	beer
bonfile	**bon**-fee-leh	fillet steak
buz	booz	ice
çay	ch-'eye'	tea
çilek	chee-**lek**	strawberry
çorba	chor-**ba**	soup
dondurma	don-door-**ma**	ice cream
ekmek	ek-**mek**	bread
elma	el-**ma**	apple
et	et	meat
fasulye	fa-**sool**-yeh	beans
fırında	fuh-ruhn-**da**	roast
gazoz	ga-**zoz**	fizzy drink
kahve	kah-**veh**	coffee
karpuz	kar-**pooz**	water melon
kavun	ka-**voon**	melon
kayısı	k-'eye'-uh-**suh**	apricots
kıyma	kuhy-**ma**	minced meat
kızartma	kuh-zart-**ma**	fried
köfte	kurf-**teh**	meatballs
kuzu eti	koo-**zoo** eh-tee	lamb
lokum	lo-**koom**	Turkish delight
maden suyu	ma-**den** soo-**yoo**	mineral water
meyve suyu	may-**veh** soo-**yoo**	fruit juice
muz	mooz	banana
patlıcan	pat-luh-**jan**	aubergine (eggplant)
peynir	pay-**neer**	cheese
pilav	pee-**lav**	rice
piliç	pee-**leech**	roast chicken
şarap	sha-**rap**	wine

sebze	seb-**zeh**	vegetables
şeftali	shef-ta-**lee**	peach
şeker	sheh-**ker**	sugar
su	soo	water
süt	sewt	milk
sütlü	sewt-**lew**	with milk
tavuk	ta-**vook**	chicken
tereyağı	teh-**reh**-yah-uh	butter
tuz	tooz	salt
üzüm	ew-**zewm**	grapes
yoğurt	yoh-**urt**	yoghurt
yumurta	yoo-moor-**ta**	egg
zeytin	zay-**teen**	olives
zeytinyağı	zay-**teen**-yah-uh	olive oil

Numbers

0	**sıfır**	**suh**-fuhr
1	**bir**	beer
2	**iki**	ee-**kee**
3	**üç**	ewch
4	**dört**	durt
5	**beş**	besh
6	**altı**	al-**tuh**
7	**yedi**	yeh-**dee**
8	**sekiz**	seh-**keez**
9	**dokuz**	doh-**kooz**
10	**on**	on
100	**yüz**	yewz
200	**iki yüz**	ee-**kee** yewz
1,000	**bin**	been
100,000	**yüz bin**	**yewz** been
1,000,000	**bir milyon**	**beer** meel-**yon**

Time

one minute	**bir dakika**	**beer** da-**kee**-ka
one hour	**bir saat**	**beer** sa-at
half an hour	**yarım saat**	ya-**ruhm** sa-at
day	**gün**	gewn
week	**hafta**	haf-**ta**
month	**ay**	'eye'
year	**yıl**	yuhl
Sunday	**pazar**	pa-**zar**
Monday	**pazartesi**	pa-**zar**-teh-see
Tuesday	**salı**	sa-**luh**
Wednesday	**çarşamba**	char-sham-**ba**
Thursday	**perşembe**	per-shem-**beh**
Friday	**cuma**	joo-**ma**
Saturday	**cumartesi**	joo-**mar**-teh-see

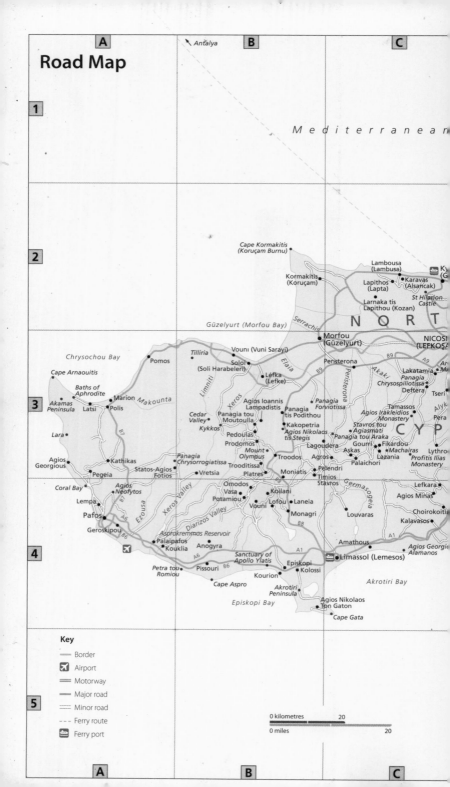

Road Map

Key
- ─── Border
- ✈ Airport
- ═══ Motorway
- ─── Major road
- ═══ Minor road
- - - - Ferry route
- ⛴ Ferry port

Mediterranean

Cape Kormakitis
(Koruçam Burnu)

Kormakitis
(Koruçam)

Lambousa
(Lambusa)

Karavas
(Alsancak)

Ky
(G

Lapithos
(Lapta)

St Hilarion
Castle

Larnaka tis
Lapithou (Kozan)

Güzelyurt (Morfou Bay)

Serrachis

N O R T

Chrysochou Bay

Pomos

Tilliria

Vouni (Vuni Sarayi)

Morfou
(Güzelyurt)

NICOSI
(LEFKOŞ

Cape Arnaouitis

Baths of
Aphrodite

Marion

Makounta

Salol
(Soli Harabeleri)

Léfka
(Lefke)

Limniti

Peristerona

Peristerona

B9

Akaki

Lakatamia
Panagia
Chrysospiliotissa
Deftera

Ar
M

Tseri

Akamas
Peninsula

Latsi

Polis

Xeros

Agios Ioannis
Lampadistis

Panagia
tis Podithou

Panagia
Forviotissa

Agios Irakleidios
Monastery

Tamassos

Pera

Alyk

C Y P

Cedar
Valley

Panagia tou
Moutoulla

Kakopetria

Stavros tou
Agiasmati

Lara

Kykkos

Pedoulas

Agios Nikolaos
tis Stegis

Panagia tou Araka

Gourri
Askas

Fikardou
Machairas

Lythro

Agios
Georgious

Kathikas

Prodomos

Mount
Olympus

Lagoudera

Agros

Lazania

Palaichori

Profitis Ilias
Monastery

Panagia
Chrysorrogiatissa

Troodos

Pelendri

Pegeia

Statos-Agios
Fotios

Trooditissa

Moniatis

Timios
Stavros

Germasogeia

Lefkara

Coral Bay

Agios
Neofytos

Vretsia

Platres

B8

Agios Minas

Lempa

Ezousa

B7

Omodos
Vasa

Potamiou

Koilani
Lofou

Laneia

Louvaras

Choirokoitia

Kalavasos

Pafos

A6

Xeros valley

Vouni

Monagri

Geroskipou

✈ B6

Diarizos Valley

A1

Amathous

A1

Agios Georgie
Alamanos

Asprokremmos Reservoir

Palaipafos
Kouklia

Anogyra

Sanctuary of
Apollo Ylatis

⛴ Limassol (Lemesos)

A6

Episkopi

Petra tou
Romiou

Pissouri

B6

Kourion

Kolossi

Akrotiri Bay

Cape Aspro

Akrotiri
Peninsula

Episkopi Bay

Agios Nikolaos
Ton Gaton

Cape Gata

| 0 kilometres | 20 |
| 0 miles | 20 |

Antalya